# JEWISH WOMEN IN

## HISTORICAL PERSPECTIVE

# JEWISH WOMEN IN
_____

## HISTORICAL PERSPECTIVE

edited by JUDITH R. BASKIN

 Wayne State University Press  Detroit

Library of Congress Cataloging-in-Publication Data
Jewish women in historical perspective / edited by Judith R. Baskin.
p.   cm.
Includes bibliographical references and index.
ISBN 0-8143-2091-0 (alk. paper). — ISBN 0-8143-2092-9
(pbk. : alk. paper).
1. Women in Judaism.   2. Women, Jewish—History.   3. Women,
Jewish—Religious life.
I. Baskin, Judith Reesa, 1950–
BM729.W6J49   1991
296′.082—dc20                                                      91-10491
CIP

*Grateful acknowledgment is made to the*
*Lucius N. Littauer Foundation for*
*financial assistance in the*
*publication of this volume.*

FOR WARREN, SAM, AND SHIRA

———————————————

# CONTENTS

# ACKNOWLEDGMENTS

I acknowledge with gratitude the enthusiastic participation of the fine scholars who have contributed to this volume. I have learned a great deal from them and from their essays.

I would like to thank Murray M. Schwartz, dean of the College of Humanities and Fine Arts at the University of Massachusetts at Amherst, for a research semester in the spring of 1988 that allowed me to complete my own essay for this volume as well as undertake the tasks connected with editing a book. I am grateful to the Faculty Research Awards Program of the State University of New York at Albany for a generous grant to assist in the costs of preparing this volume for publication.

I am also indebted to the Women's Division of the Jewish Federation of New Haven, Connecticut, whose 1982 invitation to speak on Jewish women in the Middle Ages led to chapter 4 in this volume and a continuing scholarly interest in its subject. My husband, Warren Ginsberg, and children, Sam and Shira, have patiently endured my preoccupation with the preparation of *Jewish Women in Historical Perspective*. I dedicate this volume to them with great love.

# CONTRIBUTORS

HOWARD ADELMAN is the director of the program in Jewish Studies at Smith College, where his courses include the study of Jewish women. In addition to his work on women in Italian Jewish life, he has published on Italian Jewish history, especially the life and thought of Leon Modena, a seventeenth-century Venetian rabbi.

JUDITH R. BASKIN is the chair of the Department of Judaic Studies at the State University of New York at Albany. She is the author of *Pharaoh's Counsellors: Job, Jethro, and Balaam in Rabbinic and Patristic Tradition* and has written on Jewish women in rabbinic tradition, and Jewish women in the context of medieval civilization.

DEBORAH HERTZ is associate professor of history at the State University of New York at Binghamtom. In 1989–90 she was director of women's studies. She is the author of *Jewish High Society in Old Regime Berlin* and the editor of *Briefe an Eine Freundin: Rahel Varhagen an Rebecca Friedlaender*. In 1987–88 she was a Fulbright professor at the Hebrew University in Jerusalem.

PAULA E. HYMAN is the Lucy Moses professor of modern Jewish history at Yale University. Coauthor of *The Jewish Woman in America*, she has written widely on the subject of gender and Jewish history. Her most recent book is *The Jewish Family: Myths and Reality*, coedited with Steven M. Cohen.

MARION A. KAPLAN is associate professor of history at Queens College and the Graduate Center, City University of New York. She has written *The Jewish Feminist Movement in Germany: The Campaigns of the Jüdischer Frauenbund, 1904–1938*, edited *The Marriage Bargain: Women and Dowries in European History*, and coedited *When Biology Became Destiny: Women in Weimar and Nazi Germany*. She has written on the social history of Jewish women and is currently completing a book on Jewish women in Imperial Germany.

ROSS S. KRAEMER is the editor of *Maenads, Martyrs, Matrons, Monastics: A Sourcebook on Women's Religions in the Greco-Roman World* and the author of a forthcoming companion volume that will include early Judaism, as well as numerous articles on Jewish women in the Greco-Roman Diaspora. She has been a visiting scholar in the Department of Religious Studies at the University of Pennsylvania since 1982 and is currently visiting associate professor of religious studies at Franklin and Marshall College.

RENÉE LEVINE MELAMMED lectures at Ben Gurion University in the Negev in the history department and the Center for Sephardi and Oriental Studies, as well as at the Hebrew University School for Overseas Students. She has published various articles concerning *conversos* and *conversas* based on material found in Spanish Inquisition documents. She is currently working on an analysis of the works of an eminent rabbinic family in the Ottoman Empire, and also plans to investigate the crypto-Jewish life of sixteenth-century Spanish *conversas*.

SUSAN NIDITCH has been a member of the Department of Religion at Amherst College since 1979. She is the author of *The Symbolic Vision in Biblical Tradition, Chaos to Cosmos: Studies in Biblical Patterns of Creation*, and *Underdogs and Tricksters: A Prelude to Biblical Folklore*. She has recently edited *Text and Tradition: The Hebrew Bible and Folklore*.

JOAN RINGELHEIM received a doctorate in philosophy from Boston University. She has received a number of grants in support of her work on women and the Holocaust and is currently writing a book on that topic. She produced the first conference on women and the Holocaust with a grant from the New York Council for the Humanities and coedited the conference proceedings, *Women Surviving: The Holocaust*. Her articles have appeared in *The Simon Wiesenthal Annual* and *Signs*.

ELLEN M. UMANSKY is associate professor of religion at Emory University. During 1989–90 she was visiting associate professor of modern Jewish thought at Hebrew Union College-Jewish Institute of Religion in New York City. The author of two books on Lily Montagu, founder of the Liberal Jewish movement in England, and of numerous articles on women and Judaism and modern Jewish thought, she is currently completing two works, *From Christian Science to Jewish Science: Spiritual Healing and American Jews* and *Piety, Persuasion, and Friendship: A Sourcebook of Modern Jewish Women's Spirituality*, coedited with Dianne Ashton.

JUDITH ROMNEY WEGNER teaches Judaic Studies at the University of Massachusetts at Amherst. She holds law degrees from Cambridge and Harvard and is a member of the English and U.S. bars. Her publications include articles on the relationship between Talmudic law and Islamic law and on the subject of women's status in Jewish law. She is the author of *Chattel or Person? The Status of Women in the Mishnah* and is currently planning a book on the status of women in classical Islamic hadith tradition.

CHAVA WEISSLER is associate professor of religion studies at Lehigh University and holds the Philip and Muriel Berman Chair of Jewish Civilization. *Voices of the Matriarchs*, her book on the religious lives of Ashkenazic women as seen through the *tkhine* literature, will be published by Beacon Press.

# EDITOR'S NOTE

---

Transliteration of Hebrew and Arabic varies from chapter to chapter according to the author's preference. Some words which appear frequently have been transliterated consistently throughout the volume, occasionally leading to inconsistencies within individual chapters.

# INTRODUCTION

## Judith R. Baskin

---

The perception that women's lives and experiences in any particular historical epoch may differ from men's has profoundly affected how many scholars approach and interpret their subjects of study.[1] Introducing gender as a factor in the study of human societies, endeavors, and achievements reveals a persistent pattern of limiting women's access to public activities and the status they confer and highlights how women have been excluded from the education and empowerment that would allow them to function and achieve in the cultural sphere.[2] While women were rarely a part of the events and cultural accomplishments that have been valued and taught in the Western tradition, investigation can sometimes reveal a contemporaneous and alternative women's history and culture. Indeed, gender studies have shown that historical transformations in many eras affected men and woman quite differently[3] and that when women were excluded from "sanctioned" male cultural activities or religious observances, they often created their own artifacts and rituals.[4] Moreover, in times of rapid social change and political turmoil, women have frequently become the culture bearers, preserving the essentials of cultural identity in both the domestic setting and the public sphere.[5]

The insights gained by using gender as a category of analysis are valuable in studying Jewish societies and cultures, as well. Rabbinic Judaism, which held sway over most Jewish communities from the sixth through the eighteenth century of our era, is classically rigid in the separations it ordains between male and female roles and the status pertaining to each sex. In this patriarchal system women are seen as connected to the realm of nature, as opposed to culture, and their activities, ideally, are confined to the private sphere of home, husband, and children.[6] That the reality of women's lives and endeavors was often quite different from the rabbinic design is a major theme running through the essays in this volume. Still, Jewish history has almost always been written from the point of view of the male Jew and has documented his intellectual concerns and achievements. Scholarly references to Jewish women have most often assumed that activities connected with the realm of the home are secondary, and few Jewish women before modern times possessed the skills or authority to preserve their own voices for posterity.

An early modern exception is Glückel of Hameln (1646–1724), whose autobiography, written to drive away the melancholy that followed her husband's death and to let her children know their ancestry, is an engrossing document and a major source of information on Jewish life in the seventeenth century. Its female voice and particular concerns with household and children, as well as business and the synagogue, set it apart in Jewish literature up to its time. This work is readily available and is an essential accompaniment to any study of Jewish women's history.[7] It is one of the aims of this volume to rediscover other similarly evocative expressions of Jewish women's lives and experiences.

The last decades have seen a growing debate over the status of women in contemporary Judaism. As the conditions of secular Western life have allowed women greater choice in their educational and vocational opportunities and an active and articulate feminist movement has prodded our society in general to endorse female equality with men in intellectual, spiritual and political endeavors, dissatisfaction with traditional Jewish limitations on women's participation in communal, religious, and scholarly activities has increased. Similarly, the apparently immoveable obstacles in traditional Judaism to women's personal freedom in the areas of divorce, desertion, and levirate marriage have also elicited criticism.

In response to these issues, Reform, Reconstructionist and Conservative Judaism stress egalitarianism within their movements and ordain properly prepared women as rabbis.[8] New liturgical language sensitive to women and their concerns has also been developed, as have innovative rituals for such events as the birth of a daughter, Bat Mitzvah (female religious coming of age, analogous to Bar Mitzvah), observance of Rosh Hodesh (the New Moon, a day traditionally set apart for Jewish women), and the arrival of menopause.[9] In recent years a number of books and articles have offered contemporary responses to traditional Jewish views of women's roles, obligations, and disabilities from both feminist and apologetic perspectives.[10]

Missing from this ongoing discussion have been perspectives from the past. While the growth of women's studies as a field of scholarly endeavor has led to increased academic study of women in Judaism and individual Jewish women, few recent works have attempted to illuminate contemporary dilemmas and concerns by scholarly investigations of the lives and experiences of Jewish women of previous eras.[11] *Jewish Women in Historical Perspective* is intended to provide such a historical excursion. Most of the essays presented here were written specifically for this volume by well-trained and distinguished scholars of the Jewish past. Each essay is both synthetic, providing an overview of the period in question, and analytic, asking serious questions about the general situations of Jewish women and their activities in a male-dominated public and intellectual Jewish life, as well as in a larger non-Jewish cultural environment. Although the authors take different approaches to their topics, all of the essays are accessible to the general reader, while detailed notes direct both the specialist and the interested student to primary documents and important secondary studies.

The arrangement of essays is chronological, although the essays might have been grouped by common elements. The essays of Judith Romney Wegner, Renée Levine Melammed, Howard Adelman, Chava Weissler, and myself, for example, are concerned with Jewish communities under the aegis of rabbinic Judaism; while those of Susan Niditch, Ross S. Kraemer, Ellen M. Umansky, and Joan Ringelheim are not. Those of Deborah Hertz, Marion A. Kaplan, and Paula E. Hyman chronicle Jews in transitional epochs, struggling between rabbinic tradition and rapid social, political, and intellectual change. The wide range of environments, eras, and forms of Judaism the essays delineate makes clear the diversity that has always characterized Jewish life and practice.

The nature of their sources might also have organized the essays. Some, like those of Hertz, Kaplan, Hyman and Ringelheim, ground their historical analyses on Jewish women's direct testimony as expressed in letters, personal recollections of their pasts, and oral accounts of traumatic historical events. Other essays, like those of Weissler and Umansky, are able to appraise aspects of Jewish women's spirituality based on literary and devotional documents written by women. The essays of Niditch and Wegner, on the other hand, interpret images of women created by men and preserved in the canonical literary traditions of Hebrew Scripture and rabbinic literature; while those of Kraemer, Adelman, Melammed, and myself paint portraits of women's lives from a variety of primary sources about women but not written by them. All of the essays, however, are united in their recognition of the fundamental unreliability of primary documents as unmediated testimony of the past and of the need for informed interpretation and analysis.

Common concerns among the essays include a recognition of the importance of social class, which can be as decisive a variable as gender in determining the course of a person's life. Most of the Jews we know about from the past were unusual people, whether exceptional in their intellectual abilities or in their circumstances. This is certainly the case with the Jewish women mentioned by name in these essays, particularly for premodern times; most came from privileged families, elite in their wealth and/or learning. The worlds of the dowryless girl, workingman's wife, or impoverished widow—also considered here—are less well documented and far more difficult to discover.

The interplay in any era between Jewish legal traditions and the social realities of a given milieu is also a major theme in the essays concerned with communities oriented toward rabbinic law. Such Jewish societies in the Diaspora have attempted, each in its own way, to achieve a balance between assuming the language, dress, and mores of their gentile neighbors and maintaining loyalty to the guidance and demands of Talmudic dicta. The necessary accommodations and acculturation that result are discussed by Melammed, Adelman, Weissler, and myself; while Kaplan, Hyman, and Umansky chronicle the further modifications of tradition demanded by modernity, with its political pressures and geographic relocations. Hertz's essay describes a historic moment when an unusual confluence of internal circumstances, outside influences, and previously inconceivable possibilities overpowered Jewish loyalties altogether for at least one small group of women in Berlin at the end of the eighteenth century.

A necessary criterion for measuring a woman's place and worth in any society is an evaluation of her economic roles. While rabbinic Judaism was determined that the private domain of the domestic be woman's primary place, participation in the family economy was not seen to contradict this imperative. Economic transactions, including marriage, were perceived not as public activities but as private proceedings between individuals. Thus, throughout Jewish history, women were expected to contribute to family income, whether through needlework or moneylending within the home, or through outside activities like those of the merchants, moneylenders, teachers, wet nurses, midwives, and physicians whom Kraemer, Melammed, Adelman, and I discuss. Most of the essays devote attention to women's economic activities and value, from Niditch's mention of the activities of the biblical "woman of valor" (Proverbs 31) to Wegner's discussion of rabbinic legislation pertaining to ownership of a woman's earnings to Hertz's analysis of the kinds of husbands a wealthy Jewish woman might attract in late-eighteenth-century Germany. Hyman describes a 1902 kosher meat boycott organized by women on New York's Lower East Side, while Kaplan discusses the attempted entry of middle-class German Jewish women into a world of work where gender was even a greater liability than religion. The particular economic power wielded by the widow is also a recurring theme, especially in the essays concerned with premodern periods.

The fundamental relationship for the Jewish women described in these essays was with their families, particularly their husbands. Marriage and the joys it can occasion, as well as the complications stemming from divorce, desertion, widowhood, remarriage, inheritance, and the guardianship of minor children, was the primary focus of Jewish women's lives before this century.[12] That marriage was fundamentally an economic transaction in most periods of Jewish history cannot be denied, and the first six essays, in particular, are full of details about the financial and legal ramifications and consequences of this event, which was so central in a Jewish woman's destiny.[13] That some marriages were irredeemably unhappy is also a fact, as the prevalence of Jewish divorce in a number of the periods under study reveals. Still, marriage functioned as an enduring and meaningful bond for many women and men, and the essays offer evidence of unions based on mutual respect, affection, and the shared concerns of family and livelihood from all epochs of Jewish history.

Interest in the nature of Jewish women's education is also a unifying concern. That Jewish women were generally taught differently from men is not surprising, given rabbinic Judaism's conviction that study of Torah—the general term for all literature believed to be divinely revealed—was a male prerogative.[14] Girls were taught housekeeping skills and the religious laws connected with domestic rituals, food preparation, and marital relations. Some exceptional women, generally daughters of elite families, received far more thorough trainings in traditional texts and commentaries, and some of these, as noted by Melammed, Adelman, Weissler, and myself, supervised the instruction and prayers of other, less fortunate women. Weissler discusses two such women who wrote devotional literature directed toward women and addressing their spiritual needs, while Umansky brings the discussion of Jewish women as spiritual models and creators of religious language into the twentieth century. That Jewish women of the past received sufficient vocational education to prepare them for their economic activities is obvious, but such training, since it did not involve study of sacred texts, was not considered "education" in its cultural context and is little noted in most of the surviving sources.

In transitional periods such as the Italian Renaissance, as Adelman relates, some daughters of wealthy Jews received secular educations, and a few were able to shine in the larger, non-Jewish cultural world. Sometimes this female acculturation outstripped that of the men in their families with, as Hertz documents, unexpected results. Kaplan, Hyman, and Umansky also discuss the complex ramifications for Jewish women of exposure to modernity and the world of secular learning.

Jewish history has too often been a chronicle of persecution. Kraemer, Melammed, and I discuss documents describing Jewish women's loyalty to their traditions in times of extreme crisis like the Maccabean Revolt, the Crusades, and the Inquisition. Ringelheim's reflection on women's recollections of their experiences of the Holocaust and what we can and cannot say about them is an important commentary on what has gone before, as she calls into question the entire endeavor of delving into the female past while accepting the status quo of the female present.

*Jewish Women in Historical Perspective* does not cover every era or locale of Jewish history, nor, given the richness and diversity of Jewish civilization, could it be expected to do so. Among several unavoidable lacunae are an analysis of women's economic and political activities in the Eastern European milieu[15] and a study of women's involvement in Zionism and the founding of the State of Israel.[16] A selected bibliography at the end of this chapter indicates some available sources and studies on these and other topics that do not receive full coverage in this book.

By gathering in one place significant studies of Jewish women's history by some of the foremost scholars of the subject, this volume makes an important beginning. I hope that these essays will further general knowledge of the diversity and richness of Jewish women's pasts, while encouraging similar scholarly endeavors.

## SELECTED BIBLIOGRAPHY

Every essay in *Jewish Women in Historical Perspective* provides a wealth of bibliographical information on the period being covered, as well as sources particularly concerned with Jewish women. These references, found in the notes to each essay, are intended to facilitate further inquiry for the student or interested reader. Readers are also urged to make use of the bibliographical sources mentioned in note 10 below. A forthcoming volume on themes related to some of the essays is Linda Gordon Kuzmack, *Woman's Cause. The Jewish Woman's Movement in England and the United States, 1881–1933* ( Columbus, OH, 1990).

The bibliographical data presented here provides guidance to some important topics not covered by the essays.

### Aspects of Jewish Women's Lives in Eastern Europe

Adler, Ruth. *Women of the Shtetl: Y. L. Peretz.* Rutherford, NJ, 1980.

Baum, Charlotte. "What made Yetta Work: Economic Role of Eastern European Jewish Women in the Family." *Response* 18: "The Jewish Woman" (Summer, 1973):32–38.

Biale, David. "Love, Marriage and the Modernization of the Jews." In *Approaches to Modern Judaism,* edited by Marc Lee Raphael. Chico, CA, 1983.

Davidowicz, Lucy, ed. *The Golden Tradition. Jewish Life and Thought in Eastern Europe.* Boston, 1967.

Etkes, Immanuel. "Marriage and Torah Study among the *Lomdim* in Lithuania in the Nineteenth Century." In *The Jewish Family: Metaphor and Memory,* edited by David Kraemer. New York, 1989.

Hurvitz, Nathan. "Courtship and Arranged Marriages among Eastern European Jews Prior to World War I as Depicted in a *Briefensteller.*" *Journal of Marriage and the Family* (May, 1975):422–30.

Katz, Jacob. "Family, Kinship, and Marriage Among Ashkenazim in the Sixteenth to Eighteenth Centuries." *Jewish Journal of Sociology* 1 (1959):4–22.

Pratt, Norma Fain. "Culture and Radical Politics: Yiddish Women Writers, 1880–1940." *American Jewish History* (1980):68–90.

––––––. "Anna Margolin's *Lider*: A Study in Women's History, Autobiography and Poetry." In *Studies in American Jewish Literature*. Vol. 3, *Jewish Women Writers and Women in Jewish Literature*, edited by Daniel Walden. Albany, 1983.

Rapoport-Albert, Ada. "On Women in Hasidism, S.A. Horodecky and the Maid of Ludmir Tradition." In *Jewish History. Essays in Honour of Chimen Abramsky*, edited by Ada Rapoport-Albert and Steven J. Zipperstein. London, 1988.

Weinberg, Sydney Stahl. *World of Our Mothers: The Lives of Jewish Immigrant Women.* Chapel Hill, 1988.

## Jewish Women's Involvement in Zionism and the State of Israel

Albeck, Plea. "The Status of Women in Israel." *The American Journal of Comparative Law* 20 (1972):693–715.

Aloni, Shulamit. "Israel: Up the Down Escalator." In *Sisterhood Is Global*, edited by Robin Morgan. Garden City, NY, 1984.

Bernstein, Deborah, ed. *Pioneers and Homemakers: Women in Pre-State Israeli Society.* Forthcoming.

––––––. *The Struggle for Equality: Urban Women Workers in Pre-State Israeli Society.* New York, 1987.

Bowes, Alison. "Women in the Kibbutz Movement." *Sociological Review* 26 (1978): 237–62.

Clapsaddle, Carol N. "Flight from Feminism: The Case of the Israeli Woman." In *The Jewish Woman: New Perspectives*, edited by Elizabeth Koltun. New York, 1976.

Gilad, Lisa. *Ginger and Salt: Yemeni Jewish Women in an Israeli Town.* Boulder, 1988.

Harman, Zena. "Israel." In *Women in the Modern World*, edited by Raphael Patai. New York, 1967.

Hazelton, Leslie. *Israeli Women: The Reality Behind the Myth.* New York, 1977.

Izraeli, Dafna N. "Sex Structure of Occupations: The Israeli Experience." *Sociology of Work and Occupations* 6 (1979):404–29.

––––––. "The Zionist Women's Movement in Palestine 1911–1927: A Sociological Analysis." *Signs* 6 (1981):87–114.

Janait, Rachel. "Stages." In *The Jewish Woman: New Perspectives*, edited by Elizabeth Koltun. New York, 1976.

Rein, Natalie. *Daughters of Rachel: Women in Israel.* New York, 1979.

Shazar, Rachel Katznelson, ed. *The Plough Woman: Memoirs of the Pioneer Women of Palestine.* New York, 1975.

Talmon-Garber, Yonina. *Family and Community in the Kibbutz.* Cambridge, MA, 1972.

## NOTES

1. See Paula E. Hyman's opening statements in her essay in this volume, and her article, "Gender and Jewish History," *Tikkun* 3 (January-February, 1988); and Marion A. Kaplan's remarks at the beginning of her essay. That historical change may affect men and women differently is an important insight. See Joan Kelly ("The Social Relations of the Sexes" in *Women, History and Theory: The Essays of Joan Kelly* [Chicago and London, 1984]), who writes: "What feminist historiography has done is to unsettle . . . accepted evaluations of historical periods. It has disabused us of the notion that the history of women is the same as the history of men, and that significant turning points in history have the same impact for one sex as for the other" (p. 3). It is instructive to note that scholars have made similar points in connection with the history of the Jews: the consequences of major historical events have often been profoundly different for the Jews than for other peoples, while the periodizations that characterize general historical studies are not always meaningful for Jewish history.

2. For discussions of the distinctions between public and private domains and the realms of nature and culture and how they pertain to women, see Michelle Zimbalist Rosaldo, "Woman, Culture, and Society: A Theoretical Overview" and Sherry Ortner, "Is Female to Male As Nature Is to Culture?" both in *Women, Culture, and Society*, ed. Michelle Zimbalist Rosaldo and Louise Lamphere (Stanford, 1974).

3. A classic exploration of this phenomenon is Joan Kelly, "Did Women have a Renaissance?" in *Women, History and Theory*, 19–50; and see chapters 6 and 8–10 below, which discuss the responses of Jewish women to periods of rapid social change.

4. See chapters 7 and 12 on the development of distinctive forms of female spirituality in Judaism and chapters 2, 4–6, and 9 for references to women's prayer groups or other activities in the synagogue, the development of devotional literature intended for women, and women's needlework or other donations to the synagogue as forms of communal participation.

5. See chapters 1–2, 4–5, and 9–10. For an alternative feminist view which rejects any glorification of women's abilities to survive in oppressive patriarchies, see the second part of chapter 11.

6. See chapter 3 for a study of the position of women in rabbinic Judaism.

7. *The Memoirs of Glückel of Hameln*, trans. Marvin Lowenthal, (1932; rep. New York, 1960).

8. See chapter 12 for a discussion of this phenomenon.

9. See, for example, Penina V. Adelman, *Miriam's Well* (Fresh Meadows, NY, 1986); Carol Diamant, *The Jewish Baby Book* (New York, 1989); selections in such anthologies as Elizabeth Koltun, ed., *The Jewish Woman* (New York, 1978); and Carol P. Christ and Judith Plaskow, eds., *Womanspirit Rising: A Feminist Reader in Religion* (New York, 1979); E. M. Broner, *A Weave of Women* (1978; rep. Bloomington, IN, 1985), a novel set in Israel concerned with Jewish women and ritual; and chapter 12 below.

10. A major new theological approach is Judith Plaskow, *Standing Again at Sinai: Judaism from a Feminist Perspective* (San Francisco, 1990). Among anthologies that address a variety of issues connected with women and Judaism are Koltun, *The Jewish Woman*; Susannah Heschel, ed., *On Being a Jewish Feminist* (New York, 1983); Susan Wiedman Schneider, *Jewish and Female* (New York, 1985); and Melanie Kaye/Kantrowitz and Irena Klepfisz, eds., *The Tribe of Dina: A Jewish Women's Anthology*. (1986;

rep. Boston, 1989). Rachel Biale, *Women and Jewish Law* (New York, 1984) is an excellent introduction to the position of women in rabbinic legislation and social policy. Among bibliographies that deal with women in Judaism are Aviva Cantor, *The Jewish Woman: 1900–1981. Bibliography* (Fresh Meadow, NY, 1981); Ora Hamelsdorf and Sandra Adelsberg, *Jewish Women and Jewish Law: Bibliography* (Fresh Meadows, NY, 1980); and Inger Marie Ruud, *Women and Judaism: A Select Annotated Bibliography* (New York, 1988). The notes to the essays in the present volume are an excellent source of bibliographical references, as is Sue Levi Elwell, *The Jewish Women's Studies Guide* (Lanham, MD, 1987), which compiles detailed reading lists from eighteen university courses dealing, in whole or part, with Jewish women.

11. A pioneering effort for the general reader is Sondra Henry and Emily Taitz, *Written Out of History: Our Jewish Foremothers* (Fresh Meadows, NY, 1983), which discusses extraordinary Jewish women in a number of different eras; the volume includes a good bibliography.

12. On alternative life-styles for Jewish women in the modern era, see Evelyn Torton Beck, ed., *Nice Jewish Girls: A Lesbian Anthology* (Boston, 1989); Christie Balka and Andy Rose, eds., *Twice Blessed: On Being Lesbian, Gay, and Jewish* (Boston, 1989); Carol Diamant, *Jewish Marital Status: A Hadassah Study* (Northvale, NJ, 1989); and excerpts in Kaye/Kantrowitz and Klepfisz, *Tribe of Dina.*

13. For an analysis of the subordinate roles women have held in most human societies, see Gayle Rubin, "The Traffic in Women: Notes on the 'Political Economy' of Sex," in *Toward an Anthropology of Women*, ed. Rayna R. Reiter (New York, 1975), 157–210.

14. See, in particular, Wegner's discussion in chapter 3 of whether or not women are allowed to study Torah according to rabbinic Judaism.

15. On these topics see notes to chapters 7–8 and 10 and my Selected Bibliography.

16. See my Selected Bibliography for suggested readings on these topics.

CHAPTER **1** SUSAN NIDITCH

*Portrayals of Women in the Hebrew Bible*

To study women and the Hebrew Bible is to delve into a variety of
fields including not only Bible scholarship but also women's studies,
Judaica, literary criticism, anthropology, and sociology. Primary material in the Hebrew Scriptures is rich and varied, the relevant bibliography extensive, and the methodologies employed by students of
women and the Bible interdisciplinary, daring, and often at the very
crest of scholarship. This essay explores portrayals of women in the
Hebrew Bible, discusses the challenges and problems such a study
poses, and provides a guide to major trends in recent scholarship.

## METHODOLOGICAL CHALLENGES

Challenges in the study of women and the Hebrew Bible are in many
ways parallel to challenges faced in Scripture study as a whole. The
ways in which biblical authors portray families or women or kings
do not necessarily correspond to how families and women actually

lived or kings governed in specific, historically datable and definable social realities. In the Bible's own scheme, Israelite history divides into three major periods: (1) the time before the monarchy (before c. 1000 B.C.E.), (2) the period of monarchy (c. 1000–586 B.C.E.), and (3) the post-monarchic period (586 B.C.E. on). Within the Bible's narrative framework the first era includes the patriarchs and matriarchs, the exodus from Egypt, and Moses, Aaron, and Miriam, the conquest and settlement, Joshua and Rahab, and all the judges including Deborah, Samson, and the prophet-judge Samuel. The second era includes the first king, Saul, and his successor, David; David's wives, Michal, Abigail, and Bathsheba; certain "wise women"; the other Northern and Southern kings; and the rise of prophecy. A major theme of this period is the building and maintainance of the Temple and the Holy City, Jerusalem; the epoch ends with the destruction of Solomon's Temple and the exile of the elite of Jerusalem. The third era includes the prophets Zechariah and Haggai and the leaders Ezra and Nehemiah and is the so-called Second Temple period following the Babylonian exile. During this time the Temple is rebuilt and a new theological grounding for Yahwism is established; Israelite religion begins to be Judaism.

All this being said, however, how do we date the literature of the Hebrew Bible? No modern scholars would accept, for example, that all the material pertaining to the lives of the patriarchs or the exodus was written in, or even originated in, a premonarchic period. A few texts such as Exodus 15 and Judges 5 may predate the monarchy as revealed by their language and orthography, but these are the exceptions. Two well-known scholars recently refused to include a so-called "patriarchal" period in their major history of Israel, beginning instead at "the eve of the establishment of the monarchy" (c. 1200 B.C.E.).[1] What, then, do we do with figures such as Sarah or Rachel?

Since the early twentieth century most scholars have accepted the so-called documentary hypothesis, which suggests that one can date certain layers of the Hebrew Scriptures through the names by which God is called. Thus, one chapter of Genesis will be attributed to the Yahwist and another to the Elohist (depending on whether the deity is referred to as Yahweh or Elohim). This hypothesis, too, has come under attack, and I am among those who do not accept many of the old attributions. Nevertheless, scholars do agree that many authors, sources, periods, and cultural threads lie behind the work we call the Hebrew Bible. Revisions and elaborations were essential to the biblical process, while the notion of "original" or "first" version may be completely out of place in dealing with traditional literature, which until its codification or canonization always exists in multiplicity and which is always undergoing change even while belonging to a continuum with the past.

Given that the Hebrew Bible is the product of a complex process of growth, what can we hope to learn about women in the Hebrw Scriptures? Can we place individual portraits on a historical time line or are all the portrayals archetypal and timeless? Is it possible to speak of individual authors and their life settings, or should we treat the tradition as a whole?

First, we need not forego all notions of history or sociological setting. Acknowledging that all pieces of Scripture were given final form by someone allows us to speak of composers or authors who belong to particular periods and settings. Certain values and attitudes—often contrasting ones—emerge in how women are presented; in these are found a history of worldviews and ethos, if not simple reliable fact. [2] We do not know if a character named Rahab once saved Israelite spies (Joshua 2), but we know that an author employs the traditional and cross-cultural motif of the helpful harlot at the crossroads in a way that comments on the appeal of Yahwism to non-Israelites and on the marginality of Israelites at a certain point in their history. This author implicitly comments on the potential power for directed action and on the cleverness of a woman, in particular, one who is outside the social order and who in a sense symbolizes the situation of Israel as narrated. Yahweh is with her and she with him. We might then go on to discuss at which periods in real history such a portrait with its implicit messages might be of particular interest to Israelite authors and audiences.

We must also keep in mind that the Hebrew Scriptures, even in its final composed form, is no monolith. It reflects various periods of time, as well as differences among Israelites, even of one period. As Morton Smith has shown, every attitude in favor of a particular position hints at the existence of counterattitudes. [3] "Yahweh-alone-ers" no doubt coexisted in Israel with those who worshipped Yahweh along with other personal gods, some of these perhaps female divine figures.

Hints of the attitudes of these Israelites remain in the Hebrew Scriptures in polemics against worshippers of the ancient Near Eastern goddess, Asherah, for example. So, too, while the Hebrew Bible in general is male-centered, interesting nuances and threads emerge when one goes beyond that generalization.[4] Equally misleading can be claims, difficult to substantiate, suggesting women may be responsible for one of the sources believed to underlie the Pentateuch just because many of the stories are about women, children, and the home and that 2 Isaiah may be a woman because some of the Isaianic prophecies employ female imagery to describe God (e.g., Isaiah 42:14, 49:15; and later material in 66:9 and 13).[5]

The situation becomes even more complicated when one thinks of the various life settings and orientations from which authors may have come, and the various options in life-style possible for real Israelite women, especially during the period of the monarchy and beyond. I have found, for example, at least three definable styles and worldviews in Genesis, one more baroque and courtly, one more popular, and one more homiletical and self-consciously theological.[6] Might not authors with such differing orientations present women differently? If one looks behind the literature to real lives, it becomes clear that the eighth-century B.C.E. woman surrounded by the "ivory couches" and other luxuries of the Northern Israelite aristocracy condemned by Amos (6:4–7), would have led a life quite different from the wife of a small landowner or a poor destitute widow. Issues of class within one period are as important as issues of date across several periods. Here, archaeological information becomes critically important even though major archaeological digs have often involved the sites of cities and temples rather than ordinary villages where people ate, and cooked, and worked.[7]

Finally, one must acknowledge that the canon of the Hebrew Bible, like the implicit canon of English literature or Renaissance music, is an explicitly edited work from which many women's roles and important aspects of women's lives have been excluded. As we turn to portrayals of women in the Hebrew Scriptures and explore attitudes toward women implied in its narratives and legal corpora and especially as we speculate on the lives of real Israelite women and on the historical settings of biblical composers, we must always think about what may have been excluded.

## LAW AND SOCIAL SETTING

The spiritual basis of Israel's history and law is the covenantal relationship enjoined on all believers in Yahweh, who are bound to each other through him in a vow of love and obedience. While such an exalted vision of human equality in the presence of their Creator might seem to be a positive and liberating force in Israelite religion, the statutes preserved in Scripture present the image of a strongly patrilineal culture in which women are in some instances highly marginalized and fenced out and in others neatly fenced in, enclosed, and safely bound.[8] Again, we must always remember that biblical law is material edited, preserved, codified and presented in literature and not necessarily a reflection of actual lives. In discussing this literature, the image of woman as vessel or a house is appropriate. She is to be filled with her husband's seed which (it is hoped) will develop into children, especially male children. As she contains and shelters the future child, so her realm is the home, the private realm of children and procreation. Women are legally governed by their fathers before marriage and by their husbands after marriage. In the former condition they are virgins; those discovered to be sexually active are to be stoned by their fathers' houses (Deuteronomy 22:21). As wives, they are to be faithful, child-producing spouses, a position they may share with other wives in polygynous marriage. Those who cannot bear successfully or who displease their husbands may be divorced (Deuteronomy 24:1–4, but see the protections offered in Deuteronomy 22:13–19); those who commit adultery are to suffer the same fate as nonvirgins (Deuteronomy 22:22; Leviticus 20:10), though we have no way of knowing whether these laws were consistently carried out. Those accused by their husbands of adultery, in the absence of certain proof, undergo a trial ritual rich in the symbolism of "purity and danger" (Numbers 5:11–31). Adultery involves relations with a married woman. A married man's relations with an unmarried woman are not adulterous, for intimate aspects of women's lives really have to do with relations between men. Thus, a man is executed for lying with another's wife because he has committed a crime of theft against a man. If a man seduces or rapes a virgin, he must pay bride-price to the father and marry her (Deuteronomy 22:28). Rules of incest—information about who is or who is not an appropriate marriage partner—are likewise addressed in the masculine singular to men. Leviticus 18 is a fascinating passage revealing priestly views concerning what constitutes too close a marriage tie, as this thread of Israelite culture steers a course between incest and exogamy.

Women normally do not inherit property, although exceptions are made in families without sons (see Numbers 27:1–11), and the author of the Book of Ruth assumes a wife could inherit her husband's property.[9] All of this paints a portrait of women with very little de jure political or economic autonomy. The married woman who does not bear children is in an especially marginalized position, for she is no longer a virgin in her father's home yet does not fully function in her husband's. It is the children who form her bond with her husband's clan. No specific law applies to her; but the barren wife is a favorite biblical motif, marking the birth of heroes, as in many cultures. The condition of infertility is presented as a special cultural worry for the woman, and the young childless widow is a particular problem case, for she is caught between two stages in her life. This problem is addressed in Deuteronomy 25:5 by a law requiring the dead man's brother to take her as his wife to raise up children in the name of the deceased, thereby regularizing the woman's position in the patriarchal clan.[10]

Perhaps the most noticeable laws of fencing off and boundary making vis-à-vis women are laws pertaining to purity. The menstruating woman is forbidden to her husband sexually for seven days. Her uncleanness (an invisible but real *substance*) contaminates what she sits upon, and a man can contract uncleanness by touching her or a seat or bed where she has been (Leviticus 15:21). This uncleanness from touching lasts until the transitional evening time returns the man's state to cleanness (15:19). The man who has intercourse with her is rendered unclean for seven days (15:24). So, too, the postpartum woman is unclean for seven days after the birth of a son, then must remain an additional thirty-three days in the blood of her purification. She may touch nothing "holy nor enter the sanctuary" in this period. Twice these lengths of time—fourteen and sixty-six days—are prescribed for the birth of daughters, in a sort of anticipation of the female babies' future dangerous states (Leviticus 12). This material is found in a portion of Scripture preserved by priests; it is not entirely clear exactly how rules such as these affected ordinary women's daily lives or their participation in community life. Are these purity laws premonarchic and pre-Temple in date or later? One can conclude that for at least one important group in Israelite culture, all discharges were regarded as rendering unclean. The ordinary woman of child-bearing age has regular discharges and is therefore regularly subject to uncleanness, an uncleanness associated with the psychologically and physically powerful rhythms of fertility, pregnancy, and childbirth. As such, woman becomes a monthly source of danger and power, containing an uncleanness that can spill over and contaminate, making successful mediation between God and humans in ritual impossible. Thus, in the priestly worldview, the woman is bound out of most aspects of cultic life. Do such laws reflect male priests' desires to hold power? Were there other competing options in religious expression open to women, threads not preserved in our sources?[11] There are, after all, cultures in which women's procreative powers render them influential in the realm of the religious.

A few more features of legal material should be mentioned. Men are obligated to perform conjugal duties for their wives in Exodus 21:10, pointing to a power of the woman in the private realm, emphasized in the matriarchal narratives of Genesis discussed below.

While prostitution is outlawed, as in the book law of many cultures, some of the narrative material assumes the existence of independent, working prostitutes, women who are crossroads people, beyond ordinary cultural norms assumed for women and not under the thumb of husband or father. These marginal women are of interest to biblical writers, as shown by the stories of Rahab (Joshua 2) and the disguised Tamar (Genesis 38).

Within the Bible, legal material does not always tally with narrative. Jacob marries two sisters although this is forbidden in Leviticus 18:18; the law of the levirate is contrary to Leviticus 18:16. These differences may reflect different periods and changes in the law or indicate that the priestly laws of Leviticus 18 were not "law" to all.

As we move on to portrayals of women in narrative and other genres, certain sometimes overlapping typologies emerge. Biblical women include matriarchs and tricksters, wise women and warriors, and finally a group whom Phyllis Trible calls the victims.[12]

## WOMEN IN NARRATIVE

Biblical authors portray Rebecca, wife of Isaac, and the sisters Rachel and Leah, wives of Jacob, as young women in their fathers' homes who marry their paternal cousins, that is, who participate in the time-honored custom of cross-cousin marriage[13] (see Genesis 24 and Genesis 28–30).

Except for the unloved Leah, all the wives of the patriarchs—Sarah, Rebecca, and Rachel—are able to bear children only with difficulty; they are archetypal barren women, as are Hannah, the mother of Samuel, and Samson's unnamed mother.[14] Paradoxically, however, they have power in the private realm over matters of sex and children; in this connection they often play the role of tricksters, of those who use irregular, deceiving means to gain an end.[15] Those who are marginal in their family and culture use wit to derive some benefit from, or power over, those in control. It is in child-related areas, in particular, that the women display their strength and a certain closeness to the divine. Communications about children to be born are some of the few instances in which God is seen to speak to women. The annunciation to Samson's mother in Judges 13 is of special relevance, for the divine emissary makes it quite clear that he wishes to speak to the woman—not with her husband, who is, in fact, portrayed as a doubting, fearful dolt in contrast to his more sensible, down-to-earth wife.[16] Sarah has the nerve to laugh when she hears a child is to be born (Genesis 18:12). Hannah herself prays for a child at the sanctuary and interacts with the priest Eli (1 Samuel 1:9–18). Sarah and Rebecca, moreover, further with God's blessing the careers of their favorite sons, the younger offspring, Sarah in having Hagar and Ishmael expelled and Rebecca in tricking Isaac into giving Jacob his blessing (see also Bathsheba's role in 1 Kings 1:15–21, 28–31). The women, like Manoah's wife, are perceived in these cases as having the inside track to God's will. Similarly, Rachel successfully steals her father's household gods and hides them under her, chasing her father away with the warning that she is in a menstrual state (Genesis 31:34–35). This scene, with its implicit emphasis on the woman's power grounded in her fertility places the power of the hearth over the power of the public realm. Laban, like the patriarchs, is reduced to impotency.

So the blind Isaac is deceived by his wife and son in his old age, so Abraham must acquiesce to Sarah's wishes vis-à-vis Ishmael, so Manoah sees but does not comprehend. A relevant scene is the "selling" of Jacob's marital duties. Rachel, desperate for children, buys fertility-producing mandrake plants from her sister Leah in exchange for Jacob's conjugal services. When he returns from the field Leah gives him his orders. He will sleep with her that night; meekly, without question, he goes and performs his duty (Genesis 30:14–18), yielding Leah an unexpected son. These stories fit traditional narrative patterns: youngest sons always inherit and heroes are born under special circumstances. Nevertheless, the fact that the biblical writers create special roles for the women in the working out of these patterns, that they draw the mothers and wives a certain way, does say something important about their perceptions of the feminine, an important perception apparently shared by the participants in the literary tradition. The portraits of women holding power in the private realm, a power associated with fertility and children, tallies with the portrait emerging in the legal material and is not unique to Israelite culture.[17]

In addition to the portrayals of "mothers," the matriarchs, we find equally penetrating portraits of women warriors and wise women, both of whom share traits with the tricky mothers discussed above and indeed with most of the successful men of the Hebrew Scriptures, who succeed by means of savvy and concealment, wit and deception.

The warriors, Deborah and Jael, make their appearances in the Book of Judges in the context of Israel's battles with Canaanite enemies. While Deborah is a judge, a general, and a tactician who clearly dominates and outshines Barak, her man-at-arms (Judges 4:8–9), Jael is a guerrilla assassin who welcomes the fleeing Canaanite general Sisera into her tent with promises of safety and succor and then runs him through the head with a tent peg (Judges 4–5). In language and imagery richly dripping in eroticism and death, Jael partakes of a wider Ancient Near Eastern and more universal archetype of the seductress-exterminator. Jael is an unlikely heroine, a self-appointed female soldier, who reverses the normal fate of a woman in battle (cf. Judges 5:30). She is not seduced, taken, or despoiled but herself seduces, marginalizes, and despoils a man. An Israelite author and Israelite audiences of various periods clearly identify with her when confronting enemies better armed and more powerful than themselves (so, too, the Maccabean-period Judith, based on Judges 4–5). As JoAnn Hackett has shown, the larger, more active, public, and aggressive roles given Deborah and Jael may well indicate works composed during periods of "social dysfunction" and decentralization, when women emerge from the shadows as more directed, overtly aggressive or powerful figures.[18] Certainly, such characterizations of women are found in the literature about such periods.

Jael, like Judith, seduces and kills via deception, and thus shares in the category of biblical men and women who use their wit to achieve their goals, escape danger, or improve their status. Among such figures are Abigail, Esther, Ruth, and Naomi. Abigail's beautiful appearance, clever rhetoric, and demeanor of self-effacement save her household from the future king David who appears on her husband's estate very much like a bandit or pirate as he flees from Saul (1 Samuel 25). Esther, also assuming the pose of the humble, vulnerable, and beautiful supplicant, saves herself and her people from her foolish but powerful husband, Ahasuerus, the Persian monarch who has fallen under the influence of the evil Haman. Ruth, with Naomi's help, wins a husband to efface her widow status. All of these women share two traits: their husbands are foolish or absent (in the cases of Abigail and Esther, the women clearly outstrip their husbands in intelligence); and they present an appearance of subservient "female behavior," dressing for success, dealing obsequiously with spouses or future spouses, flattering, and using language well and convincingly. The wisdom tradition in Proverbs suggests a similar combination of savvy and subservience as the means of obtaining political success in dealing with the powerful, for spheres of politics and gender are often mirror images. Proverbs 31:10–31 presents a slightly different portrait, that of the respected, capable wife, the jewel in her husband's crown, having various economic as well as familial responsibilities.

Quite different are the so-called "wise women" who appear in two fascinating passages in 2 Samuel. Does the term *wise woman* simply refer to a woman who is wise, or were there professional wise women in ancient Israel? If so, what were their roles? In 2 Samuel 14 a wise woman from Tekoa is summoned to become a living *mashal*, or parable. Joab, general to King David, instructs her as a director would direct an actress to portray the role of bereaved mother and spin a tale to David that will convince him to allow his son Absalom to return to court. She plays the part beautifully, convincing the king. She is, in short, a professional mediator, an improvisationist skilled in the dramatic weaving and enactment of mediating parables.[19] In a similar role, the wise woman of 2 Samuel 20:16 intervenes between her town and the general Joab, who has come on a search-and-destroy mission to capture the rebel Shimei ben Bichri. She uses appropriate proverbs, rhetoric, and skills of mediation to convince her townsmen to give up the offender to the agent of the king and in this way prevents great destruction. These wise women are not unlike Abigail and Esther in their mediating roles but appear also to be titled professionals. Their activities, moreover, have much in common with those of prophets like Nathan, who weaves a parable to mediate between God and David, indirectly accusing the king of murder. Numerous other prophets, named and unnamed, become living dramatizations or symbols of God's message (see 1 Kings 11:29–40, 20:35–43; Jeremiah 13:1–11). These women and men employ a creative, artistic, and formalized technique to accuse an offender of wrongdoing or to reveal a true situation in order to resolve tensions, ease conflict, and render justice, sometimes shaming a person or persons into acting justly.[20]

One might wonder if women also played the prophetic mediating role or any prophetic role, for prophecy is a form of wisdom. In other Near Eastern cultures women were prophets, dream interpreters, diviners, and singers (and perhaps ecstatic composers) of sacred texts.[21] The Hebrew Bible does include some portrayals of such female figures involved in leadership roles in the publically religious sphere (see Isaiah 8:3; 2 Kings 22:14–20; and Nehemiah 6:14).[22] Hulda, the prophetess (2 Kings 22:14–20), provides the seventh-century B.C.E. King Josiah with a divine warning of doom unless he becomes a pro-Yahwist reformer, casting out idols. Her oracle is framed in rubrics typical of biblical prophecy, although all other examples are delivered by male prophets. The accusations, suggestions for reform, and acceptance of the king's confession and repentance are presented in language completely at home in the canon of prophetic speech. Her prophetic gift is not treated as unusual for a woman. Petition to her is made in the most matter-of-fact way, leading one to wonder whether she was one of a score of female prophets not included in the Hebrew Scriptures or at least a characterization based on such real-life figures. Miriam, sister of Moses, is called "the prophetess" in Exodus 15:20. Passages such as Numbers 12 reveal another thread in the tradition. In its criticism of Moses' sister, the tale of Miriam's "gossiping" about Moses' wife is an attempt to squelch Miriam's pretentions—or more

precisely the claims of priestly groups and leaders, perhaps female
leaders, claiming Miriam as ancestress heroine.[23] One also thinks of
the female spirit medium who raises the ghost of the prophet Samuel
for Saul in an eerie and powerful adumbration of the latter's final defeat (1 Samuel 28:7). In an apparent trance state she brings forth the
crusty old man to predict Saul's death and then emerges from her state
and professional role to offer the depressed king food. Much like
Achilles to Priam after the death of Hector in Homer's *Iliad,* she attempts to bring Saul and his thoughts out of the realm of death to the
realm of the mundane and ordinary, the realm of eating. Thus the
spirit medium is also the nurturer, Woman.

In discussing women able to cross the boundary from earthly to
divine, this-worldly to otherworldly, we raise several important issues
touched upon above: (1) the question of ordinary women's cultic and
religious activities: How did women reach God? (2) special cultic roles
for women in various forms of Yahwism; (3) the question of women
goddesses in the Ancient Near East and in some forms of Yahwism;
(4) images of Yahweh as female.

We do not have the space to discuss each of these matters in detail
but direct the reader to fine secondary readings. Phyllis Bird's essay
and a forthcoming book discuss the first two of these issues, including
biblical and extra-biblical evidence for forms of Israelite popular religion not sanctioned by the framers of the Hebrew Scriptures.[24] For an
overview of ancient Near Eastern goddesses, places to start are E. O.
James, *The Cult of the Mother Goddess,* an older but still useful work;[25]
articles by Judith Ochshorn and C. J. Bleeker in C. Olson's edited
*Book of the Goddess Past and Present;*[26] and Carole Fontaine's study of
goddess tricksters.[27]

In one spot in the Hebrew Scriptures a goddess-like figure meets
Yahwism in the female personification of Wisdom, whose alter ego, or
Jungian negative counterpart, is the "strange" woman personifying
Antiwisdom. The biblical figure of Wisdom of Proverbs 8 has a certain
grand stature, accompanying God at the Creation and exhorting men
to follow her ways. Claudia Camp has explored the female Wisdom
figure in detail.[28] Another important area involves the place of the
Near Eastern goddess Asherah in the religious life of some Israelites
who worshipped her, much to the horror of, and in spite of the condemnation of purist Yahwists (see 1 Kings 15:13, 18:19; 2 Kings
21:7, 23:4, 7). As noted by P. D. Miller, inscriptions from Kuntillet

Ajrud described by William Dever as "a 9th–8th century B.C.E. Isra-
elite-Judaean caravanserai and attached shrine" refer more than once
to "Yahweh of Samaria and his *'ašerah.*" Scholars debate about *'ašerah's* status, though many believe her to have been a regarded as a
consort of Yahweh.[29] Also relevant are the prophet Jeremiah's condemnations of worship practices involving "the Queen of Heaven"
(see Jeremiah 7:17–18, 44:15–25). The possibility that in some
forms of Israelite religion women played greater roles in cult or that
some Israelites may have worshipped female deities, of course, does
not necessarily imply that the workaday lives of women in these traditions differed markedly from the lives of women whose Yahwism is
sanctioned by the biblical framers nor that the former enjoyed better
or fuller lives, socioeconomically or politically. As for images of Yahweh as mother or nurturer, as a starting point, I recommend Phyllis
Trible's *God and the Rhetoric of Sexuality.*[30]

Having raised questions concerning the connections between the
patterns of literature and the patterns of real lives, we turn to a group
of women whom, after Phyllis Trible, we call the victims. Phyllis
Trible explores a number of these characters with her usual great literary sensitivity and thoughtfulness in the book *Texts of Terror.*[31] By
*victims* we refer to women who suffer physical and/or mental abuse at
the hands of some of the male characters of Scripture. Most troubling
is the narrators' neutrality and seeming lack of sympathy for the victims. As Eve Sedgwick has shown for a different corpus of literature,
the stories featuring women are not necessarily about women but
about relations between men.[32] Thus, the rape of David's daughter
Tamar, about which David does nothing, becomes the cause of the
blood feud between Absalom, Tamar's brother, and Amnon, the half
brother, who has his way with her (2 Samuel 13–18). The rape of
Jacob's daughter Dinah similarly becomes the cause for Jacob's sons'
vengeance against the men of Shechem (Genesis 34). The nameless
concubine in Judges 19 is another rape victim thrown to her fate by
her husband to save his own skin from rapists, "evil fellows" among
the Benjaminites. The evil deed spills over into a full-scale civil war.
Michal, David's first wife, daughter of Saul, is caught between her
father and husband, given to David, taken away, retaken by David,
and then cast off by him.[33] Jephthah promises as a sacrifice to God the
first thing he sees upon return from battle if God helps him to succeed.
He succeeds, but the first thing he sees is his daughter. She meekly

agrees to become a sacrifice and goes off to the the hills to mourn her virginity with friends her age (Judges 11:29–40). Hagar, Abraham's concubine, is sent away with her son, alone and deserted (Genesis 21:8–21). She is caught in the Ishmael-Isaac contest for succession, though they are both children at the time. The complex texts that present these women are open to interpretation. Do the authors of these tales mean us to sympathize with the women? A modern reader of this material cannot but do so, but is the sympathy reader-generated or author-generated? The men of the narratives are variants of the folk motif of the incompetent, stupid father-husband mentioned above. Like Beauty's foolish father, or the father of the "Girl without Hands" (*Grimms' Fairy Tales*, nos. 88 and 31, respectively), Jephthah thoughtlessly and with concern only for his own success makes a vow dooming his daughter. So the Levite in a more visceral way sacrifices his concubine to a barbaric mob. When Jacob hears of the rape of his daughter, he is more concerned to make peace with the rapist's father than to defend his child. Abraham—and indeed his advisor, God— cast off the mother Hagar. David and Amnon use young women and then discard them, later suffering—or in the case of Amnon, dying—because of the family strife they create. Even the pro-Davidic writer of David's court narratives portrays David as a weak and impotent father and husband, a man whose personal life never reaches the successes of his public achievements. It is as if the artistic demands on this creative and traditional-style author outweigh his pro-Davidic propagandistic motivations. Even the men who defend women, Dinah's brothers and Absalom, might be accused of being self-serving— with honor in the case of Jacob's sons, concerned with ridding himself of a senior prince in the case of Absalom (though this is not certain). These narratives may reflect an interesting anthropological, psychological, and mythological pattern whereby the brother-sister relationship is the love relationship rather than the relationship between father and child (e.g., the birth narratives of Cronos and Zeus and his siblings in *Theogony* 145–210, 453–506, and the folktale "Hansel and Gretel," *Grimms' Fairy Tales* no. 15).

The women submit silently (Dinah, concubine, Hagar) or verbally (Jephthah's daughter) or protest in vain (Tamar). Are the authors of these narratives providing models of how women should be or how they must be? Are the characterizations typological reflections of a cultural reality? How does each author judge this reality if it exists?

Do the authors sympathize with the women, or are the narrative voices too silent, too neutral, to read? Jephthah's daughter displays a certain nobility and is described as the founder of a ritual for young women; Tamar and Hagar certainly evoke pathos. These women are surely presented as the heroines of their stories; the men around them are bumbling, cruel, foolish, or all three.

## CONCLUSION

To study women in the Hebrew Bible is to reexamine and reassess a lengthy history of biblical hermeneutics; it is to pose new questions about legal and nonlegal texts and to make what will strike some readers as radical suggestions concerning the religion and culture of Israel. I have explored the characterizations of women, and the tone, texture, and point of view of the compositions in which they appear as a student of literature, asking what sorts of authors and audiences would have found these portrayals meaningful and why. As a student of history, I have faced the challenge that even the so-called historical books of the Bible and the legal texts are not simple reflections of historical fact or verifiable data. Most important, I have tried to convey a sense of the varieties of Israelite religion and culture both in any one period of time and over time as relevant to a study of women. An examination of the provenance and biases of particular authors is critical, as is the realization that information about women's modes of religious expression, about alternate forms of Yahwism, and about particular women leaders and positions of leadership held by women, may have been excluded from the canon. We have explored some of the hints left behind in the edited texts. Perhaps most interesting in our study is the realization that the laws of the Hebrew Bible come from various periods and groups responding to, and reflecting, various perceptions of Israelite mores and worldviews.[34] The priestly view of women, emerging in laws of purity, for example, may not have been the most characteristic view of women in all periods or segments of Israelite culture. Just as Jacob Neusner and other feminist scholars have suggested that early rabbinic law originally may have reflected the cosmology of the rabbis and not Jews in general,[35] so, too, priestly law may reveal the worldview of a small group of Israelites and not the worldview of all or even most participants in Israelite culture.

**NOTES**

1. J. Maxwell Miller and John H. Hayes, *A History of Ancient Israel and Judah* (Philadelphia, 1986), 79.

2. For a judicious as well as creative approach to the reconstruction of Israelite women's history see, JoAnn Hackett, "In the Days of Jael: Reclaiming the History of Women in Ancient Israel," in *Immaculate and Powerful. The Female in Sacred Image and Social Reality*, ed. Clarissa W. Atkinson, Constance H. Buchanan, and Margaret R. Miles (Boston, 1985), 15–38.

3. Morton Smith, *Palestinian Parties and Politics That Shaped the Old Testament* (New York, 1971).

4. A less-than-adequately complex approach to patriarchalism is Esther Fuchs, "The Literary Characterization of Mothers and Sexual Politics in the Hebrew Bible," and "Who Is Hiding the Truth? Deceptive Women and Biblical Androcentrism," both in *Feminist Perspectives on Biblical Scholarship*, ed. Adela Yarbro Collins (Chico, CA, 1985).

5. For conclusions too quickly drawn, see Richard E. Friedman, *Who Wrote the Bible?* (San Francisco, 1987), 86. A more interesting and careful—if controversial—analysis of the issue of female authorship and the female composer's voice is found in Mieke Bal, *Murder and Difference. Gender, Genre, and Scholarship on Sisera's Death* (Bloomington, 1988).

6. See my *Underdogs and Tricksters: A Prelude to Biblical Folklore* (San Francisco, 1987), 22–69.

7. For application of anthropological, sociological, and archaeological perspectives to some questions about the lives of "ordinary people" in Israelite culture, see Carol Meyers, "Procreation, Production, and Protection: Male-female Balance in Early Israel," *Journal of the American Academy of Religion* 51 (1983): 569–94; idem, *Discovering Eve: Ancient Israelite Women in Context* (New York, 1988), 16–20. See also her earlier article "The Roots of Restriction: Women in Early Israel," *Biblical Archaeologist* 41 (1978): 91–103. This paper interestingly contrasts with suggestions offered in Hackett, "In the Days of Jael." For additional material on the lives of women in the Ancient Near East, see Sue Rollin, "Women and Witchcraft in Ancient Assyria," Jackie Pringle, "Hittite Birth Rituals," and Katarzyna Grosz, "Bridewealth and Dowry in Nuzi," all in *Images of Women in Antiquity*, ed. Averil Cameron and Amélie Kuhrt (Detroit, 1983). The reader might also consult resources in *La femme dans le Proche Orient antique*, ed. J. M. Durand (Paris, 1987).

8. For a thorough but concise examination of Israelite law and women, see Phyllis Bird, "Images of Women in the Old Testament," in *Religion and Sexism*, ed. Rosemary Radford Ruether (New York, 1974), 48–57.

9. See Bird, "Images," 53.

10. See my "Wronged Woman Righted: An Analysis of Genesis 38," *Harvard Theological Review* 72 (1979): 143–49.

11. On this matter see Phyllis Bird, "The Place of Women in the Israelite Cultus," in *Ancient Israelite Religion*, ed. Patrick D. Miller, Jr., Paul D. Hanson, and S. Dean McBride (Philadelphia, 1987), 408–9.

12. See Phyllis Trible, *Texts of Terror: Literary-feminist Readings of Biblical Narratives* (Philadelphia, 1984), 102, 104–6, and 114 n. 43.

13. On cross-cousin marriage and the patriarchal narratives see Robert Oden, *The Bible without Theology* (San Francisco, 1987), 106–30.

14. For a fine study of the matriarchal narratives see J. Cheryl Exum, "Mother in Israel: A Familiar Figure Reconsidered," in *Feminist Interpretation of the Bible*, ed. Letty M. Russell (Philadelphia, 1985), 73–85; for a different but equally interesting perspective see Fuchs, "Literary Characterization of Mothers."

15. See my *Underdogs and Tricksters*, and the various articles in J. Cheryl Exum and Johanna W. H. Bos, eds., *Reasoning with the Foxes: Female Wit in a World of Male Power, Semeia* 42 (1988).

16. On Manoah's wife see J. Cheryl Exum, "Promise and Fulfillment: Narrative Art in Judges 13," *Journal of Biblical Literature* 99 (1980): 43–59.

17. The classic discussion of issues of public and private in gender roles is Michelle Zimbalist Rosaldo, "Woman, Culture, and Society: A Theoretical Overview," in *Woman, Culture, and Society*, ed. Michelle Zimbalist Rosaldo and Louise Lamphere (Stanford, 1974), 17–42.

18. Hackett, "In the Days of Jael," 24–26.

19. See Claudia V. Camp, "The Wise Women of 2 Samuel: A Role Model for Women in Early Israel," *Catholic Biblical Quarterly* 43 (1981): 14–29, esp. 24, 26.

20. See Camp, "Wise Women."

21. For a review of comparative Ancient Near Eastern sources see Judith Ochshorn, "Ishtar and Her Cult," in *The Book of the Goddess Past and Present*, ed. Carl Olson (New York, 1983), 16–28; Gay Robins, "The God's Wife of Anun in the 18th Dynasty in Egypt," and Ulla Jeyes, "The Nadītu Women of Sippar," both in *Images of Women*, ed. Cameron and Kuhrt.

22. See also the fuller discussion in Bird, "Images of Women," 67–69.

23. See Rita J. Burns, *Has the Lord Indeed Spoken Only through Moses? A Study of the Biblical Portrait of Miriam* (Atlanta, 1987).

24. Bird, "Place of Women," 404–5.

25. E. O. James, *The Cult of the Mother Goddess* (London, 1959), 47–90.

26. Ochshorn, "Ishtar and Her Cult," and C. J. Bleeker, "Isis and Hathor: Two Ancient Egyptian Goddesses," in *Book of the Goddess*, ed. Olson.

27. Carole Fontaine, "The Deceptive Goddess in Ancient Near Eastern Myth: Inanna and Inaras," *Semeia* 42 (1988): 84–102. Also see material listed in n. 7.

28. See Claudia V. Camp, *Wisdom and the Feminine in the Book of Proverbs*, Bible and Literature Series no. 11 (Sheffield, UK, 1985); and "Woman Wisdom as Root Metaphor: A Theological Consideration," in *The Listening Heart: Essays on Wisdom and the Psalms*, ed. K. Hogland et al. (Sheffield, UK, 1987), 45–76.

29. See P. D. Miller, "The Absence of the Goddess in Israelite Religion," *Hebrew Annual Review* 10 (1986): 239–48, esp. 246 and nn. On the topic of goddesses among ancient Israelites, see also Peter R. Ackroyd, "Goddesses, Women, and Jezebel," in *Images of Women in Antiquity*, ed. Cameron and Kuhrt.

30. Phyllis Trible, *God and the Rhetoric of Sexuality* (Philadelphia, 1978), 31–72. See also Virginia Ramey Mollenkott, *The Divine Feminine: The Biblical Imagery of God As Female* (Philadelphia, 1983).

31. For readings of the tales of Jephthah's daughter, the unnamed woman in Judges 19, Tamar, and Hagar see Trible, *Texts of Terror*.

32. Eve Kosofsky Sedgwick, *Between Men: English Literature and Male Homosocial Desire* (New York, 1985). See also Gayle Rubin, "The Traffic in Women: Notes on the 'Political Economy' of Sex," in *Toward an Anthropology of Women*, ed. Rayna P. Reiter (New York, 1975), 157–210.

33. For an insightful study of the role of David's wives in the characterization of

the king himself, see Adele Berlin, "Characterization in Biblical Narrative: David's Wives," *Journal for the Study of the Old Testament* 23 (1982): 69–85.

34. R. R. Wilson points to some of the ways in which the varying legal traditions of the Hebrew Bible reflect variations in world-view and culture in "Ethics in Conflict. Sociological Aspects of Ancient Israel," in *Text and Tradition: The Hebrew Bible and Folklore*, ed. Susan Niditch (Atlanta, 1990).

35. See Jacob Neusner's excellent articles, "Anthropology and the Study of Talmudic Literature" and "Thematic or Systemic Description: The Case of the Mishnah's Division of Women," in *Method and Meaning in Judaism* (Missoula, MT, 1979), esp. 95–96; and chapters 2–3 below.

CHAPTER **2** **ROSS S. KRAEMER**

*Jewish Women in the Diaspora World of
Late Antiquity*

In the second century C.E., in the city of Smyrna on the western coast
of Asia Minor, a Jewish woman named Rufina commissioned the following Greek inscription on a marble slab: "Rufina, a Jewess, head of
the synagogue built this tomb for her freed slaves and the slaves raised
in her household. No one else has the right to bury anyone [here].
Anyone who dares to do [so] will pay 1500 denaria to the sacred treasury and 1000 denaria to the Jewish people. A copy of this inscription
has been placed in the [public] archives."[1]

Rufina's inscription seems surprising for many reasons: Rufina, who
has a Latin name, commissions an inscription in Greek, calls herself
"head" or "president" of the synagogue, acts both autonomously and
publicly without any reference to a father, husband, son, or male
guardian; oversees her own household of slaves and former slaves; and
lives in sufficient social proximity to the non-Jewish community to
prescribe a double penalty for anyone audacious enough to violate the
tomb. By considering each of these aspects of Rufina's inscription in

detail, we may address most of the issues central to the study of Judaism and Jewish women in late antiquity.

## BACKGROUND AND CONTEXT

From the third century B.C.E. on, like Rufina, the majority of Jews lived outside ancient Judea. Major cities such as Alexandria in Egypt, Antioch in Syria, and Rome itself all had large thriving Jewish communities at one time or another, while inscriptional evidence for Jewish communities has been found virtually throughout the entire Roman Empire.[2] The primary language of Jews living outside Judea was neither Hebrew nor Aramaic but rather Greek, and occasionally Latin, and as early as the third century B.C.E. Hebrew scriptures had been translated into Greek. Even Jews living within Judea were often bilingual in Greek and Aramaic.

Significantly, although there is virtually no evidence for the presence of rabbis in the Diaspora cities and towns of the Greco-Roman world where most Jews lived,[3] many scholars continue to rely heavily on rabbinic sources, especially the Mishnah and the Talmud, for evidence of the way Jews lived and thought in late antiquity. The assumption that rabbinic texts reflect even the social reality of the towns and villages in which the rabbis lived, let alone the social reality of Jewish communities removed from the rabbis in time or space or both, has been subject to increasing challenge.[4] Yet rabbinic sources still dominate many studies of early Judaism, including those on the study of Jewish women, and rabbinic evidence is considered to portray the realities of Jewish social and religious life.[5]

This study, by contrast, emphasizes nonrabbinic evidence for Jewish women in Diaspora communities and attempts to assess its historical reliability.[6] By focusing predominantly on nonrabbinic sources, especially inscriptions, papyri, and less well known literature, I hope to demonstrate that there is considerable other evidence for the lives of Jewish women in late antiquity. These sources not only serve as an important corrective to the rabbinic model but allow us to see that rabbinic Judaism is only one strand in the rich tapestry of diverse Judaisms in Greco-Roman antiquity.

## WOMEN'S ECONOMIC LIVES

To have commissioned such an inscription, Rufina of Smyrna must have been of substantial economic means. Not only were such inscriptions costly in and of themselves, the very content of the inscription reveals that Rufina owned property (the burial site) and slaves and was the head of a household. Regrettably, we cannot tell from this inscription how Rufina acquired her wealth, whether through inheritance[7] or business or some combination.

How unique Rufina was in her economic status can only be considered within the context of the varied economic conditions of Jews in different communities and at different times in the Greco-Roman world. A substantial proportion of the Jews in Rome may have been slaves or freedpersons,[8] although in the ancient world financial status and social status were not always closely correlated: slaves and freedpersons could and did control substantial financial resources.[9] The cumulative evidence from pagan writers, Christian sources, and the Jewish catacombs themselves, with their inscriptions suggests that while some Jews in Rome had substantial wealth and perhaps social position, the majority did not.

Similarly, the relative poverty of the Jewish community at Leontopolis in Egypt may be inferred from the physical nature of the burial inscriptions found there, most of which are brief and stereotypical. Tax registers, commercial documents, and other papyri suggest that Jews who lived in rural Egyptian villages were also of modest means: the amount of the dowry in a Greek divorce decree reflects the low economic status of the wife's family.[10] But the literary evidence and some of the epigraphical and papyrological evidence supports the view that many Jews living in Alexandria were financially comfortable. Like Rufina, Jews in the cities and towns of Asia Minor seem frequently to have been as well off as their neighbors and well integrated into the social and economic life of their communities.

Rufina's inscription is typical in containing no information about her occupation, if any. The occupations of Jewish women are rarely mentioned in burial and donative inscriptions. However, the papyri from Egypt make it clear that Jewish women engaged in commercial transactions of various sorts. In a document from the Fayum dated to 172/171 b.c.e., a woman named Sara guarantees a loan contracted by an unknown party.[11] A fragment from the same region dated to the middle of the second century B.C.E. lists the cattle, sheep, and goats owned by four Jewish women, while a tax register from Arsinoe in the same period lists six Jewish landowners, four of them women (*Corpus papyrorum judaicarum* [hereafter *CPJ*], nos. 28, 47). Jewish wet nurses are known from at least two papyri: in one the man engaging the woman's services is clearly not Jewish, although the identity of the foundling baby she is to nurse is less certain.[12]

Inscriptions from Asia Minor suggest that, like Rufina, Jewish women there had considerable financial independence and were publicly active. The individual names of women are routinely given in burial and other inscriptions, rather than identifying them only as the wife or daughter of some man. Aurelia Augusta, of Hierapolis, a city whose Jewish population is well documented for the second and third centuries C.E., owned a burial site reserved for herself, her husband and their children (*Corpus inscriptionum judaicarum* [hereafter *CIJ*], no. 775). Ammia of Acmonia, a village not very far from Hierapolis that also had a considerable Jewish population in the late Roman period, paid for the burial monument for herself, her husband, her son, and her daughter-in-law out of her own dowry funds (*CIJ*, no. 763). Other women in Jewish communities in Asia Minor made substantial contributions to local synagogues out of their own resources, often with no mention of a spouse.

## EDUCATION

Regrettably, Rufina's inscription sheds no direct light on the question of her formal education, although her role as *archisynagogos*, head of the synagogue, may well be indirect attestation of her ability to read and write. In general, the limited discussions of the education of Jewish women in late antiquity have, as usual, relied heavily on rabbinic sources for evidence. Leonard Swidler, for example, assumes that Jewish education in this period is more or less identical with study of Torah and cites the standard rabbinic references against teaching women Torah.[13] It is worth remembering that on this subject, as on many others regarding women, different rabbis had different opinions; and, as I noted earlier, many if not most Jews in this period did not, in any case, abide by rabbinic interpretations.

In reality, educated Jews in the Greco-Roman period, especially those in the Diaspora, undoubtedly studied far more than Jewish Scripture and its interpretation, Paul of Tarsus being one prominent example. Jesus ben Sira advised his students to travel abroad to gain knowledge, and his own writing reflects exposure to Greek and Egyptian learning (Wisdom of ben Sira 34:9–12). Philo of Alexandria was well trained not only in Scripture and its (allegorical) exegesis but in classical Greek texts and techniques as well. While it is highly unlikely that many Jews (men or women) were well educated in this period, some women clearly were, and that education consisted not only of the study of Jewish scriptures (primarily, like Philo, in Greek rather than in Hebrew) but of pagan literature as well.

The papyri, however, are replete with instances of women, both Jewish and non-Jewish, who could not write and therefore needed literate persons to sign legal documents on their behalf. This function was frequently met by a male relative acting as guardian, or *kyrios*. The phrase "So-and-so wrote for her, because she is illiterate" is found on many papyri: it is also found often for men, most of whom were similarly illiterate.[14] While most of the epigraphical evidence does not allow us to decide whether the women mentioned could read and write (which is essentially what we mean by *educated*), occasional references allude to this. One woman from Rome is called *discuplina bona* (a good pupil or disciple, *CIJ*, no. 215). The term *philentolos* (lover of the commandments), which is applied to several men and women, may also connote formal education (*CIJ*, no. 132). Similarly, as in the case of Rufina, women who held important synagogue offices may have needed to read and write in order to perform their duties. For our purposes, it is important to consider not only to what extent Jewish women were likely to have learned to read and write but whether they were any more or less likely to have done so than their pagan and Christian sisters, especially when social class and geographic factors are taken into consideration. Swidler claims that the young age at which Jewish girls routinely married would have curtailed their opportunities for any advanced education. However, Swidler's calculated average age at first marriage for Jewish women relied exclusively on rabbinic evidence, which is not consistent with the available demographic evidence from inscriptions and papyri.[15] If age at first marriage is related to educational attainments, young Jewish women may have had more opportunity to study before marriage than Swidler suggests.

Furthermore, some scholars have suggested that early marriage would have been an impediment to the education of pagan women, indicating that Jewish women would not have been any more or less likely to have been educated than other women in similar economic and social circumstances.[16]

## WOMEN'S JUDAISM:
## PARTICIPATION IN SYNAGOGUE LIFE

One of the most compelling and significant features of Rufina's inscription is her designation as an *archisynagogos*, the head or president of a synagogue. Rufina is not unique in this regard. At least two other women heads of synagogues are known from inscriptions: Sophia of Gortyn, who was head of a synagogue at Kissamos on Crete, probably in the fourth or fifth century C.E. (*CIJ*, no. 731c; Kraemer, *Maenads*, no. 85), and Theopempte of Myndos in Caria, Asia Minor in the same period (*CIJ*, no. 756, Kraemer, *Maenads*, no. 86). Women are also attested as members of the councils of elders in Crete, in Thrace, on the island of Malta, in North Africa, and in Venosa, Italy[17] and as "mothers of the synagogue" in Rome, Venetia, and Venosa, all in Italy.[18]

Epitaphs and inscriptions commemorating financial contributions to synagogues confirm that women played a significant role not only in the governance of synagogues throughout the ancient Diaspora but also in maintaining the financial health of their communities. Women donors to synagogues are widely documented: in Ionia, Caria, Apamea in Syria, Cyrenaica, and Hamman Lif (North Africa), together with donations to synagogues in Judea.[19] We have no record of specific financial contributions by women to synagogues in ancient Rome, since no ancient synagogues have yet been identified and excavated there.

Literary sources ranging from rabbinic texts to the New Testament and other early Christian writings make it clear that Jewish women routinely attended synagogue services.[20] This evidence receives vivid confirmation from an inscription found at Kyme in Western Asia Minor: "Tation, daughter of Straton, son of Empedon, having erected the assembly hall and the enclosure of the open courtyard with her own funds, gave them as a gift to the Jews. The synagogue of the Jews honored Tation, daughter of Straton, son of Empedon, with a golden crown and the privilege of sitting in the seat of honor."[21] That Tation sits in the seat of honor may surprise those who assume, as have many scholars in the past, that men and women were separated in the synagogue, as is the case in contemporary orthodox Jewish practice. However, Bernadette Brooten's exhaustive survey of the archaeological, literary, and epigraphical evidence[22] reveals that there is currently no evidence from antiquity that women were routinely separated from men in synagogue worship nor that women sat in upstairs galleries or adjacent rooms.[23]

## WOMEN'S RELIGIOUS PRACTICES

Ironically, outside rabbinic texts, the sources we have tell us nothing about the religious practices we most commonly associate with Jewish women, such as the baking of Sabbath bread, the blessing of Sabbath candles, the maintenance of a kosher household, and the observance of the laws of menstrual purity. When the piety of Jewish women receives praise in epitaphs, it is in vague, general terms, as in the epitaph of a Roman woman, dating perhaps to the second century c.e.:

> Here lies Regina, covered by such a tomb, which her husband set up as fitting to his love. After twice ten years, she spent with him one year, four months, and eight days more. She will live again, return to the light again, for she can hope that she will rise to the life promised as is our true faith, to the worthy and the pious, in that she has deserved to possess an abode in the hallowed land. This your piety has assured you, this your chaste life, this your love for your people, this your observance of the Law, your devotion to your wedlock, the glory of which was dear to you. For all these deeds your hope of the future is assured. In this your sorrowing husband seeks his comfort.[24]

We do not know, for example, exactly how Regina manifested her love for her people or her observance of the Law, whether through charitable service, synagogue office (though perhaps her husband would have been explicit about that), or formal study of Torah.

Some texts suggest that the observance of certain festivals was of particular importance to women, especially the fall holidays of Rosh Hashanah, Yom Kippur, and Sukkoth.[25] The Book of Judith, an

anonymous work that circulated in Greek, whose exact date and pro-
venience are unknown, offers a fascinating portrait of women's religious practices.[26] Judith, a widow, fasts[27] every day except Fridays,
Saturdays (Shabbat), the day before and of the New Moon, and the
day before and of festivals (Judith 8:4–7). She convinces the enemy
camp that she goes out nightly to pray, which provides her alibi and
subterfuge when she ultimately kills Holofernes, the commander of
the besieging "Assyrian" army. When Judith succeeds in saving her
people, the women of Israel come and bless her, and dance for her.
She distributes branches to the women, who crown both themselves
and Judith with olive wood. Then, led by Judith, the women dance
in a procession to Jerusalem, with the men following behind, bearing
garlands and singing hymns of praise to God. Finally, Judith sings a
hymn of praise, which recounts her deeds in the third person (Judith
15:12–16:17).[28]

The religious life of ordinary Jewish women doubtless also involved
the use of what we call magic, of which the following papyrus is but
one example:

> I bind you by oath, divine spirit who is present here, in the holy name
> Aoth Abaoth, the god of Abraam [Abraan], Iao of Jacob [Iakos], Iao
> Aoth Abaoth, the god of Israel [Israma]. Hear the honored, the fearful
> and the great name and lead [the spirit] to depart from [here] and [go]
> to Urbanus, whom Urbana bore, bring him to Domitiana, whom Can-
> dida bore, [making him] full of love, raging with jealousy and without
> sleep over his love and passion for her, and make him ask her to return
> to his house as wife. . . . I bind you by oath, the one who has separated
> the sea with the staff, to lead and yoke Urbanus, whom Urbana bore,
> to Domitiana, whom Candida bore, [making him] full of love, tor-
> mented and sleepless on account of his passion and desire for her, in
> order that he may lead her back to his house as his wife. (Kraemer,
> Maenads, no. 54)

Similarly, a Greek magical amulet from Syria, dating to the fourth
century C.E. or later, seeks the protection of Iao, Michael, Gabriel
and others for the newborn daughter of an unnamed woman (CIJ,
no. 849).

It is difficult to tell which of these were written by Jews, or used by
Jews. Previous generations of scholarship, constrained by the paradigm

of Judaism as uniformly and consumingly monotheistic rejected the possibility that spells that mix Jewish and pagan names for divinities could have been used by Jews. Recent scholarship has begun to mount a sustained attack on the insufficiency of this interpretation, making it all the more important for us to rethink the significance of these sources, particularly when what we seek is some reconstruction of the history of Jewish women. Moreover, many of the papyri, like the inscription of Domitiana, contain no references that are explicitly "pagan" and contain many references that point directly to Judaism. It seems quite likely that Jews in the villages of Egypt and elsewhere shared the inclinations of their pagan neighbors to utilize magical means to procure the objects of their social and economic desires.[29]

A small number of upper-class, well-educated Jewish women joined the contemplative monastic Therapeutic community known to us only from the testimony of Philo. Apparently, most of those women were older virgins, about whom Philo says that they preferred the immortal children which come from marriage with Wisdom above mortal children.[30] Like their male counterparts, they spent their days reading Jewish scriptures and allegorical commentaries (*On the Contemplative Life* 27–29). Members of the community, both men and women, broke their solitude weekly for Shabbat prayers and a common meal, as well as for occasional festival observances; otherwise they lived in their small cells, abstaining from all but the most modest nourishment, and living a life of rigorous asceticism (*On the Contemplative Life* 30, 34–39).

## PUBLIC ACTIVITY
## AND THE PRESENCE OF WOMEN

Everything about Rufina's inscription testifies to her involvement in public life, and we have ample evidence that other Jewish women participated in the social, economic, and religious life of their communities across the Roman Empire. Such participation would have required their physical presence in public places, such as synagogues, at least some of the time. Yet some scholars contend that Jewish women were physically secluded within their houses, and there are ample literary references to such practices. For example, Philo reports the indignation of Alexandrian Jewish men when their houses were searched for weapons during the prefecture of the violently anti-Jewish Flaccus: "They were . . . indignant . . . that their women kept in seclusion, never even approaching the outer doors, and their maidens confined to the inner chambers, who for modesty's sake avoided the sight of men, even of their closest relations, were displayed to eyes, not merely unfamiliar, but terrorizing through the fear of military violence."[31] Apparently describing the customs of Jews in Jerusalem, 2 Maccabees is also among several sources referring to the seclusion of young unmarried women, though not married women (2 Maccabees 3:19). It is not easy to decide how reliable such evidence is, how widespread such practices might have been, and how (if at all) different Jewish practices were from those of their non-Jewish neighbors. Philo, for example, presents ambiguous information; for while he seems to applaud the seclusion of women within their houses, his attacks on the inappropriate public behavior of some women suggests that social reality and Philo's ideals, here as elsewhere, did not always coincide. It is also conceivable that Jews in late antiquity were not of one mind about the seclusion of women and that the whole question was part of a larger debate over appropriate Jewish beliefs and behavior.[32]

In her pioneering study of early Christian women, Elisabeth Schüssler Fiorenza makes the point that male attempts to control women, evident particularly in prescriptive statements about appropriate behavior for women, intensify precisely when women are achieving some degree of success in escaping or circumventing male control.[33] It is not inconceivable that such a situation is precisely what exists in many Jewish communities in late antiquity. This is how, for example, she understands much of the restrictive rabbinic regulation of women.[34]

It is interesting that the portrait of Jewish women that may be gleaned from the New Testament contradicts the evidence for the routine seclusion of Jewish women, both for women portrayed as living in Judea and for women portrayed as residents of the Diaspora.[35] The Gospel According to Luke claims that the financial support for the Jesus movement was provided by a group of women whom Jesus had cured of evil spirits and infirmities and who traveled with him and the Twelve. The author identifies three specifically: Mary of Magdala; Joanna, the wife of Chuza, Herod's steward; and Susanna (Luke 8:2). Whether the Gospel of Luke is historically reliable here is not the point: what is crucial is the cumulative and, I would argue, unintended evidence for the pervasive public presence of women that is assumed throughout the Gospel accounts, the Acts of the Apostles and the letters of Paul, among other early Christian evidence for Judaism in this period.

What we should conclude from this contradictory evidence is that some Jewish women probably did live their lives in relative seclusion, rarely leaving their homes except under carefully defined circumstances. Social class, geographic location, and religious perspective may all have been factors in this. Slaves, for example, would not have been secluded; their responsibilities to their owners would have made this impossible. Secluding women may have been limited to what we would call middle- and upper-class households, where there were enough slaves and servants to permit other women to remain at home. Even then, only some such households may have considered the seclusion of women desirable.

In some communities marital status may have been a further factor: only young unmarried women may have been secluded. *The Conversion and Marriage of Aseneth*, a Greek Jewish text probably dating to first-century-c.e. Egypt (which recounts how Joseph married the daughter of an Egyptian priest), describes the seclusion of the future bride, who lives in a high tower in her family compound and who has seen no men other than her immediate family.[36] Among other things, her seclusion apparently guarantees the preservation of her chastity before marriage. One recent study suggests that the emphasis on Aseneth's seclusion is designed to combat (unjustified) Jewish prejudice that female gentile converts were sexually impure.[37] Once she marries Joseph, however, Aseneth leaves her tower and engages in various public activities, including overseeing her estate.

It is regrettable that we do not know how women themselves might have viewed the whole issue of seclusion. The author of 4 Maccabees places into the mouth of the martyred mother Hannah a speech to her seven sons that seems less designed to exhort them to martyrdom than to propound the author's values to the audience: "I was a pure virgin and did not go outside my father's house; but I guarded the rib that was built" (4 Maccabees 18:7). Aseneth's seclusion is represented as clearly acceptable to her if not of her own choosing altogether. Yet we cannot be sure that these representations are not simply male projections onto women who actually viewed their seclusion quite differently. On the other hand, it is also likely that many women were sufficiently socialized into believing their seclusion appropriate and acceptable.

## JEWISH WOMEN: GENTILE POLIS

One of the most unusual features of Rufina's inscription is its stipulation that whoever violates the tomb of her slaves and freedpersons shall be liable for fines both to the Jewish community and to the imperial treasury. Very few other Jewish inscriptions prescribe such a dual penalty, and there are several conceivable explanations for Rufina's action, which lie outside the scope of this paper.[38] However, at the very least, this provision testifies to Rufina's connections with the public life of the non-Jewish community in Smyrna. We have very little indication that Jewish women participated directly in ancient politics, whatever that comprised. Josephus does provide some information about several Hellenistic Jewish queens, whose political influence was sometimes quite substantial.[39] Two inscriptions from ancient Venosa may be interpreted as evidence that Jewish women in that city held public office toward the end of our period (CIJ, nos. 606, 619d). Five women there also held synagogue titles in the same period, and Bernadette J. Brooten suggests that Venosa may have had a tradition of women holding public offices both civil and religious.[40]

While the evidence for the direct participation of women in the political systems of antiquity may be thin, we have some idea of how political issues affected Jewish women's lives. Along with Jewish men, many Jewish women were enslaved as a consequence of the many wars fought for political control of Judea.[41] Apparently, Jewish communities considered it their duty to redeem Jewish slaves whenever possible, as reflected in a manumission document from Oxyrhynchos, Egypt in the third century C.E., in which Aurelius Dioskoros and Aurelius Justus, called "senator of Ono in Syrian Palestine" and "father of the synagogue" paid fourteen talents of silver to free a forty-year-old Jewish woman and her two children, aged four and ten.[42]

The lives of Jewish women were also affected by the tax structures of the Roman empire, which for most people were onerous. Except for the laographia, or poll tax, which was imposed only on adult males, Jewish women were liable for all the same taxes as men. After the revolt of 66–73 C.E., which resulted in the destruction of the Temple in Jerusalem, this also included the Jewish tax, which the Romans levied against all Jews in place of the Temple tax.[43]

## MARRIAGE AND MOTHERHOOD

On one aspect of women's lives Rufina's inscription is conspicuously silent: marriage, motherhood, and relationships with men. In fact, given the presumed centrality of marriage and childraising for women in virtually any period of Jewish history, it is interesting how little we really know about these issues in the Greco-Roman Diaspora. We are mostly dependent on a few literary texts whose fictive nature makes it difficult for us to use them as evidence for social reality. The Book of Tobit,[44] for example, offers some interesting details about the marriage customs of the characters: marriage with a member of one's own tribe is extremely important, and marriage is presumed to be patrilocal (the wife goes to live with her husband's family). The marriage of the heroine, Sarah, to seven husbands, each of whom is killed off by a jealous demon, follows the biblical rules of levirate marriage, but when Tobias, the young hero, seeks to marry Sarah, he must not only demonstrate his kinship ties but receive her father's permission as well. Nevertheless, their marriage is not portrayed as a simple arrangement between men but as a love match between Sarah and Tobias, whom God had chosen for one another (Tobit 6:17). Once all parties have verbally agreed to the marriage, Sarah's mother and father sign the marriage contract, ultimately finalized by a wedding meal (8:19). There are some other interesting tidbits: both Sarah and Tobias are said to be only children (1:20, 6:10). When Tobit goes blind and can no longer earn a living, Anna, his wife, earns money by unspecified "women's work"—presumably weaving, spinning, and so forth, which she does at home and sends out to her employer.[45] Unfortunately, there are too many unanswered questions about the social matrix out of which Tobit comes for us to rely fully on its presentation of Jewish social practices in the Greco-Roman Diaspora.

The romantic fiction *The Conversion and Marriage of Aseneth* may be a more appropriate source for extracting clues about the practices of Egyptian Jews in the late Hellenistic and early Roman period. There, it is Aseneth's father who first proposes marriage between Aseneth and Joseph, whom Aseneth rejects in favor of the son of Pharaoh, whom his father has betrothed to another woman, in spite of the son's preference for Aseneth (*Conversion and Marriage of Aseneth* 4.11–15). In the beginning of the novel Aseneth is still an idol-worshipping pagan; so conceivably, the customs for contracting marriages depicted here should not be taken as evidence of social practice for Egyptian Jews. However, the tale is manifestly a Jewish one, in which even the father of Aseneth, an Egyptian priest, is depicted as a man who praises God (3.4), so it seems plausible that the process for contracting marriage depicted in this text does have some social verisimilitude. Interestingly, Aseneth's father does not force her to marry Joseph or anyone else who sought her hand: rather, when Aseneth refuses his choice, her father simply lets the matter rest (4.16)[46]

Whatever formal roles fathers played in the selection of mates, sexual attraction between the prospective spouses almost certainly played a role in actual marriage arrangements. The magical tablet of Domitiana quoted above has marriage as its explicit goal.[47] A poignant burial inscription from the first century B.C.E. in Egypt also provides some information on Jewish marriage customs:

> Weep for me, stranger, a maiden ripe for marriage, who formerly shone in a great house. For, decked in fair bridal garments, I, untimely, have received this hateful tomb as my bridal chamber. For when a noise of revellers already at my doors told that I was leaving my father's house, like a rose in a garden nurtured by fresh rain, suddenly Hades came and snatched me away. And I, stranger, who had accomplished twenty revolving years. . . . (*CPJ*, no. 1508; Kraemer, *Maenads*, no. 39)

Twenty was probably a little older than the average age of fifteen for a first marriage, as derived from the inscriptions that give direct or indirect evidence for the age at which Jewish women first married.[48] A number of inscriptions and papyri testify to women who married closer to age eighteen, which is the age of Aseneth.[49] The average age at first marriage for Roman women was probably somewhat younger, closer to thirteen.[50] Rabbinic literature supposes that Jewish women were married at age twelve (and often betrothed at a much younger age); but we have little evidence with which to test the accuracy of this even for communities in Galilee, Babylonia, and so forth, known to have had major rabbinic academies.

Papyri from the Judean desert have yielded a few marriage contracts, including several Aramaic *ketuboth* and two Greek documents:
one a marriage contract, the other, more unusual, a remarriage.[51] Two
marriage documents are among the papers belonging to a Jewish
woman named Babata who lived at the time of Bar Kochba in the
early second century c.e.:[52] the contract for her own second marriage,
which has not yet been published, and the contract for her second
husband's daughter by his first wife.[53] No Jewish marriage contracts are
known from Egypt during the heyday of Alexandrian Jewry (prior to
117 c.e.) but one survives from Antinoopolis, dated 417 c.e.[54]

Despite their fragmentary nature, the marriage papyri from Judea
seem to be relatively similar. They are in the form of a declaration by
the husband to his wife in which he formally acknowledges her as his
wife and promises to feed and clothe her. He acknowledges receipt of
the dowry and guarantees its return in case of their divorce. In the
event that the wife predeceases the husband, he guarantees that her
sons will inherit her dowry, while her daughters will be supported up
until their own marriage. In the event that the husband dies first, she
will have the right to continue living in the house and to receive food
and clothing from his estate. He further guarantees to reproduce a
copy of the agreement whenever his wife so demands. Only a few of
these papyri have signatures intact: in one the bride may sign for herself rather than needing a surrogate to compensate for her illiteracy.[55]
The Antinoopolis contract, between one Samuel, son of Sampati ( =
Sambathi) and Metra, daughter of Leazar and Esther(?), is in Aramaic
and Greek, both written in Aramaic letters. Since virtually every line
is mutilated, it is difficult to know exactly how the contract read.
Samuel declares that he hereby takes Metra as his wife. A few phrases
suggest that he promises to feed and support her and that she has made
reciprocal promises of some sort. Most of the document is a detailed
list of the dowry, in Greek, together with Samuel's guarantees of the
dowry. These are presumably in the event that the marriage termi-
nates, but the clauses found in the Judean contracts stipulating the
disposal of marital property in the event of death or divorce are not
found in this contract, at least as it survives. One particularly interesting feature of this *ketubah* is that the dowry of the bride was provided by her mother, although her father is apparently also living.

We also have an Aramaic divorce document from the Judean desert
in which the husband declares to his (former) wife that he formally

repudiates her, confirms that she is free to go out and become the wife of some other Jewish man, conveys to her the divorce decree and her dowry, and guarantees that he will provide her with a replacement copy of the document on demand, as long as he lives. The document is signed only by the husband, and witnessed by three men (*Discoveries in the Judean Desert* 2.19). Intriguing and problematic is a Greek papyrus divorce decree of 13 B.C.E. that actually antedates the Aramaic decree by several centuries.[56] It differs significantly from the Aramaic document and from rabbinic divorce regulations.[57] The husband and wife jointly agree that their marriage is dissolved, that neither will proceed against the other on any grounds relating to the marriage since the husband has returned the dowry to the wife and that both are now free to contract another marriage. Although the document is included in the corpus of Jewish papyri, it is not absolutely certain that it dissolves a marriage between two Jews.

## MALE-FEMALE RELATIONSHIPS

Although we have little evidence for the true nature of personal relationships between Jewish men and women, especially between husbands and wives, some clues exist. Divorces themselves might be considered evidence of poor relationships between men and women, as would a third-century-B.C.E. papyrus from Egypt in which a woman named Helladote sues her Jewish husband, apparently for failure to support her (*CPJ*, no. 1509; Kraemer, *Maenads*, no. 40). But there is also evidence of deep affection between spouses. Philo of Alexandria, whose scathing indictment of the deleterious effects of marriage on men may be considered a classic example of ancient male misogynism (*Hypothetica* 11.14–17), could also write sympathetically of the man who chooses not to divorce his barren wife on grounds of love and affection for her even though Jewish law allows him, and arguably even compels him, to do so in order to fulfill the commandment to be fruitful and multiply (*On the Special Laws* 3.35). *The Conversion and Marriage of Aseneth* (3.7, 4.1, and *passim*) portrays the relationship between the couple after their marriage as one of great affection and mutual respect: a similar portrait is offered of the marriage of Aseneth's parents.

While the expressions of marital affection and devotion found on some burial inscriptions are surely conventional expressions of socially acceptable sentiment, others provide glimpses into the private emotions of women and men in antiquity. One such example is the Roman epitaph for Regina quoted above. Another comes from Egypt in the first century B.C.E.:

> This is the tomb of Horaia, wayfarer. Shed a tear. The daughter of Nikolaos, who was unfortunate in all things in her thirty years. Three of us are here, husband, daughter, and I whom they struck down with grief. [My husband died] on the 3rd, then on the 5th my daughter Eirene, to whom marriage was not granted. I then with no place or joy was laid here after them under the earth on the 7th of Choiak. But stranger, you have clearly all there is to know from us to tell all of the swiftness of death. In the 10th year, Choiak 7. (*CPJ*, no. 1509; Kraemer, *Maenads*, no. 40)

## MOTHERHOOD

However seriously Jews in the Greco-Roman diaspora may have taken the injunction in Genesis 1:22 to be fruitful and multiply, the epigraphical and papyrological evidence points to relatively small families, which probably reflects concomitantly low birthrates, especially in Egypt. Of the burial inscriptions from Leontopolis, for example, only one woman has more than one child (*CPJ*, no. 1490). In a tax register from Arsinoe from 73 C.E. a twenty-year-old woman has two children, ages three and five; two other women, both twenty-two, have one child apiece (*CPJ*, no. 421; Kraemer, *Maenads*, no. 48). In this regard, Jewish women may not have differed from non-Jewish women in the same geographic communities, and a variety of factors, including everything from diet to Roman proclivities for hot baths to fundamental attitudes about sexual activity may have been involved. Interestingly, Jewish fiction of this period also features a number of only children, including Sarah and Tobias (in Tobit), and Aseneth; but as I noted earlier, it is difficult to draw very many social conclusions from these texts with any certainty.

Jewish women, like their Greco-Roman sisters, risked dying in childbirth with each pregnancy, although I know of no studies that have tried to correlate the evidently low birthrates with unusual maternal mortality. The actual maternal mortality rates cannot be computed from the epigraphic and papyrological evidence, since many burial inscriptions give no information about the cause of death. The relatively high percentage of women commemorated in burial inscriptions who died during childbearing years might be taken to reflect the maternal mortality rate, but Keith Hopkins has shown that this really reflects the higher probability that a woman who died young would still have a husband alive to commemorate her.[58] Still, the epitaph of Arsinoe (probably erected by her husband), who died in the first century B.C.E. in Egypt could probably stand for many Jewish women of her era:

> This is the grave of Arsinoe, wayfarer. Stand by and weep for her, unfortunate in all things, whose lot was hard and terrible. For I was bereaved of my mother when I was a little girl [perhaps in her bearing another child?], and when the flower of my youth made me ready for a bridegroom, my father married me to Phabeis, and Fate brought me to the end of my life in bearing my firstborn child. I had a small span of years, but great grace flowered in the beauty of my spirit. This grave hides in its bosom my chaste body, but my soul has flown to the holy ones. Lament for Arsinoe. In the 25th year, Mechir 2. (*CPJ*, no. 1510; Kraemer, *Maenads*, no. 41)

We know very little about Jewish childrearing practices in this period or whether they differed significantly from those of others in the communities in which Jews lived. 2 Maccabees implies that Jewish children were nursed for a period of three years, which accords with what we know of Greco-Roman practices.[59] As we have already seen, some lactating Jewish women earned money by nursing other children, including the children of non-Jews. A few inscriptions suggest that Jewish families sometimes raised abandoned babies in their own households (*CIJ*, nos. 3, 21).

## CONTROL BY MEN

In contrast to much of the evidence for women's activity in antiquity, Rufina's inscription lacks any reference to male relatives or agents, raising the important question of to what extent Jewish women were under the control of Jewish men. Feminist scholarship on women in antiquity has frequently stressed the extent to which most women were under the control of men all their lives, whether as daughters subject to their fathers, wives subject to their husbands, fatherless daughters subject to their father's male relatives, widows subject to their own sons, slaves subject to their masters, and so forth. Yet while not minimizing women's very low place in ancient hierarchies of social power, we must not forget that most men were also under the control of other men, and virtually everyone in the Greco-Roman world felt little if any control over his or her own life not only because of the political and social realities but because the real control over human lives was held by Fate and/or malicious demons. Many sought refuge from the malevolence of these beings and of the cosmos itself in cults ranging from the mysteries of Isis to the Judaism of Aseneth to Gnosticism and even to "orthodox" Christianity.

In some of the papyri, women were represented in legal and financial proceedings by a male *kyrios*, or guardian. Numerous scholars are quick to point out that such representation by a male guardian derives from Greek law and that "no such disability existed under Jewish [i.e., biblical and Talmudic] law."[60] Such distinctions, while they may have some basis in fact, are also intended to show that women actually fared better under "Jewish" law but fail to see that distinctions of degree within second-class status may not be compelling. Moreover, the representation of Jewish women by male guardians in commercial dealings transacted in Greek is documented both for Egypt and for Judea (see, e.g., *CPJ*, nos. 19, 143–44, 146) and deserves further study within the context of the representation of women by male guardians in Greek transactions in these communities generally. The connection of guardianship with literacy is also worthy of exploration.

## CONCLUSION

The Greek inscription of Rufina, head of a Jewish synagogue in the city of Smyrna in the Roman province of Asia in the early part of our era impelled us to ask a series of fruitful questions about Jewish women in the Greco-Roman Diaspora. From Rufina's dedication of burial space for her slaves and freedpersons and from numerous other evidence for Jewish communities at this time, we have drawn a much richer and significantly different portrait of Jewish women and their participation in the lives of their communities than can be obtained from early rabbinic sources. Yet, like the inscription by Rufina, there are many issues to which these sources do not speak, not the least of which is the perceptions of women themselves. While the discovery and publication of new sources such as the archives of Babata may from time to time offer real new evidence to study, we must continue to pursue ever more sophisticated and subtle ways to wring the evidence for Jewish women's lives out of the mostly androcentric sources that survive.

## NOTES

I wish to thank the National Endowment for the Humanities for a fellowship held during 1982–83 on women in Greek-speaking Jewish communities in the Greco-Roman period, which enabled me to do most of the research reflected in this essay.

1. Jean-Baptiste Frey, ed., *Corpus inscriptionum judaicarum* [hereafter *CIJ*] (Rome, 1936–52), no. 741. (Volume 1 has been reprinted with prolegomenon by Baruch Lifshitz [New York, 1975]). English translation in my edited *Maenads, Martyrs, Matrons, Monastics: A Sourcebook on Women's Religions in the Greco-Roman World* (Philadelphia, 1988), no. 84. Important discussion of this inscription may be found in Bernadette J. Brooten, *Women Leaders in the Ancient Synagogue*, Brown Judaic Studies no. 36 (Chico, CA, 1982), 5–12.

2. The literature on Judaism in the Greco-Roman period is vast. An excellent introduction is Shaye J. D. Cohen, *From the Maccabees to the Mishnah*, Library of Early Christianity no. 7, ed. Wayne A. Meeks (Philadelphia, 1987). See also Robert A. Kraft and George W. E. Nickelsburg, eds., *Early Judaism and Its Modern Interpreters* (Atlanta, 1986).

3. Jack Lightstone, "Christian Anti-Judaism in Its Judaic Mirror: The Judaic Context of Early Christianity Revised," in *Separation and Polemic: Anti-Judaism in Early Christianity*, vol. 2, ed. Stephen G. Wilson (Waterloo, Canada, 1986), 103–32.

4. Ibid. See also Martin Goodman, *State and Society in Roman Galilee, A.D. 132–212* (Totowa, NJ, 1983), esp. chap. 7.

5. Outstanding exceptions to this are Bernadette Brooten, *Women Leaders*; idem "Jewish Women's History in the Roman Period: A Task for Christian Theology," in *Christians Among Jews and Gentiles*, ed. G. W. E. Nickelsburg and George W. MacRae, *Harvard Theological Review* 79 (1986): 22–30. For a discussion of research prior to 1983, see my "Women in the Religions of the Greco-Roman World," *Religious Studies Review* 9, no. 2 (1983): 127–39, esp. 130–31. Two works too recent for me to utilize to any degree for this paper are Günter Mayer, *Die jüdische Frau in der hellenistich-römischen Antike* (Stuttgart, 1987), which takes account of some of the

epigraphical evidence, and Leonie Archer, *Her Price Is Beyond Rubies: The Jewish Women in Graeco-Roman Palestine. Journal for the Study of Old Testament*, suppl. vol. 60 (Leiden, 1988). An earlier article by Archer, "The Role of Jewish Women in the Religion, Ritual, and Cult of Graeco-Roman Palestine," in *Images of Women in Antiquity*, ed. A. Cameron and A. Kuhrt (Detroit, 1983), was essentially an uncritical survey of Josephus and biblical, Mishnaic and Talmudic references. The principal value of Leonard Swidler, *Women in Judaism: The Status of Women in Formative Judaism* (Metuchen, NJ, 1976) lies in its amassing of references.

6. See also Brooten, *Women Leaders*; and my three articles: "Jewish Women in Rome and Egypt," in *Rescuing Creusa: New Methodological Approaches to Women in Antiquity*, ed. Marilyn B. Skinner, *Helios* 13, no. 2 (1986): 85–101; "Hellenistic Jewish Women: The Epigraphical Evidence," in *Society of Biblical Literature Seminar Papers*, vol. 25, ed. Kent Harold Richards (Atlanta, 1986) 183–200; and "Monastic Jewish Women in Greco-Roman Egypt: Philo Judaeus on the Therapeutrides," *Signs: Journal of Women in Culture and Society* 14, no. 2 (1989): 342–70.

7. The ability of Jewish women to inherit and bequeath property is complicated in the Greco-Roman period, and probably varied considerably from one region to another, depending as much on local law and custom as on any possible "standard" of Jewish jurisprudence. A discussion of Jewish inheritance and property laws, based on biblical and rabbinic evidence may be found in Z. W. Falk, "Jewish Private Law," in *The Jewish People in the First Century*, ed. S. Safrai and M. Stern, *Compendia rerum iudaicarum ad Novum Testamentum* vol. 1 (Philadelphia, 1974), 504–34, esp. 518–26. Discussion of women's legal status in the Mishnah may be found in Judith Romney Wegner, *Chattel or Person? The Status of Women in the Mishnah* (New York, 1989) and chapter 3 below.

8. G. Fuks, "Where Have All the Freedmen Gone? On an Anomaly in the Jewish Grave-Inscriptions from Rome," *Journal of Jewish Studies* 36 (1985): 25–32.

9. For a concise treatment of slavery in ancient Rome, see Paul Veyne, in *A History of Private Life*, vol. 1, *From Pagan Rome to Byzantium*, ed. Paul Veyne, trans. by Arthur Goldhammer (Cambridge, MA, 1987), 51–69.

10. V. Tcherikover, A. Fuks, M. Stern, and D. Lewis, *Corpus papyrorum judaicarum* [hereafter, *CPJ*], 3 vols. (Cambridge, MA, 1957–64), 2:12, n. 20.

11. *CPJ*, no. 26. See also *CPJ*, no. 483 (Kraemer, *Maenads*, no. 47): the sale of a house by a woman who is probably Jewish to a woman who is probably not.

12. *CPJ*, no. 146 (Kraemer, *Maenads*, no. 44); *CPJ*, no. 147. Ways women might earn money in Galilean villages are named by Goodman (*State and Society*, 37 and n. 156), particularly breadselling, shopkeeping and wetnursing. An Egyptian tax register from 173–74 c.e. identifies three married women (all non-Jewish) as having no trade; see *New Documents Illustrating Early Christianity* [hereafter *NewDocs*] (North Ryde, Australia) 4 (1979 [1987]): p. 91. This may indicate that women with trades would have been so specified.

13. Swidler, *Women in Judaism*, 114 and, on apparent exceptions to rabbinic restrictions on women studying Torah, 93–111; and see Wegner, *Chattel or Person?*; and chapter 3 below.

14. Among the Jewish examples are *CPJ*, nos. 468 and 483. There may be instances of women who were not illiterate and signed their own legal transactions (such as the unnamed wife in an Aramaic marriage document from the early second century c.e. found in the Judean desert or Shalom, wife of Hadar, who is a signatory to a deed of sale); but Yigael Yadin argues that the phrase ʿal nafsha does not mean "wrote for

him/herself" but "merely that the signatory was one of the parties to the deed, as distinct from its witnesses ("Expedition D—The Cave of the Letters," *Israel Exploration Journal* 12 [1962]: 253–54).

15. Swidler, *Women in Judaism*, 114. For discussion of Jewish women's ages at first marriage, see below.

16. Sarah Pomeroy makes a similar argument about the impediment to education caused by the early marriage of Roman women in *Goddesses, Whores, Wives, and Slaves: Women in Classical Antiquity* (New York, 1975), 170.

17. *CIJ*, nos. 400, 581, 590, 597, 692, 731c; Kraemer, *Maenads*, nos. 85, 88–89; *Supplementum epigraphicum graecum* 27 (1977), no. 1201; and my "A New Inscription from Malta and the Question of Women Elders in the Diaspora Jewish Communities," *Harvard Theological Review* 78, nos. 3–4 (1985): 431–38.

18. *CIJ*, nos. 496, 523, 639; also perhaps 166, 606, 619d. See Brooten, *Women Leaders*, 57–72.

19. An appendix giving text and translation of inscriptions mentioning women as donors in the ancient synagogues may be found in Brooten, *Women Leaders*, 157–65.

20. See, e.g., Acts 17:1–4; 18:26; Babylonian Talmud Sotah 22b.

21. *CIJ*, no. 738 (Kraemer, *Maenads*, no. 60). The seat of honor might have been located in rows of seats facing the congregation, as have been found at the synagogue in Sardis and also in Western Asia Minor. Similar honors are recorded for women benefactors and priestesses in many cities and towns of Asia Minor. See, e.g., Kraemer, *Maenads*, nos. 81–83; *NewDocs* 1 (1976), no. 111.

22. Brooten, *Women Leaders*, 103–38.

23. The first-century Jewish writer Philo of Alexandria remarks that when the Therapeutic Society gathered for Sabbath discourse and services, the men were separated from the women by a divider preventing them from seeing each other but allowing the women to hear the speaker. See *On the Contemplative Life* 19 (Kraemer, *Maenads*, no. 14). However, Philo is not describing an Egyptian Jewish synagogue here, and the fact that he must mention such a wall might suggest that his readers would be unfamiliar with such a phenomenon. In any case, the Therapeutics were an ascetic, monastic community for whom the separation of the sexes was a somewhat different issue. Also, we need to keep in mind that seating at public events such as athletic games and the theater was routinely segregated by gender and other status determinants in the Greco-Roman world. See, e.g., Pomeroy, *Women in Classical Antiquity*, 213.

24. *CIJ*, no. 476 (Kraemer, *Maenads*, no. 120). On burial epithets for women, see *NewDocs* 3 (1978 [1983]), no. 11; *NewDocs* 2 (1977 [1982]), no. 80.

25. John Chrysostom, *Against Judaizing Christians* 2.3.4 (Kraemer, *Maenads*, no. 31).

26. The Greek text of Judith may be found in any edition of the Septuagint and also in Morton S. Enslin and Solomon Zeitlin, *The Book of Judith*, Jewish Apocryphal Literature no. 7 (Leiden, 1972). Translation of Judith also appears in any Bible with the Apocrypha. Although the story is set in ancient Israel, it is clearly a much later tale, which scholars have variously assigned to the Persian or Maccabean periods. For a summary of recent discussion, see Robert Doran, "Narrative Literature," in *Early Judaism*, ed. Kraft and Nickelsburg, 302–4.

27. In her marvelous discussion of fasting and sexual abstinence in late antiquity, Aline Rousselle (*Porneia: On Desire and the Body in Antiquity* [London, 1988], 167ff.) writes, "The term fasting referred to the practice of imposing restrictions within a diet and not generally to abstaining from food altogether"—which may shed light on

Judith's regular fasting. Perhaps we are to understand that she ate only at night, or drank only liquids, or some such.

28. For another example of female piety and courage, see the story of the woman and her seven sons in the first-century-C.E. anonymous Greek-Jewish work, 4 Maccabees (14:11–17:10, 18:6–19), found in the pseudepigraphical writings (Kraemer, *Maenads*, no. 118).

29. See H. D. Betz, *The Greek Magical Papyri in Translation* (Chicago, 1986), xli–xlviii; Lightstone, "Christian Anti-Judaism." For some literary references to Jewish women's involvement in mysticism and prophesying, see Juvenal, *Satire* 6 (Kraemer, *Maenads*, no. 25); *Testament of Job* 46–52 (text and translation in Robert A. Kraft et al., eds., *The Testament of Job: Greek Text and English Translation*, Society of Biblical Literature Texts and Translations no. 5, Pseudepigrapha series 4 [Missoula, MT, 1974]); also translated in H. D. F. Sparks, ed., *The Apocryphal Old Testament* (Oxford, 1984), 617–48.

30. Philo, *On The Contemplative Life* 68–69; and see my "Monastic Jewish Women."

31. Philo, *Against Flaccus* 89; and see P. van der Horst, *The Sentences of Pseudo-Phocylides*, Studia in Veteris Testamenti Pseudepigrapha no. 4 (Leiden, 1978), 11:215–16. Also in J. H. Charlesworth, *The Old Testament Pseudepigrapha*, 2 vols. (Garden City, 1983–85), 2:565–82. This first-century Jewish work advises the strict guarding of unmarried daughters.

32. *On the Special Laws* 3.169 assumes the seclusion of Jewish women within their homes. But the sections immediately following, which castigate women for their improper behavior in public, are predicated on the assumption that women do appear in public (3.171–77). Both here and in *Against Flaccus*, Philo assumes that the degree of seclusion was dependent on marital status, unmarried virgins being more sheltered than their married mothers.

33. Elisabeth Schüssler Fiorenza, *In Memory of Her: A Feminist Theological Reconstruction of Christian Origins* (New York, 1983), 109.

34. Ibid., 59.

35. For example, the woman with the twelve-year flow of blood who touches Jesus' robe (Luke 8:43 and parallels); the women and children who are present in the crowds fed with loaves of bread and fishes, and who are in addition to the five thousand (Matthew 14:21), and the four thousand (Matthew 15:38); the sisters of Jesus in the synagogue in Galilee (Matthew 13:56), and so forth.

36. *The Conversion and Marriage of Aseneth*. English translation in Kraemer, *Maenads*, no. 113. *Aseneth* was probably written in Greek, by the early second century C.E. For a summary of recent scholarly discussion, see Robert Doran, "Narrative Literature," 290–93.

37. Randall Chesnutt, *Conversion in Joseph and Aseneth: Its Nature, Function, and Relation to Contemporary Paradigms of Conversion and Initiation* (Ph.D. diss., Duke University, 1986), 224. See also Wegner, who notes (*Chattel or Person*, 22–23) that the framers of the Mishnah believed that all gentile women could be presumed to have been sexually violated by age three.

38. See my "Hellenistic Jewish Women"; and my "On the Meaning of the Term 'Jew' in Greco-Roman Inscriptions," *Harvard Theological Review* 92 (1989).

39. Joseph Sievers, "The Role of Women in the Hasmonean Dynasty" in *Josephus, the Bible, and History*, ed. L. H. Feldman and G. Hata (Detroit, 1989), 132–46.

40. Brooten, *Women Leaders*, 61–63. The inscriptions from Venosa are difficult to date: Brooten gives only the range of the third to sixth century C.E.

41. See Fuks, "Where Have All the Freedmen Gone."

42. CPJ, no. 473: also see the discussion, CPJ 3:36, n. 9. Later Jewish marriage contracts required husbands to redeem their wives if taken captive, but the ones we have for this period do not contain such clauses. See also CIJ, no. 709 from Delphi, dating to the mid-second century B.C.E., which records the manumission of a Jewish woman named Antigona and her daughters Theodora and Dorothea through a procedure in which their owner sold them to Pythian Apollo and they then paid the purchase price to the god for their freedom.

43. Two instances of women who pay the Jewish tax are recorded in CPJ, no. 223 (114 C.E.) and CPJ, no. 227 (116 C.E.). On the Jewish tax, see CPJ 2:114. Sarah Pomeroy notes that women in Syria were liable for the laographia imposed by Rome ("Women in Roman Egypt: A Preliminary Study Based on Papyri," in Reflections of Women in Antiquity, ed. H. Foley [London, 1981], 306).

44. English translations of Tobit may be found in the Oxford Annotated Apocrypha, Charlesworth, Old Testament Pseudepigrapha, and Sparks, Apocryphal Old Testament. Extant now in Greek, Tobit was almost certainly written originally in Aramaic by about 200 B.C.E. and probably reflects the social concerns of some Diaspora Jews in Babylon or perhaps some other Aramaic-speaking community. Since Tobit is ostensibly set in the Assyrian diaspora which followed the conquest of the ten Northern tribes of ancient Israel in the eighth century B.C.E., it is hard for us to know whether the author's description of marriage and other social customs reflect social reality in the author's own times, projected back onto antiquity or the author's perception of how things were in ancient times. For a summary of recent discussion on Tobit, see Robert Doran, "Narrative Literature," 296–99.

45. See n. 12.

46. The idea that daughters should have a say in the selection of their husbands is found in a Talmudic passage: "For Rab Judah said in Rab's name: One may not give his daughter in betrothal when a minor [but must wait] until she grows up and says, "I want so-and-so" (B. Qiddushin 41a). But Wegner (Chattel or Person?, 33) argues that in the Mishnah a minor daughter could not refuse her father's choice. Beryl Rawson ("The Roman Family," in The Family in Ancient Rome: New Perspectives, ed. Beryl Rawson [Ithaca, NY, 1986], 21), observes that Roman first marriages were normally arranged by the parents of the couple and that although daughters (and sons) had to consent, the grounds on which a daughter could refuse were limited to claims that the proposed groom was of bad moral character. It is interesting that the grounds on which Aseneth refuses to marry Joseph are precisely that: he is the abandoned son of a disreputable person, who was sold into slavery and who had illicit sex with the wife of his owner (4.12–14).

47. Many magical papyri from Egypt are spells to attract a lover, although this one is unusual both because it seeks to attract a marriage partner and because it is written for a woman. Another love charm to bring a man to a woman also comes from Hadrumetum in North Africa; it is cited in H. Dessau, Inscriptiones latinae selectae no. 8757 and translated in F. Grant, Ancient Roman Religion (New York, 1975), 241–42. Most of the love spells in the Greek magical papyrii seek to attract women to men, and a small number are homosexual. One or two seek to lure women away from their husbands.

48. These are listed and discussed in NewDocs 4 (1979 [1987]), no. 114.

49. Conversion and Marriage of Aseneth 1.6. Since the majority of Greco-Roman inscriptions, whether Jewish or otherwise, do not provide age at marriage for women,

it is difficult to tell how representative are the data that can be distilled from the relatively small number of inscriptions with this information.

50. Some discussion and bibliography for average age of Roman women at first marriage may be found in *NewDocs* 4; see also Rawson, "Roman Family," 21–22.

51. P. Benoit, J. T. Milik and R. de Vaux, *Les grottes du Murabba'at. Discoveries in the Judean Desert* [hereafter *DJD*] vol. 2 (Oxford, 1961), nos. 20–21 [Aramaic]; 115 (the Greek remarriage), 116. *DJD* 2.20 may also be found in Solomon A. Birnbaum, *The Bar Menasheh Marriage Deed. Its Relation with Other Jewish Marriage Deeds* (Istanbul, 1962).

52. The archives of Babata, who lived in the time of Bar Kochba, leader of the rebellion against Rome in 132–135 C.E., were found in 1960 in a cave in the Judean desert. Brief descriptions and discussion may be found in Yigael Yadin, "Expedition D—The Cave of the Letters," *Israel Exploration Journal* [hereafter *IEJ*] 12 (1962): 243 and in H. Polotsky, "The Greek Papyri from the Cave of the Letters," *IEJ* 12 (1962): 258–62. Recently, a few of the papyri have been published: Naphtali Lewis ("Two Greek Documents from Provincia Arabia," *Illinois Classical Studies* 3 [1978]: 100–114) provides the Greek texts, translation, and discussion of two documents pertaining to the guardianship of Babata's son after the death of her husband. The Greek text of these two, together with a third papyrus, were printed in *Sammelbuch Griechischer Urkunden aus Agypten* (Wiesbaden, 1969), no. 10288. See also n. 53. The entire archive appeared in print shortly before this volume went to press, and too late to be used in this chapter: *The Documents from the Bar Kokhba Period in the Cave of Letters: Greek Papyri*, ed. Naphtali Lewis. Judean Desert Studies no. 2 (Jerusalem, 1989).

53. The marriage contract of Babata's second husband's daughter by his first wife has now been published by N. Lewis, B. Katzoff, and J. Greenfield, in "Papyrus Yadin 18," *IEJ* 37, no. 4 (1987): 229–50.

54. C. Sirat, P. Cauderlier, M. Dukan, and M. A. Friedman, *La Ketouba de Cologne. Un contrat de mariage juif à Antinoopolis*, Papyrologia coloniensia no. 12 (Opladen, 1986).

55. See n. 24. In *DJD* 2.21, published after Yadin's Babata article, the editors still read line 23 as evidence that the bride signed for herself.

56. *CPJ*, no. 144 (Kraemer, *Maenads*, no. 45). There is also an extremely interesting Samaritan divorce decree from 586 C.E. from Hermoupolis (*CPJ*, no. 513) characterized by a strong degree of reciprocity and mutuality.

57. Discussion of Jewish women's ability to initiate divorce proceedings in late antiquity may be found in B. Brooten, "Konnten die Frauen im alten Judentum sich von ihren Männern scheiden? Überlegungen zu Mk 10, 11–12 und I Kor 7, 10–11," *Evangelische Theologie* 42 (1982): 65–80. On the Roman side, see Myles McDonnell, "Divorce Initiated by Women," *American Journal of Ancient History* 8 (1983): 54–80.

58. Keith Hopkins, "On the Probable Age Structure of the Roman Population," *Population Studies* 20 (1966): 245–64.

59. Beryl Rawson, "Children in the Roman Familia," in *Family in Ancient Rome*, ed. Rawson, 170–200; Rousselle, *Porneia*, chap. 3.

60. Z. W. Falk, "Jewish Private Law," 507.

**3** **JUDITH ROMNEY WEGNER**

*The Image and Status of Women*
*in Classical Rabbinic Judaism*

The Babylonian Talmud relates that whenever the blind rabbi Joseph bar Hiyya heard his mother's footsteps approaching, he would stand up, saying, "Let me rise up before the approaching Shekhinah [Divine Presence]" (B. Qid. 31b).[1] The same Talmud records elsewhere the unattributed statement of another sage that "a woman is a pitcher of filth with its mouth full of blood—yet all men run after her" (B. Shab. 152a).[2] In analyzing the image and status of women in classical rabbinic Judaism, this essay explains how two such polarized assessments of women can appear in the same sacred text.

In exploring the rabbinic portrayal of women's place in the life of "Israel,"[3] we discover a system in which woman's cultural image, social function and legal status combine to perpetuate patriarchal norms that had already governed Jewish and surrounding cultures for many centuries. The classical rabbinic texts include the Mishnah, Tosefta, Talmud, and Midrash collections. The Mishnah, a juristic handbook edited by Judah the Patriarch (Rabbi) about 200 c.e., covers a wide range of topics of Jewish law. The Tosefta, a supplemental collection of legal rulings (slightly later than the Mishnah), follows the arrangement of, and further elaborates, the Mishnaic material. The Palestinian and Babylonian Talmuds are voluminous commentaries on the Mishnah, produced in the land of Israel between 200 and 400 c.e. and in Babylonia between 200 and 600 c.e., respectively; while Midrash is the generic term for a large body of exegetical material compiled over several centuries that interprets Scripture and contains some material in common with Mishnah and Talmud. The primary texts of rabbinic Judaism span a vast expanse of time (some fifteen hundred years if we start with the Torah, edited about 450 b.c.e.) and space (from Palestine to Babylonia).

Fully two-thirds of the Mishnah discusses matters having to do with the Temple and its cult, which had no practical application at the time of editing of the Mishnah, but the remaining third contains rules concerning personal status and civil and criminal law that may well have been followed by that small portion of the Jewish people over whom the sages held moral sway.[4] Since the social reality reflected in the Mishnaic and Talmudic texts is unavoidably distorted by the perspective of the framers and interpreters, rabbinic statements about the nature and role of women cannot provide an objective view of women's history; rather, they offer us an androcentric vision, sometimes colored by men's fears or wishful thinking about female sexuality.

The formulators of rabbinic literature were also inevitably influenced by various surrounding cultures. The Mishnah, Tosefta, early Midrash collections and Palestinian Talmud are imbued with the hellenistic culture of the Roman Empire, while the Babylonian Talmud (edited about 600 c.e.) and later Midrash compilations bear the stamp of Zoroastrian Persia. Furthermore, virtually our sole source for the history of Jewish women within the ambit of Mishnaic and Talmudic culture is rabbinic literature itself, a fact that gives rise to some methodological problems.[5] We find scant external corroboration beyond some parallels in contemporaneous Hellenism or Zoroastrianism. We cannot be sure that the Mishnah and Talmud's reflections on the nature of women or the rules governing their legal status represent an actual sociopolitical system—the way things were—rather than the rabbis' idealized view of the way things should be. More important, we do not know what percentage of Jews in those centuries voluntarily submitted themselves to the rabbinic interpretation of the divine will.[6] Nonetheless, the legal-cultural-social system now called rabbinic Judaism, which developed in Palestine and Babylonia during the first six centuries c.e., was destined to become normative for virtually all Jewish communities for the next twelve hundred years.

## WOMEN'S STATUS IN THE MISHNAH

In discussing the image and status of women in classical rabbinic texts, it makes sense to begin with the Mishnah,[7] which predates the Talmud and much of the Midrashic corpus. The Order of Women, one of the six Mishnaic divisions, certainly reflects ingrained cultural attitudes toward real, live women that significantly impinged on women's reality. But that reality was more complex than feminist scholarship has tended to assume. In particular, the evidence of the Mishnah belies the global assertion of Simone de Beauvoir that women in classical antiquity were mere chattels of their patriarchal owners.[8] A legal *chattel* is a piece of property, having by definition neither rights nor duties, while a legal *person* is an entity possessing both entitlements and obligations; an individual's *level of personhood* in a hierarchical society depends on his or her specific mixture of rights, duties, and powers. Analysis of the Mishnaic rules of women's status reveals two important facts. First, the system does not treat all women alike; some women are independent of male control and hence can *never* be treated as chattels. Second, even women who fall under the authority of specified men are treated as persons in all contexts but one.

In the private domain of personal status, the Mishnah divides women into two opposed categories: dependent and autonomous. Each of these classes, in turn, breaks down into three subclasses defined by who has control of the women's sexual and reproductive function, as set forth in chart 1.

The Mishnah recognizes three classes of dependent woman: minor

## CHART 1

| Owner of Biological function | Dependent Woman | Autonomous Woman | Owner of Biological function |
|---|---|---|---|
| father | minor daughter | adult daughter | herself |
| husband | wife | divorcée | herself |
| levir | levirate widow | widow | herself |

daughter, wife, and levirate widow.[9] Each woman is legally controlled by the man who owns the sole right to use or profit from her biological function: her father, husband, or brother-in-law as the case may be. Corresponding to these dependent women are three classes of autonomous women: emancipated (i.e., adult unmarried) daughter,[10] divorcée, and regular widow.[11] In their legal entitlements and obligations, these three subgroups form mirror images of their dependent counterparts.

This feature is especially evident in cases involving the disposition of a woman's sexual and reproductive function. Thus, a minor daughter's marriage is arranged by her father (M. Ket. 4:4), while an adult daughter negotiates her own (M. Qid. 2:1). Penalties for the rape of a minor accrue to her father (M. Ket. 4:1), but if she is of full age they go to the woman herself (M. Ket. 3:6). These distinctions reflect the fact that the minor daughter's biological function is the legal property of her father while that of an adult daughter belongs to herself alone. As for wife and divorcée, here too the rules follow ownership of sexuality. Thus, because he owns the sole right to benefit from her sexuality, a husband can revoke his wife's vows that may impair conjugal relations (M. Ned. 11:11–12, M. Naz. 4:5); but no one can countermand the vows of a divorcée, since no one owns her sexual function (Numbers 30:10, M. Ned. 11:9). A husband who divorces his wife for adultery (or simply at will, M. Git. 9:10) can place no limits on her sexual freedom once released (M. Git. 9:1, 3). Similarly with levirate widows and normal widows: the brother-in-law inherits the sexual function of his brother's widow, who cannot remarry unless he chooses to release her (M. Yeb. 4:7); but a normal widow may remarry at will, as her sexuality is entirely at her own disposal. In all these cases, we observe the mirror image effect produced by the Mishnaic "penchant for combining symmetry and alternatives."[12]

A woman's biological function is an economic asset, as witness the formalities for transferring women from one man to another. An Israelite father technically sells his daughter's virginity for bride-price, although by Mishnaic times it had become customary to assign the bride-price (*mohar*, Exodus 22:16) to the bride herself as part of her marriage deed (*ketubbah*, M. Ket. 4:7).[13] If the bride is not intact, the bridegroom can claim damages because the goods did not meet the specification (M. Ket. 1:1). Conversely, a father collects damages from a man who rapes or seduces his minor daughter (M. Ket. 4:1), because her reduced value on the marriage market leaves him out of pocket. The unilateral form of the marriage ceremony (M. Qid. 1:1), epitomized in the bridegroom's declaration to the bride, "Thou art set apart [*mequddeshet*] for me" (M. Qid. 2:1), highlights the fact that an item of property (namely, the bride's virginity) is being transferred from father to husband. Likewise, the divorcing husband formally discards his wife by unilaterally renouncing his sexual rights over her body: "Thou art now permitted to any man" (M. Git. 9:3). But property can no more release itself than it could acquire its owner; so Mishnaic law gives the wife no corresponding power to divorce her husband (a severe disadvantage that wreaks social havoc for Jewish women to this day).[14] The same basic approach governs the levirate widow (*yebamah*), who figures as chattel in the automatic inheritance of her sexual function by her late husband's brother (M. Yeb. 4:5). She has no option unless this man chooses to release her; as with wife and minor daughter, her personhood is sacrificed to her socio-sexual function. The Mishnaic system thus inextricably links a woman's social identity to ownership of her sexuality.

In the patriarchal culture of the sages, this comes as no great surprise. What may surprise us, though, is the striking contrast between the low status of woman as sexual chattel and her far higher status in all other aspects of Mishnaic private law. In private transactions generally, the law treats women unequivocally as persons. Thus, a wife participates in a reciprocal arrangement of matrimonial entitlements and obligations, performing specified household chores and producing a requisite amount of cloth in return for maintenance at a prescribed standard that befits her social class (M. Ket. 5:5, 9). The catalog of spouses' conjugal rights and duties (M. Ket. 5:6–7) treats intercourse as primarily the wife's right and the husband's duty, presenting an interesting contrast to other traditional legal systems, such as Anglo-American common law, which have generally construed it as primarily the husband's right and the wife's duty.[15] Another interesting rule preserves the wife's title to property she brings to the marriage (again in contrast to Anglo-American common law) and even her power of sale (though this requires her husband's consent, because of his legal right to the earnings of her property). Likewise, a husband cannot sell his wife's property without her consent (M. Git. 5:6).

A wife can appoint agents to transact her business (M. Git. 6:1) and can act as her husband's agent to sell his goods (M. Ket. 9:4).

She even possesses a right of action against him, for she can petition the court to compel a divorce for specified infringements of her rights (M. Ket. 7:1–5, 10). True, the husband alone can execute the divorce; but the court will endorse draconian measures to secure his compliance (M. Git. 9:8). At the same time, the court expects the wife, as a person, to honor her obligations (which, in all legal systems, are as much a mark of personhood as is the possession of rights). A wife forfeits her marriage settlement if she violates Jewish law or custom, for instance, by breaking the rules of menstrual separation or by being a "loudmouth" whose voice can be heard by her neighbors when she speaks inside her house (M. Ket. 7:6).

The common denominator of all the wife's rights so far described is that the husband's exclusive ownership of his wife's sexuality is unchallenged. Only in that context is the wife ever treated as chattel; and even then, the law usually preserves her other rights incidental to the case. For instance, biblical law permits a suspicious husband to put his wife to the ordeal without actual witnesses to her adultery (Numbers 5:11–31). If he divorces her on suspicion, the Mishnah requires two witnesses to state that he had warned her to stay away from the suspected lover (M. Sot. 1:1); otherwise, she retains her right to collect her marriage settlement, because (like any other Israelite) she may not be deprived of her property without due process (Deuteronomy 19:15).[16]

The same emphasis on exclusive ownership of a wife's sexuality informs the laws governing the *'agunah*, the "chained woman" whose husband either has disappeared without trace or refuses to issue her a *get* (divorce decree). If such a woman "remarries" without proof of widowhood or divorce, she suffers enormous legal penalties (losing all her rights in the first, genuine marriage as well as the second, spurious one). These penalties apply even where the woman is innocent of moral wrongdoing, having remarried in reliance on a *get* that later proves technically defective or on witnesses' testimony to her husband's death, which later turns out to be false or mistaken (M. Git. 8:6, M. Yeb. 10:1). In such cases, the true husband's ownership of the wife's biological function overrides her normal rights of personhood and reduces the whole woman to the status of chattel.

So far, we have spoken only of the dependent woman. The autonomous woman's legal status and level of personhood theoretically surpass that of the dependent woman in that she controls every aspect of her private life. Thus, an emancipated daughter or divorcée may keep anything she finds, unlike the minor daughter or wife, who must turn it over to father or husband (M. B.M. 1:5). While a minor daughter's earnings accrue to her father and those of a wife to her husband (M. Ket. 4:4, M. Ket. 6:1), an adult daughter may keep whatever she makes (M. Nid. 5:7). The autonomous woman can buy and sell without impediment, for no man has a claim on her property (M. B.M. 1:5). Her vows are not subject to revocation by any man (M. Ned. 10:2, 11:9). She can bring suit for damages (M. B.Q. 1:3), or for the return of her marriage portion upon widowhood or divorce (M. Ket. 2:1), for the right to sell part of her marriage portion still in the hands of her husband's heirs, or for maintenance pending collection of her settlement (M. Ket. 11:2). In a special exception to the rule that women are incompetent as witnesses (M. Shebu. 4:1), the autonomous woman can even testify to her right to the bride-price of virgins when arranging her marriage or when recovering her marriage settlement on termination of the marriage (M. Ket. 1:6–7, 2:5–6). Her high level of personhood emerges also in the criteria for assessing her credibility, which are precisely the same as for a man, both sexes being judged by whether their statements do or do not stem from self-interest (M. Ket. 2:5–7, M. Dem. 6:11). A woman is deemed as competent as a man to swear certain business-related oaths (M. Shebu. 5:1, M. Ket. 9:4). But by far the most significant power of the autonomous woman is her control over her sexual-reproductive function, which belongs to no man and hence is hers to bestow. As noted earlier, this control enables her to negotiate (either personally or through her selected agent) with the suitor of her choice (M. Qid. 2:1). For the same reason, the Mishnah points out that a jealous husband cannot complain of his wife's sexual conduct before betrothal or after divorce, since this gives him no grounds for putting her to the ordeal (M. Sot. 2:6), nor can he restrict the future sexual relations of his divorcée (M. Git. 9:1–3).

According to the Mishnaic rules, then, in the private domain in all respects but the control of her sexuality even the dependent woman remains a person. As a member of the Israelite community, she is bound by the responsibilities of Jewish personhood and must in principle observe the rules of Jewish law and custom (M. Ket. 7:6). As for the autonomous woman, on whom no man has a legal claim, nothing can ever justify treating her as a legal chattel so long as she chooses to remain unattached.[17]

Rules governing women in the public domain, however, tell a different story. It is a commonplace that patriarchal cultures significantly diminish the personhood of women by systematically depriving them of access to the life of the mind, which men reserve for themselves in universities or other academies of higher learning.[18] The Mishnah is no exception: the sages systematically exclude women from the intellectual and spiritual forms and forums of Mishnaic culture. This result is achieved, first, by arbitrarily exempting women from performance of "time-contingent positive precepts" (M. Qid. 1:7) including the recitation of specified prayers (M. Ber. 3:3).[19] Then the sages effectively turn that exemption into a disqualification of women from leadership roles by applying a rule, articulated elsewhere (in a totally different context), that persons not bound by a particular precept cannot validly perform it on behalf of persons who are so obligated (M. R.H. 3:8). Further discouraged by some sages' objections to women's studying Torah at all (M. Sot. 3:4) and by male fears of female sexuality both as a source of cultic pollution and as a distraction from men's serious business of serving God, women are ultimately barred from leadership roles in synagogue, study house and courthouse. Nor do the sages stop there; the Mishnah even prohibits the formation of women's fellowship groups (*ḥaburot*, M. Pes. 8:7), thereby precluding women from engaging together in Torah study. This array of devices deprives women of the most intellectually and spiritually rewarding practices of traditional Judaism, which were also the most prestigious enterprises of rabbinic culture, as the sages themselves acknowledge in the maxim that the merit gained by study of Torah outweighs the combined merit of practicing several of its most important ethical precepts (M. Peah 1:1).

This brief survey cannot cover every aspect of "woman's place" in the doctrine and practice of Mishnaic sages. But the Mishnah clearly depicts a society that expects women to spend their lives largely in the domestic realm. Systematic restriction of a woman's options and even her physical movements in the public domain of the culture made it virtually impossible for women to choose an alternative lifestyle, even had societal pressures not sufficed to preclude such a choice.

## WOMEN IN THE TALMUD AND MIDRASH

While the Mishnah is the primary source for the status of women in Jewish law, the Talmud and Midrash complement its rulings by presenting a vivid picture of women's cultural role and social function in the rabbinical worldview. The many references to women (with all their contradictions and inconsistencies) project the rabbis' collective understanding of women's raison d'être in the cosmic scheme. But here, as before, there are methodological problems.

So far as named women are concerned, we cannot authenticate their historicity (unless corroborated by external sources).[20] A case in point is Beruriah, the unique woman scholar whom the Talmud mentions several times (B. Ber. 10a, B. Erub. 53b-54a, B. Pes. 62b). She is presented as the wife of R. Meir, one of the most prominent sages of the Mishnah. Yet the Mishnah itself, which refers to Meir hundreds of times, does not mention Beruriah even once. So we may be forgiven for wondering whether she is a figment of the Talmudic imagination and, more importantly, what literary purpose she serves. She is the sole Talmudic instance of a woman well versed in both written and oral law, who "learned three hundred *halakhot* from three hundred scholars in a single day" (B. Pes. 62b). It is by no means clear whether Beruriah represents tokenism ("Women *are* allowed to study Torah!") or functions as a cultural countertype that proves the very rule sages wish to enforce ("Women should *not* study Torah," M. Sot. 3:4). She may have served as a sop to the rabbinic conscience for excluding women from study of sacred texts, or possibly she emphasizes the risks of admitting women into the rabbinic fellowship. By medieval times Beruriah had come to symbolize the folly of permitting women access to sacred learning, for the eleventh-century commentator Rashi records a tradition (found nowhere in the classical texts) to the effect that after she derided the Talmudic statement "Women are weak-minded" (or, better, "women's judgment is unstable," B. Qid. 80b, B. Shab. 31b), she was seduced by one of her husband's students and committed suicide.[21] This story, with its implication that women who deviate from the female "norm" will come to a bad end, reflects the negative attitude that has denied women access to the highest cultural expression of rabbinic Judaism throughout most of Jewish history.[22]

As we move from named women to generic references to the female, we must repeat the question, What do such statements tell us
about women in Talmudic times? We have here no record of women's
lives as experienced and reported by themselves but, rather, a collection of observations made by men about "women's attributes" and
"women's work," based on an explicit assumption that "women are a
breed apart" (B. Shab. 62a). Such statements, colored as they are by
an androcentric lens, must be treated with caution; men in traditional
societies tend to see women not as persons in their own right but only
as they impinge on men's lives. Rabbinic comments about women fit
this pattern, focusing on one or another of three main concerns: wom-
en's physical attributes, their cognitive and affective faculties, and
their standards of morality. In each of these respects, the sages claim
that women are not merely different from men but also somehow inferior to them.

A striking feature of both biblical and rabbinic literature is its preoccupation with the mysterious female processes of menstruation and
childbirth. Women's ability to give birth, a capacity manifestly denied
to men, seems to have had threatening implications for the hierarchical ranking of men and women. The ancient myth of Adam's rib
(Genesis 2:22) nipped the problem in the bud by insisting (counter
to all human experience) that "in the beginning" it was not the first
woman whose body produced the first man, but precisely the reverse.[23]
Significantly, the apostle Paul cites this story to justify the subordination of women (I Corinthians 11:8–10). With the problem of gender
hierarchy neatly resolved in favor of men, cultures lacking biological
knowledge naturally perceived childbirth as resulting from a man's
planting his seed in a woman, much as he ploughs and sows his field.
This "field" motif, frequent in rabbinic as in other ancient literatures,[24] reinforces man's dominance over woman in the very aspect of
human activity that is most peculiarly her own. Even when acknowledging the complementary roles of male and female in the creation of
a child, sages maintained that the "higher" parts of the human being
came from the father and the "lower" parts from the mother. Thus,
we learn that male semen (white) provides the child's brain tissue,
while menstrual blood (red) provides its skin and flesh (B. Nid. 31a).[25]

As for menstruation, the ancients saw this phenomenon as em-
bodying the dangerous power of contamination that lurks within
women. Both Mishnah and Talmud (Tractate Niddah and elsewhere)

pay much attention to the problem of avoiding cultic pollution through contact with a menstruant or with things she has touched. The menstrual taboo is not unique to Judaism but appears in many primitive cultures.[26] But menstrual pollution assumes paramount importance in the Temple cult described in the Priestly Code,[27] where, according to some scholars, circumstantial evidence suggests the influence of Israelite exposure to Zoroastrian doctrines and practices during the Babylonian exile.

In rabbinic Judaism pollution was important not to the menstruant herself (since women, excluded from participating in cultic rites, did not need to maintain cultic purity for that purpose) but to her male contacts. From the male standpoint, the disqualification of polluted persons from sacred activities stamps women as a separate and cultically inferior entity.[28]

The rabbinic view that woman's physical qualities justify her social subordination is also present in the meaning attached to the "normal" position for sexual intercourse; the sages explained that the man, on top, looks toward his origins in the earth (i.e., to the cosmic substance from which God created him) while the woman, facing upward, looks toward the man from whose body she was created (B. Nid. 31b). The symbolism is transparent: the male communicates directly with God and the cosmos; the woman experiences that relationship only indirectly, if at all—through her subordinate relationship to the man.[29]

The sages' perceptions of intrinsic differences between men and women include the conviction that women's mental grasp of the world rests not on knowledge acquired through formal study and intellectual ratiocination (*ḥokhmah*), but rather on an intuitive understanding or commonsense (*binah*), closer to instinct than to reason. According to R. Eleazar (citing R. Jose b. Zimra), the proof that God endowed women with an extra measure of *binah* can be derived from the description of Eve's creation.[30] God did this because "a woman generally stays at home, whereas a man goes out into the streets and learns understanding from people" (Genesis Rabbah 18:1).[31] Traditional apologists, using the *binah* argument to rationalize the fact that men were privileged to perform many more precepts, claim that women were exempted from certain mitzvot (like putting on *tefillin* [phylacteries], praying with the congregation, or reading from the Torah scroll) because their intuitive closeness to the Divine obviated the

need.[32] But the Midrash can equally be interpreted as making an in-
vidious distinction between male cognition-by-intellect (*hokhmah*)
and female cognition-by-instinct (*binah*), with the latter as more of an
animal attribute than a human one, as is clear from the commence-
ment of traditional morning prayers with a blessing that praises God
for giving the rooster sufficient *binah* to distinguish night from day.[33]

These examples become even more striking when we recall that
nothing in biblical literature defines women as less intelligent than
men. On the contrary, the Genesis legends of the matriarchs and the
stories of other biblical women tend to present women as rather clever
creatures who, possessing no *de jure* authority, get their way by exercising *de facto* powers of cajolery and trickery.[34] But the fact that
women's actions often implement God's scripturally declared will, as
when Sarah banishes Hagar (Genesis 21:12) or Rebecca promotes
Jacob over Esau (Genesis 25:23), does not save them from rabbinic
censure. Indeed, the sages sometimes both blame and praise the same
action. Thus, they fault Rachel for stealing her father's idols (Genesis
Rabbah 18:2) yet laud her for thereby delivering him from theological
error (Genesis Rabbah 74:5). But such criticism never takes the form
of disparaging a woman's intelligence. Those wishing to bar women
from male pursuits had to seek some other rationale.

This explains why rabbis who speak of women's mental and emotional processes usually relate these to women's "lower" standards of
morality. Consider the following midrash in Genesis Rabbah 18:2 on
the creation of Eve, which puns on *wayyiben*, "and he built":

> Rabbi Joshua of Siknin said in R. Levi's name: *Wayyiben* is written,
> signifying that He considered well [*hithbonen*] from what part to create
> her. Said He, "I will not create her from [Adam's] head, lest she be
> swelled-headed; nor from the eye, lest she be a coquette; nor from the
> ear, lest she be an eavesdropper; nor from the mouth, lest she be a
> gossip; nor from the heart, lest she be prone to jealousy; nor from the
> hand, lest she be light-fingered; nor from the foot, lest she be a gad-
> about; but from the modest part of man, for even when he stands
> naked, that part [sc. the rib] is covered." And as He created each
> limb He ordered her "Be a modest woman." Yet in spite of all this, she
> is . . . swelled-headed . . . a coquette . . . an eavesdropper . . . prone
> to jealousy . . . light-fingered . . . a gadabout [citing prooftexts from
> Genesis and elsewhere in support of these judgments].

Lest these appraisals not suffice, the Talmud goes beyond both Scripture and Mishnah in tying women's affective behavior, especially sexual conduct, to a lack of judgment. The rabbinic dictum about women's unreliability, variously translated as "Women are weak-minded" or "light-headed" or "frivolous," has been generally understood to point to woman's unstable temperament, which will inevitably lead to sexual misconduct unless she is kept under strict control. This convenient imposition of the blame for sexual transgressions on women, rather than men, illustrates the power of interpretation in patriarchal culture; and in fact, no subject exercises the sages more than sex in general, and woman's sexual ethics in particular. Beliefs about women's morality seem to be shaped largely by two factors: male wishful thinking about the female capacity to satisfy male lust, and male fear that women (in a polygynous but not polyandrous culture) might cuckold their husbands and produce children of doubtful paternity. For these reasons, the Talmud adopts Mishnaic rules that keep women under wraps, while the Midrash (see, e.g., Tanḥuma Wayyishlaḥ 36) uses the proof text, "All the glory of the king's daughter lies within" (Psalms 45:14), as a justification for keeping wives chastely confined to the house.

We find frequent claims that a woman's sexual appetite exceeds that of a man. Rabbi Joshua said, "A woman prefers a poor husband who makes love to her, to a wealthy one who ignores her" (M. Sot. 3:4). As for conjugal relations, most Talmudic comments seem designed to secure wifely compliance with the husband's demands. Thus, the verse, "And thy desire shall be for thy husband" (Genesis 3:16) is said to teach that a wife desires her husband most strongly when he is about to set forth on a journey (B. ʿErub. 100b, B. Yeb. 62a), while a man returning from a journey may assume that his wife is in the requisite state of cultic purity unless she tells him otherwise (M. Nid. 2:4). As to the permissibility of various sexual practices, sages were divided. On the one hand, Abaye defines an "evil woman" as one who, having aroused her husband by "preparing the dish," offers him her mouth instead and Raba reviles the wife who "prepares the dish, then turns her back" (B. Yeb. 63b). Of course, these objections may stem less from prudery than from disapproval of clumsy attempts at birth control by wives overburdened with children. In fact, R. Johanan b. Dahabai discourages "deviant" practices by threatening divine punishment in the form of defective offspring (B. Ned. 20a). On the other hand, lest wives resist a husband's personal desires, the Talmud (B. San. 54b), interpreting Leviticus 18:22, points out that the halakha specifically permits any sexual practice, so long as it takes place between a man and a woman. Here, as elsewhere, we find the rabbis making the virtually universal analogy between sex and food: "Just as meat may be cooked according to preference, so a man may do as he pleases with his wife" (B. Ned. 20b).[35] One woman who complained to Rabbi Judah the Patriarch (editor of the Mishnah) of her husband's proclivity for anal intercourse was told, "My daughter, the Torah has permitted you to him [in this manner], so there's nothing I can do for you" (B. Ned. 20b); another, who complained to Rav, was told, "It's no different from [cooking] a fish" (ibid.).

In all fairness, some Talmudic rabbis declared that a man must not compel his wife but may have intercourse only with her consent (B. ʿErub. 100b). But they mitigated the force of this assertion by assuring their disciples that "a woman solicits silently while a man solicits verbally" (ibid.) and by adopting the Mishnaic rule that penalizes a recalcitrant wife more heavily than a reluctant husband (M. Ket. 5:7).[36] As a further incentive, they claimed that a woman who actually invites her husband to have intercourse will produce "children such as did not exist even in the generation of Moses" (B. ʿErub. 100b).

## PERCEPTIONS OF WOMEN'S SOCIAL ROLE AND FUNCTION

The rabbinic views of "women's place" are largely compatible with those held by surrounding cultures of the Eastern Mediterranean before, during, and after the Talmudic period. Perhaps the best-known Talmudic comment on women's place is R. Eliezer's sharp rejoinder to a woman who asked him an abstruse question on a point of scriptural exegesis. Instead of commending her perspicacity, he peremptorily sent her back to her domestic pursuits with the caustic comment that "women's wisdom [ḥokhmah] is only with the spindle," basing himself on a scriptural proof text that refers to women's manual skills as a form of ḥokhmah (Exodus 35:25).[37] Eliezer's stance that a woman had no business asking clever questions about the meaning of sacred texts recalls Hector's equally firm (if less jaundiced) response to Andromache's unsolicited advice on the conduct of the Trojan War: "Go home, attend to your own handiwork at loom and spindle. . . . As for the war, that is for men."[38] A thousand years after Homer, in Eliezer's day, working in wool remained the normal occupation for women in Eastern Mediterranean culture; the Mishnah prescribes spinning and weaving as the wife's economic tasks beyond the standard domestic chores of grinding corn, baking bread, cooking food, and nursing her child (M. Ket. 5:5, 9), while the epitaph of a Roman matron of the second century B.C.E. records that "[h]er conduct was appropriate. She kept house, she made wool."[39]

This is not to say that women never went outside. The Mishnah speaks of women who gossip together as they spin their yarn by moonlight (M. Sot. 6:1) and of a wife's right to leave the house to visit her parents or to attend festival or funeral celebrations at neighbors' homes (M. Ket. 7:4–5). But we learn little else about women's social contacts from an androcentric text (with no interest in chronicling women's lives) beyond a few sparse references incidental to a legal discussion, such as whether in the interests of social harmony the wife of a scholar may lend household utensils to the wife of a common person unschooled in the proper handling of cooking pots, despite the attendant risk of cultic pollution (M. Git. 5:9). The Talmud permits a scholar's wife to grind corn with the unschooled wife only if the former is already in a state of cultic impurity due to menstruation and thus has nothing to lose (B. Git. 61b, B. Hul. 6b).[40]

In classical rabbinic times Jewish women played an economic role in the cottage industry of spinning and weaving above and beyond their normal domestic duties. Here the Mishnah offers a fascinating glimpse into the prevalence of class distinctions in Israel;[41] for the number of tasks a wife must perform varies depending on how many slaves she brings to the marriage as part of her dowry from her father. If she owns as many as four slaves, one opinion has it, "she may lounge in a chair [all day long]" (M. Ket. 5:5). Most wives, no doubt, lacked slaves and did their own household chores. Some husbands appreciated this; one midrash has the prophet Elijah pointing out to R. Jose that a wife helps her husband by processing the raw materials he brings home: "if a man brings home wheat, does he chew the [raw] wheat? If flax, does he wear the [raw] flax?" (B. Yeb. 62b). Conversely, a wife whose industry brought in more than the husband's cost of maintaining her could profit from a rule permitting her to opt out of most domestic duties if she chose to maintain herself and keep the surplus (B. Ket. 58b). Particularly fascinating is the sages' perception of the hazards of wifely idleness; the Mishnah records the comment of Rabbi Eliezer, supported by the Talmud, that even if she brought one hundred slaves, her husband could compel her to work in wool lest idleness tempt her to dally with other men (M. Ket. 5:5), while R. Simeon b. Gamaliel in the same text forbade husbands to *prevent* their wives from wool-working because of the stultifying effect of boredom. To the wife's Mishnaic chores the Talmud adds personal ministrations like filling the husband's wine cup and washing his face, hands, and feet as expressions of wifely subservience (B. Ket. 61a).

## WOMAN AND THE PUBLIC DOMAIN

Just as most women in Greek society stayed by their spindle or loom while men went out to talk politics in the public square or to wage war in foreign lands, so Talmudic culture approves women who stay home spinning or weaving while men go to the synagogue to pray and the academy to study Torah. Both systems confined women to the private sphere, while men went forth into the public cultural domain. A few rabbis seem to have recognized the constricting effect of female seclusion: R. Dimi states that among the ten curses of Eve was her condemnation to be "wrapped up like a mourner, banished from the company of all men [except her husband], and confined within a prison [the home]" (B. ʿErub. 100b).

Some modern scholars have misconstrued women's capacity to engage in commercial and legal transactions as indicating participation in the public cultural domain of rabbinic culture. But this overlooks the fact that from a juristic standpoint such activities are merely transactions between individuals in the private domain. Indeed, this is how rabbinic jurists perceived them. The distinction is illustrated by the fact that while the Mishnah explicitly permits women to bring and defend lawsuits (M. B.Q. 1:3), it denies them the right to testify personally in the public courthouse (M. Shebu. 4:1), where they must rely on the testimony of men to plead their cause. The apparent discrepancy stems precisely from the perception of commercial and other legal transactions between private parties, including lawsuits, as pri-

vate domain activities for which women qualify; whereas the courthouse (along with synagogue and study house) is a forum of the public
domain in which they may not appear.

By Talmudic times, the exclusion of women from the public domain
was taken for granted. A midrash comments on "Be sure to set as king
over yourself one of your own people" (Deuteronomy 17:15): "A
king—but not a queen. . . . A man may be appointed leader of the
community, but not a woman."[42] As for the barring of women from
synagogue and study house, the Talmud remarks casually that despite
the superstition that pregnant women would miscarry if they stepped
on discarded nail parings, R. Yohanan's discarding his nail parings on
the study house floor was acceptable, because "women don't [usually]
come to the study house" (B. M.Q. 18a).[43]

Not only is the study house off limits; we learn that "women don't
go out [alone] into the fields" (B. Ber. 3a). Those who do must expect
to be taken for harlots and hence deserve what they get, as witness
rabbinic censure of Jacob's daughter Dinah in Genesis Rabbah 80:12,
who is said to have "provoked" her rape by Shekhem b. Hamor simply
by going out "to visit the daughters of the land" (Genesis 34:1).
Genesis Rabbah 80:11 adds insult to injury by insisting that Dinah
actually enjoyed the experience; her brothers had to drag her away
from Shekhem, because "when a woman has intercourse with an un-
circumcised man, she finds it hard to tear herself away."

It is highly significant that the rabbis of the Talmud felt a special
need to justify the exclusion of women from the study house. A scriptural proof text was essential because, following M. Qiddushin 1:7,
Torah study (a positive but not time-contingent commandment)
should be required of women as well as of men. To prove that women
were exempt from this precept, the rabbis claim that the biblical injunction "And you shall teach [the precepts of the Torah] to your
children" (Deuteronomy 11:19) referred only to sons and not to
daughters (B. Qid. 29b-36a).[44] Even so, some sages worried about
women's exclusion from the greatest intellectual experience of rabbinic culture; hints of subliminal guilt pervade Talmudic statements
on the topic. For instance, R. Hiyya consoles women with the assurance that while men acquire merit in Heaven by their devotion to
study, wives and mothers gain merit by "sending their sons to learn in
the synagogue and their husbands to study in the schools of the rabbis,
and waiting patiently for them to return home" (B. Ber. 17a).[45] But

the rabbis never explicitly acknowledge the fact that no amount of sugarcoating can mask the bitterness of women's systematic exclusion from the life of the mind and spirit.[46]

In Talmudic terms, in fact, a woman who appears in public in any context is up to no good. Most likely, she is a prostitute; scholars are exhorted not to speak with women in the marketplace (not even to their own wives and daughters) lest bystanders erroneously conclude that if a scholar may accost strange women on the street, common people may do so with impunity (B. Ber. 43b). If she is not a prostitute, a woman encountered abroad may well be a witch: "Two women seated at a crossroads, facing each other across the highway, are certainly engaged in witchcraft" (B. Pes. 111a). In like vein, women returning from preparing a corpse for burial should be avoided, as they may be accompanied by the Angel of Death (B. Ber. 51a). Incidental or gratuitous observations of this kind, which pepper the Talmud, give a good indication of male perceptions of the female who appears in public. Even rabbinic commentary on Deborah and Huldah, two women who in biblical tradition had functioned in highly praiseworthy ways within the public domain, viciously downgrades the achievements of these remarkable women, as in B. Megillah 14b:

> Said R. Nahman: Haughtiness is unbecoming to women. There were two haughty women whose names were [appropriately] hateful: one was called Wasp [*zibortah*, which like *deborah* means "wasp" or "bee"] and one was called Weasel [*karkushta*, which like *huldah* means "weasel"]. Of the Wasp it is written, "And she sent and summoned Barak" (Judges 4:6). Why didn't she go to him? Of the Weasel it is written, "[she said,] 'Tell the man' [King Josiah]" (2 Kings 22:15). She should have said, "Tell the King."

Every rule has its exception. B. Shabbat 62a describes a woman as a *gizbarit*, a word that in its masculine form means "manager" or "treasurer" and generally signifies one who makes disbursements from charity funds. A modern translator of Tractate Shabbat comments that "it is interesting to observe a woman occupying this position."[47] Possibly this woman, clearly filling a position of public trust, kept the community chest in her home and disbursed the funds from there. Whatever the case, the *gizbarit* reminds us of women in hellenistic Jewish cultures contemporaneous with Mishnah and Talmud whose lay leadership role in the synagogue has been revealed by study of epitaphs and other inscriptions commemorating those activities.[48] But the Talmud records no other case of a woman functioning in such a public capacity within rabbinic culture.[49]

## RABBINIC AMBIVALENCE: THE HUMAN TOUCH

We began with the shocking contrast between R. Joseph's perception of his mother as the embodiment of the divine Shekhinah and an anonymous sage's reviling of woman "as a pitcher of filth with its mouth full of blood," a contrast that seemed to express an irrational ambivalence toward women. But in truth, there was no contradiction: favorable comments are not lacking for women fulfilling the traditional roles of wife and mother, while unfavorable comments are directed at unattached (hence dangerous) women who in some way threaten male control of sexuality, reproduction, paternity, and in the end patriarchal society itself.

Beyond the exclusion of women from the life of mind and spirit, we find yet another reflection of ambivalence in the discrepant assessments of women in Talmudic descriptions of men's domestic experience, which appear to emerge from the rabbis' sometimes affectionate, sometimes caustic comments about their own wives. While some statements are complimentary, others are disparaging. No doubt this partly reflects different psychological responses on the part of individual sages.[50] But this familiar phenomenon, transcending time, space, and culture, perhaps more than anything else brings the Talmud to life for the modern reader. It represents the human factor, pure and simple, of men's deep-rooted ambivalence toward the women who figure most prominently in their daily lives.

Consider, for instance, the statements "A man who has no wife is not a [complete] man. . . . A man who has no wife lives without joy, without blessing and without goodness . . . without Torah . . . and without peace" (B. Yeb. 62b), contrasted with Raba's complaint that "a bad wife is as hard [to bear] as a stormy day" (B. Yeb. 63b). Or again, "When a man divorces the wife of his youth, even the altar sheds tears" (B. San. 22a) versus Raba's statement that "It is a pious deed [*mitzvah*] to divorce a bad wife" (B. Yeb. 63b). And again, "If your wife is a short woman, bend down to listen to her" (B. B.M. 59a), contrasted with "He who follows a woman's advice will end up

in *Gehinnom* [Hell]" (ibid). These last two pieces of conflicting advice
are neatly harmonized by the assurance of a third rabbi that the first
statement speaks of "domestic matters," while the second refers to
"worldly affairs."

Statements about women are sometimes explicitly equivocal, as in
the following exegesis, in B. Yebamot 63b, of the text, "I find woman
more bitter than death" (Ecclesiastes 7:26):

> Rab Judah was reading to his son R. Isaac the scripture: "I find woman
> more bitter than death." When [his son] asked him, "For instance,
> whom?" [he replied], "For instance, your mother!" But did not Rab
> Judah [also] teach his son R. Isaac, "A man finds happiness only with
> his first wife, as it is said, 'Let your fountain be blessed; find joy with
> the wife of your youth' (Proverbs 5:18)." When [his son] asked him,
> "For instance, whom?" [he replied], "For instance, your mother!" She
> was irascible, but she could easily be appeased with a word.

In the same text we find the similar observation: "In the West [i.e.,
in Palestine], when a man married a woman, people would ask him,
'Is it [a case of] "found" or "find?"' *Found*, as it is written, 'He who has
found [*matsa*] a wife has found happiness' Proverbs 18:22). *Find*, as it
is written, 'I find (*motse*) woman more bitter than death' (Ecclesiastes
7:26)."

Not only their wives but also their daughters were the objects of
the sages' strictures; and some of their paternal concerns are expressed
in B. Sanhedrin 100b:

> "A daughter is a false treasure to her father; through worrying about
> her he cannot sleep at night—while she is a minor, lest she be seduced;
> at puberty, lest she play the harlot; when she is grown, lest she not get
> married; when she is married, lest she bear no children; when she grows
> old, lest she engage in witchcraft" (Wisdom of ben Sira 42:9–10). Our
> rabbis likewise have said this. The world cannot exist without both
> males and females. [But] happy is he whose children are males and woe
> to him whose children are female.

Still, the Talmudic rabbis express more concern for their daughters'
happiness than did the sages of the Mishnah. The latter had permitted
fathers to marry off their daughters in childhood without their consent; but Babylonian rabbis asserted that "a man is forbidden to marry

off his daughter while she is a child, [he must wait] until she is old enough to say, 'I want so-and-so'" (B. Qid. 41a, but see M. Yeb. 13:2).

Despite their preoccupation with the sexual conduct of their wives and daughters, the rabbis' assessments of women include on balance more expressions of approval than of condemnation. One could multiply examples; but suffice it to say that we gain an overall impression that the authors of rabbinic literature appear most human in their sometimes grumbling, often grudging, but withal affectionate acknowledgment of the vital role of women in their domestic lives.

## CONCLUSIONS

A literature produced by men offers very little testimony to the actual experience of real, historical women. The Talmud rarely speaks of individual women, treating them for the most part in a generic and stereotypical way. What we get, in the end, is the rabbinic understanding of women's nature and place in the social fabric, along with a set of rules delineating the (perhaps theoretical, perhaps actual) legal status of women in a patriarchal culture.

If rabbinic literature fails to speak directly of women's actual experience, it does offer glimpses, often tantalizing, sometimes frustrating, of how things may have been for the Jewish women of late antiquity who, voluntarily or otherwise, subjected themselves to rabbinic regulation. Chances are that *most* Jewish women's daily lives during the centuries of Mishnah and Talmud differed little from those of *most* women in surrounding patriarchal cultures. It seems certain that Jewish women in Talmudic society, legally confined to a world of domesticity and of private commercial transactions, were largely excluded from the stimulating world of ideas available (at least in principle) to the male inheritors and transmitters of the Jewish intellectual past. True, the king's daughter "all glorious within" may have ruled the roost at home, craftily wielding a power of manipulation that undermined her husband's legal authority over her; but it was never true of classical rabbinic culture that "the hand that rocks the cradle rules the world." We cannot hope to recover, from rabbinic literature alone, the whole truth about the lives of the women in its orbit—above all, how they may have channeled their intellectual and emotional energies to create an inner life of mind and spirit. What they knew, what they thought, and what they felt have not come down to us.

## NOTES

The abbreviations M. (Mishnah) and B. (Babylonian Talmud) are used regularly in the text and notes. Titles of mishnaic/talmudic tractates are abbreviated as follows:

| | | | |
|---|---|---|---|
| **A.Z.** | Abodah Zarah | **Naz.** | Nazir |
| **B.M.** | Baba Metzia | **Ned.** | Nedarim |
| **B.Q.** | Baba Qamma | **Nid.** | Niddah |
| **Ber.** | Berakot | **Pes.** | Pesahim |
| **Dem.** | Demai | **Qid.** | Qiddushin |
| **'Erub.** | 'Erubin | **R.H.** | Rosh ha-Shanah |
| **Git.** | Gittin | **San.** | Sanhedrin |
| **Hul.** | Hullin | **Shab.** | Shabbat |
| **Ket.** | Ketubot | **Shebu.** | Shebuot |
| **Meg.** | Megillah | **Sot.** | Sotah |
| **M.Q.** | Moed Qatan | **Yeb.** | Yebamot |

1. In classical rabbinic literature, Shekhinah (a feminine noun in Hebrew) denotes the divine presence of God dwelling in the world.

2. In this context, *mouth* is an obvious euphemism. The Hebrew *tso'ah*, here translated as "filth," means literally "excrement."

3. Israel (*yisra'el*) is the name used consistently and exclusively to denote the Jewish people in all classical rabbinic texts.

4. For an exposition of these matters, see Jacob Neusner, *Judaism: The Evidence of the Mishnah*, 2d ed. (Atlanta, 1988).

5. Other Judaisms certainly coexisted with the rabbinic mode both before and during the centuries of the halakhic source texts. On the general subject of Judaism in Greco-Roman culture, see Shaye J. D. Cohen, *From the Maccabees to the Mishnah* (Philadelphia, 1987). For women in hellenistic Jewish cultures contemporaneous with Mishnah and Talmud, see chapter 2 above.

6. Some recent assessments of rabbinic authority in late antiquity include Jack Lightstone, "Christian Anti-Judaism in Its Judaic Mirror: The Judaic Context of Early Christianity Revised," in *Separation and Polemic: Anti-Judaism in Early Christianity*, ed. Stephen Wilson, vol. 2 (Waterloo, Canada, 1986), 103–32; Martin Goodman, *State and Society in Roman Galilee, A.D. 132–212* (Totowa, NJ, 1983), chap. 7. See also Erwin R. Goodenough, *Jewish Symbols of the Greco-Roman Period*, ed. and abr. Jacob Neusner (Princeton, 1988), xiii.

7. On the Mishnah, see Jacob Neusner, *Judaism: The Evidence of the Mishnah*; idem, *The Mishnah: An Introduction* (Northvale, NJ, 1989). For a detailed analysis of

the status of women in Mishnaic law, see my Chattel or Person? The Status of Women in the Mishnah (N.Y., 1988).

8. Simone DeBeauvoir, The Second Sex (New York, 1953; rep. 1974), 93 and passim.

9. A levirate widow (yebamah) is one whose husband has died without lineal heirs (meaning, in the mishnaic context, without male issue). Mishnaic law, following Deuteronomy 25:5–10, requires her to marry her husband's brother (levir in Latin) unless he agrees to a release ritual of unshoeing (halitzah). The primary object of levirate law was to produce a surrogate son, that is, a lineal heir, for the deceased; it could also provide protection within the patriarchal group for an unattached woman.

10. In Mishnaic law, "adult daughter" (bogeret) means one who has reached the age of twelve-and-a-half years and a day. Between the ages of twelve and twelve-and-a-half she is a "maiden" (na'arah), liable to keep precepts of Torah but not yet emancipated. Unless married off by her father during this six-month period (as normally happens), she will acquire full autonomy at the end of it.

11. A "regular" widow is one who has borne her husband a son (or whose husband already had a son by another wife).

12. Sarah B. Pomeroy (Goddesses, Whores, Wives and Slaves: Women in Classical Antiquity [New York, 1975], 25) employs this felicitous characterization of the hellenistic mode of thought.

13. The historical origins of the ketubbah are cloaked in obscurity. Tradition ascribes it to Simeon b. Shetah, a sage of the first century B.C.E. (B. Ket. 82b). See M. J. Geller, "Some New Light on the Origins of the Rabbinic Ketubah," Hebrew Union College Annual 49 (1978).

14. In accordance with halakha (rabbinic law), a civil divorcée cannot remarry Jewishly until her husband gives her a unilateral writ of divorce called a get, nor can a yebamah contract a legal Jewish marriage without performing the release ceremony of halitzah. Any children such women may later bear without having received a get or undergone halitzah are considered illegitimate (mamzerim) and may only marry others of the same status.

15. This unusual stance probably resulted from the sages' misconstrual of a technical term 'onah (Exodus 21:10), whose meaning had apparently changed during the many centuries separating Torah from Mishnah. The Mishnah takes the word to mean "set time" (for intercourse), rather than the contextually more appropriate meaning of "shelter." See my Chattel or Person?, 232, n. 143 for a fuller discussion of this point.

16. See my "Tragelaphos Revisited: The Anomaly of Woman in the Mishnah," Judaism 37 (1988): 160–72; and Jacob Neusner, Method and Meaning in Ancient Israel Brown Judaic Studies 10 (Missoula, MT, 1979), 96–97.

17. See my Chattel or Person, chap. 5.

18. Ibid., 194; and see Judith R. Baskin, "The Separation of Women in Rabbinic Judaism," in Women, Religion, and Social Change, ed. Yvonne Y. Haddad and Ellison B. Findly (Albany, NY, 1985), 3–18.

19. Contrary to the popular belief that the sages exempted the woman to free her for domestic duties, none of the classical rabbinic sources gives this reason. (In fact, no reason at all is given in either the Mishnah, the Talmud, Maimonides' Commentary to the Mishnah, or Rashi's Commentary to the Talmud on M. Qid. 1:7.) It is first articulated in a medieval tract whose author claims that God absolved women from their duties to him so as to free them to serve their husbands (Sefer Abudarham, pt. 3, "The Blessing over [Fulfilling] the Commandments"). On the question of wom-

en's exemptions, see Rachel Biale, *Women and Jewish Law* (New York, 1984), esp. 13–14, and my *Chattel or Person?*, chap. 6.

20. The same is true in principle of every person named in the Talmud, male or female. But since Talmudic rabbis are routinely named in recording their opinions, it seems fair to assume that most, if not all, were historical characters, even if there is reason to doubt the accuracy of many Talmudic attributions.

21. Rashi on B. A.Z. 18b., s.v. *we-ikka de-amrei mi-shum ma'aseh diBeruriah*. The Hebrew phrase in question, *nashim da 'atan qallah 'aleihen*, looks like an attempted rendition of a well-known maxim of contemporary Roman law, which insisted that women, including those of full age, should remain under guardianship all of their lives *propter animi laevitatem*, "because of their instability of judgment" (Gaius, *Institutes* 1.144; *animus* = Heb. *da'at*, *laevitas* = Heb. *qallut*).

22. See also Rachel Adler, "The Virgin in the Brothel and Other Anomalies: Character and Context in the Legend of Beruriah," *Tikkun*, November/December 1988, 28–32, 102–105; idem, "The Jew Who Wasn't There: *Halakhah* and the Jewish Woman," *Response* 7 (1973): 77–82.

23. The sages also prove by means of creative wordplay that God's commandment to "be fruitful and multiply" (Genesis 1:28) applies only to men and not women, despite the fact that both verbs appear in the plural form (B. Yeb. 65b). This was obviously crucial to establish men's right to control the reproductive process and also to ensure that unmarried women would not claim the right to reproduce in the guise of a divinely imposed obligation. On the restriction of the obligation of procreation to men, see Judith R. Baskin, "Rabbinic Reflections on the Barren Wife," *Harvard Theological Review* 82 (1989): 103–5.

24. See, e.g., M. Ket. 1:6, where the betrothed maiden must tell her bridegroom: "After you betrothed me, I was raped and your field was flooded," and Qur'ān, 2:223, "Your women are a field for you: plough your field as ye will." Similar metaphors are found in classical Greek literature; e.g., Plato (*Timaeus* 91d) compares the womb to "ploughed soil" (*arouran*).

25. Credit for creating a child's spirit and intellect goes not to the man, however, but to God (B. Nid. 31a).

26. The best-known treatment of the subject is found in Mary Douglas, *Purity and Danger* (Boston, 1966), esp. 140–158. See also Howard Eilberg-Schwartz, "Menstrual Blood, Semen and Discharge," in his *The Savage in Judaism* (Bloomington, 1990), 177–194.

27. The Priestly Code comprises the Book of Leviticus (together with the conclusion of the Book of Exodus and portions of the Book of Numbers).

28. Islamic tradition expresses a similar view. Since an early *ḥadīth* collection introduces the rules of menstruation with the statement that "some say Allah first sent menstruation among the children of Israel," it would seem that Islamic law "borrowed" the Talmudic law of the menstruant (along with much other Judaic material). See Muḥammad al-Bukhārī (*al-Jamiʿ al-Ṣaḥiḥ* 1.6 ["The Book of Menses"] chap. 2), who also writes that the Prophet forbade women to pray while menstruating (chap. 8), because in Islamic, as in Jewish, law, menstruation generates cultic pollution ("It is a noxious thing," Qur'ān 2:222). The Qur'ān forbids an individual in such a state to perform cultic acts like prayer and fasting (4:43).

29. The analogy between a man's relation to God and a woman's relation to her husband is found explicitly in all three of the monotheistic religions. See, e.g., Hosea 2–3 and the statements of Paul in 1 Corinthians 11. We find an even more explicit statement of this analogy in Islamic *ḥadīth* traditions that postdate the Talmud by a

92 Judith Romney Wegner

century or more. See Jane Smith and Yvonne Haddad, "Women in the Afterlife: The Islamic View as seen from Qur'an and Tradition," *Journal of the American Academy of Religion* 43 (1975): 44–45.

30. The phrase "and He built [*wayyiben*] [Adam's rib] into a woman" (Genesis 2:22) was read as a wordplay on the verb "to build" (*b-n-y*)and the verb "to understand" (*b-y-n*); a slight change in vocalization can yield the alternative rendition, "and he gave intuitive understanding [*wayyaben*] to the woman."

31. H. Freedman and M. Simon, trans. and eds., *Midrash Rabbah* 1, Genesis, 3rd ed. (New York, 1983), 141–42.

32. Apologists whose work would be more useful were it not sadly flawed by selective use of primary texts (ignoring those unfavorable to women) include Moshe Meiselman, *Women in Jewish Law* (New York, 1978) and Menahem Brayer, *The Jewish Woman in Rabbinic Literature* (Hoboken, NJ, 1986). On the other side of the line, the same criticism may be directed at Leonard Swidler's polemically selective book, *Women in Judaism* (Metuchen, NJ, 1976), which ignores Mishnaic rules and Talmudic texts that favor women.

33. Philip Birnbaum (trans., *Daily Prayer Book* [*Ha-Siddur Ha-Shalem*], 16) comments on this blessing as follows: "The worshiper expresses his appreciation of nature's super-senses and the exact timing of animals, for there are many kinds of 'knowingness' in which animals far surpass us by means of their exquisite ability to 'feel' things." Perhaps it is no accident that the male worshiper continues immediately with three blessings praising God for not making him a gentile, a slave, or a woman.

34. See chapter 1 above.

35. See, e.g., Genesis Rabbah 80:5 on the rape of Dinah, which states that when Dinah exposed herself by going out of the house, the result was "like an eagle who swoops down to grab a piece of meat."

36. The husband may reduce the rebellious wife's marriage settlement by seven dinars for each refusal but need augment it by only three dinars for each refusal on his part. This is not because her services are worth more than his; the rule simply aims to establish that despite the sages' interpretation of intercourse as the husband's duty and the wife's right, in the last analysis her compliance is her duty and his right.

37. B. Yoma 66b (*Ein ḥokhmah la-'ishah ella ba-pelekh*). The creators of the Talmud, treating the Torah as a unitary text proceeding directly from God, failed to recognize that the same word used by different biblical writers might not have the same meaning. The term *ḥakhmat lev beyadeha* in Exodus 35:25 (from the author of the Priestly Code) connotes "manual dexterity." In Deuteronomy, however, *ḥakham* has (as in the Talmud) the quite different connotation of cognitive knowledge and intellect.

38. Homer, Iliad 6.490–93 (trans. Robert Fitzgerald [New York, 1975], 157). Centuries later, Islamic culture would combine both Greek and Jewish notions of appropriate male and female activities. Muslim women stayed home under wraps, while Muslim men engaged in the struggle for Allah, both in the literal sense of holy war (*jihād*) and in the metaphorical sense of studying the sacred laws (*ijtihād*).

39. Pomeroy, *Women in Classical Antiquity*, 199. See also M. R. Lefkowitz and M. B. Fant, eds., *Women's Life in Greece and Rome* (Baltimore, 1982), 170.

40. This discussion illuminates our ignorance of what proportion of Jews, male or female, actually followed Mishnaic or Talmudic regulations, even in communities where rabbinic Judaism flourished.

41. While there were certainly class distinctions among the Jews of late antiquity, it seems doubtful that social class was a primary factor in the learning-based culture

of rabbinic Judaism (except in so far as the learned themselves constituted a separate class), since distinguished rabbis like R. Eliezer and R. Joshua are known to have come from the wealthiest (patrician) and most impoverished (plebeian) strata of Jewish society, respectively.

42. Sifre Deuteronomy, Pisqa 157. Similar is Pisqa 13, which asks in connection with the choosing of male tribal leaders, "[Why does it say] men? Would we ever think of appointing women?" (trans. Reuven Hammer, in *Sifre: A Tannaitic Commentary on the Book of Deuteronomy* [New Haven, CT, 1988], 37 and 192).

43. For anecdotes involving women who do enter the study house, see B. Ber. 23a, and B. Shab. 13a–b, both involving autonomous women (a prostitute and a widow), on errands having to do with *tefillin* (phylacteries).

44. Since the Hebrew word *banim* often means "children" in the generic sense but sometimes does mean "sons" as opposed to daughters, the language in Deuteronomy is ambiguous. Hence, an intention to exclude daughters could not be taken for granted but had to be proved. The sages based that proof partly on the fact that the word *welimmad'tem* (and you shall teach) can also be read as *ulemad'tem*, (and you shall learn). Thus, they said, the Torah clearly intended that only those having the obligation to teach their offspring (according to M. Qid. 1:7, this meant fathers, i.e., men) needed to learn; hence Torah had to be taught only to sons.

45. And see B. Ned. 50a, where R. Akiba, returning home after twenty-four years' absence at the academy, declares that the merit for his learning and that of his disciples belongs to his long-suffering wife Rachel.

46. With the development of feminist theory, social-scientific explanations of the exclusion of women from the public domain (both in general and in Judaic culture) have been appearing with increasing frequency in recent years. One of the first such analyses of this phenomenon in Judaism is Baskin, "Separation of Women"; see also my *Chattel or Person?*, chap. 8.

47. I. Epstein, ed., *The Babylonian Talmud. Seder Moed: Shabbat*, trans. H. Freedman (London, 1936), 290, n. 2.

48. See Bernadette Brooten, *Women Leaders of the Ancient Syagogue* (Chico, CA, 1982); and chapter 2 above.

49. The case of a woman whose husband sets her up as a stallkeeper, *henwanit*, discussed in M. Ket. 9:4, is equally mysterious. A *henwani* was normally a man who operated a *hanut*, or stall, in the marketplace. It seems unlikely that a man would send his wife out to do this; the Mishnah may perhaps refer to a woman selling goods from a stall in a room of her house that opens onto the public courtyard, this being a common architectural plan. But in any case, the sale and purchase of goods is a private domain activity, something which we know women could legally perform in Mishnaic and Talmudic law. It sheds no light, however, on the case of the *gizbarit*, which remains a mystery.

50. For instance, one can easily distinguish the consistently limiting positions of R. Eliezer b. Hyrcanus from the equally consistent championship of women's rights by R. Judah b. Ilai. For Eliezer, see, e.g., M. Ket. 5:5, 9:4; M. Ned. 10:5–6; M. Sot. 1:1, 3:4, 6:1; M. Git. 6:3, 9:1. For Judah, see M. Ket. 3:2, 4:4, 9:1, 11:10; M. Git. 7:4, 7:6, 9:3.

CHAPTER **4** **JUDITH R. BASKIN**

*Jewish Women in the Middle Ages*

The main expectations for a Jewish woman of the Middle Ages were
domestic: "May she sew, spin, weave and be brought up to a life of
good deeds" is the prayer with which one set of parents in medieval
Northern Europe recorded their daughter's birth.[1] With the additional
desire, declared in another milieu of the Jewish Middle Ages, Moslem
Egypt, that a newborn daughter "might come into a blessed and auspicious home,"[2] that is, be well married, the essential hopes for medieval Jewish women have been expressed. Yet the evidence shows,
particularly in Christian Europe, that women were also active in transacting business, often supporting their families, and fulfilled public
religious roles such as teaching other women and leading them in
prayer.[3] This conflict between pious expectations and the realities of
women's lives is paradigimatic of the ambiguities that must inform
any study of Jewish women in periods when rabbinic Judaism was
dominant.

For Jewish history, the Middle Ages span a thousand years, from the
completion of the Babylonian Talmud in circa 600 c.e. to the imposition of ghetto restrictions in Western Europe in the sixteenth cen-

tury. Within this wide span of centuries diverse Jewish communities supported themselves in a variety of settings. While large populations thrived in the Moslem worlds of Iran and Iraq, Egypt, Spain, and North Africa, far smaller and more insecure Jewish communities were dispersed across Christian Europe in France, Germany, Italy, and England. No matter where Jews lived, the Talmud provided a uniform pattern for family, business, community, and religious life. Still, local environments always played a vital role in the ways Jewish social and family life developed, and to study Jewish societies in the Diaspora is to observe the ambivalence of a people assuming the language, dress, and mores of their gentile neighbors while endeavoring to maintain an allegiance to the guidance and demands of Jewish legal dicta and rabbinic leadership.

Discovering texts that reflect the spiritual lives and personal aspirations of Jewish women of the Middle Ages is an all-but-impossible task, since almost no contemporary documents from women themselves are extant. Medieval Jewish women's feelings about the expectations imposed upon them and the limitations for their sex inherent in rabbinic social policy are also virtually unrecoverable. While a number of sources relevant to medieval Jewish women survive, they generally reveal male understandings of what women's roles should be and offer praise for exemplary women who appeared to have fulfilled these criteria.

Thus, a major source of information about Jewish women in the Middle Ages, the *responsa* literature, is intimately connected with the rabbinic legal process. Through *responsa* the rabbinic authorities kept halacha (Jewish law and law-making) a living process after the Talmud had been completed.[4] Individuals or communities, confused over a problem for which the Talmud did not offer an obvious answer, would address a letter to a recognized rabbinic leader setting forth the difficulty. The authority would consult the legal traditions at his disposal and formulate a response that would be circulated among many Jewish communities; *responsa* of major rabbinic authorities were usually collected and published, and the issues they address cover all aspects of life and religious practice. Additional medieval sources that provide information about medieval Jewish women include marriage contracts and other legal records, historical chronicles by Jewish and non-Jewish authors, personal documents, and legal, economic, and ecclesiastical documents.[5]

## JEWISH WOMEN'S LIVES IN THE MOSLEM WORLD

Study of the documents of the Cairo Genizah has provided modern scholars with an abundance of information on Jewish society and institutions under Islam. A *genizah* is a place where unusable sacred writings were stored in order to preserve them from desecration. The treasure trove of late antique and medieval documents which were deposited in the *genizah* of the synagogue of Rabbanite Jews in Fostat, a suburb of Cairo, has been known to scholars since early modern times.[6] While much of this material has a religious or literary character, the Cairo Genizah also included a huge quantity of discarded secular writings such as official, business, learned, and private correspondence, court records, contracts, and other legal documents.[7] The letters this *genizah* preserves come from almost every country of the Islamic Jewish world; most are written in Arabic, the language of Jewish everyday life in this milieu. Among the legal documents are marriage contracts, which often enumerate all of the dresses, ornaments, and furniture brought into marriage by the bride, providing a material gauge of a given community's standard of living.

The *genizah* documents are most relevant to Jewish life in the Islamic world from the ninth to twelfth centuries, a period when conditions tended to be peaceful and prosperous. Jews did not have the full rights of Moslems; but, like Christians, they were tolerated and protected from persecution so long as they paid a substantial tax. Many of these Mediterranean Jews were involved in trade, and their undertakings often involved overseas travel. A number became quite wealthy, and a Jewish community like that of Cairo was solidly middle-class. Social life was strongly influenced by Islamic norms. Thus, polygyny was not uncommon,[8] and while Jewish women of prosperous families were not literally isolated in women's quarters (as were Moslem women of comparable social status), community norms dictated that woman's place was in the home. The twelfth century traveler, Petachia of Ratisbon, wrote of the Jewish community of Baghdad, "Nobody sees there any woman, nor does anybody go into the house of his friend, lest he should see the wife of his neighbor. But he knocks with a tin knocker, and the other comes forth and speaks to him."[9] The observation of the preeminent medieval sage Maimonides (1135–1204) that "there is nothing more beautiful for a wife than sitting in the corner of her house, as it is written, 'The most honored place for a princess is inside' (Psalms 45 : 14),"[10] reflects the high degree of Jewish acculturation to Islamic custom. Maimonides, however, did allow that a woman is not a prisoner to be prevented from going and coming, although he also suggested that outside visits to family and friends should not exceed one or two a month. In fact, however, a Jewish woman usually insisted on her freedom of movement, and many *genizah* accounts of marital squabbles make this an explicit right for the wife if reconciliation is to be achieved.[11]

The marriage her parents arranged for her when she was thirteen or fourteen, usually to a considerably older man, would determine the course of a young woman's life. The community, following Talmudic norms, took it for granted that marriage was the natural state for both men and women. A sermon found in the *genizah*, explains that the wife is a wall around her husband, bringing atonement for his sins and peace to his domicile. And marriage, the text continues, preserves a man from sin and, through sons who study Torah and fulfil the commandments, ensures physical and spiritual continuity.[12] "I was happy to learn about the joy [wedding] of our elder," a letter from the *genizah* reads. "May God make your happiness full and complete. May the wife who comes into the house of our elder be like Rachel and Leah, who both built the house of Israel, and may God give you male children studying the Torah and fulfilling its commandments. May you see the erection of the House of God, the ingathering of the people, and the advent of the [Messiah]."[13]

The first preference for a spouse—generally a first cousin or other suitable relative—was intended to preserve prosperity within the extended family while also offering security and familiarity to the young bride. Marrying outside the family, however, was an opportunity for merchant families to widen their connections and enhance their strength. It was not uncommon for marriages to be arranged between young men in Persia and young girls from Syria or Egypt to strengthen business ties between two trading houses by establishing family alliances. Sometimes young businessmen from abroad would endeavor to marry into a successful local family as a way of establishing a foothold and eventually attaining a prominent position in the new country.[14] Thus, an elder brother writes from Tunisia when he learns of the younger's marriage in Egypt: "I took notice of the description of your blessed and most auspicious wedding and understand that God has granted you to become connected with the most illustrious and finest people, those of whom one can boast in East and West. This is more precious than the earth and the fullness thereof. Thank and praise God that he has cast your lot with the grandees of Israel."[15] Nor were all marriages contracted on purely economic grounds; there was often an effort to marry a girl from a scholarly family in the expectation that she would produce "sons studying the Torah."[16]

The marriage contract, or *ketubah*, was a prerequisite for marriage, since marriages were regarded as economic agreements in which, first and foremost, the husband obligated himself to provide his wife with food and clothing and to maintain her in general. He also contributed a marriage gift, part of which was payable at the time of the wedding, with a portion reserved for the bride in the event of a divorce or her husband's death. This provided a form of security for her and was certainly a deterrent against rash divorce. Similarly, the bride brought property into the marriage in the form of her dowry. This was generally worth many times more than the husband's marriage gift, and marrying off several daughters could be extremely expensive. The value of the dowry was not left to chance but was carefully evaluated by professional assessors; an itemized list of its contents was attached to the marriage contract. S. D. Goitein, the preeminent scholar of the *genizah* documents, writes:

> A properly executed and well-preserved appraisal of a dowry is apt to provide us with a complete picture of the economic circumstances of a marriage. It lists the price of each item and describes it by provenance, material, color and size. The totals of each group, such as gold and silver jewelry, clothing, bedding, copper, carpets and hangings and other household goods are also noted. The total of the entire outfit is followed by other possessions of the bride, such as houses, or usually, parts of a house, one or more maidservants and occasionally books.[17]

A marriage contract also contained various social safeguards protecting the wife. These were a way of effecting alterations in Jewish laws and practices that were unfavorable to women, and they provided security against many of the known pitfalls of married life, as the following betrothal agreement illustrates:

> 1. Should separation occur, the [divorce] document freeing Sitt al-Dalal [Lady Bold] will be produced by her husband without delay.

2. She is trustworthy in her statements concerning everything and no oath of any kind may be imposed on her.

3. He will not marry another wife [nor keep a slave girl disliked by her].

4. He will not beat her.

5. He will not leave Fustat and travel anywhere [except with her consent].

6. Before setting out on a journey he will write her a conditional bill of divorce, and deposit the delayed installment of her marriage gift as well as the sums needed for her maintenance during his absence.

7. The young couple will live in her parents' house. The husband owes yearly rent of 6 dinars and will never be late in paying it.

8. He will not separate her from her parents, as long as the latter are alive and cannot force her to live anywhere else.

9. A fine of 50 dinars is imposed on him in case he fails to fulfill any of the preceding conditions.[18]

Although the husband promised to support his wife, it was not un-usual for her to earn money on her own, most often through needle-work, especially embroidery. Usually, a wife was permitted to keep her earnings for her own private use, although clauses in some marriage agreements stipulate that she provide her own clothing out of her earnings. It seems clear, however, that these earnings were often a source of marital friction. In a petition to a rabbinical court in the twelfth century, the wife of a miller—also described as the daughter of a cantor—requests that her husband not have the right to tell her to do embroidery in the houses of other people and bring him her earnings, and if she does chose to work, she requests that she be per-mitted to retain her wages.[19]

While the poorest women might find it necessary to sell wares or produce in the marketplace, a wealthy wife's economic worth would probably be based on her property, including gifts and inheritances she received during her married life. There are many records of quite sub-stantial women of property who handled their own financial affairs and represented themselves in court.[20]

Marriages were far from being purely financial arrangements. Al-though brides were typically considerably younger than their hus-bands, through the passage of years and the development of shared concerns a marriage could grow into a warm and meaningful bond. As S. D. Goitein has written, "When *genizah* husbands speak of love, we should take them seriously. They were not people from another planet."[21] Certainly, deep marital devotion is evident in the following letter:

> Abundant greetings and wishes for speedy salvation come from East and West to my pure and chaste wife. Now I know how good your doings are, although I have no mouth to express this in words. I am sure you are well, but my well-being is bitter, because of my separation from you and from the eyes of the boy, my dear, beloved and most cherished son. I weep and groan and cry, day and night, and lift my eyes unto the four quarters of the world, but there is no one who has mercy upon me, except the Holy One, Blessed be He. Although you need no admonition from me, please lift your eyes to Heaven and act for the sake of your soul by taking utmost care of our cherished and dear boy, and do not neglect him. This will be the best proof of your love.[22]

Still, divorce was by no means uncommon in this time and place of Jewish history. Not only did Islamic social custom accept divorce, but arranged marriages, geographic mobility, and the "greater attentiveness to a wife's sufferings to be expected in a cosmopolitan bourgeois society" all contributed to marital strife.[23] Some women emerged unscathed, particularly if they had favored the divorce and been supported by prosperous families, and remarriage was very common. Less fortunate divorcées were left in want and joined society's other outcast females, the widowed and the deserted who were dependent on public charity. One such woman, a deserted wife, made the following plea:

> I am a poor foreigner reporting what I had to endure from my husband, Saʿid b. ʿammar [Lucky, son of Long-Lived] the silk weaver. He left me pregnant and traveled away. [No mention of a birth is made here.] Then he came back and stayed a while until I was with child. He left me again, I delivered a boy and took care of him until he was a year old, whereupon Saʿid came back. Then there was that incident with Ibn al-Zuqilliya, who drove us out of our place. We arrived in Jaffa, where Saʿid abandoned me, leaving me alone in a town where I was a stranger. Thus I was forced to get back with my family. From them, however, I suffered their hard words which only God knows. I decided to leave and, uncovering my face [living on public charity], I finally arrived here, where I learned that Saʿid had come to Malij, where a brother of his lives. I went there, but was told that he had

returned to Sham [the Holy Land]. I ask you now to write to someone there who would induce him to have compassion on me and my child; for the boy is now like an orphan; anyone looking at him has compassion upon him and blames his father. If he responds, fine; otherwise have him set me free [through divorce]. I do not blame him. I call upon God as judge, day and night. I am now looking forward to the action to be taken by you and ask God to accept my prayers for you in his mercy.[24]

A series of *responsa* to Maimonides tell of one deserted wife who was able to make herself independent by running a school, assisted by her elder son. Suddenly her husband reappeared and demanded that she give up the school because it injured his dignity for his wife to be a teacher; and besides, he had no one to serve him. He insisted that she give up her teaching and stay with him; otherwise he demanded permission to take a second wife. The suggested solution is a divorce, after which, Maimonides says, "She will have disposition over herself, she may teach what she likes, and do what she likes"; but he rules that "if she stays with her husband, he has the right to forbid her to teach."[25]

This incident raises questions about Jewish women's educations and their involvement in Jewish communal religious life: our schoolmistress had certainly received an elementary education from someone, possibly from her unworthy husband, perhaps in her childhood home. Nor was she unique in her learning, however limited. A twelfth-century Jewish traveler from Spain reported that a community leader in Baghdad, Samuel ben Ali, had no sons but had a daughter who was expert in the Scriptures and Talmud. He wrote that "she gives instruction in Scripture to young men through a window. She herself is within the building, whilst the disciples are below outside and do not see her."[26] On the whole, however, in line with traditional rabbinic norms and the practice of the surrounding Moslem environment, significant learning among women was rare. In all the Cairo Genizah, there is no single piece of writing, religious or otherwise, that may be attributed with certainty to a woman. Yet despite their general lack of learning, references in *genizah* documents report that Jewish women were pious in their observance of the home-based laws incumbent upon them, and there are many indications that their attendance at synagogue was regular. Moreover, women also donated Torah scrolls for the service and oil and books for study and left legacies for the upkeep of the synagogue; and it is not farfetched to interpret these activities—found among Jewish women in Christian Europe, as well—as female strategies for imprinting their existences on a communal religious life from which they were otherwise barred. Still, it was as a mother of sons learned in Torah that the Jewish woman in the Islamic world earned her spiritual reward in the eyes of her family and her society.[27]

## JEWISH WOMEN IN WESTERN EUROPE IN THE CHRISTIAN MIDDLE AGES

Jews began settling in Western Europe in Roman times, primarily as merchants and traders. As Europe became Christian, Jews found themselves subject to increasing legal disabilities, a process that continued throughout the medieval period. Eventually, Jews were barred from virtually any source of livelihood but moneylending. They were often compelled to wear distinctive clothing and badges, and ultimately, toward the end of the Middle Ages, they were either expelled altogether from areas where they had long lived or were forced to live in crowded and unpleasant ghettos (beginning in Rome in 1555). The number of Jews in Western Europe was far smaller than in the Moslem world; and although Western European Jews were also urban, they lived in tiny communities in cities a great deal smaller than those of the East.[28] Despite the legal disabilities they suffered and their ultimate insecurity as to property and life, these Jews tended to be quite prosperous and enjoyed a standard of living comparable to the Christian lower nobility and upper bourgeoisie.[29]

Jewish women were active participants in the family economy; and their status was certainly higher than that enjoyed by their sisters in the Islamic milieu, indicated, in part, by the large dowries they brought into marriage.[30] Girls in this society, despite Talmudic prohibitions to the contrary, were betrothed very young, often at the age of eight or nine. A young woman might be married at eleven or twelve, while her husband would be almost the same age. One young woman, an orphan whose brothers had arranged her engagement, married and established her own household while she was still eleven-and-one-half years old. A year later, "when she reached her majority [according to

Jewish law, twelve-and-one-half] she sued her brothers for her proper share of her father's estate."[31]

Why were children married so young? One Talmudic commentary of the thirteenth century gives the following explanation: "The reason we nowadays are accustomed to betroth our daughters even while they are minors is that our life in the Diaspora is becoming harder; consequently, if a person is now in a financial position to give his daughter an adequate dowry, he is apprehensive lest after the lapse of some years he will be in no position to do so and his daughter will remain unwed forever."[32] But there were other, less negative motivations as well. One would be the religious desire to remove young people from the sexual tensions and temptations that might lead to sin. Economic factors were also operative. Favorable business conditions meant that a well-dowered young couple could support themselves immediately, learning the business at the same time. Moreover, marriage could form an enduring and profitable partnership between two wealthy families, contributing to the prosperity of all. Marriages might also have a social aspect, for settling a young daughter well proved her desirability and increased her family's prestige.[33]

Daughters were given large portions of their parents' property as dowries, and the size of the dowry could also enhance the social standing of the bride's relations. Since the capital with which a young couple started life had its origin mainly in the bride's portion, parents demanded strong guarantees in the marriage contract that the bride would be treated with respect, that her marriage would have some permanence, and that she would have financial security. Thus, the high level of dowries could assure a wife a prominent position in her household. As a tenth-century rabbi remarked in a *responsum* addressing a family quarrel, "It is the custom of men to appoint their wives as masters over their possessions."[34] In recognition of this social reality, as well as under the influence of the prevailing mores of the Christian environment, Rabbi Gershom ben Judah (c. 960-1028), the first great rabbinic authority of Ashkenazic Jewry, is credited with the ruling that polygyny (already rare in this Jewish community, although still legally permitted) was forbidden[35] and more significantly, in opposition to established rabbinic law and practice, that no woman could be divorced against her will.[36]

Familiarity with money led many women to take the initiative in business matters, and often they supplied a part or even the whole of the family income, sometimes allowing their husbands to devote themselves to study. During their husbands' absences on business, women ran the family's affairs. As one scholar points out, "In spite of the rules of modesty formally imposed upon women by the *halacha*, many of them went out to conduct negotiations with feudal princes and with other Jewish and gentile merchants."[37] Women engaged in all kinds of commercial operations and occupations, but money-lending was especially preferred.[38] Widows would frequently continue their financial activities, occasionally in partnership with another woman.[39] Such undertakings, which could be extremely complex, undoubtedly required literacy and training in mathematics and book-keeping skills.[40] Some women were probably involved in craft activities, as well, and there are also some references in Christian sources to independent Jewish women who practiced medicine.[41]

The level of religious education among Western European Jewry certainly included literacy in Hebrew for all men, and for a small elite, considerably more. Occasionally these higher standards also applied to women, particularly those from families distinguished for their learning. In the early twelfth century one of the daughters of Rabbi Shlomo ben Isaac (Rashi), the preeminent biblical and Talmudic commentator of the Ashkenazic Middle Ages, is known to have recorded a *responsum* from her father's dictation, an undertaking requiring knowledge of rabbinic Hebrew.[42] Among women who are described as women's prayer leaders are the twelfth century Dolce of Worms, discussed below, and Urania of Worms, of the thirteenth century, whose headstone epitaph commemorates her as "the daughter of the chief of the synagogue singers. His prayer for his people rose up to glory. And as to her, she, too, with sweet tunefulness officiated before the women to whom she sang the hymnal portions."[43] The intellectual roles of learned Jewish women, however, remained ancillary to mainstream "male" Judaism, consisting either of assisting the male members of their family or providing elementary instruction and synagogue leadership to young girls and other less privileged women. To call these women's activities "ancillary," of course, is not to invalidate their spiritual depth and religious meaning for the participants.

Many ideals of medieval Jewish family life, including the value placed on education, are evident in the medieval ethical *will*. Such moral testaments, left by a parent for his or her children, sum up the author's life experience and values, and advise offspring on the proper conduct of their lives. A good example of such a document is the will of Eleazar b. Samuel of Mainz, a fourteenth-century Jew of whom nothing else is known. Eleazar's will urges all his children to attend synagogue in the morning and evening and to occupy themselves a little afterwards with "Torah, the Psalms or with works of charity." His daughters are particularly requested to obey the laws applying to women: "modesty, sanctity, and reverence should mark their married lives"; and they must "respect their husbands and be invariably amiable to them." Daughters, as well as sons, are admonished to live in communities among other Jews so that their children may learn the ways of Judaism; and, significantly, he insists that "they must not let the young, of either sex, go without instruction in the Torah."

Marriages are to be celebrated as early as possible, according to Eleazar, and prospective spouses should come from respectable families. Distinguished lineage is far more important on the father's than on the mother's side, however, "for all Israel counts descent from the father's side." Eleazar specifically requests that his daughters prepare beautiful candles for the Sabbath and that they refrain from risking money in games of chance, although they may amuse themselves for trifling stakes on New Moons, days customarily celebrated as holidays by Jewish women.

The actual mores of Jewish life must have strayed rather far from Talmudic ideals in Eleazar's time, for he urges his children to avoid "mixed bathing and mixed dancing and all frivolous conversation." He further desires that his daughters "ought to be always at home and not be gadding about." Nor should they stand at the door, watching whatever passes: "I ask, I command, that the daughters of my house be never without work to do, for idleness leads first to boredom, then to sin. But let them spin, cook, or sew." [44]

It is difficult to know where the personal overtakes the formulaic in a document like this; but Eleazar's obvious concern for his daughters' education and mode of life and his knowledge of the pitfalls they might encounter is vibrant, if uneasy, testimony to a Jewish society in which women played many active roles.

The esteem granted a beloved wife, and a description of her activities, is found in the lament of a member of the learned elite and an important spiritual leader, R. Eliezer ben Judah of Worms, for his ex-

emplary wife, Dolce, and his two daughters, killed by Crusaders in
1196:

> Crown of her husband, daughter of nobles . . . her husband's heart
> trusted in her, she fed him and clothed him in honor to sit with the
> elders of the land and garner Torah and good deeds. . . . All the time
> she was with him, she made him books from her toil . . . she sought
> for white wool to spin fringes . . . she spun thread for phylacteries,
> scrolls and books. She was as swift as a deer to cook for her children,
> and to do the will of the students . . . she sewed together about forty
> Torah scrolls . . . adorned brides and brought them [to the wedding]
> with honor. Her hands stitched clothes for the students and repaired
> torn books. She opened her hands to the poor and gave food to her
> sons and daughters and husband. She made wicks [for the candles of
> the] synagogue . . . and recited Psalms. She sang hymns and prayers
> . . . in all the cities she instructed women and sang sweetly, coming
> early to the synagogue and staying late. Throughout the Day of Atone-
> ment she stood singing and taking care of the candles . . . she opened
> her mouth with wisdom and knew what is forbidden and what is per-
> mitted. . . . On the Sabbath day she would sit enquiring, absorbing
> her husband's words. . . . Wise in speech was she . . . buying milk for
> those who studied and hiring teachers by means of her toil. . . . She
> ran to visit the sick . . . fed her sons and urged them to study . . .
> rejoicing to perform her husband's will, and never at any time angering
> him.[45]

Of his thirteen-year-old daughter, the father wrote that she had
"learnt all the prayers and melodies from her mother. She was pious
and wise, a beautiful virgin. She prepared my bed and pulled off my
boots every night. Bellette was nimble about the house, and spoke
only truth, serving her Maker and spinning and sewing and embroi-
dering." And of his younger daughter, Hannah, Rabbi Eliezer remembers: "Each day she recited *Shema Yisrael* and the prayer that follows
it. She was six years old and could spin, sew and embroider, and entertain me by singing."[46]

Since most ordinary Jewish women were cut off from the knowledge
of Hebrew that would enable them to read the traditional liturgy and
holy books, during the later Middle Ages a separate woman's vernacular literature of *tkhines* (supplicatory prayers specially directed towards
women's needs and concerns) began to be produced—sometimes by
women—and simplified "women's Bibles" to fill women's spiritual

needs were written.[47] These volumes had great appeal for less-educated male members of the Jewish community, as well.

The evidence indicates that many unlearned Jewish women, although unconcerned with enlarging their religious knowledge or obligations beyond the household sphere, were genuinely pious. The early thirteenth-century *Sefer Hasidim*, preserves the following account praising a woman's religious philanthropy, and its result:

> A certain man, leaving on a journey, told his wife: "On such and such a day, I shall return and be with thee." The woman, knowing the time of her husband's return, prepared for his return by going to the ritual bath. Her husband thereupon said: "Since you've bathed in anticipation of my return, I shall present you with a gold piece with which to buy a garment." The woman replied: "Allow me, with that gold piece, to purchase a book or to hire a scribe to copy a book for lending to students, enabling them to pursue their studies." Subsequently the woman became pregnant and gave birth to a boy. While all of the brothers of the boy were devoid of learning, that boy himself was the exception.[48]

Another anecdote in the same source tells of a woman who refused to have sexual relations with her miserly husband until he agreed to purchase books and devote them to charitable purposes. The husband complained to a wise man, who told him: "Blessed is she for having brought upon thee pressure to perform a worthy deed. Any other way of constraining thee she knows not." To the wife, however, the sage remarked: "If you cannot be effective in matters related to his doing good, such tactics are commendable. But, when it comes to disputes between him and you as regards sexual intercourse, do not thwart his wishes, lest he indulge in sinful imaginings and lest you keep yourself from becoming pregnant and aggravate his wrath."[49]

Throughout the Middle Ages conversion to Christianity was always an available choice and many Jews, most often men attracted by the wide range of opportunities available after conversion, became apostates. A number of *responsa* deal with the question of the divorce of a Jewish wife from a converted husband. The rabbinic authorities displayed all their flexibility in devising ways to help extricate a Jewish wife from such a marriage and guarantee the return of her property so that remarriage might be a possibility. Rabbi Jacob ben Meir, known as Rabbenu Tam, ends one such twelfth-century *responsum*, "You, noble father of the girl, marry your daughter to someone worthy of her, for one should pay no attention to those who question the validity of a divorce in these circumstances."[50]

In times of persecution, too, Jewish women stood firm. When the crusading fervor swept France and Germany, beginning in 1096, many Jewish communities were massacred by overzealous crusaders. Time and again, the chronicles detail the steadfastness and courage of Jewish women who preferred death for themselves and their children to apostasy. One ruler gave the Jews of his realm the choice of conversion to Christianity or destruction by the sword. "At that time," a Hebrew chronicle relates, "there arose noble women who took hold of one another's hands, saying: 'Let us go to the river and drown ourselves, so that the name of God not be desecrated through us, for the sacred is trodden down in the mire of the streets and our treasures are burned in the fire and altogether death is better for us than life.'"[51] And of the daughters of Mainz, the chronicler relates: "There the women girt their loins with strength and slew their sons and daughters and then themselves. . . . The tender and delicate woman slaughtered her darling child. . . . See, O Lord, what we do for the sanctification of your great name."[52]

An unusual case of a woman's loyalty to her people is that of Polcelina, the Jewish mistress of Count Theobald of Blois.[53] In 1171, apparently as a result of political intrigues at the court of Blois, fed in particular by the hatred that had grown out of the count's fondness for Polcelina, the Jews of Blois were accused of murdering a Christian boy, although no body was ever found.[54] Ultimately, under clerical pressures and when Jewish attempts at ransoming their imprisoned coreligionists failed, the count had more than thirty Jews burned, including, at her own wish, the formerly powerful Polcelina.

Christian writers were aware of the role played by Jewish women in discouraging Jewish conversion to Christianity, and they condemn Jewish wives who "enticed their husbands to repudiate the crucified one."[55] Church legislation also discriminated against the Jewish woman, decreeing that she wear a distinguishing badge at a younger age than was required for Jewish men and often insisting that she wear distinctive and humiliating garb, such as one red slipper and one black, even when Jewish men did not have to.[56]

Particularly good records, both Jewish and Christian, are available to document the lives of Jews in England. These records relay a vivid picture of a community in which Jewish women appear to have possessed complete freedom within the limits of rabbinic law. Here women played a considerable part in the economic life of the Jewish community. In numerous cases of the sale of houses, land, or debts women appeared alone before the Beth Din (the Jewish court) to carry out the legal arrangements. Some women owned land and houses and conducted business operations on a large scale, often in partnership with a husband or son or other prominent financiers. Documents show wives transacting business on behalf of husbands and bringing court actions of all kinds against both Jews and non-Jews.[57]

The large majority of Jewish women in England had French or English names like Alemandina, Belassez, Blanche, Brunetta, Chera, Columbina, Duzelina, Fleur de Lys, Floretta, and Glorietta; few Sarahs, Hannahs or Rachels are documented, an indication of significant Jewish acculturation. In England, moreover, many men were denoted as the sons of their mothers, as in "Leo, son of Preciosa" or "Abraham the son of Muriel." In these instances their mothers may have been more prominent in business than their fathers; perhaps some of the fathers had become converts, and the sons refused to be called by their names.[58]

One particularly famous Jewish woman in medieval England was Licoricia of Winchester. She had direct business dealings with the king and the court and was a successful businesswoman on a large scale. She was twice imprisoned on charges that were later dismissed and made large contributions toward the building of Westminster Abbey. Her five sons also became moneylenders, and they invariably described themselves as "sons of Licoricia." Yet the Jew's life was always a precarious one, and Licoricia's ended violently when she was murdered in 1277.[59]

This essay has sketched the general outlines of Jewish women's lives in the Middle Ages, but the details that allow for immediacy are still lacking, as are the women's voices, themselves. As increasing research is completed on Jewish women in specific locales, as well as in the larger context of women in medieval society, more accurate judgements on the respective influences of rabbinic law and local social custom and culture on the conduct of everyday life will be possible, as will more detailed understandings of the involvement of women in business activities and Jewish communal and religious life.

## NOTES

1. I. Epstein, "The Jewish Woman in the Responsa (900 C.E.–1500 C.E.)," in *The Jewish Woman*, ed. Leo Jung, Jewish Library 3 (New York, 1934), 123, quoting from an inscription entered into a book used as a family register, cited by A. Berliner, *Aus dem inneren Leben der deutschen Juden im Mittelalter* (Berlin, 1900), 7. Other works presenting general studies of medieval Jewish women or the medieval Jewish family in the Ashkenazic (Christian European) milieu include Irving Agus, *The Heroic Age of Franco-German Jewry* (New York, 1969); Z. W. Falk, "The Status of Women in the Communities of Germany and France during the Middle Ages" [Hebrew] *Sinai* 48 (1961), 361–67 ; Ivan Marcus, "Mothers, Martyrs, and Moneymakers: Some Jewish Women in Medieval Europe," *Conservative Judaism* 38 (1986), 34–45; Kenneth R. Stow, "The Jewish Family in the Rhineland in the High Middle Ages: Form and Function," *American Historical Review* 92 (1987): 1085–1110. Thérèse and Mendel Metzger, *Jewish Life in the Middle Ages* (New York, 1982) is copiously illustrated with representations of everyday scenes from a variety of illuminated Hebrew manuscripts.

2. S. D. Goitein, *A Mediterranean Society*, vol. 3, *The Family* (Berkeley, 1978), 49. Goitein's multivolume work, *A Mediterranean Society*, based on Cairo Genizah documents (discussed below), is the major source for Jewish social history in the Islamic environment. See Mark R. Cohen, "Jews under Islam," in *Bibliographical Essays in Medieval Jewish Studies* (New York, 1976), 169–232 for a thorough essay and bibliography of scholarship on Jewish life under Islam.

3. Although these activities did not take place in "male space" in the public sphere, they did take place in the "public space" of the synagogue and should be reckoned as communal activities. Medieval Jewish women were barred from being counted as participants in "authorized" communal prayer, but too little notice has been taken of the fact that they sometimes created their own religious communities. See nn. 17, 20.

4. For an introduction to Responsa literature, see Solomon Freehof, *The Responsa Literature* and *A Treasury of Responsa* (two volumes in one) (New York, 1973); Jacob Bazak and Stephen Passamanek, *Jewish Law and Jewish Life: Selected Rabbinical Responsa* (Cincinnati, 1979); and Bernard Weinryb, "Responsa As a Source for History (Methodological Problems)," in *Essays Presented to Chief Rabbi Israel Brodie* (London, 1967), 399–417.

5. A good review of the kinds of primary documents and secondary sources available can be found in Stow, "Jewish Family in the Rhineland"; also see Ivan Marcus, "The Jews in Western Europe: Fourth to Sixteenth Century," in *Bibliographical Essays in Medieval Jewish Studies*, 17–108. Useful sources on women and family in the medieval world, in general, include C. Erickson and K. Casey, "Women in the Middle Ages. A Working Bibliography," *Medieval Studies* 37 (1978): 340–359; M. Sheehan and K. Scardellato, *Family and Marriage in Medieval Europe: A Working Bibliography* (Vancouver, 1976); and most recently, Susan Mosher Stuart, ed. *Women in Medieval History and Historiography* (Philadelphia, 1987). Important books on the subject include Philippe Ariès, *Centuries of Childhood: A Social History of Family Life* (New York, 1962); Jack Goody, *The Development of the Family and Marriage in Europe* (New York, 1983); David Herlihy, *Medieval Households* (Cambridge, MA and London, 1985); Eileen Power, *Medieval Women*, ed. M. M . Postan (Cambridge, 1975); Shulamit

Shahar, *The Fourth Estate: A History of Women in the Middle Ages* (New York, 1983); and Susan Mosher Stuard, ed. *Women in Medieval Society* (Philadelphia, 1976).

6. S. D. Goitein, *Letters of Medieval Jewish Traders, Translated from the Arabic* (Princeton, 1973), 3; and see "Cairo Genizah," *Encyclopedia Judaica* (Jerusalem, 1972), 16:1333.

7. S. D. Goitein, *Jews and Arabs* (New York, 1955), 93–94.

8. On polygyny among the Jews of Islamic countries, see Mordechai A. Friedman, *Jewish Polygyny in the Middle Ages: New Documents from the Cairo Genizah* [Hebrew] (Jerusalem, 1986); and Z. W. Falk, *Jewish Matrimonial Law in the Middle Ages* (Oxford, 1966).

9. *Travels of Rabbi Petachia of Ratisbon*, ed. and trans. A. Benisch, 2d. ed. (London, 1861), 15. Rabbi Petachia's account of his travels can also be found in Elkan N. Adler, *Jewish Travellers* (New York, 1930), 64–91.

10. Moses Maimonides, *Mishneh Torah*, "Code of Women, Marriage" 13:11; and see chapter 3 above for this interpretation in rabbinic sources.

11. Goitein, *Mediterranean Society* 3:153–55; and see Mordechai A. Friedman, "The Ethics of Medieval Jewish Marriage," in *Religion in a Religious Age*, ed. S. D. Goitein (Cambridge, MA, 1974), 83–102, esp. 87–95; idem, *Jewish Marriage in Palestine: A Cairo Genizah Study*, 2 vols. (New York and Tel Aviv, 1980–81). It should be noted that conditions in prosperous Egypt, the main provenance for the *genizah* documents, may have been more favorable for Jewish women in this period than in some other places and times in the Moslem world. See Avraham Grossman, "The Historical Background to the Ordinances on Family Affairs Attributed to Rabbenu Gershom Me'or ha-Golah ('The Light of the Exile')," in *Jewish History: Essays in Honor of Chimen Abramsky*, ed. Ada Rapoport-Albert and Steven J. Zipperstein (London, 1988), 15.

12. Goitein, *Mediterranean Society* 3:53.

13. Ibid., 118.

14. Ibid., 56. And see Grossman ("Ordinances on Family Affairs," 11–15), who discusses the likelihood that German Jewish merchants, who often spent years in Moslem lands, married local women while away from home.

15. Goitein, *Mediterranean Society* 3:56.

16. Ibid., 58.

17. Ibid., 125.

18. Ibid., 114.

19. Ibid., 133. See chapter 3 above for rabbinic views of the disposition of a wife's earnings.

20. Ibid.

21. Ibid., 165.

22. Ibid., 220.

23. Ibid., 263.

24. Ibid., 197.

25. Moses Maimonides, *Responsa of R. Moses b. Maimon*, vol. 1 [Hebrew], ed. Yehoshua Blau (Jerusalem, 1958), no. 34, no. 45.

26. Benisch, ed., *Travels of R. Petachia b. Jacob*, 19. It must be admitted that the story of Samuel ben Ali's daughter exhibits folklore motifs and may be apocryphal. The same motif of the veiled woman teaching male students reappears in both Jewish and Christian literary sources of the later Middle Ages. See my "Some Parallels in the Education of Medieval Jewish and Christian Women," *Jewish History* 5 (1991).

27. Goitein, *Mediterranean Society* 3:358.

28. Irving Agus, *Urban Civilization in Pre-Crusade Europe*, 2 vols. (New York, 1965) is a major source in English of pre-1096 *responsa* literature; chap. 9, "Family," is particularly relevant. Idem, *Rabbi Meir of Rothenburg* 2d ed. (New York, 1970), provides a broad selection of the *responsa* of the thirteenth-century R. Meir, a number of which deal with women or family issues. On how medieval Jewish communities functioned, see Salo Baron, *The Jewish Community*, 3 vols. (Westport, CT, 1973); Jacob Katz, *Exclusiveness and Tolerance: Studies in Jewish-Christian Relations in Medieval and Modern Times* (New York, 1961). On communal decisionmaking, see Louis Finkelstein, *Jewish Self-Government in the Middle Ages* (New York, 1964), and D. M. Shohet, *The Jewish Court in the Middle Ages* (New York, 1931).

29. Haim Hillel Ben Sasson ("The Middle Ages," in *A History of the Jewish People*, ed. H. H. Ben Sasson [Cambridge, MA, 1976], 401) writes of the pre-Crusade period that "the Jewish city dweller lived on an aristocratic level, as befitted international merchants and honored local financiers" and speaks of the "economic well-being and social stability" of post-Crusade Jewish communities as well (p. 463).

30. Irving Agus, *Heroic Age*, 278; idem, "The Development of the Money Clause in the Ashkenazic Ketubah," *Jewish Quarterly Review* 42 (1951): 221–56; and see below, n. 33. Grossman ("Ordinances on Family Affairs," 14) points to "the high level of compensation which husbands bound themselves by their marriage contracts to secure to their wives in the event of death or divorce," as well as "the honorable position of the woman in the conduct of domestic and business affairs" as indicative of women's relatively high status in these communities.

31. Agus, *Heroic Age*, 278. This anonymous *responsum*, probably of R. Gershom, can be found in Joel Müller, *Responsa of the Sages of France and Germany* [Hebrew] (Vienna, 1881), no. 94, and appears in English in Agus, *Urban Civilization* 2:581–84.

32. Agus, *Heroic Age*, 281, citing *tosaphot* (thirteenth-century Talmudic commentary) to Babylonian Talmud Kiddushin 41a.

33. Ibid., 303.

34. Rabbi Meshullam b. Kalonymus (c. 910–85), in a responsum printed in Louis Ginzberg, *Ginzei Shechter* (1928–29; rep. New York, 1969), 275, no. 6; English version in Agus, *Urban Civilization*, 2:607.

35. See Falk, *Matrimonial Law*, 1–15. He points out that "the early founders of the French/German communities acquired the monogamous structure of the Christian family and turned it into an integral element of their piety and way of life" (p. 34). Grossman ("Ordinances on Family Affairs") stresses the high status of women in Ashkenazic society as a major motivation for this ruling, writing that the status of women in this milieu "was better and more firmly based than in any other part of the contemporary Jewish world" (p. 14). Grossman agrees with Falk that the influence from Christian society has to be taken into account, but he also suggests the possibility that the ordinance was intended to put a stop to Ashkenazic merchants' taking second wives during their sojourns in Moslem lands (pp. 11–15).

36. Grossman ("Ordinances on Family Affairs") suggests that here, too, "[fear of] marriage to a second wife while far from home, and the solid status of women" underlie this ordinance (p. 15).

37. Ibid., 14.

38. Agus, *Heroic Age*, 295, 305. On Jewish women's involvement in moneylending, see William C. Jordan, "Jews on Top: Women and the Availability of Consumption Loans in Northern France in the Mid-Thirteenth Century," *Journal of Jewish*

*Studies* 29 (1978): 39–56; Andrée Courtemanche, "Les femmes juives et le crédit à Manosque au tournant du XIVe siècle," *Provence historique* 37, no. 150 (1987): 545–58; Louis Stouff, "Isaac Nathan et les siens: Une famille juive d'Arles des XIVe et XVe siècles," *Provence historique* 37, no. 150 (1987): 499–512.

39. On the unique opportunities available to widows see Richard Emery, "Les veuves juives de Perpignan," *Provence historique* 37, no. 150 (1987): 559–69; Cheryl Tallan, "Medieval Jewish Widows: Their Control of Resources," *Jewish History* 5 (1991); ibid, "The Position of the Medieval Jewish Widow as a Function of Family Structure," *Proceedings of the Tenth World Congress of Jewish Studies* (forthcoming); ibid, "Opportunities for Medieval Northern-European Jewish Widows in the Public and Domestic Spheres," in *Widows in the Histories and Literatures of Medieval Europe*, ed. Louise Mirrer (Ann Arbor, MI, forthcoming); and chapter 5 below.

40. On Jewish women's vocational training, see my "Some Parallels in the Education of Medieval Jewish and Christian Women."

41. On medieval women's general involvement in medicine, see Eileen Power, *Medieval Women* (Cambridge, 1975), 86–88; Margaret Wade Labarge, *A Small Sound of the Trumpet* (Boston, 1986), 169–94. For references to Jewish female physicians, see Power, *Medieval Women*, 88; Labarge, *Small Sound*, 173, 178; Harry Friedenwald, *The Jews and Medicine*, 2 vols. (1946; rep. New York, 1967), 1:217–20; Marcello Segre, "Dottoresse Ebree nel Medioevo," *Pagina di storia della medicina* 14 (1970): 98–106; and chapters 5–6 below. On Jewish women as midwives, see Ron Barkai, "A Medieval Hebrew Treatise on Obstetrics," *Medical History* 33 (1988): 96–119.

42. In *Shibbolei HaLeket*, a code of Jewish law compiled by the thirteenth-century Italian Talmudist Zedekiah ben Abraham Anav, whose teachings were highly influenced by Rashi and his school, Rashi is quoted as having said that because of his infirmity, his daughter Rachel served as his secretary, recording one of his *responsum*. This anecdote is cited in Moritz Güdemann, *Geschichte des Erziehungswesens und der Cultur der abendländischen Juden während des Mittelalters und der neueren Zeit*, vol. 1 (1880–88; rep. Amsterdam, 1966), 189.

43. On Jewish women's roles as women's prayer leaders, see Emily Taitz, "Kol Ishah—The Voice of Woman: Where Was It Heard in Medieval Europe?" *Conservative Judaism* 38 (1986): 46–61, esp. 53–56; and the discussion of Dolce of Worms, below.

44. I. Abrahams, *Hebrew Ethical Wills* (Philadelphia, 1926), 207–18.

45. As reproduced in Haim Ben Sasson, *History of the Jewish People*, 523. The poem is in the form of a verse-by-verse commentary on Proverbs 31:10–31, an acrostic poem discussing the "woman of valor." A rendering of the eulogy along with the biblical verses on which it comments may be found in Ivan Marcus, "Mothers, Martyrs, and Moneymakers," 41–42. The Hebrew text is found in A. M. Haberman, *Sefer Gezerot Ashkenaz ve-Zarfat* (Jerusalem, 1945) 164–67.

46. Ben Sasson, *History of the Jewish People*, 523.

47. Certainly, it was the invention of printing that allowed this religious literature intended specifically for women and less learned men to develop and spread as widely as it did. Its great success, however, indicates that it was meeting some deeply felt needs. See "Literature for Jewish Women in Medieval and Later Times," in Jung, *The Jewish Woman*, 213–243; Chava Weissler, "The Traditional Piety of Ashkenazic Women," in *Jewish Spirituality: From the Sixteenth Century to the Present*, ed. Arthur Green (New York, 1987), 245–75; and chapter 7 below.

48. Judah b. Samuel the Pious, *Sefer Hasidim*, Bologna, 1538, ed. J. Wistinetzki and J. Freimann (Frankfurt, 1924), sec. 669; trans. in Abraham Cronbach, "Social Thinking in the *Sefer Hasidim*," *Hebrew Union College Annual* 22 (1949): 53. A recent

study of the milieu of *Sefer Hasidim* is Ivan Marcus, *Piety and Society: The Jewish Pietists of Medieval Germany* (Leiden, 1981).

49. *Sefer Hasidim*, sec. 670; trans. in Cronbach, "Social Thinking," 59. Disputes between husband and wife over giving charity must have been frequent, for a third comment (sec. 1715, trans. in Cronbach, "Social Thinking," 135) instructs: "Should an irascible man say to his wife: 'Understand, if thou givest anything to charity, I shall chastise thee,' or if he vexes her in any other way and if the solicitor knows about the husband's antipathy, the solicitor shall not accept anything from the wife, not even a small contribution. But, if there should issue a communal decree specifying so and so much per pound of one's possessions—a decree whose violation is punishable by ex-communication—and the husband violates the decree, then let the wife give, and blessings will come upon her. However, anything that the son or the wife may steal must be returned."

50. Jacob ben Meir, *Sefer ha-Yashar*, ed. F. Rosenthal (Berlin, 1898), no. 25; trans. in Freehof, *Treasury of Responsa*, 35.

51. Shlomo Noble, "The Jewish Woman in Medieval Martyrology," *Studies in Jewish Bibliography in History and Literature*, ed. C. Berlin (New York, 1971), 349; original text may be found in Haberman, *Gezerot Ashkenaz*, 19.

52. Noble, "Jewish Woman," 349. The original text may be found in A. Neubauer and M. Stern, *Hebräische Berichte über die Judenverfolgungen während der Kreuzzüge* (Berlin, 1892), 7. Grossman ("Ordinances on Family Affairs," 22, n. 32) writes that these women were "distinguished in the chronicles by epithets the like of which, in general, it is hard to find applied to women [elsewhere] in medieval Jewish literature: 'saintly,' 'esteemed,' 'holy.'"

53. Robert Chazan, *Medieval Jewry in Northern France* (Baltimore, 1973), 37, 56; idem, "The Blois Incident of 1171: A Study in Jewish Intercommunal Organization," *Proceedings of the American Academy for Jewish Research* 37 (1969): 13–31; and see Jacob R. Marcus, *The Jew in the Medieval World: A Source Book: 315-1791* (1938; rep. New York, 1969), 127–30, where an excerpt from a twelfth-century Hebrew chron-icle describing the Blois tragedy, Ephraim ben Jacob's (1132-c. 1200) *A Book of His-torical Records*, appears in English translation. The issues raised by historical docu-mentation of a Jewish woman who was the mistress of a Christian noble are many; on other Jewish-Christian sexual contacts in the Middle Ages and Renaissance, see chap-ters 5–6 below.

54. Chazan, *Medieval Jewry*, 37, 55.

55. Noble, "Medieval Martyology," 351, citing Neubauer and Stern, *Hebräische Berichte*, 27.

56. Noble ("Medieval Martryology," 351) cites the yellow badge imposed upon the Jews by Pope Innocent III where the minimum age was thirteen for male wearers and eleven for female, along with other examples of such discriminations directed at women. See chapters 5–6 below for other references to distinctive dress required for Jewish women.

57. Michael Adler, "The Jewish Woman in Medieval England," in idem, *The Jews of Medieval England*, (London, 1939), 18.

58. Ibid., 23. Jewish women throughout the medieval period, both in the Moslem and Christian spheres, tended to have non-Hebrew names. See chapter 5 below for similar data on Sephardi women.

59. Adler, "Jewish Woman," 39–42.

CHAPTER  **RENÉE LEVINE MELAMMED**

*Sephardi Women in the Medieval and*
*Early Modern Periods*

The world of Sephardi[1] women is without a doubt one of the most
neglected fields in Jewish history. The history and heritage of Sephardi
Jewry itself was virgin ground until Yitzhak Baer and Eliyahu Ashtor
contributed their respective histories in 1929–36 and 1966.[2] Subsequent scholarship has advanced this discipline in an impressive manner but is far less impressive regarding its treatment of women.[3] This
study will present Sephardi women's history with two aims in mind: to
indicate available sources on medieval and early modern Sephardi
women and to assess the present state of the field, as well as the ave-
nues of research available to interested historians.

The Sephardi woman emerges from a land where three religions and
cultures interacted and affected one another in various spheres and in
numerous ways.[4] During the period of Moslem rule, Arabic language
and culture deeply influenced the Jewish community in Spain, producing levels of interaction ranging from the sciences and poetry to the
marketplace. The Spanish and Portuguese languages became so deeply
rooted in Jewish life that the Sephardim continued to speak and create

in their distinctive dialects of Judeo-Spanish, or Ladino, for hundreds of years after the expulsion of Jews from the Peninsula in the late fifteenth century.[5] During Christian rule, by contrast, a cultural dichotomy developed because the written language of the church, Latin, never became part of the Jewish experience.

One of the most obvious manifestations of contact with non-Jewish cultures is the assortment of female names of the pre-expulsion Jewish community. While girls were sometimes given biblical names,[6] far more common were names that "were altogether or partly Arabic or Romance."[7] Thus, the occasional Esther or Azter, Miriam, and Simah or Simha are overwhelmingly outnumbered by the vast array of Astruga-, Bona-, Dolso-, Dueña-, Oro-, or Sol-based names of Romance origin; also appearing are Arabic names such as Aljofar, Amira, Belor, Jamila, Saledina, Sitbora, Yamen, and the like. In one list of seventy-six female names only six are of Hebrew origin, whereas the majority derive from Romance languages. These names, whether Arabic or Romance, transmit generally positive images such as beauty (Jamila), gold (Ora), precious (Preciosa) or precious stone (Belor), just (Justa), happiness (Yamen), and a few images of power like queen (Reyna), or princess (Amira), and mistress-owner (Dueña).

Names were also affected by political events. The year 1391 began a century marked by waves of forced and voluntary conversions in Spain and Portugal, which created a new phenomenon and eventually a new class, the *converso* (convert), also known by the derogatory designation, *marrano*. Many of these *conversos* regretted their decision but could not openly revert to Judaism; the church would not permit such deprecation of the holy rite of baptism. Those who secretly professed Judaism, outwardly living as good Catholics, were known as *crypto-Jews*. These converts also had to adopt good Spanish-Christian names, although some crypto-Jews secretly retained their Hebrew names. Thus, an unexpected continuity in women's names developed, however inadvertently, once Jewish women became members of *converso* and crypto-Jewish society.[8] The Spanish tradition is to pass on to the child both the mother's and father's family names, thus creating a genealogy with both maternal and paternal lineage. Since this custom was universally adopted in Christian Spain, all the crypto-Jewish women who had converted or whose ancestors had converted between 1391 and 1492, inadvertently acquired a genealogy and a sense of family continuity unavailable to other Jewish women.

Rather different influences on Sephardi women came from Islam. Prior to the invasion of the Moslem Umayyads in 711 C.E., Spain was under Christian Visigothic rule. After 711 the defeated Christian princes were forced to retreat to the northernmost borders; there they bided their time, consolidating and reinforcing their power, awaiting the day when Spain would again be in Christian hands. The long-awaited Reconquest (Reconquista) began in the eleventh century and the Christian warriors proceeded, in a piecemeal fashion, to push the Moslems southward. By 1492 Granada, the last Moslem stronghold, fell and the Reconquista was formally completed. But the restrictive, overprotective attitude toward women in Islam[9] had long-term effects on both Jewish and Christian society during and after the Reconquista.

Moslem women were expected to remain at home; and should they leave those confines, their required mode of dress scarcely allowed for recognition.[10] Christian Iberian society absorbed these attitudes and customs, and as late as the seventeenth and eighteenth centuries, one could perceive an "almost Arabic obsession with protecting women from being seen in the streets."[11] Even within the confines of the home the women were exhorted not to appear at windows and expected to sit on low cushions rather than on chairs.[12] The Portuguese men, in particular, were well known for being unreasonably overprotective of their women and were even ridiculed by the Spaniards on this count because they kept them in "harem-like seclusion."[13]

Jewish women were expected to behave more or less accordingly, and such expectations were even carried over to the Sephardi Diaspora. Seventeenth-century Amsterdam received numerous Portuguese Jews and former *conversos* into its midst, and one discovers even here that "the close watch and strict seclusion by which Portuguese Jews tried to keep their females under control is strikingly similar to the way women in the Iberian Peninsula were guarded and in sharp contrast to the independent and free conduct of the Dutch female population at large."[14] Even in Amsterdam, Sephardi women were to be kept secluded and out of the public eye as much as possible, whereas unmarried maidens were never to go out into the street.

Moslem society strove to restrict a woman to the home and eventually succeeded in barring her from participating in the mosque service.[15] On the other hand, both Christian and Jewish societies made allowances for women's attendance at the house of worship.[16] Ironically enough, Moslem proclivities still affected Jewish women in the Spanish synagogue, for they were assigned to separate seating arrangements from the men.[17] It is possible that this custom was initiated early in Moslem Spain while the seating in medieval Ashkenazi synagogues was still mixed.[18] Nevertheless, women were indeed present at the site of the most central social and religious activities, even if there were occasional objections to their attendance at evening services or an insistence by the elders on stationing a guard at the entrance to the women's section of the Amsterdam synagogue.[19]

The Moslem practice of polygyny also had serious repercussions for Jewish women on the peninsula, since the famous ban of R. Gershom was never universally accepted in Spain.[20] While some individual Jewish communities attempted to proscribe this practice, which was clearly forbidden by the church and generally opposed by the Crown, special royal permission could be obtained for a fee.[21] As a result, there are instances of men taking a second wife for numerous reasons, the most acceptable being due to fertility problems, usually after ten years of marriage without producing progeny. Others did so after the first wife ceased childbearing or when the marital relationship was an unhappy one.[22]

In his study of this subject, Yom Tov Assis singles out "human nature" (i.e., greed, lust) as the most common factor leading to polygyny; one might note as well the lower status of the Sephardi as compared to the Ashkenazi woman.[23] Although men of all classes married more than one woman, on the whole the wealthy were far more prone to such action. Some women were fortunate enough to have a clause in their marriage contract prohibiting the taking of a second wife, and as a result, the husband might resort to consorting with a concubine. Unprotected first wives had to turn to outsiders, be they members of their family, the community, or even the Crown, for aid in attempts to defend their position.[24] While the rabbis often tried to control such situations, the most eminent of Spanish bigamists was none other than R. Hasdai Crescas, a major figure in the second half of the fourteenth century.[25]

Essentially, the rabbis preferred second wives and concubines to prostitutes.[26] While no form of extramarital sexual relations was espoused, society as well as religious leaders reacted differently to each alternative. Of the three, concubinage appears to have been most accepted, however reluctantly; and this was true of Islam and Christianity, as well. Concubinage was common in the Moslem world,[27] lawful in Christian society only for the bachelor,[28] and preferable to prostitution in Jewish society when both the man and woman were Jewish. In both the Christian and Jewish upper class, affairs with servants, who were often of different religion, were commonplace and accepted.[29]

There is additional evidence of religiously mixed couples, especially during the Reconquista period. The very nature of this "frontier" society allowed for laxer moral standards; thus the *barragana*, or domiciled mistress, appears on the scene, with an occasional Jewish or Moslem woman becoming the *barragana* of a Christian man.[30] Christian society allowed its men to consort or cohabit with minority women who often mothered their children;[31] the fathers could ransom their offspring if they so pleased.[32]

Prostitution was prevalent and condoned in both Moslem and Christian Spain. Cases of Jewish prostitutes are rarely mentioned, but Assis has documentation to prove that there were Jewish prostitutes in Aragon and Castile.[33] In some fifteenth century communities the local rabbis overlooked the existence of these women, rationalizing that it was preferable for a single Jewish male to turn to them rather than to commit adultery with a married woman. During this period R. ʿArāma reported that there were even instances of stipends provided by the community for its prostitutes.[34] In Amsterdam a Jewish madame could be found, but she employed only Christian women; Tirtsah Levie claims that in this community "no Sephardi woman sank so low as to make a living as a prostitute."[35]

Contact between Jewish women and non-Jews existed on various levels, including sexual liasons. Ashtor writes of a military leader, Saʾid ibn Djudi, "handsome" and "licentious," who was slain in the house of his Jewish mistress;[36] in 1320, the case of a Jewish woman who had intercourse with a Christian man came before the Christian ruler, who preferred to let her be judged by Jewish law. Two rabbis recommended cutting off her nose.[37] Between 1481 and 1490 a very wealthy widow, Doña Vellida of Trujillo, was arrested for "scandalous behavior," namely, adultery with Christians in three distinct affairs.[38]

Jewish women also encountered gentiles in more acceptable social and occupational connections. On the social level, there were places where women, Jews as well as non-Jews, would come to execute chores such as obtaining drinking and cooking water at the spring, laundering at specified spots,[39] using the oven, utilizing the water mill for processing grain, or spinning and weaving in courtyards.[40] An additional meeting place was the bathhouse which was attended by Jewish, Moslem, and Christian women together on the days and hours reserved for them. One Moslem theologian objected vehemently to this practice; in his eyes, the fact that unclothed non-Moslem women were indistinguishable from Moslem women was particularly disturbing.[41] In Christian Spain bathhouses were privately owned; the men of the different faiths bathed separately, but "Christian, Jewish and Muslim women must have used a municipal bath house simultaneously."[42] Attending the bathhouse was definitely a social event; for the Spanish lady, regardless of her religion, was often accompanied by her daughters, servants, and neighbors.

Jewish women are required to undergo ritual immersion postmenstruation and postpartum; one assumes that a *mikveh* (ritual bath)[43] was available for them, either as an institution of the Jewish community or possibly at these public bathhouses. Childbirth often resulted in additional contact between Jews and non-Jews. The wet nurse, or *rodriza*, appeared in wealthier households; and wealthy Jews might employ non-Jewish women just as wealthy non-Jews employed Jewish women.[44] Jewish midwives or *comadronas* can also be found, frequently in the service of royalty. Some of them were well known and were specifically sought out by the royal families of Castile and Aragon; apparently they were skillful, for the records show that they were paid well for their services.[45] In addition, there were Jewish women who practiced medicine; some were even sued for malpractice, while others obtained authorizations to practice from the king himself.[46]

The discovery that Jewish women participated in the medical profession in medieval Spain is unexpected in light of the meager education usually provided for girls of all faiths in Spain.[47] Most women were illiterate, although their "illiteracy was not an obstacle to carrying on practical business."[48] Ashtor explains that a girl's education was the responsibility of her mother, who taught her spinning and various other forms of domestic work.[49] Both Jewish and non-Jewish women supported themselves by spinning, knitting, or weaving,[50] while those in more comfortable financial situations learned these crafts as pastimes.[51] Beyond needlework, the poor Jewish woman had very limited options. There are examples of Jewish girls as servants in Jewish homes, but this was the exception rather than the rule, and most household servants were not Jewish.[52] Sometimes the community provided means of livelihood for less fortunate women. For instance, "Jewish and Moslem women were engaged as professional wailers by Christians as well as by their own coreligionists."[53] In Amsterdam older women would work in the *mikveh*, and widows would serve as *mortalhadeyras*, those who washed the dead and prepared the shrouds.[54]

Urban middle-class women were clearly limited as to available occupational options; women in towns and in the working class enjoyed more extensive freedom and could undertake more activities, at times approaching a level of equality with male workers.[55] In fourteenth-century Navarre one finds "many men and women of the Jewish communities who went to market and sold chicken, eggs and wine there, peasants like the other peasants."[56]

Women of greater means chose livelihoods as merchants and money-lenders;[57] their activities can at times be uncovered in court litigations as well as in records of royal privileges granted to the wealthier individuals who often provided the Crown with services. For example, a wealthy Jewish woman from Pamplona was also a well-established merchant in the second half of the fourteenth century. This woman, Doña Encave, received special privileges from the king and supplied the court with some of the merchandise she sold, such as embroidered purses, silk, silver, jewels, and the like.[58]

How these and other women of means achieved their status needs to be examined further. The Pamplonan merchant was a member of an old, established Jewish family; she most likely acquired her wealth by means of her dowry and gifts or by inheritance from either her parents or husband. As early as the ninth century, Jewish women in Spain were acquiring land "as a dowry and in fulfillment of a marriage contract, or as a gift."[59]

The dowry, while present in all three religious communities in medieval Spain, took various shapes and forms. In Islam the *mahr*, or *sadaq*, was given to the bride by the groom as protection in case of divorce or widowhood. She was entitled to manage the dowry and all other personal income in any way she pleased, exclusively for her own benefit.[60] The Christian medieval bride witnessed a complete turnabout vis-à-vis matrimonial customs. While at first, as in Islam, the bridegroom provided the bride with a dowry, by the eleventh century demographical changes created a competition for grooms, forcing the bride and her family to provide the finances.[61] Herlihy points out that in Spain the older custom of the groom's providing the *donatio* is longer lived, still being practiced in the thirteenth century: "but even there the true dowry triumphs in the late Middle Ages."[62]

This "true dowry," which the parents furnish, prevailed in the Jewish community as well. A daughter of a wealthy family would be given a substantial dowry to guarantee her social position. Reports of Jewish bridal dowries appear in marriage contracts, in wills, and, quite often, in litigations. The kings of Aragon, for example, were often involved in protecting women's dowries and their rights to them.[63] A poor girl or woman, on the other hand, would be at the mercy of charitable institutions. In seventeenth-century Amsterdam, the dowry society, or *dotar*, had the candidates draw lots; a prospective bride with no dowry might have to wait as long as ten years for her turn. In addition, the society's statutes demanded that the girls maintain a virtuous, unblemished life-style.[64] Once property or other possessions were acquired, women could buy, sell, exchange or donate as they pleased. Women also became active in family financial affairs when their husbands were absent; many professions necessitated travel, often for extended periods of time, leaving the wife with no alternative but to attend to the business at hand.[65]

Women gained control of family resources through inheritance from parents or husbands; in the latter case, in order to survive, a widow frequently assumed a new status. In her husband's absence she became the head of household, exceptionally independent and accepted by society in that role. In Navarre "women played their part, engaging in commerce in their names alone, deciding about the purchase of land, lending a certain sum of money or quantity of wheat, sometimes while their husbands were living, and more frequently when they had become widows."[66]

Widowhood granted the greatest degree of freedom to the woman: now she was a single woman, but one who did not have to return to her parents; she controlled her dowry and inheritances and was responsible for herself and her children. Her subsequent financial situation was dependent on inheritance laws, which varied from community to community in medieval Spain. Islamic law, for example, gives both women and children only a fixed share in inheritances and provides the daughter in a family with half of what the male family members receive.[67] The inheritance laws of Christian Spain provided more generously for female survivors. "All capital acquired during a marriage belonged equally to both partners, so that at the death of either spouse, the survivor was only entitled to half the estate. The deceased person's share was then divided in equal portions among all the children of the marriage, male and female alike."[68]

The Jewish community had obviously begun to imitate this custom, for there is a conflict between two fourteenth-century rabbis about an ordinance in Toledo pertaining to the spouse's inheritance rights: the crux of the debate between R. Asher and R. Israel ben Joseph Israeli was whether or not conditions guaranteeing equal rights of inheritance of a wife or husband's property can be included in contracts. R. Asher refused to consider anything other than Talmudic law, while R. Israel insisted on upholding the local ordinance.[69] Clearly, in wealthier families the matter of inheritance was significant, for "women gained considerable power as heiresses to their fathers and husbands."[70] In the long run, the widow of means—of whatever religious tradition—enjoyed a freedom unique among medieval women: "She almost certainly enjoyed not merely legal independence but also a relatively broad degree of freedom in her everyday life."[71]

Examples of a few eminent Sephardi widows are illustrative. Benvenida Abarvanel, niece of the statesman-philosopher Isaac Abarvanel, married her first cousin Samuel. The couple left Spain in 1492 for Italy, and Don Samuel became the head of the Jewish community in Naples. His wife was an educated woman, who established, among other things, a good relationship with the duchess of Tuscany. As a matter of fact, when the Jews of Southern Italy were threatened with an expulsion in 1541, Benvenida used her influence with the duchess to negotiate a postponement of the decree. Following her husband's death in 1547, she took over his business concerns and even attained important trade privileges. Doña Benvenida gained renown as a pious and extremely charitable woman whose home was a center of study and culture.[72]

Esther Kiera was a Turkish-born Sephardi of far more modest origins. She and her husband, Elias Handeli, began as petty merchants, dealing mainly in trinkets and cosmetics. Esther was widowed in 1548 while still a young woman near or in her twenties. Since the women of the sultan's harem were among her clientele, Esther chose to concentrate on providing various services to them. Slowly but surely, she rose in importance as she became "the" contact for the world of the harem with the outside world. The Moslem women could not have contact with men outside their families; the only men allowed inside the harem were the sultan and his eunuchs. Thus, a Jewish woman was an ideal candidate for such an intermediary position. Esther was enterprising and ambitious; she successfully served three sultans. In recognition of her services she received various privileges (firmans) from the Ottoman sovereign. Unfortunately, Esther had a penchant for intrigue and bribery and used her power to influence political appointments. On the other hand, she did not abandon her fellow Jews, for as her wealth accumulated, she used it generously to aid in the printing of Hebrew books, to support scholars, and to help merchants whose businesses had suffered either due to fire or theft. Her negative qualities, however, proved to be her downfall; for after she effected an unpopular military appointment, the masses displayed their wrath. In 1600 a mob burst into the harem in order to seize Esther and then located two of her sons. All three were murdered and Kiera's limbs were disengaged and nailed to the doorposts of her friends' homes.[73]

Benvenida Abarvanel came from a wealthy family, married into wealth, and as a widow took advantage of her station in society. Esther Kiera built up her wealth and reputation after her husband's demise. Doña Gracia Nasi, on the other hand, began with a solid financial base and continued to amass huge fortunes with and without the aid of her male relatives. Like Esther, Gracia was born after the expulsion of the Jews from Spain. Because all of the Jews in Portugal were converted en masse in 1497, Gracia was born as a New Christian and baptized following her birth in 1510 as Beatriz de Luna.

Her husband, on the other hand, was born in Spain into the wealthy Benveniste family that dealt in banking, gems, and spices. Five years after seeking refuge in Portugal, the family was forced to convert and adopted the name Mendes. Francisco, who wed Gracia in 1528, died in 1536, leaving a daughter Brianda (Reyna) and his wife. Francisco bequeathed half of his property to his wife and half to his brother Diogo Mendes, who was his partner and business representative in Antwerp. Once the Inquisition was established in 1536, Doña Gracia realized that Portugal was no longer a viable home for a crypto-Jew.[74] While a move to a haven such as Turkey was one option, the family decided to proceed step by step, taking care to preserve the maximum amount of its fortunes and simultaneously planning its return to an open observance of Judaism.

Since Doña Gracia's life and numerous activities are the subjects of various books and articles,[75] only a few germane details of her life will be mentioned. As a widow, Gracia had the freedom to pursue the family's business interests; she and her brother-in-law, a financial genius, worked well together up until his death in 1542. Diogo left his partner, Gracia Nasi, half his fortune and gave her custody of the other half bequeathed to his wife and daughter. This Sephardi lady continued to build up the business, maintained a network for aiding *conversos* who had fled the peninsula, and evaded the clutches of the Inquisition by moving from Antwerp to different cities in Italy and ultimately to Constantinople. She supported numerous scholars and rabbis and aided in the publication of scholarly works, many of which were dedicated to her. This *conversa* also initiated an attempted boycott of the port of Ancona in Italy in 1556. This plan was intended to achieve revenge for the burning at the stake of twenty-four Judaizers who had been promised a haven; an additional intention was to demonstrate Jewish solidarity. Doña Gracia also planned the resettlement of Tiberias by Jews who would be economically self-sufficient.[76] While she was able to enlist the aid of her nephews and the various agents she employed in cities throughout Europe and the Ottoman Empire, it was Doña Gracia's widowed status combined with her brilliant and visionary mind that enabled her to become the outstanding businesswoman, patroness, philanthropist, and activist that she was.

There is little doubt that the Nasi-Mendes experience as *converso* Judaizers influenced their careers. While living as Christians in Portugal, extensive contacts were made, even with the Crown. Subsequent mobility was invariably a delicate matter, for crypto-Jews would have to continue their facade as observant Christians whenever they chose a Christian country of residence. Once the decision openly to revert to Judaism was made in the late fifteenth and early sixteenth centuries (prior to the option of Amsterdam), they would have to go to a Moslem country such as Turkey or come to a special arrangement with the authorities that would guarantee protection from a possible Inquisition. While the latter arrangement occasionally succeeded in some Italian city-states, the Ancona incident proved its inherent precariousness and indicated that no guarantee was truly final. When the church and the Holy Inquisition set out to extirpate heresy, the baptized Christian observing Jewish rituals was a sure target.

Because of her connections, wealth, mobility, and foresight, Doña Gracia managed to escape the long-reaching tentacles of the Inquisition. But countless others were not so fortunate. The Spanish and Portuguese Inquisitions, established in 1478 and 1536, respectively, became obsessed with the phenomenon of the crypto-Jew and the danger inherent in having unfaithful converts in the midst of a Catholic state. As a matter of fact, Inquisitorial courts were established in the New World, as well, for fear that these unfaithful New Christians were relocating, hoping to practice Judaism far from the reach of the Holy Tribunal. The crypto-Jewish woman played a crucial role in the perpetuation of Judaism in the postexpulsion period. With no Jewish community available to provide teachers, rabbis, schools, or texts, the only institution that remained more or less intact and viable was the family. As a result, the home was transformed into the one and only center of crypto-Jewish life. Yet even the home was not necessarily safe for clandestine religious observance, since the Inquisition discovered a formidable collection of eye-witnesses among the numerous servants, some of whom would report their masters' and mistresses' activities.

Analysis of Inquisition documents reveals that women were outstanding in their devotion to Judaism, religious observances, and awareness of the need to perpetuate their traditions.[77] Seymour Liebman writes that "these women were stalwart defenders of their faith and bulwarks of strength to their husbands. If one were to measure degrees of orthodox observances, unquestionably the females would scale the highest."[78] This contention is confirmed by Arnold Witznitzer in his study of seventeenth-century crypto-Jews in Mexico. He writes: "The Judaizing woman, in Mexico as in other countries of the dispersion, played an enormous part in holding the torch of Judaism for centuries after the forced conversion to Catholicism at the end of the fifteenth century. They taught their children Jewish rites and prayers, and often they endured tortures in the prisons of the Inquisition with greater fortitude than men."[79]

Some of these women maintained a surprisingly high level of observance, while others only managed to observe minimally. Dietary laws and the Sabbath were the most widely kept precepts. Fasting was also common, especially as an act of purification and in the hope of having one's sins forgiven. Many observances were forgotten over the course of time or were simply too risky to attempt (i.e., circumcision). Nevertheless, some holidays, such as Passover, were indeed celebrated; and many rituals related to the birth and death experiences were preserved. Any and every custom and ceremony observed was a declaration of loyalty to Judaism,[80] a clear rejection of Catholicism,[81] and a dangerous act whenever the Inquisition was in the vicinity.

Crypto-Jewish women sometimes observed Jewish rituals together with their husbands, but often they did so without their husbands' or childrens' knowledge.[82] Mothers and grandmothers most frequently served as teachers; their concern with the past and the future is strikingly apparent.[83] Examples of Judaizing women abound; some were even leaders and central communal figures.[84] Many sacrificed their lives for their faith, withstanding the tortures of the Inquisition and facing death at the stake at public executions (autos-da-fé). Shulamit Shahar has wondered about the motivations of these martyrs: "Was it their fidelity to their faith and their conviction that after their agonies they would win the kingdom of heaven; was it fidelity to their fellow heretics, with whom they had lived in joint devotion, some of whom had already died for the faith or been sentenced to life imprisonment; or was it a supreme expression of protest against the existing form of society and the world and the situation of women in them?"[85]

While religious devotion may well have been a means of protest, it most certainly provided an opportunity for self-expression in a society that rarely allowed female voices to be heard.[86] The late medieval period in Europe witnessed two particular religious phenomena: female saints, who often functioned as teachers or preachers, and a proclivity for mysticism. Spanish-Jewish and crypto-Jewish women were affected by both of them.[87] *Conversas*, observing Judaism in secret in the hope of salvation, were the more likely candidates for a mystical or even messianic penchant; and during the postexpulsion period there were various women and girls who experienced visions and delivered messianic prophecies. In the region of Extremadura an incredible revival of Judaism transpired among the *conversos*, many of whom began to fast on Mondays and Thursdays.[88] Both Mari Gómez of Chillón and Inés, the twelve-year-old daughter of Juan Esteban of Herrera, claimed to have had prophetic visions, thus creating a major stir in numerous *converso* communities, particularly in the La Mancha and Extremadura regions of Castile.[89] From 1499 until 1502, as their prophesies spread, they inspired a renewal of observance with a special emphasis on fasting and heightened the belief in the arrival of Elijah and the Messiah, heralding redemption in the Promised Land. This postexpulsion movement was quickly and rigorously extinguished by the Inquisition; Inés was burned at the stake in 1500, while Mari Gómez escaped to Portugal. Nevertheless, these two *conversas* symbolized the spiritual readiness of the crypto-Jew for messianic tidings, while exemplifying the leadership role assumed by women in popular mystical movements.

Women in medieval Spain and Portugal and the later Sephardi Diaspora lived in a world of paradox and contradiction. While societal guidelines appeared restrictive, urging women of all faiths to remain at home, our documents show Sephardi women venturing into the world for both occupational and personal reasons. Still, the world in which Sephardi women lived was powerfully influenced by Islamic culture, with all its negative implications for female autonomy. It is truly remarkable that a few Sephardi women, like Doña Gracia Nasi, rose to levels of wealth and power and that others ascended to spiritual heights and martyrdom like the messianic *conversa* prophetesses and other Judaizing *conversas*. The wealth of material still awaiting study suggests that our picture of the world of Sephardi women is far from complete and that further research and new perspectives will add to our comprehension of a complex period and allow a fuller reconstruction of the lives of medieval and early modern women of Sephardi heritage.

## NOTES

I would like to thank my dear friend and colleague Jay Berkovitz for his invaluable aid and my Israeli colleague Yom Tov Assis for giving me access to his research prior to its publication.

1. Sepharad is the biblical name for Spain. Jews who were born in the Iberian peninsula or can trace their ancestors to either Spain or Portugal are considered to be Sephardim.

2. Yitzhak Baer, *A History of the Jews in Christian Spain*, 2 vols. (Philadelphia, 1961, 1966), a modified version of the German original (1929, 1936–37); and its

Hebrew translation (1945). Eliyahu Ashtor, *The Jews of Moslem Spain*, 3 vols. (Philadelphia, 1984), translated from the original Hebrew version (1966).

3. An exception is Shlomo Dov Goitein, who devoted an entire section (3:312–59) of his four-volume, *A Mediterranean Society* (California, 1967–1983) to the "world of women." Scholars of medieval Iberian history, in general, lag far behind specialists in other regions of medieval Europe in investigating the history of women. A recent collection of essays, *Las mujeres en las ciudades medievales* [hereafter *LM*] (Madrid, 1984) is a groundbreaking exception.

4. See Americo Castro, *The Structure of Spanish History* (Princeton, NJ, 1954).

5. The Jews of Spain were expelled in 1492, whereas those in Portugal, being less expendable to the state, were all forcibly converted in 1497. See Mina Rozen, "The House of Nasi and the Renewal of Settlement in Tiberias" [Hebrew], *Skira Hodshit* 9 (September 1979): 40.

6. Goitein, *Mediterranean Society*, 3:315.

7. Ashtor, *Jews of Moslem Spain*, 3:146.

8. Antonio Domínguez Ortiz, "La mujer en el tránsito de la edad media a la moderna," *LM*, 176. See Goitein, *A Mediterranean Society* 3:318 on genealogies.

9. See Wiebke Walther, *Woman in Islam* (London, 1981), 24, 40; Raphael Patai, *The Seed of Abraham: Jews and Arabs in Contact and Conflict* ( Salt Lake City, UT, 1986), 237, 240; Barbara Freyer Stowassser, "The Status of Women in Early Islam," in *Muslim Women*, ed. Freda Hussain (New York, 1984), 34.

10. On the development of the law of the veil, see Stowasser, "Status," 27–28, 34; Rashda Sharif, "Women in Islam," *European History* 21, no. 1 (1987): 34; and Walther, *Woman*, 43. For long-term effects of such customs, even in Spanish-ruled Sardinia, see John Day, "On the Status of Women in Medieval Sardinia," in *Women of the Medieval World.*, ed. Julius Kirshner and Suzanne F. Wemple (Oxford, 1985), 316.

11. Asunción Lavrin, "In Search of the Colonial Woman in Mexico: the Seventeenth and Eighteenth Centuries," in *Latin American Women: Historical Perspectives*, ed. Asunción Lavrin (Westport, CT, 1978), 27. The Spanish Christian women wore a cloak that covered their faces and a veil, or *tapado*, that made them almost unrecognizable. See Marcelin Defournaux, *La vie quotidienne en Espagne au siècle d'or* (Paris, 1964), 183.

12. Ann M. Pescatello, *Power and Pawn: The Female in Iberian Families, Societies and Cultures* (Westport, CT., 1976), 20.

13. For a marvelous description of women's long veils covering all but their eyes, recorded in an English seaman's journal, see C. R. Boxer, *Women in Iberian Expansion Overseas 1415–1815* [henceforth Boxer, *WIEO*] (New York, 1975), 30–31. As late as the nineteenth century, according to Pescatello (*Power and Pawn*, 40), "Portuguese women veiled and concealed themselves and did not descend from their carriages in public."

14. Tirtsah Levie, "Poor Sephardi Women in Seventeenth Century Amsterdam" (presented at the Third International Congress on the Sephardi-Oriental Heritage, Jerusalem, July 5, 1988), 6–7.

15. Nabia Abbott, "Women and the State in Early Islam," *Journal of Near Eastern Studies* 1 (1941): 111; and see Stowasser, "Status," 26, 30, 35; and Patai, *Seed of Abraham*, 222.

16. Stowasser, "Status," 25, 30; Walther, *Woman*, 24.

17. Ashtor, *Jews of Moslem Spain*, 3:140. Initially, the Moslems all prayed to-

gether; but according to Walther (*Woman*, 24), in the first centuries of Islam, "a recommendation that was regularly observed by women entering the mosque for prayer was that they should pray separately from men and place themselves in a row behind them."

18. No precise date is available concerning the time of the appearance of the women's gallery or of separate seating. Shmuel Safrai ("Was There a Woman's Gallery in the Synagogue of Antiquity?" [Hebrew], *Tarbiz* 32 [1963]: 329–38) claims that during the First Temple and Talmudic periods, no such institution existed. By the eleventh century, traces of a "women's house" (*beit nashim*) can be found in Egypt, as recorded in *genizah* material. See S. D. Goitein, "Women's Galleries in the Synagogues of the Genizah Period" [Hebrew], *Tarbiz* 33 (1964): 314; and see, regarding women and participation in the synagogue, idem, (*Mediterranean Society* 3:359).

19. Levie, "Poor Sephardi Women," 6–7.

20. See Yom Tov Assis, "The 'Ordinance of Rabbenu Gershom' and Polygamous Marriages in Spain" [Hebrew], *Zion* 46 (1981): 251–77. He points out (p. 257) that the rabbis of Aragon never took a clear-cut stand on the issue; on the other hand, in Castile, traditionally the site of stronger Islamic influence, attempts to prevent polygyny occurred.

21. Ibid., 253.

22. Ibid., 262.

23. Ibid., 257–58, esp. n. 35; idem, "Sexual Behavior in Mediaeval Hispano-Jewish Society," in *Jewish History*, ed. A. Rapoport Albert and S. J. Zipperstein (London, 1988), 42–46.

24. Assis, "Ordinance of Rabbenu Gershom," 263.

25. Ibid., 263.

26. Ibid., 276; idem, "Sexual Behavior," 47.

27. Patai, *Seed of Abraham*, 249.

28. Heath Dillard, *Daughters of the Reconquest: Women in Castilian Town Society 1100–1300* (Cambridge, 1984), 127. In Christian society, there was no taboo on the taking of a Moslem concubine by a Jewish male. See Assis, "Sexual Behavior," 43.

29. See Assis, "Sexual Behavior," 62, n. 10 on Moslem slaves as mistresses of their Jewish employers.

30. Dillard, *Daughters*, 207.

31. See Pescatello, *Power and Pawn*, 30, 33; on non-Christian mistresses, see Assis, "Sexual Behavior," 30.

32. Dillard, *Daughters*, 206–7.

33. Assis, "Sexual Behavior," 52–53.

34. Simha Assaf, "The 'Anusim' of Spain and Portugal in the Responsa Literature" [Hebrew], *Me'assef Zion* 5 (1933): 35–36, esp. n. 1.

35. Levie, "Poor Sephardi Women," 9. Neither Ashtor nor Baer mentions Jewish prostitutes.

36. Ashtor, *Jews of Muslim Spain* 1:316 and 2:127.

37. Baer, *Jews in Christian Spain* 1:322.

38. Haim Beinart, *Trujillo: A Jewish Community in Extremadura on the Eve of the Expulsion from Spain* (Jerusalem, 1980), 20–24.

39. Dillard (*Daughters*, 150) cites a municipal privilege granted by Alfonso VIII to Jewish women permitting them to launder outside the castle walls.

40. See Shulamit Shahar, *The Fourth Estate: A History of Women in the Middle Ages* (London, 1983), 246 for a discussion of sites of informal contact among women.

41. See Ashtor, *Jews of Moslem Spain* 3:132–33 and 277, n. 263. In Egypt, Jews

and Christians were assigned badges to wear in the bathhouse or had to use separate bathhouses.

42. Dillard, *Daughters*, 152.

43. Assis mentions the *mikveh* in "Sexual Behavior" (p. 37) and *The Jews of Santa Coloma de Queralt* (Jerusalem, 1988), 31.

44. See José Hinojosa Montalvo, "La mujer en las ordenanzas municipales en el reino de Valencia durante la Edad Media," in *LM*, 53. Toward the end of the thirteenth century, restrictive laws began to appear in order to discourage contact at the domestic level. See Dillard, *Daughters*, 207, on laws to prevent Christian women from nursing Jewish and Moslem children. See also Baer, *Jews in Christian Spain* 1:234, regarding a fine imposed on a Christian whose Jewish wet nurse bathed in the river on the last day of Passover.

45. For details regarding these obstetric services, see A. Cardoner Planas, "Seis mujeres hebreas practicando la medicina en el reino de Aragon," *Sefarad* 9 (1949): 442–43.

46. Ibid., 442–45, for details about these women and their practices.

47. Generally, Moslem women were illiterate; as girls, most were only taught domestic activities such as needlework. In wealthier families, some education—albeit segregated from the boys—was provided. See Walther, *Woman* and Patai, *Seed of Abraham*, 241–42. Regarding the neglect of Christian girls' education and their illiteracy, see Defournaux, *La Vie*, 177–78. See also Pescatello, *Power and Pawn*, 27–28; she explains (p. 25), "Among the elites and professional classes, there were no women lawyers, doctors, professors, notaries, or merchants." Levie ("Poor Sephardi Women," 7) discusses the education at a Sephardi girls' orphanage in Amsterdam where the wards were taught to read a bit, to sew, to knit, and to fear God. She also examined civil matrimonial contracts belonging to seventeenth-century Sephardim in this city and concluded that most of the brides could not sign their names.

48. Lavrin, "Colonial Woman in Mexico," 43.

49. Ashtor, *Jews in Muslim Spain* 3:93.

50. Christian European women of the lower class even took part in craft guilds as spinners. See, e.g., Jo Ann McNamara and Suzanne Wemple, "Sanctity and Power: The Dual Pursuit of Medieval Women," in *Becoming Visible: Women in European History*, ed. Renate Bridenthal and Claudia Koonz (Boston, 1977), 114. Regarding Jewish women supporting themselves by crafts, see Ashtor, *Jews in Muslim Spain* 3:270, n. 119; Baer, *Jews in Christian Spain* 2:335 (he refers to a mother and her three daughters who were professional weavers); and Levie, "Poor Sephardi Women," 9.

51. Ashtor, *Jews in Muslim Spain* 3:93.

52. See Baer, *Jews in Christian Spain* 1:259 on Jewish servants. The joint study by Escobar Camacho and colleagues, "La mujer cordobesa," in *LM* shows (p.157) that in the fifteenth century, 54 percent of the working Christian women in Cordoba were employed in domestic service. Similar figures appear in José Manuel Escobar Camacho, Manuel Nieto Cumplido and Jesús Padilla González, "Vida y presencia de la mujer en la Cordoba del siglo XIII," in *L.M.*, 136. Here maidservants represent 45 percent of the urban women in thirteenth-century Cordoba.

53. Baer, *Jews in Christian Spain* 1:313.

54. Levie mentions these tasks in "Poor Sephardi Women," 8–9.

55. See, e.g., in Shahar, *Fourth Estate*, 174–219, as well as 220–50. Diliard (*Daughters*, 116, 127, 165–67) shows how women in frontier town society took advantage of expanding opportunities, noting (p. 2) that Jewish women were also present. See also Fitzmaurice-Kelly, "Women in Sixteenth-Century," 622.

56. Beatrice Leroy, *The Jews of Navarre in the Late Middle Ages* (Jerusalem, 1985), 40. Portugal was a more agriculturally centered society; see Pescatello, *Power and Pawn*, 27, 36 on women's economic participation there.

57. Moneylenders are discussed in Leroy, *Jews of Navarre*, 67–68. Assis (*Jews of Santa Coloma*, 36–37) discovered eight women who engaged in moneylending in a community comprising between fifty and a hundred Jewish families (and see 99, on two female cloth merchants).

58. See Assis, *Jews of Santa Coloma*, 33 and 47–48.

59. Ashtor, *Jews of Muslim Spain*, 1:207.

60. Walther, *Woman*, 33; Sharif, "Women in Islam," 29. See also Saadawi, "Woman and Islam," 200; Stowasser, "Status," 17.

61. David Herlihy, "Life Expectancies for Women in Medieval Society," in *The Role of Woman in the Middle Ages*, ed. Rosemarie Thee Morewedge (Albany, 1975), 11–12; and see also Diane Owen Hughes, "From Brideprice to Dowry in Mediterranean Europe," *Journal of Family History* 3 (1978): 263–96.

62. Herlihy, *Medieval Households* (Cambridge, MA, 1985), 100.

63. Jean Regné, *History of the Jews in Aragon* (Jerusalem, 1978), 197, 265, 281, 309, 378, 449.

64. Levie, "Poor Sephardi Women," 3–4, 6. Christians also made contributions to charities to supply the less fortunate maidens with dowries.

65. See Goitein, *Mediterranean Society* 3:336–37.

66. Leroy, *Jews of Navarre*, 19.

67. Saadawi, "Woman and Islam," 201; Hibri, "Study," 212. The widower is entitled to half of what his wife leaves if there are no children and one quarter if there are; the childless widow is entitled to one quarter of her husband's property but one eighth if there are progeny. See Sharif, "Women in Islam," 30 and Patai, *Seed of Abraham*, 239 on Moslem widows.

68. Boxer, *WIEO*, 52–53.

69. See Baer, *Jews in Christian Spain* 1:318, on this conflict. Generally speaking, according to Jewish law, widows do not inherit from their husbands. Rather, they either receive their *ketubah* (marriage portion) or are maintained out of their husband's estate. It was not uncommon for husbands in many periods of Jewish history to have recourse to non-Jewish legal systems in order to leave a greater part of their estates to their wives. See, e.g., chapter 6 below.

70. Lavrin, "Colonial Woman in Mexico," 41.

71. Shahar, *Fourth Estate*, 95.

72. Cecil Roth, *The Jews in the Renaissance* (New York, 1965), 54–55.

73. Abraham Galanté, *Esther Kyra d'après de nouveaux documents* (Constantinople, 1926); A. M. Haberman, *Jewish Women As Printers, Typesetters, Publishers and Backers (Patronesses) of Writers* [Hebrew] (Berlin, 1933), 8.

74. An *inquisition* was a temporary legal institution or court set up by the Roman Catholic Church in order to extirpate suspected heresy. Its jurisdiction was solely over baptized Catholics; thus, it could bring to trial converted Jews or Moslems, suspected witches, sectarians, and the like. In Spain and Portugal and most of their territories, numerous *conversos* and their descendants were accused by the unusually powerful and long-lived Spanish and Portuguese Inquisitions and tried for Judaizing. Those convicted as crypto-Jews faced an array of sentences ranging from penances and fines to expropriation of property and public execution by the secular arm at an auto-da-fé.

75. See, for example, Cecil Roth, *Doña Gracia of the House of Nasi* (Philadelphia, 1977); Rozen, "House of Nasi," 40–47.

76. The Tiberias project has often been falsely attributed to her nephew, Don Joseph Nasi. See Rozen, "House of Nasi," 44–45.

77. See Renée Levine, *Women in Spanish Crypto-Judaism 1492–1520* (Ph.D. diss., Brandeis University, 1983); and Renée Levine Melammed, "The Ultimate Challenge: Safeguarding the Crypto-Judaic Heritage," *Proceedings of the American Academy for Jewish Research* 53 (1986): 91–109.

78. Seymour B. Liebman, *New World Jewry, 1493–1825: Requiem for the Forgotten* (New York, 1982), 71.

79. Arnold Witznitzer, "Crypto-Jews in Mexico during the Seventeenth Century," in *The Jewish Experience in Latin America*, ed. Martin Cohen (New York, 1971), 1:177.

80. In the eyes of the church and the Inquisition, these crypto-Jews were Jews. For the rabbis, however, determining whether or not a *converso* or his descendants were Jewish was a more complex matter, especially in light of such legal intricacies as the status of an *ʿagunah* (abandoned woman) and her children. As a result, contrasting and conflicting rabbinical opinions and tensions developed. For interpretations of these rabbinical opinions, see Simha Assaf, "The Marranos of Spain and Portugal in the Responsa Literature" [Hebrew], *Meʾassef Zion* 5 (1933): 19–60; B. Netanyahu, "The Marranos According to the Hebrew Sources of the 15th and Early 16th Centuries," *Proceedings of the American Academy for Jewish Research* 31 (1963): 81–164, idem, *The Marranos of Spain from the Late Fourteenth to the Early Sixteenth Centuries According to the Hebrew Sources* (New York, 1966); Gershon D. Cohen, review of *The Marranos of Spain* by B. Netanyahu, *Jewish Social Studies* 29 (1967): 178–84; and Jacob Katz, "Though He Sinned, He Remains an Israelite" [Hebrew], *Tarbiz* 27 (1958): 203–17.

81. See I. S. Révah, "L'hérésie marrane dans l'Europe catholique du 15e au 18e siècle," in *Hérésies et sociétés dans l'Europe pré-industrielle 11e-18e siècles*, ed. J. Le Goff (Paris, 1968), 328.

82. I. S. Révah, "La religion d'Uriel da Costa, Marrane de Porto," *Revue de l'Histoire des Religions* 161 (1962): 59; B. S. Pullan, "The Inquisition and the Jews of Venice: The Case of Gaspare Ribeiro 1580–1591," *Bulletin of the John Rylands Library* 62 (1979): 230.

83. See Solange Alberro, "Mujeres ante el Tribunal del Santo Oficio de la Inquisición en la Nueva España," *El Colegio de México Boletín Editorial* 15 (September–October, 1987): 20; George Alexander Kohut, "Jewish Martyrs in the Inquisition in South America," and Arnold Witznitzer, "Crypto-Jews in Mexico during the Sixteenth Century," in *The Jewish Experience in Latin America*, ed. Goodman, 1: 18–19, 151, 154, 156, 157–158.

84. The Carvajals of Mexico were among the best known families of Judaizers. The Carvajal women are discussed in Salo W. Baron, *A Social and Economic History of the Jews* vol. 15 (Philadelphia, 1973), 285, 287; Witznitzer, "Crypto-Jews in Mexico," 106–7; Martin Cohen, *The Martyr* (Philadelphia, 1973); Seymour B. Liebman, *The Jews in New Spain* (Coral Gables, FL, 1970), 159–82. Boleslao Lewin has a series of four articles on a Mexican crypto-Jewish woman, "Isabel Machado, fiel hija de un 'dogmatizador' judío del Siglo XVI," *Mundo Israelita* (Buenos Aires), January 20, 1979, p. 10; January 27, 1979, p. 10; February 3, 1979, p. 10, and February 10, 1979, pp. 10–11.

85. Shahar, *The Fourth Estate,* 268.

86. See Beatrice Gottlieb, "The Problem of Feminism in the Fifteenth Century," in *Women of the Medieval World,* ed. Kirschner and Wemple, 361; and Suzanne Fonay Wemple, *Women in Frankish Society* (Philadelphia, 1982), 149.

87. Herlihy, *Medieval Households,* 113, 122; see also Yitzhak Baer, "The Messianic Movement in Spain during the Period of the Expulsion" [Hebrew], *Me' assef Zion* 5 (1933): 61–78.

88. Haim Beinart, "The Spanish Inquisition and a 'Converso Community' in Extremadura," *Medieval Studies* 43 (1981): 445–71; idem, "Herrera: Its Conversos and Jews" [Hebrew], *Proceedings of the Seventh World Congress of Jewish Studies* B (Jerusalem, 1981), 53–85; and see also Levine, *Women,* 106–15.

89. Haim Beinart, "The Prophetess Inés and Her Movement in Her Hometown, Herrera" [Hebrew], in *Studies in Jewish Mysticism, Philosophy and Ethical Literature* (Jerusalem, 1986), 459–506; idem, "A Prophesying Movement in Cordova in 1499–1502" [Hebrew], *Zion* 44 (1980): 190–200; idem, "The Prophetess Inés and Her Movement in Pueblo de Alcocer and Talarrubias" [Hebrew], *Tarbiz* 51 (1982): 633–58; idem, "Conversos of Chillón and the Prophecies of Mari Gómez and Inés, the Daughter of Juan Esteban" [Hebrew], *Zion* 48 (1983): 241–72.

# **6** HOWARD ADELMAN

## *Italian Jewish Women*

---

Jews have lived in Italy uninterruptedly since antiquity. Over the centuries Italy has been ruled by diverse empires and attracted immigration from many lands; consequently, Italian Jewry has reflected the cultures and traditions of a variety of Jewish communities. After enjoying a privileged status under pagan Roman emperors, with the rise of Christianity Italian Jewry was soon subjected to restrictive legislation separating Jews and Christians, especially in matters of sex and marriage. During the early Middle Ages, sectors of Italian Jewry lived under the Ostrogoths, Byzantines, and the Arabs. By the high Middle Ages Italian Jewry was, for the most part, concentrated in the Southern part of the peninsula. During the later Middle Ages, despite growing religious animosity toward the Jews by the papacy, the Jews of Rome continued to enjoy the protection and the patronage of the pope himself because of their economic usefulness. Gradually, hostile papal policies in the South and favorable treatment in the North caused a reversal in the distribution of the Jews in Italy. In the thirteenth and fourteenth centuries the Jews of Italy began to flourish as loan bankers in many of the cities and small towns of Northern Italy.

As antagonism against the Jews increased in France and the Germanic lands, many fled across the Alps to take part in the opportunities available in Italy. Spanish Jews began to go to Italy after the persecutions of 1391, building to a substantial wave of immigration after the expulsion of the Jews in 1492 from Spain and her possessions, which included Sicily and Sardinia and after 1503 the Kingdom of Naples. After the forced mass conversion of the Jews of Portugal in 1497, which included many refugees from Spain, many of these Jews started making their way to Italy. Since they provided valuable services, usually as moneylenders or merchants, these Jews often received generous charters allowing them to live comfortably in many of the small towns and growing cities of northern Italy. Prosperous, well connected with all levels of Christian society, and living in relatively small Jewish communities, these Jews cultivated the tastes and culture of upper-class Christian society. These tendencies became particularly pronounced during the Renaissance, a time when cultural creativity also flourished among the Jews of Italy. Although the fifteenth century saw an increase in anti-Jewish agitation by churchmen in Italy and many cities established ghettos in the sixteenth, the fact that Italy was not unified provided the Jews with opportunities to leave one city-state to go to another that offered greater promise for better conditions. At various times, despite intermittent expulsions, their protectors included the popes in Rome, Ancona, and Bologna, the Medici in Florence, the Gonzaga in Mantua, the Este in Ferrara, the Sforza in Milan, and the Republic of Venice. During the sixteenth and seventeenth centuries many Jews from the Ottoman Empire (including Palestine) and from Eastern Europe began to trade, travel, study, and settle in Italy. Thus, in Italy, Ashkenazic and Sephardic customs were practiced in close proximity to each other by Jews who spoke a mixture of Italian, Spanish, German, Hebrew, Turkish, and French, in addition to dialects of Judeo-German, Judeo-Spanish, and Judeo-Italian.

In Italy, therefore, Jewish attitudes and behavior toward women were shaped by Ashkenazic customs from France and Germany; Sephardic practices from Spain and Portugal; Islam-inspired attitudes from Spain, Northern Africa, Southern Italy, and the Levant; native Italian Jewish patterns; and the thinking of contemporary Christians. The latter are often identified as new developments, which, under the influence of Renaissance humanism, may have had a salutary effect on the status of women. At least since the nineteenth century, historians, mostly following Jacob Burckhardt, have asserted that the Renaissance was a period in which women attained equality. Jewish writers, following Cecil Roth and Moses Shulvass, accepted this position concerning Jewish women as well.[1] In recent years, however, several historians have challenged many of Burkhardt's assumptions, including his assertions about the equality of women during the Renaissance. These challenges can be applied to Jewish historiography about women as well.

There are very few sources relevant to the history of Jewish women in Italy written by women themselves; and the number of "great" Jewish women known during this period is small, although more are known than from earlier eras. Therefore, to reconstruct the lives of Jewish women in Italy we must use primarily documents written by men, many of whom wished to limit the role and authority of women. However, by using gender as a category of analysis in reading these texts, it is possible to see how the system of Jewish law provided opportunities for women to enter the public realm, how they could arrogate power for themselves even without the authority to do so, and how men consciously invoked not only Jewish law but extralegal considerations to subordinate women.

If we are to understand the texts available about Jewish women, it must be kept in mind that each Jewish community in Italy was autonomous. The charters of the Jews and their own internal communal regulations allowed for wealthy Jewish lay leaders to manage the affairs of their communities. The rabbis in each locale usually served at the pleasure of the lay leaders; nor did they serve as officials but in various capacities such as teachers, preachers, and deciders of Jewish law. These services were rendered for a fee, and their rulings were not necessarily binding. The lay leaders did not always accept rabbinic authority; and on many burning questions of the day, especially those of personal status such as marriage or divorce, there were often controversies in which the rabbis of Italy would take opposing positions.

A very important source for the study of Jewish women in Italy, therefore, is the legal rulings of the rabbis, *sheelot uteshuvot*, or *responsa*, about specific cases. These provide rich documentation about the details of complex interactions, as well as insights into the thinking of particular rabbis, and anecdotal material about similar cases.

*Responsa* are not the only source of information about women in Italian Jewish history. Each Jewish community kept extensive records of its transactions, in Hebrew or Italian; although many are lost, a few are extant. Jewish communities or Jewish individuals, often without the approval of the community, corresponded with the governments of the various Italian city-states. These letters, usually in Italian or Latin, can be found in the archives of Italy. In addition, the records of governmental deliberation on Jewish matters are extant and useful for the study of Jewish women. Finally, the personal correspondence of individual Jews offers important insight into the lives of women.

The categories of "public" and "private," applied by different writers to the experience of women, are extremely useful but not totally satisfactory. Jewish women did function in certain capacities in public, social, religious, commercial, legal, and cultural matters. These areas included participating in Jewish worship, working as ritual slaughterers, writing books, and conducting businesses. Nevertheless, it cannot be argued that Italy represented a radical departure from the limited authority granted women in the traditional Jewish community, in which rabbis, lay leaders, and Jewish men in general saw the role of women as centered in the domestic realm and deterred women's exercising power and influence. However, it cannot be taken for granted that the lives of Italian Jewish women only concerned members of their own family at home, because even in these matters crucial transitions could not be made without involving the public, political, and legal authority of rabbis and Jewish lay leaders. Each stage of transition and activity in a woman's life from her birth to her death, including education, courtship, marriage, childbirth, domestic strife, divorce, widowhood, inheritance, guardianship of children, and remarriage, involved tensions between the prescribed norms of Jewish life embodied in the transmitted corpus of rabbinic textual tradition, in terms of the privileges reserved for males, and the actual behavior of Jews as sanctioned by leading authorities based on local customs or alternative traditions, especially those that allowed for women to exercise power and influence. In other words, the opportunities for women to exercise power, even in the domestic realm, were not constant but emerged as a result of ambivalent instructions in the traditional religious literature, women's attempts to control their own destiny and influence their community, the needs of the family, and the methods employed by males to try to curtail female autonomy.

## WOMEN IN THE PUBLIC SPHERE

When Jewish women fulfilled roles in the public sphere, the reasons were the needs of Jewish society rather than a change in the status of women. In general, women continued to act under the aegis, and for the benefit, of men. In each case where occasion arose for a woman to appear and function publicly there were voices that reacted against her. Thus, women's public activities were not an aspect of Renaissance values, a new status in the Jewish community, or the liberation of women but reflections of the normal give-and-take between traditional halachic texts, which were read very carefully, and the ongoing needs of the Jewish community, which under certain conditions women could serve, or, if necessary, defy.

Sumptuary laws were enacted by men to control what women wore in public, although these laws were regularly defied to assert family pride and female power. In Padua some Jewish communal legislation from 1599 and 1630 also attempted to limit the public appearances of women by forbidding those under thirty to appear in public at all. Violators would be excommunicated and fined; husbands were responsible for the behavior of their wives.[2]

## WOMEN AND WORSHIP

Closely connected with the question of women's public behavior is a discussion of their role in Jewish worship in Italy. Women who could read Hebrew prayed daily and on the Sabbath,[3] some wearing tefillin;[4] but they were not counted for the quorum of ten. Others led prayer for the women's section.[5] During the fifteenth and sixteenth centuries translations of the service appeared, possibly for the women;[6] however, there were plenty of men in Italy who did not know enough Hebrew to pray. Women also participated in worship services by disrupting them. In Modena, when the Torah was taken out of the ark, women would loudly curse men and ask for vengeance against those who had slighted them. In 1534 R. Azriel Diena (d. 1536), wrote a *responsum* against this practice, stating, "Over his women, every man shall be ruler in his house and rebuke his wife."[7] However, men, too, used the service as an arena to air marital grievances, particularly in cases where their wives refused to have intercourse with them.[8]

Denied direct access to the Torah during the service, Italian women made the *mappot*, the binders with which the Torah scrolls were wrapped, and dedicated them to the synagogue. In their lavishly embroidered Hebrew inscriptions they always identified themselves in relationship to a man—husband, father, or even grandfather.[9] Benvenida Abravanel of Naples, a supporter of the messianic pretensions of David Hareuveni, displayed another type of piety. She was known not only for her charitable donations and redemption of captives but for her ascetic practices, particularly fasting.[10]

## PUBLISHED WOMEN WRITERS

Jewish women in Italy did write and publish works of their own. Regrettably, much of their poetry is now lost. For example, Giustina Levi-Perotti sent the eminent poet and scholar Francesco Petrarca (1304–1374) a sonnet, to which he replied with one of his own.[11] At least two women did become distinguished, published Italian authors. Debora Ascarelli of Rome gained recognition for her *Abitacolo degli oranti*, rhymed Italian translations of Hebrew liturgical poetry completed about 1537 and published in 1601.[12] Roth suggested that this may be "the earliest independently published work in Jewish literary history which was written by a woman."[13]

The most accomplished—and therefore the least typical—Jewish woman of this period in terms of education and literary productivity was Sarra Copia Sullam (1592–1641). The details of her life are instructive as an indication of the great opportunities available for at least one woman of wealth and talent. Born to a prominent Italian Jewish family in Venice, Sarra received a good classical education. She was married to Jacob Sullam, an important figure in the ghetto. Sarra gathered around her a salon of mostly Christian men of letters who gave her lessons, sonnets, and letters in exchange for which she provided financial backing as well as intellectual conversation. But gradually many of her male admirers betrayed her; some humiliated her by accusing her of plagiarism. As a Jewish woman writer who had both captivated and bested Christian clerics in public, Sarra was an ideal target for accusations that would undermine her accomplishments as a woman and a Jew. In addition to much of her poetry (which was published with the letters of one of her male correspondents, *Lettere d'Ansaldo Ceba' scritte a Sarra Copia*, in Genoa in 1623), her polemic against one of her other admirers, *Manifesto di Sarra Copia Sulam hebrea nel quale e' da lei riprovate, e detestata l'opinione negante l'immortalita' dell'anima, falsemente attribuitale da Sig. Baldassare Bonifaccio*, was published in Venice in 1621. Sarra's defenders saw her in the tradition of women writers of the Renaissance, and her Jewishness was noted regularly in their praise of her.[14]

## WOMEN AS RITUAL SLAUGHTERERS

Some women in Italy had acquired knowledge sufficient for them to serve as ritual slaughterers. However, this was not a situation unique to Italy. Prior to the Italian Renaissance, the question of women's slaughtering had been debated in rabbinic literature and affirmative answers had been offered,[15] although there are no examples given of such a practice having been performed. Even during the Renaissance it is clear that the circumstances under which women could slaughter were extremely limited. On the question of women's being allowed to *porge* (a process of removing the fat, veins, nerves, and sinews after the animal has been ritually slaughtered), one *responsum* saw a connection between trusting women in matters of porging and in other matters of law. It acknowledged the leniency of most authorities toward trusting properly qualified women in some matters but admitted that some rabbis were not so enthusiastic when it came to ritual slaughtering and cited arguments concerning female weak-mindedness and tendency to faint.[16] The reason women were permitted to slaughter was not to encourage their liberation or emancipation but so that women in isolated locations (such as summer houses in the mountains) and sometimes in distressed circumstances could provide food for their families.[17] Whatever the reasons for allowing women to slaughter, it is clear that it was only in special, private circumstances; and there is no indication that this was a change in the traditional attitudes toward the limits placed on the women's public roles.

## WOMEN AND BUSINESS

Despite the reservations developed over the years in rabbinic literature concerning the acceptability of the testimony of women, Jewish women were *allowed* to take oaths and to bring cases to court, especially in matters related to business practices—though it is still to be ascertained how often they actually testified.[18] Thus, it was possible for the males of the family to enlist their wives in business activities.[19] In Italy women acted as financial agents for their husbands, continuing in this role during their husbands' absence or after their death.[20] These businesses included work as moneylenders,[21] silk and button manufacturers and merchants,[22] developers and sellers of cosmetics (there is a well-known letter from Anna the Hebrew to Catherine Sforza on these matters from 1508),[23] brokers of merchandise,[24] experts in precious metals,[25] partners in stores,[26] healers proficient in medicine,[27] publishers of Hebrew books,[28] and occasional involvement with stolen goods.[29]

Although business could be conducted in private, one *responsum* by Meir Katzenellenbogen (1473–1506) lashes out at women in Castel Maggiore, near Bologna, who went to fairs and markets on their own to conduct business as merchants. He called them *yotzaniot* (gadabouts), and invoked Psalms 45:14: "The honor of the daughter of the king is inside"; since all Jewish women are daughters of kings, this kind of behavior was improper. He ended with an appeal to the rabbis of the area to use their power to stop the women from going out.[30]

## EDUCATION AND PRIVATE LIFE

When girls came into the world they were blessed, "May she grow up to be married and have children,"[31] omitting the hope offered for boys at the time of their circumcision that they would pursue Torah study. The birth of a girl brought with it certain anxieties: "If it is a daughter and she lives she will require vigilance, dispersion, and expense."[32] In his Italian compilation of Jewish law Leon Modena noted that it was the father who named the girl,[33] yet he reported in his autobiography that his granddaughter was named by her mother.[34] Italian Jewish women were often known by their Italian names, but usually they had a Hebrew name as well.[35]

To foster female domestic roles, many rabbis opposed the education of girls. Nevertheless, in Italy as early as the thirteenth century there were rabbis who allowed Jewish girls to receive a Jewish education. Many of the reasons given against educating Jewish girls were the same as those offered in non-Jewish society: fear that the honor of the woman would be compromised or that she would become manly. However, Jews realized that female illiteracy was not good for a household, a business, or a family; so daughters were taught at least Italian and sometimes some Hebrew as well—often at home, sometimes at school. Letters also show that Jewish women corresponded with parents, fiancés, sons, brothers, grandsons, and teachers.[36] Jewish women in Italy also taught young girls Italian and sometimes Hebrew; some even were called *rabbit* or *rabbanit*.[37] Women teachers were involved with healing and birthing; others, often widows, offered instruction in domestic skills in their homes. Two of the most scholarly women we know about were sisters, Fioretta (Bat Sheva) Modena and Diana Rieti. They had mastered Torah, Mishnah, Talmud, Midrash, Jewish law, and Kabbalah. At the age of seventy-five, after the death of her husband, Fioretta set out to live in Safed, a struggling community with many mystics in Palestine.

Young women were often engaged as soon as they reached puberty; after a period of engagement (*shiddukhin*), which could last a year or more, the usual age for betrothal (*erusin* or *kiddushin*) and marriage (*nissuin*) was between fourteen and eighteen for young women, although sometimes it could be as high as nineteen; it was twenty-four to twenty-eight for young men.[38]

Given the late age of marriage for men, it is not surprising that prostitution was found among Italian Jews. In addition to providing a sexual outlet for young men, it was an opportunity for young women who did not have a sufficient dowry to marry. One of the main problems with Jewish prostitutes was that they had intercourse with Christian clients as well, a major violation of church and civil law. In Venice, magistracies were charged with enforcing the laws separating Jews and Christians, by making sure the Jews wore their special yellow hats (the same color assigned to prostitutes), by controlling Christians who worked in the ghetto, and by watching Jews who entered Christian

homes.[39] Evidence of Jewish-Christian sexual relations during the fifteenth century, probably associated with prostitution, is found in
Rome (where between 1490–1500 more than fifty Jewish women were
burned at the stake for sexual relations with Christians), Florence
(where at least thirty-four out of eighty-eight condemnations of Jews
were for sexual offenses), Bologna (where a rabbinical synod acted to
curb such relations), Cremona (where in 1575 the church was concerned with extensive Jewish-Christian social contacts), and Padua
(where complaints from the cardinal prompted the Jewish leaders to
prohibit Jewish men from having sex with Christian women).[40]

Like prostitution, sexual promiscuity was often a result of the structural impediments that Jewish law and custom placed in the way of
marriage, such as the inability to find a suitable spouse, the lack of
means to secure the spouse with a dowry or *ketubah* amount, the im-
possibility of marriage for a woman who had been abandoned, the
opportunities created when a husband was traveling for long periods
of time, and the possibility of men's taking advantage of female servants.[41] Cases of children conceived or born out of wedlock are found
among the Jews of Italy. Jewish community leaders often had to determine who must support an unwed mother. Their tendency to ignore
such situations was corrected when the woman threatened to take
matters in her own hands by bringing the infant to the synagogue to
interrupt the service and embarrass the alleged father unless she received the child support she requested.[42] Cases of foundlings in the
ghettos were not unknown. In such instances the main concern of
both Jewish and secular authorities was to determine whether the
child was Jewish or not rather than to establish the guilt or innocence
of those who were responsible for abandoning the child. In one epi-
sode from Venice in 1691, when the mother of the baby asked the
father what had happened to her baby, he replied, "I did what I
pleased."[43]

Engagement and marriage for a daughter, of course, were the hope
and expectation of all parents. In such an environment it was considered important that Jewish women be married with their hymens intact, to guarantee their chastity. When that of a young girl was acci-
dentally ruptured while at play, *mukat etz* ("hit by a stick") entries
were often made in the public records of Italian Jewish communities
based on the testimony of competent witnesses (usually women, for
reasons of modesty), so that when she married there would be no

suspicions about her conduct and she would be entitled to the rights and privileges of a virgin in matters of her *ketubah* amount and whether she could marry a member of a priestly family.[44]

Engagements in Italy reflect a mixture of parental arrangements and the couple's spontaneity and choice. Traditionally, matches were made by the fathers; but there were cases where the father was alive but the mother made the match, shook hands, and made the symbolic exchange of property.[45] When acting in this capacity the mother was required to make the arrangements in the presence of two witnesses, a requirement not always followed.[46] The engagement was of a contractual nature—either between parents when the children were young or between adults on their own—and expenses for an engagement could be great for both families. These included costs of banquets, lodging, transportation, emissaries, and wardrobe.[47] One who broke such an agreement was often subject to a fine agreed upon ahead of time.[48] In Italy there were both forced marriages[49] and young women who refused the matches made for them.[50] Some women become betrothed to one man after their parents had already engaged them to another.[51]

Another key aspect of courtship was exchanging gifts, often accompanied by love notes.[52] In some Jewish communities, the receipt of a gift indicated that a woman was betrothed, and a severance of the relationship would require a bill of divorce, while in others, it simply was taken as a sign of affection on the part of the man. There were even cases where a woman would receive gifts from several suitors who were wooing her at once, either for her beauty or her money. In Italy the giving of gifts to one's fiancée usually preceded the betrothal, although a very small minority reversed the order. Thus, the presentation of gifts by a suitor did not automatically signify that a woman was betrothed.[53] If a couple separated, the gifts were to be returned.[54]

The major consideration in making a match was financial. There was a tremendous financial burden on both parties, especially the woman's family. In Venice, where Jewish dowries could run as high as twelve thousand ducats for the rich and as low as ten to eighteen ducats for the poor, the usual amount was five hundred to a thousand ducats for families with an annual income of about two hundred ducats.[55] Fathers were notorious for seeking out matches on the basis of the wealth of the family, rather than the merits of the people involved. For this reason less-affluent Jews often found it difficult to make a match.[56] Many communities provided assistance by raising dowries for young women. The groom also supplied the bride with a *ketubah* sum (usually ritually stipulated at one hundred or two hundred *zuzim*) and a *tosefet* (an additional amount, which often was his principal contribution, ranging from a quarter of the dowry to its equal).[57] The *ketubah* amount and the dowry were debts owed by the man to the woman in the event of divorce, his going to jail, or his death.[58] The dowry and other sums raised allowed the woman to retain a certain amount of economic power in the home.[59] At various times decrees were made to ensure that a woman would be betrothed and married in the presence of her parents, two blood relatives, or ten proper witnesses.[60] These concerns indicate the likelihood of people marrying on their own out of romantic, rather than financial, familial, or communal, considerations.

When a woman married, despite the financial expenditure lavished upon her by her family, she often left them both emotionally and physically. The expectation was that the woman would join the family of her husband, perhaps even living in her father-in-law's house. There she would assume domestic duties. Such an arrangement would be necessary because often the husband could not afford to support his bride on his own. In one case, responding to his daughter's anxiety over keeping house for a large family, a father made a vow that upon her marriage his daughter would do no housework. Contrary to most vows a father made concerning his daughter that became invalid at the time of her marriage, this one was unknown to her father-in-law and her husband; and when it was revealed, even though her father promised to provide her with a Jewish servant to do work expected of her, the in-laws insisted she leave the house. They made it clear that not economics but power was the issue by invoking Genesis 3:16, "He will rule over you,"—adding, "He and not her father" and invoking Esther 1:22, "so that every man will be ruler in his house." The woman, nevertheless, sought rabbinic help to have the vow annulled.[61]

Childbirth was an expected but perilous part of a woman's life. In especially difficult deliveries a Torah scroll was sometimes brought into the birthing room for the woman to hold. In Viadina using a Torah in this way was condemned by some rabbis because it used the holy Torah for theurgical purposes as well as allowing women a measure of religious control. In 1526 Azriel Diena argued that it was sacrilegious to place the Torah on the breast of a woman so that a "foul valley will be a door for hope" (Hosea 2:17). Diena caustically asked how use of the Torah could actually help during distressful deliveries and stated that since there was doubt as to its effectiveness, the honor of the Torah must not be violated by placing it on the "impure" bosom of a woman, who was, to borrow an expression from the Talmud, "a pitcher of filth with its mouth full of blood."[62] When a birth was successful, it was a cause for joy. Celebrations accompanying new mothers to the synagogue became so extravagant that some communities included in the sumptuary laws limits on the number of women who could join them.[63]

Marriage was not always harmonious, and rabbinic records give insights into marital quarrels presented for adjudication. Difficulties were frequently linked to how men and women attempted to exercise power over each other, and it was not unusual for the woman to have the upper hand. One left her husband after six weeks of marriage and took with her almost all their money and gifts.[64] Another was regularly able to force her husband out of the house; finally, she collected her dowry from him by using the secular courts and returned to her father's house.

Often spouses did not live together. If the man was a teacher, he might be employed far from his home, sometimes for up to a year at a time. Women sometimes did not want to bring their entire households to where their husbands had found work, and sometimes the man did not continue in his position.[65] One man whose wife tried to lure him back from a distant teaching job asked that, "She should set her mind as his . . . because the way of mankind is that the woman serves the man in thought, word, and deed."[66]

In the Italian *responsa* very few instances of domestic violence are noted. In conformity with the views in rabbinic literature, Italian rabbis maintained a distinction between justified and unjustified violence against one's wife. However, breaking with most previous discussions, these rabbis were more willing to force a man who beat his wife to divorce her.[67] These attitudes are corroborated by findings in the Jewish communal archives of Rome and in governmental documents from Milan.[68] Women, in turn, often leveled charges of violence by husbands as a way of extricating themselves from their marriages. Women also hit men, sometimes in the genitals.[69] Some men, however, attempted to avoid intricate legal proceedings by simply trying to have their wives murdered.[70]

Another charge leveled by women against their husbands was that they were impotent and incapable of fulfilling their obligations to satisfy them or to produce offspring.[71] Rabbis were reluctant to grant an immediate divorce. They feared that such charges were being made only because the woman had developed an attraction for another man. The tradition was to disregard her and to require that the couple remain together for ten years; if, after that time, there were no offspring he could be forced to divorce her. Attempts were also made to blame his condition on the woman, either because of the nature of her hymen or because of her use of magic.[72]

Cases of marital infidelity are found in Italian rabbinic and archival material. One case reported to the duke of Milan involved a Jewish woman who gave birth to a child soon after she was divorced from her husband because she claimed that he was impotent.[73] The key to understanding the charge of adultery is the provision in Jewish law that if the man so wanted he could divorce his wife on the basis of suspicions without giving her her *ketubah* payment. Some rabbis held that the ban of R. Gershom against divorcing a woman against her will did not apply in cases of adultery even if there was only one witness and she a woman.[74] Similarly, if a woman wanted to extricate herself from a marriage, she could claim that she had committed adultery. One woman, either revolted by her husband's lame condition, his poverty, and his gambling or attracted to another man, told him that she had had sexual relations with another man several years earlier.[75]

Married men, however, often had mistresses, referred to in Hebrew as an *ishah meyuhedet* (special woman) or *pilegesh* (a concubine), with whom they had sexual relations and sometimes children in addition to those born to their wives.[76] There were cases where provisions would be made by these fathers for these sons, *naturale o bastardo*, to receive an inheritance. Such provisions often created conflicts between the legitimate and the illegitimate heirs.[77] Some men took a mistress for procreative purposes when their wives did not produce offspring.[78] It was unclear if the ordinance of R. Gershom against polygyny also applied to *pilegesh* relationships.[79]

Conversion from Judaism to Christianity was another way for either spouse to control the other. In one famous *responsum* a women who did not want her husband to be an innkeeper threatened to become a Christian. Conversion would not have invalidated the marriage; the problem concerned her permissibility to her priestly husband were she to spend time in the house of a Christian and in a house for catechumens. Moreover, since the local bishop expressed concern about the sincerity of the putative conversion, it appears that such threats and even actual conversions may have been recognized as attempts to coerce stubborn spouses. Converted women might charge their husbands with apostasy to have them removed from the scene by the authorities, perhaps so that they could be with a lover. Young women might convert to be provided with dowries by the house of the catechumens, enabling them to marry, or to enter a nunnery. Some young women (like young men) would convert several times to Christianity to take advantage of the benefits received by new converts, although a second conversion was considered a sacrilege and punishable by the Inquisition.[80]

Wives and children over twelve could not be forcibly converted from Judaism to Christianity according to Christian law. However, the consent of one parent, usually the father, was enough to permit a minor child to be converted; while women were often subjected to ordeals and tricks in order to effect their conversions. One man had his wife put in prison for forty days to force her conversion, a strategy that proved unsuccessful. A man who wished to convert to Christianity connived with the officials of Cremona to trick his wife into converting with him by having himself arrested on a capital charge from which he could be saved only by her conversion. If a woman chose to retain her Judaism despite efforts by her husband to have her convert, she could be divorced by her husband and separated from her children. If the apostate husband chose not to divorce her (which was his choice according to Jewish law), she could never remarry as long as he was alive.[81]

Since women did not have the right to petition for divorce in Jewish law, several attempted to violate laws or appear to have done so, as a way to extricate themselves from a difficult marriage. Similarly, one woman accused her husband of coin clipping, probably as a way to get him jailed and to regain her dowry.[82] A woman might also claim that her husband had an intolerable odor—acceptable grounds, according to rabbinic law, for arranging a divorce.[83] A woman, revolted by her husband's epilepsy, asserted that had she known about it she would never have married him and that she now wanted him to be forced to divorce her and to pay her her *ketubah* and her *tosefet*. He argued that this condition began after he married her, that it was not one for which he could be forced to divorce her, and that it had not bothered her through many years of marriage during which they had many children together. It only became an issue after she developed an interest in another man whom she wanted to marry. He also felt that since his wife could work, there was no reason for him to have to pay her full support. The rabbi's reply asserted that her silence could not be considered acceptance; it may have been because she did not know she could protest. However, he concurred that the husband did not have to support her fully, because a woman was supported only in exchange for the services she provided to her husband.[84]

Occasionally, marriages took place between Jews and Christians. Sometimes it was as simple as a Jewish woman marrying a Christian and living as a Christian without having converted.[85] Jewish women could also find themselves unwillingly married to a Christian if their husbands converted, since Jewish law considered an apostate still a Jew in matters such as marriage, divorce, *yibbum*, or *halitzah*.[86] A woman could remain bound to a convert, whether he was her fiancé, husband, or brother-in-law. He would still have to provide a Jewish divorce or release in order for the woman to remarry, but the Jewish community had no power to force him to do so.[87] Although attempts were made to remedy this contingency in Jewish law, challenges were usually limited to finding loopholes in specific cases. If a woman committed apostasy it was routine for her husband simply to dissolve the marriage.[88]

While polygyny was not an everyday occurrence among Sephardic Jews, its theoretical acceptance made it possible for Jewish men to take more than one wife or to have relations with more than one woman under certain conditions, such as ten years of an infertile marriage,[89] the death of a childless brother,[90] inability to correct a contentious wife who would not accept a divorce, the wife's apostasy,[91] the wife's insanity,[92] a desire to take a mistress[93] or escape from a betrothal made when he was a minor.[94] However, in 1554 a synod of Italian Jews ruled that if there was offspring, a man was not allowed to marry a second wife unless he received the permission of his first wife and one of her relatives.[95] In Italy, it was also necessary to receive the permission of the pope before marrying a second wife. This permission was often granted for a fee, even without the permission of the first wife, as long as the second wife lived in a different city.[96] The tendency towards polygyny was enhanced during the sixteenth century when some rabbis, most notably Joseph Colon (1410–1480), following the lead of Solomon ibn Adret of Spain (c. 1235–c. 1310), questioned whether R. Gershon had intended his ban to be valid after 1240. However, voices against polygyny rose up in the seventeenth century. Leon Modena asserted that rabbinic authorities after 1240 continued to accept the ban of Rabbenu Gershom. He also stated that if a marriage had been infertile for ten years, a man could not take another wife until he had divorced the first and given her her *ketubah* payment.[97]

According to the rabbinic understanding of the biblical laws of levirate marriage (*yibbum*), a childless widow could not receive her dowry (or half her husband's possessions) or marry another man without going through *halitzah*, the ceremony of release from her brother-in-law.[98] As Modena noted, "Therefore do many of these kinsmen hold them off, and bear them in hand a long while, that so they may vex them, and get money out of them for their release." In order to avoid these situations of blackmail,[99] part of the engagement contract sometimes called for the brothers of the man to release the woman willingly, "without cost or claim," in the event of their brother's death, for the wife to be named *donna e madonna* of all her husband's property in the marital document, or for the man to write his wife a bill of divorce whenever he became sick or set out on a journey.[100] Nevertheless, Italian rabbis faced cases where married men tried to enter a levirate marriage despite already having a wife. Some women would agree to this, and some rabbis would support it, although most opposed such arrangements.

Despite reluctance in the Talmud, a woman did retain the right to serve as guardian of her children after her husband's death—"according to Jewish law", in the words of several Italian archival documents from Milan,[101] although a mother was not automatically entitled to custody of her children. Often, she would have to share guardianship with others.[102]

Women frequently received the right to serve as guardians for their children only on the condition that they not remarry.[103] If a widow was pregnant or had a newborn baby, she had to wait until the child was two before she could remarry, so that the child would not be neglected.[104] An exception was made if the woman was no longer nursing the baby either because it had been weaned or because she was no longer producing milk—but not if the services of a wet nurse were required, unless they had been procured three months before the death of the husband. A divorcée was free from all obligations to her husband, including nursing the child. It is not clear whether a husband had to support his wife's children from her earlier marriages. There were cases where a mother remarrying would stipulate that her children from a previous marriage had the right to live with her and her new husband.[105] However, usually it was easier for a woman to remarry if she was in possession of her dowry and free of obligations to care for children. In order to prevent the neglect or abandonment of children, some Italian rabbis adopted a more lenient position concerning the early remarriage of widows with young children.[106]

Essential to the widow's physical well-being was retrieving her *ketubah* amount, including the dowry.[107] This was not automatic or even easy, because Jewish law is based on the premise that a wife does not inherit from her husband. Often her husband's family, if it was in possession of the estate, was reluctant to part with it. Sometimes she would receive sustenance from them instead of the *ketubah* amount itself. In some attempts to recover a dowry, documents were prepared for the secular courts.[108] This was risky since the *Talmud* ruled that the widow or divorcée lost her sustenance if she requested her dowry in any court, Jewish or secular (even if it were not awarded), or became betrothed to another.[109] In 1556 Yehiel Nissim of Pisa allowed women to go to Jewish courts to claim their *ketubot*; however, as long as they were receiving adequate sustenance, they could not go to secular courts.[110] In other cases in Padua the Jewish community would appoint a representative to help with the affairs of the widow, especially the recovery of her dowry.[111] Nevertheless, according to general practices around Italy, it was customary for either surviving spouse to retain control of some funds on the death of the other when there was no issue.[112]

Given the uncertainties of providing for a female relative under Jewish law, some men, husbands or fathers, made their wills with a Christian notary.[113] Thus, some widows would survive with independent control of their own possessions, and even as executors of estates.[114] Other widows remained dependent on members of their family, and some had to rely on public assistance.[115] Those unable to procure even basic assistance in their community had to beg from town to town.[116] Italian rabbis conceded that widows faced a confusing situation in matters of inheritance, because beyond the inequities present in Jewish law, there was little agreement on women's rights among different rabbis and different communities.[117]

When women died they were mourned, like men, by close relatives tearing their garments. Candles were lit in the synagogue, especially for a wealthy woman. Soon after the interment a tombstone with lavish Hebrew inscriptions was erected. On these monuments, women were referred to in terms of their relationship with the men in their family, usually their husband or their father, and were regularly praised for their kindness, charity, and modesty.[118]

## CONCLUSION

One of the key issues in a feminist critique of Jewish law is whether the expressions of male superiority and female inferiority that appear with some frequency are an inherent aspect of the halachic system. Italian rabbis appear to have thought so, regularly invoking Genesis 3:16, "He will rule over you,"[119] and urging wives to obey and to serve their husbands.[120] Often they went beyond this and based their case on the "weakness," or even "imbecility," of women.[121]

Jewish women's domain in the Italian milieu was clearly distinct from men's, but not totally separate. An unsuccessful man was seen as entering the world of woman.[122] Conversely, the successful woman was seen as entering the realm of men, as when Modena described his mother's attempts to free his father from jail: "She girded her loins like a man and rode to Ferrara to speak to noblemen and judges."[123]

These views—essential to understanding rabbinic attitudes toward women in Italy—cannot be the only word or the final word. There was a mutual interdependence between Jewish men and Jewish women. The realm of men was, despite very limited views of women, seen as deficient without them. The Jewish leaders of Padua ruled (although only once) that a man who was not married could not be a lay leader and that marriage to a woman from Padua would convey residence rights to a man from another city.[124] Jewish women were, for the most part, extremely loyal to their religion and their community, sometimes even more than the men who enjoyed vastly superior positions. Nevertheless, they continued to function under male authority. Such apparent changes in their roles as occurred during this period were not a function of Renaissance values or a new status for women but reflections of the normal give-and-take between traditional halachic mandates and the ongoing needs of the Jewish community. Between these shifting poles women had to balance themselves as best they could.

## NOTES

I would like to thank Judith R. Baskin for inviting me to contribute to this book and thereby inaugurating a research project which has led to several additional papers: "Public Activities of Jewish Women in Italy during the Renaissance and Catholic Restoration," *Jewish History* 5 (1991); "The Educational and Literary Activities of Jewish Women in Italy during the Renaissance and the Catholic Restoration," *Shlomo Simonsohn Festschrift* (forthcoming); and "Images of Women in Italian Jewish Literature of the Late Middle Ages," *Proceedings of the Tenth World Congress of Jewish Studies* (Jerusalem, forthcoming). I would also like to acknowledge the support of the Smith College Committee on Faculty Compensation and Development, which provided funding for obtaining research materials used in preparing this study.

1. Cecil Roth, *The Jews in the Renaissance*, (Philadelphia, 1959), 49; Moses Shulvass, *The Jews in the World of the Renaissance*, trans. Elvin I. Kose (Leiden, 1973), 166.

2. Daniel Carpi, *Pinkas vaad k. k. Padova* (Jerusalem, 1973 and 1980), vol. 1, no. 652, and vol. 2, app. 17, no. 27. On restrictions placed on Jewish women's dress by Christian authorities, see Diane Owen Hughes, "Distinguishing Signs: Ear-rings, Jews and Franciscan Rhetoric in the Italian Renaissance City," *Past and Present* 112 (1986): 3–50.

3. Simhah Assaf, *Mekorot letoledot hahinnukh beyisrael* (Jerusalem, 1930–1943), 2:112.

4. Alexander Marx, "R. Yosef ish arli betor moreh verosh yeshivah besienna," in *Sefer hayovel likhvod levi ginzberg lemelat lo shivim shanah* (New York, 1945), 294.

5. Kenneth B. Stow and Sandra Debenedetti Stow, "Donne ebree a Roma nell'eta' del ghetto: Affetto, dipendenza, autonomia," *La Rassegna mensile di Israel* 52 (1986): 81.

6. Umberto Cassuto, "Les traductions judeo-italiennes du rituel," *Revue des études juives* 89 (1930): 260–80.

7. Azriel Diena, *Sheelot uteshuvot*, ed. Yacov Boksenboim (Tel Aviv, 1977), no. 6.

8. Menahem Azariah Fano, *Sheelot uteshuvot* (Venice, 1600), no. 54.

9. Cissy Grossman, "Womanly Arts: A Study of Italian Torah Binders in the New York Jewish Museum Collection," *Journal of Jewish Art* 7 (1980): 35–43.

10. A. Z. Aescoly, *Sippur David Hareuveni* (Jerusalem, 1940), 57, 82.

11. Meyer Kayserling, *Die Jüdischen Frauen in der Geschichte, Literatur und Kunst* (Leipzig, 1879; rep. New York, 1980), 158.

12. Pellegrino Ascarelli, *Debora Ascarelli Poetessa* (Rome, 1925).

13. Roth, *Renaissance*, 57.

14. Carla Boccato, "Sara Copio Sullam, La poetessa del ghetto di Venezia: Episodi sua vita in un manoscritto del secolo XVII," *Italia* 6 (1987): 104–218.

15. C. Dushinsky, "May a Woman Act As Shoheteth?" in *Occident and Orient*, ed. Bruno Schindler and A. Marmorstein (London, 1936), 96–106.

16. Samuel Aboab, *Devar shemuel* (Jerusalem, 1983), no. 353.

17. Robert Bonfil, "The Historian's Perception of the Jews in the Renaissance," *Revue des études juives* 143 (1984): 71–75.

18. See my "Simonsohn's *The Jews in Milan*," *Jewish Quarterly Review*, n.s. 77 (1986–87), 202; Stow, "Donne ebree," 68–69.

19. See my "Simonsohn's," 202.

20. Ibid.

21. Stow, "Donne ebree," 67–68; Betzalel Roth, "Tzevatah veazvonah shel eshet-hayyil miverona," *Zion* 2 (1936): 130–32.

22. Stow, "Donne ebree," 66

23. The note is translated in Jacob Marcus, *The Jew in the Medieval World* (Cincinnati, 1938), 399–400.

24. Carpi, *Padova*, vol. 1, nos. 98, 525, and vol. 2, app. 17, nos. 25–26.

25. See my "Simonsohn's," 202.

26. Carpi, *Padova*, vol. 1, no. 103.

27. On Jewish women physicians, see Assaf, *Mekorot* 2: 197–98; Diena, *Sheelot*, no. 240; Leon Modena, *Hayyei yehudah, Autobiography of a Seventeenth-Century Venetian Rabbi: Leon Modena's Life of Judah*, ed. and trans. Mark Cohen (Princeton, 1988), fols. 7a, 12a; Roth, *Renaissance*, 50; Marcello Segre, "Dottoresse ebree nel medioevo," *Pagina di storia della Medicina* 14 (1970): 98–106.

28. Abraham Yaari, *Mehkarei sefer* (Jerusalem, 1958), 256–302.

29. Carpi, *Padova*, vol.2, app.17, no. 36.

30. Meir Katzenellenbogen, *Sheelot uteshuvot* (Jerusalem, 1980), no. 26.

31. Modena, *Hayyei*, fol. 14a.

32. Leon Modena, *Ziknei yehudah*, ed. Shlomo Simonsohn (Jerusalem, 1956), no. 4.

33. Leon Modena, *Historia degli riti hebraici* (Paris, 1637), 4.8.

34. Modena, *Hayyei*, fol. 21b.

35. Roth, *Renaissance*, 47.

36. Yakov Boksenboim, *Iggerot melamedim* (Tel Aviv, 1985), Iggeron 1, nos. 36, 49, 51; Iggeron 3, no. 166; idem, *Iggerot beit carmi* (Tel Aviv, 1983), nos. 73, 178–9, 198, 276; Diena, *Sheelot*, no. 110; Assaf, *Mekorot* 2:106.

37. Brian Pullan, *The Inquisition of Venice and the Jews of Europe* (Totowa, NJ, 1983), 161; Assaf, *Mekorot* 2:112–3, 236; Boksenboim, *Carmi*, no. 129; and my "Educational and Literary Activities," esp. nn. 24, 30–31.

38. Stow, "Donne ebree," 71–72; Modena, *Hayyei*, fol. 15b; Aboab, *Devar*, no. 48.

39. Pullan, *Jews*, 61, 79–80, 226, 239.

40. Elliot Horowitz, "'Hakhnasat kalah' begetto venetziah: bein masoret uvein idial lemetziut," *Tarbiz* 56 (1987): 255; Modena, *Hayyei*, fol. 19b; Pullan, *Jews*, 80, 157, 162, 277; Roth, *Renaissance*, 45; Shulvass, *Renaissance*, 165.

41. Katzenellenbogen, *Sheelot*, no. 33.

42. Carpi, *Padova*, vol. 1, nos. 200, 204–5, 210. Joseph Colon, *Sheelot uteshuvot ufiskei maharik hahadashim*, ed. Eliahu Pines (Jerusalem, 1984), no. 36; Moses Zacuto, *Sheelot uteshuvot* (Jerusalem, 1983), no. 5; Judah Minz, *Sheelot uteshuvot* (Jerusalem, 1980), no. 5; Diena, *Sheelot*, no. 138.

43. Carla Boccato, "Il caso di un neonato esposto nel Ghetto di Venezia alla fine del '600," *La rassegna mensile di Israel* 44 (1978): 179–202.

44. Diena, *Sheelot*, no. 137.

45. Modena, *Hayyei*, fol. 9b.

46. Diena, *Sheelot*, no. 116; Katzenellenbogen, *Sheelot*, no. 74.

47. Aboab, *Devar*, no. 48.

48. Yacov Boksenboim, *Sheelot uteshuvot matanot baadam* (Tel Aviv, 1983), no. 82; Diena, *Sheelot*, no. 216; Modena, *Ziknei*, no. 99.

49. Stow, "Donne ebree," 63–64.

50. Diena, *Sheelot*, no. 134; Modena, *Historia degli riti*, 4.4.1; *Ziknei*, no. 72.

51. Modena, *Ziknei*, no. 85.

52. Colon, *Hadashim*, no. 46. For an example of an extremely passionate love letter, see Franz Kobler, *Letters of Jews throughout the Ages* (New York, 1952), 378–79; Yacov Boksenboim, ed., *Iggerot beit karmi* (Tel Aviv, 1983), 332–36.

53. Diena, *Sheelot*, 116–17.

54. Aboab, *Devar*, no. 48.

55. Pullan, *Jews*, 196, 238; Paul Grendler, *The Roman Inquistion and the Venetian Press, 1540–1605* (Princeton, NJ, 1977), 18. Horowitz, "Hakhnasat kalah," 362–71; Modena, *Hayyei*, fols. 16a-b, 18a, 20a, 21a.

56. Aaron Berechiah of Modena, *Ma 'avar Yabbok* (Mantua, 1626; Zhitomir, Russia, 1851), art. 4, sec. 14.

57. Attilio Milano, "The Private Life of a Family of Jewish Bankers at Rome in the Sixteenth Century," *Jewish Quarterly Review*, n.s. 30 (1939–40): 170.

58. Diena, *Sheelot*, no. 170; and my "Simonsohn's," 201.

59. Patricia H. Labalme, "Women's Roles in Early Modern Venice: An Exceptional Case," in *Beyond Their Sex: Learned Women of the European Past*, ed. Patricia H. Labalme (New York, 1980), 131–32; Stanley Chojnacki, "Patrician Women in Venice," *Studies in the Renaissance* 21 (1974): 185–97.

60. Louis Finkelstein, *Jewish Self-Government in the Middle Ages* (New York, 1924), 305–6, 308.

61. Aboab, *Devar*, no. 336.

62. Diena, *Sheelot*, nos. 8, 9.

63. Carpi, *Padova* vol. 2, nos. 378 and 475.

64. Colon, *Hadashim*, no. 23.

65. Boksenboim, *Melamedim*, Iggeron 1, nos. 34, 35.

66. Ibid., Iggeron 1, no. 43.

67. Idem, *Matanot*, no. 188.

68. Stow, "Donne ebree," 82–87, 105–6.

69. Diena, *Sheelot*, no. 121.

70. See my "Simonsohn's," 205.

71. Stow, "Donne ebree," 70.

72. Diena, *Sheelot*, nos. 125, 129.

73. See my "Simonsohn's," 204.

74. Diena, *Sheelot*, nos. 123, 128; Boksenboim, *Matanot*, no. 164.

75. Katzenellenbogen, *Sheelot*, no. 34.

76. Aboab, *Devar*, nos. 7, 20; Katzenellenbogen, *Sheelot*, no. 19.

77. Boksenboim, *Matanot*, no. 288.

78. Katzenellenbogen, *Sheelot*, no. 19; Aboab, *Devar*, no. 7.

79. Boksenboim, *Matanot*, no. 161; Katzenellenbogen, *Sheelot*, no. 19.

80. See my "Simonsohn's," 202.

81. Pullan, *Jews*, 103, 268–69, 272, 277, 278–79.

82. See my "Simonsohn's," 204.

83. Boksenboim, *Matanot*, nos. 176–77.

84. Colon, *Hadashim*, no. 24.

85. Pullan, *Jews*, 50–51, 54, 69–70, 227–28.

86. Benzion Netanyahu, *The Marranos of Spain* (New York, 1966), 18, 39–41.

87. Aboab, *Devar*, no. 208; Katzenellenbogen, *Sheelot*, nos. 5, 11.

88. Katzenellenbogen, *Sheelot*, no. 13.

89. Diena, *Sheelot*, no. 157; and see Z. W. Falk, *Jewish Matrimonial Law in the Middle Ages* (Oxford, 1966).

90. Modena, *Historia degli riti*, 4.2.2.

91. Katzenellenbogen, *Sheelot*, no. 13.

92. Diena, *Sheelot*, no. 122.

93. Boksenboim, *Matanot*, no. 161.

94. Katzenellenbogen, *Sheelot*, no. 8; Colon, *Sheelot*, no. 101.

95. Finkelstein, *Self-Government*, 304–5.

96. P. L. Bruzzone, "Documents sur les juifs des états pontificaux," *Revue des études juives* 19 (1889): 131–33. Stow, "Donne ebree," 75; Milano, "Family," 154–55.

97. Modena, *Ziknei*, nos. 3, 7; Katzenellenbogen, *Sheelot*, no. 13.

98. Katzenellenbogen, *Sheelot*, no. 17.

99. Ibid., no. 18.

100. Modena, *Historia degli riti*, 7; Milano, "Family," 148–49, 177–78; Stow, "Donne ebree," 92.

101. See my "Simonsohn's," 202; Stow, "Donne ebree," 77.

102. Diena, "*Sheelot*," no. 2

103. See my "Simonsohn's," 202.

104. Modena, *Historia degli riti*, 4.2.5–6; idem, *Ziknei*, no. 110.

105. Stow, "Donna ebree," 93, 99.

106. Katzenellenbogen, *Sheelot*, no. 30; Aboab, *Devar*, no. 82.

107. Boksenboim, *Matanot*, no. 155.

108. See my "Simonsohn's," 201.

109. Boksenboim, *Matanot*, no. 129; Diena, *Sheelot*, no. 199.

110. Boksenboim, *Matanot*, no. 155; see also Diena, *Sheelot*, no. 199.

111. Carpi, *Padova*, vol. 1, nos. 27, 486.

112. See my "Simonsohn's," 202; Milano, "Family," 158, 172; Modena, *Ziknei*, no. 65; Fano, *Sheelot*, no. 89.

113. Modena, *Hayyei*, ed. Cohen, 32.1.

114. Aboab, *Devar*, no. 72.

115. Stow, "Donne ebree," 88–91.

116. Carpi, *Padova*, vol.2, app.17, nos. 12, 32.

117. Aboab, *Devar*, no. 72.

118. Simon Bernstein, "Luhot Abanim II," *Hebrew Union College Annual* 10 (1935): 483–552.

119. Modena, *Ziknei*, no. 103; Aboab, *Devar*, no. 336.

120. Diena, *Sheelot*, no. 124.
121. Modena, *Historia degli riti*, 5.5.1.
122. See, e.g., Boksenboim, *Carmi*, no. 238.
123. Modena, *Hayyei*, fol. 7b.
124. Carpi, *Padova*, vol. 1, no. 572; vol. 2, app. 17, no. 44.

CHAPTER **7** CHAVA WEISSLER

*Prayers in Yiddish and the Religious World*
*of Ashkenazic Women*

---

> [The woman] says this when she puts the loaf of *berkhes*
> into the oven: Lord of all the world, in your hand is all
> blessing. I come now to revere your holiness, and I pray
> you to bestow your blessing on the baked goods. Send an
> angel to guard the baking, so that all will be well-baked,
> will rise nicely, and will not burn, to honor the holy Sab-
> bath (which you have chosen so that Israel your children
> may rest thereon) and over which one recites the holy
> blessing—as you blessed the dough of Sarah and Rebecca
> our mothers. My Lord God, listen to my voice; you are the
> God who hears the voices of those who call to you with the
> whole heart. May you be praised to eternity.
> —Yiddish Prayer

This lovely prayer is a *tkhine*,[1] one of the supplicatory prayers in Yiddish recited by Central and Eastern European Jewish women. As a
historical document, it illumines the lives of Jewish women, reflecting
what they might have been thinking as they performed their religious
duties and household tasks.

Like other genres of popular religious literature, these prayers began
to appear in print in the sixteenth century. Because *tkhines*, as well as
ethical works, collections of pious tales, and Bible paraphrases were in

Yiddish (the vernacular of Ashkenazic Jews), they were available to women, who rarely mastered Hebrew, the sacred tongue and the language of scholarly communication. An analysis of women's religious lives forms a necessary corrective to the overwhelming majority of studies of the history of Judaism relying primarily on sources produced by and for learned men, always a small minority of the Jewish people. Taking the religion of women and other nonlearned Jews into account must inevitably cause us to revise our view of Ashkenazic Judaism.

## THE *TKHINES* AS A SOURCE
## FOR WOMEN'S HISTORY

Yiddish *tkhines* and other popular religious material enable us to reconstruct the religious lives of "ordinary Jews." Because women so rarely received more than the rudiments of a Jewish education, they left only a scant literary legacy of their own. Further, they were excluded from the major arenas of Jewish public life: the government of the *kehillah*, the rabbinical court, the yeshiva, the house of study, the kabbalistic conventicle, and the hasidic gathering. Even in the synagogue, they could not lead services, read from the Torah, or count in a *minyan* (the required quorum of adults for public prayer); and they sat screened from men's eyes behind a curtain, in a balcony or completely separate room.

Modern critics of the role of women in Jewish life have often assumed that this must have meant that women had no religious lives to speak of or that their religion was only a pale shadow of the religious lives of men, who had more direct access to the great classics of Jewish tradition, and to the important arenas of Jewish religious life. Others have suggested that women had a religious culture of their own, influenced by the scholarly and male formulations of Judaism but also in part independent of them, or that women adapted the religious language created by men for their own purposes.

For many periods in Jewish history, because of the paucity of sources, it is nearly impossible to decide which of these views might be correct. In the search for evidence concerning women's religious culture, the popular religious literature in Yiddish, including the *tkhines*, is an especially precious historical resource. The very fact that these works were published shows that important religious movements, such as the Lurianic revival, Sabbatian messianism, and has-idism, could have had some impact on women.

Yet there are certain difficulties involved in using this material to write the religious history of Ashkenazic women. The central issue is that most of this literature, written by men for women, represents *men's* conceptions of women's religious lives and as evidence about women is necessarily indirect. Since these works were enormously popular among women, they must have appealed to women in some ways; but this material is not about "real" women in the same way that women's letters and diaries, or even rabbinical responsa would be. Rather, these texts contain evidence about what was made *available* to women as part of the raw materials for their own conceptualization of their religious lives. As to what women did with these raw materi-als, in some cases it may be possible to suggest an answer.[2]

While most popular religious literature in Yiddish was written by men, some *tkhines* were written by women. Thus, *tkhines* in particular are a suggestive body of material for the examination of the religious language that was made available to women and of women's transfor-mations of this language. *Tkhines* can show us what women prayed about and how they understood the meanings of their religious acts. *Tkhines* also shed light on how women viewed the areas defined by Ashkenazic culture as women's religious domain and how they felt about the areas of religious life reserved for men.

There are two main categories of *tkhines*. The first group appeared in Western Europe in the seventeenth and eighteenth centuries, and were probably written or compiled by men for women; the second group originated in Eastern Europe in the eighteenth and early nine-teenth centuries, and some of these were written or reworked by women.

## THE WESTERN EUROPEAN *TKHINES*

Although there are scattered instances of *tkhines* published in the six-teenth century and although a short, atypical collection of *tkhines*, entitled *Tkhine zu* (This *tkhine*), was published in 1590 in Prague, the real appearance of this genre is in the mid-seventeenth century.[3] Be-ginning in 1648, and up through the first few decades of the eigh-teenth century, collections of about thirty *tkhines* were published in

Prague, Amsterdam, and various German towns. Then some time about the middle of the eighteenth century, these various collections were combined into one longer, standard work containing about a hundred and twenty *tkhines*, which was published in many different editions in German towns such as Fürth and Sulzbach, usually under the title of *Seder tkhines u-vakoshes* (Order of supplications and petitions). This collection became very popular, and was reprinted with only minor variations, first in Western and then in Eastern Europe. Many of the texts it contains are reworkings or paraphrases of Hebrew literary models.[4] As in all collections of *tkhines*, the individual prayers contained in the *Seder tkhines u-vakoshes*[5] have headings explaining when they should be said, for example: "Every woman should say this every day, morning and evening" (no. 38); "When a woman's husband is travelling, for his benefit she should say this *tkhine* for him with great devotion" (no. 59); "When a woman becomes pregnant, she should say this every day or when she is giving birth" (no. 95); and "On the eve of the Day of Atonement at nightfall before *Kol nidrei* one should say this *tkhine* with devotion" (no. 85). Thus, an examination of the "table of contents" of a representative work such as *Seder tkhines u-vakoshes* can reveal a great deal about the structuring of women's religious lives. Nonetheless, we do need to keep in mind the question whether *tkhine* collections can best be analyzed as *descriptive* or *prescriptive* of women's lives. After using this material to map out the domains and occasions of women's religious activity, we shall examine in greater detail one set of *tkhines* in particular, those for *niddah*, pregnancy, and childbirth. There we shall see that even in material probably compiled by men there may be echoes of women's voices and that in any case there is a range of views about the meaning of particular religious acts.

The distinctiveness of *tkhines* as prayers for women can be thrown into greater relief by comparing them to the standard liturgy. *Tkhines* are quite different from the prayers of the Hebrew liturgy, which are regulated by clock and calendar: morning, afternoon, and evening prayers, weekday, Sabbath, and festival prayers. The prayers of the *siddur* (the Hebrew prayerbook) are most typically phrased in the plural; by preference they are recited in public, in the midst of the worshiping community, defined primarily as a community of men. *Tkhines*, by contrast, were almost always phrased in the singular and often had space for the petitioner to insert her own name, thus making her address to God intensely personal. Further, *tkhines* were voluntary prayers, recited when the woman wished and most typically at home. And although *tkhines* were voluntary, we can reasonably assume if a *tkhine* exists for a particular event—and especially if many *tkhines* exist for an event—that that event had religious significance for at least some women.

Some of the occasions for which *tkhines* were written are those we might expect, knowing that all women certainly participated in the round of the liturgical calendar and that some women did regularly attend synagogue. In fact, there was a special prayer leader, a learned woman known as the *firzogerin* or *zogerke*, who led the women's section of the synagogue in reciting the liturgy and the *tkhines*. Not surprisingly, then, the *Seder tkhines u-vakoshes* contains prayers connected with the liturgy or the synagogue service, for each day of the week and for the Sabbath. Other *tkhines* concern the penitential season (from the beginning of the month of Elul, one month before the New Year, through the Day of Atonement), confessions of sins, and the festivals. There are *tkhines* for each of the fast days and several prayers for days on which one undertakes a private fast.

All these occasions were common to the religious lives of women and men. Other *tkhines* fall more squarely into areas of concern that were defined as belonging to women. Foremost among them were the special "women's commandments," three religious duties singled out as incumbent especially on women: *ḥallah* (separating out a small portion of the dough in memory of the priestly tithes), *hadlaqah* (lighting candles on the eve of Sabbaths and festivals); and *niddah* (marital separation during menstruation and ritual immersion after menstruation).[6] Connected with *niddah* are the *tkhines* for pregnancy and childbirth, indubitably in women's biological domain. And while both women and men die and both seem to have visited the cemetery to pay respects to the dead, contact with and petitioning the dead was also an important topic for *tkhines* and an arena of piety that seems overwhelmingly to have been associated with women.

Some *tkhines* are personal petitions concerning children and family; one is for "a widow [to] say with great devotion so that the dear God may once again give her what she asks of him" (no. 71). Several *tkhines* contain petitions for recovery from illness, for rain during a drought, and for sustenance and livelihood. There are also a few prayers for the New Moon (Rosh Hodesh), which was a minor holiday for women.[7]

From the list of nonliturgical *tkhines*, there emerges a set of occasions of special importance to women. They were defined, whether biologically or culturally, as being in the women's domain: pregnancy and childbirth, the family, the "women's commandments." Events that were also important to men but which seem to have had distinctive significance for women were the New Moon; the Days of Awe; and contact with, and petitioning of, the dead. *Tkhines* hallowed women's biological lives and domestic routines. Menstruation, pregnancy, and childbirth were considered *religious* events, important subjects for prayer. And by reciting *tkhines*, women could also sanctify the ordinary events of home life: baking bread, preparing for the Sabbath, bringing up children.

Indeed, the *tkhines* give us the sense that women's religious lives were less public and communal than men's. Women's domain was the home (and the marketplace, although this was not conceived of in *religious* terms); and most *tkhines* are clearly intended to be recited individually, at home or in other settings, such as the bathhouse or the cemetery.[8]

Thus, the liturgy of the siddur (prayerbook containing the synagogue liturgy) and the literature of the *tkhines* contrast in many ways: the siddur is in Hebrew, the sacred and scholarly language, while the *tkhines* are in the vernacular Yiddish; the prayers of the siddur are fixed and obligatory, while those of the *tkhine* collections are voluntary and thus flexible; and the prayers of the siddur are recited, by preference, communally, while *tkhines* are recited individually.

This summary raises a methodological issue. This discussion has treated the *tkhines* as neutral evidence about women's religious lives. By noting the occasions for which *tkhines* existed, I have sought to show what events were of religious importance to women. Yet to the extent that *tkhines*, written by men, actually *shaped* women's religious identitities, this approach is probably too simple, or perhaps naive. Thus, it may be more precise to say that the list of *tkhine* topics shows how the religious lives of women were constructed by Ashkenazic culture; the domains, occasions, and understandings of religious life that the *tkhines* made available to women were part of the definition of women's roles in that culture.

This process of construction is exemplified in the *tkhines* for *niddah*, pregnancy, and childbirth. The *Seder tkhines u-vakoshes* contains a sequence of thirteen consecutive prayers connected to these topics.[9] The sequence begins with "A *tkhine* for when a woman bites off the stem of the *etrog*" (no. 89) and includes such items as "When a woman wishes to immerse herself [in the ritual bath] she says this *tkhine*" (no. 92), "A *tkhine* for when the woman goes to give birth" (no. 100), and "A *tkhine* for the mother to say when her child is carried to circumcision" (no. 102). A close examination and contrast of two of these texts, the *tkhine* for post-menstrual self-inspection during the seven "clean" days (no. 91) and the *tkhine* for biting off the end of the *etrog* (no. 89) reveals two rather different responses to the biblical story explaining the pains of childbirth—and by rabbinic extension, also the pains of menstruation—as the punishment for Eve's sin.[10]

According to Jewish law, all physical contact between husband and wife is forbidden during the wife's menstrual period, and for seven days thereafter. During these seven "clean" or "white" days, the wife must inspect herself to make certain the flow of blood has completely ceased. At the end of the seven days, she immerses herself in the *mikveh*, the ritual bath, and resumes marital relations and other forms of physical contact with her husband. Although there are no *tkhines* for the onset of menstruation (either a girl's first menstruation—a subject for ritual and celebration in some other cultures—or subsequent regular menses), *tkhines* do exist for the other stages of the cycle. These quite-physical aspects of women's biological lives are considered fit topics for prayer, as the first text illustrates:

> She says this *tkhine* when she has put on white [for postmenstrual inspection] with great devotion:
>
> God and my King, you are merciful. Who can tell or know your justice or your judgment? They are as deep as brooks of water and the depths of springs. You punished Eve, our old Mother, because she persuaded her husband to trespass against your commandment, and he ate from the tree which was forbidden them. You spoke with anger that in sadness she would give birth [cf. Genesis 3:16]. So we women must suffer each time, and have our regular periods, with heavy hearts. Thus, I have had my period with a heavy heart, and with sadness, and I thank your holy Name and your judgment, and I have received it with great love from my great Friend[11] as a punishment. And I have waited until

the time when every pious woman in Israel waits, according to the command of our sages, following our holy Torah. Now comes the time for me to purify myself according to the command of our sages, up until the time of my immersion. God, my God, may my putting on [white] be acceptable, and let me remain pure up till the time when I go to immerse myself. You are he who helps to purify those who desire to be pure. May the speech of my mouth and the thoughts of my heart be acceptable before you, God, my creator and redeemer.

While this prayer contains several themes, such as the desire for purity and a sense of community with the pious women of Israel, it seems chiefly designed to reconcile the women who recited it both with the discomfort of their menstrual cycles and with an interpretation of this discomfort as a just punishment of all women for Eve's sin. By voicing a question about God's justice, the *tkhine* does recognize, indirectly, that women's situation might seem unjust but goes on to squelch this thought by having the reciter thank God for her periodic punishment.

The second text, for biting off the end of the *etrog*, refers to a folk religious practice. The *etrog* (citron) is used, along with the *lulav* (palm branch) together with myrtle and willow twigs during the liturgy of the week-long fall harvest festival of Sukkot. For the *etrog* to be fit for ritual use, it must be intact; in particular, the *pittam* (raised blossom-end tip of the fruit) must not have been broken off. There were two, probably interrelated, folk beliefs concerning the *pittam* of the *etrog*. The first, attested in twentieth-century ethnographic materials, was the belief that childless women would conceive if they bit off and swallowed the *pittam*.[12] The second, attested in the seventeenth- and eighteenth-century *tkhines*,[13] was the belief that by biting off the end of the *etrog*, pregnant women would ensure a safe and easy childbirth. Of course, in either case, the woman was supposed to wait until the end of the holiday so as not to render the *etrog* unfit for ritual use. Apparently, there were tales of desperate childless women who would snatch the *etrog* and defiantly bite off the *pittam* in the middle of the holiday. (Citrons were far more rare and expensive in seventeeth-, eighteenth-, and nineteenth-century Europe than in modern Jewish communities, and there might only have been one in a town.)[14]

The *tkhine* for biting off the end of the *etrog* appears in the *Seder tkhines u-vakoshes*; but it is also found in an older source, the *Tsenerene*

(Go forth and see). This work, which contains Yiddish homilies on the biblical portions of the week, was so beloved it became known as "the women's Bible." The *Tsenerene* was first published around 1600, although the earliest editions are no longer extant; it went through well over three hundred editions in the next three centuries.[15] The way the *Tsenerene* introduces this *tkhine* gives some indication of its possible origin and the setting in which it was recited. The context is a discussion deriving from the Midrash[16] about what kind of tree the Tree of Knowledge was:

> Some sages say that it was a citron tree. Therefore, the custom is that women take the *etrog* and bite off the end on Hoshana Rabba [the seventh day of Sukkot], and give money to charity, since charity saves from death [cf. Proverbs 6:2], and they pray to God to be protected from the sufferings of bearing the children they are carrying, that they may give birth easily. Had Eve not eaten from the Tree of Knowledge, each woman would give birth as easily as a hen lays an egg, without pain. The woman should pray and should say:[17]
>
> "Lord of the World, because Eve ate of the fruit all of us women must suffer such great pangs as [almost] to die. Had I been there, I would not have had any enjoyment from [the fruit]. Just so, now I have not wanted to render the *etrog* unfit during the whole seven days when it was used for a mitzvah. But now, on Hoshana Rabba, the mitzvah is no longer applicable, but I am [still] not in a hurry to eat it. And just as little enjoyment as I get from the stem of the *etrog* would I have gotten from the fruit which you forbade."[18]

This is a fascinating text on two counts. First, the account of it in the *Tsenerene* suggests that it may represent an oral tradition among women.[19] Second, here, in contrast to the *tkhine* for putting on white, the reciter repudiates Eve's sin and, by implication, *its consequences for her*. She points out that unlike Eve, who disobeyed God, she has kept God's commandment concerning the *etrog* and strongly implies that if she had been in Eve's place, she would not have eaten of the forbidden fruit of the Tree of Knowledge. Therefore, the text suggests, she ought not suffer the pains of childbirth with which Eve was punished.

Thus, two *tkhines* (which are, incidentally, printed on the same page of the *Seder tkhines u-vakoshes*) express two quite different views of the relationship of women both to Eve, the first woman, and to their own biological processes. It is perhaps tempting to speculate that the first text was composed by a man while the second does indeed

reflect some women's traditions; but this would be no more than specu-
lation. What is clear is that even in a work that was in all likelihood
compiled and edited by a man or men, no monolithic view of women
was present. If the *tkhines* shaped women's religious self-understand-
ing, they at least presented women with a variety of images.

## THE EASTERN EUROPEAN *TKHINES*

Our discussion of the Western European *tkhines* has shown us the
range of occasions that made up the framework of women's religious
lives and a few of the themes and images connected with menstruation
and childbirth. A consideration of the Eastern European materials will
show how the conventions of the genre were transformed. The *tkhines*
published in Eastern Europe treat a more limited repertoire of topics
than the Western European collections but present a much more diverse world of individual authors. Because there are some women authors, these texts can show us women's concerns and women's appro-
priation of religious language and concepts more clearly than could
the Western European materials.

Although some *tkhines* were probably published in Eastern Europe
as early as the sixteenth century, the texts that appeared before the
eighteenth century seem to have been almost entirely lost.[20] It is difficult to be specific about dates because, unlike the Western European
*tkhines*, Eastern European texts were published in little booklets with
no place of publication or date noted, until well into the nineteenth
century. The extant earlier Eastern European collections, which can
be dated on the basis of typography to the late eighteenth or early
nineteenth century, were rather different from the Western European
material. These *tkhines* usually appeared in quite short collections of
eight to twelve pages, and some were as short as four pages. (Sometimes, these short texts could also be assembled into larger booklets.)
These texts display a distinct shift in the range of subjects they address. Unlike the broad range of occasions covered by the Western
European *Seder tkhines u-vakoshes*, which, it is important to remember,
was also being reprinted in Eastern Europe, the Eastern European texts
usually confined themselves to just one theme or a few related topics.
But even if we take all the material in the aggregate, the range of
subjects is more limited than that found in the Western European

materials and more closely tied to the synagogue and the liturgical calendar. By far the most popular topic is the penitential season, including *tkhines* for the month of Elul, and for Rosh Hashanah and Yom Kippur. Other common themes are the Sabbath and the New Moon. There are also scattered texts dealing with other subjects such as the women's mitzvot, the struggle for sustenance and livelihood, and spiritual preparation for prayer. The overall emphasis on liturgical events suggests that in contrast to their counterparts in Western Europe, Eastern European *tkhine* authors and/or readers were more interested in women's relationship to the communal religious domain of men and somewhat less interested in the religious meanings of other aspects of their lives.

In addition, unlike most Western European *tkhine* collections, the Eastern European texts often name a woman as author or translator or as in some other way connected with the work. These author statements appear in fascinating variety. They range from prosaic attributions to historically documentable or perfectly ordinary-sounding women to such statements as "We found this *tkhine* in the possession of the righteous, famous rabbi's wife, Mistress Hene . . . who received it from her mother-in-law, the pious, famous, righteous rabbi's wife, Mistress Leah Rayzel," "The righteous woman who thought this up, because of her great piety, did not mention her name," or, "This was found in the *tkhine* pouch [*be-amtahat ha-tehinnot*] left by the righteous rabbi's wife, Mistress Rachel Hinde." If all this is not simply printers' hyperbole, this language may indicate some sort of women's tradition of writing and collecting *tkhines*. Some of the Eastern *tkhines* were also attributed to male authors, named or unnamed; and many were also anonymous.

The question of whether or not any of the texts attributed to female authors were actually written by women is a vexed one, and I cannot enter into all the arguments here.[21] Despite the fact that beginning in the mid-nineteenth century, *maskilim*, Jewish intellectuals influenced by the Enlightenment, did write *tkhines* to which they attached, for commercial motives, fictitious women's names, there is good evidence that at least some of the eighteenth-century texts attributed to women were actually written by women.

An examination of the *tkhines* attributed to two East European women reveals quite different approaches. Sarah Rebecca Rachel Leah Horowitz (c. 1720–c. 1800), author of the *Tkhine imohes* (Tkhine of the matriarchs), was concerned with the power and importance of women's prayer. Sarah bas Tovim, the legendary figure to whom the *Tkhine Shloyshe she'orim* (Tkhine of three gates) is attributed, combined eschatological and domestic concerns in a single tightly woven fabric and looked beyond this world to another, where women could study Torah like men. Both authors were interested in ways of appropriating aspects of men's religiosity such as public prayer, mystical prayer, and Torah study for the use of women. Both authors, although their level of learning differs, were also far more knowledgeable of Jewish classic texts, whether in the original or in translation, than the average Ashkenazic woman, exemplifying the historiographic problem that written texts are produced by intellectual elites. Nonetheless, their writings can shed light on women's religious lives generally, since other women shared their concerns.

Sarah Rebecca Rachel Leah Horowitz, usually called Leah by her family and friends, is referred to in several independent sources. The memoirist Ber of Bolechow recalls meeting her when she was a young married woman living in the home of her brother, then rabbi of Bolechow in Southern Poland.[22] The sources depict her as an accomplished Talmudic scholar (a very rare achievement for a woman) and as possessing something of a sharp tongue when her rights to rabbinic learning were challenged. Leah was part of a distinguished rabbinical family; the Horowitzes belonged to the scholarly aristocracy of Ashkenazic Jewry. Her father seems to have been involved in the prehasidic circle of mystics known as the *kloyz* in the Galician city of Brody, where he was rabbi from 1735 to circa 1742.[23] The indications in Leah's writings that she was familiar with the esoteric literature of the Kabbalah suggest that she, too, was influenced by the religious ferment surrounding the rise of hasidism.

Although at least one other *tkhine* was attributed to her,[24] Leah's only extant work is the *Tkhine imohes*,[25] a work unique in the genre because its three sections are in three different languages. The work begins with an introduction in Hebrew; it contains a *piyyut* (a liturgical poem) in Aramaic, and concludes with a Yiddish prose paraphrase of the *piyyut*. Except for a very few early editions, the later reprints of this *tkhine* include *only* the Yiddish section, which was intended to be recited in synagogue on the Sabbath preceding the New Moon. While the *piyyut* and its Yiddish paraphrase are of considerable interest, in particular for the use they make of the figures of the four matriarchs,[26] the discussion here will focus on the introduction.

Leah Horowitz was passionately concerned with the religious place and role of Jewish women and keenly felt her own anomalous status as a learned woman. Her views about women seem ambivalent: while she defended her own right to her knowledge of classical sources, she seems to have considered herself so exceptional that she could not imagine other similarly learned women. Nonetheless, she believed that women had the potential for real spiritual power.

Leah addresses these issues explicitly in the Hebrew introduction to her *tkhine*. This is the only premodern text known to me in which an Ashkenazic woman discusses such issues as the significance of women's prayer, the proper way for women to pray, and the circumstances under which women should and should not submit to their husband's authority. Thus, the two-page introduction to this *tkhine* is an extremely precious historical document. Yet it must be read with pain: writing for and about women in Hebrew, Leah literally had no audience. Since men were not interested and women could not read Hebrew, Leah's efforts to speak about women's prayer and women's power and attempts to legitimate her own voice as authoritative were ignored. After one or two editions, printers simply omitted the Hebrew introduction (and usually the *piyyut* as well) from their reissues of this popular work.

From the outset, Leah was particularly concerned to establish the legitimacy of her participation in the traditionally male domains of Talmudic discussion and halachic argument. Near the beginning of the introduction, she writes, "Although you may say that a woman is not competent in reasoned argument, nonetheless, 'the crown of Torah is left [for the generations],' and in my view, I am bringing merit to the many." Quoting Ecclesiastes Rabbah 7:2 here, Leah may also be thinking of Avot de-Rabbi Nathan 41 which declares that although the crowns of priesthood and kingship are restricted to certain segments of the population, "the crown of Torah is not thus. Whoever wishes to undertake to toil in the Torah may do so"—even (Leah implies) herself, a woman. Indeed, throughout the introduction, Leah's densely textured argument, couched in the traditional phraseology of source citation, is direct evidence of her mastery of classical Jewish literature.

Leah also discusses the proper religious role for women in general, especially the nature and importance of women's prayer. In the introduction she carries on an explicit polemic about several aspects of women's religious activity. Two major interrelated themes are the importance of women's prayer and the nature of proper prayer (which is understood kabbalistically). Secondary themes include critiques of behaviors and practices Leah considered improper and a discussion of the proper balance of authority between husband and wife. Throughout, Leah argues that women have greater religious importance than is usually thought.

In the course of the introduction Leah underlines the power of women's prayer when that prayer is undertaken with proper devotion. Part of the point of the introduction is to prove that "there can be prayer for the sake of heaven" from women. After supporting this point with reference to a medieval commentary,[27] Leah remarks tartly, "I have many other proofs. . . . This matter has certainly not escaped the discerning eye, and I will not speak in the ears of a fool."

She also stresses that despite the fact that more commandments apply to men, women have the power to bring redemption. This is partly because of the redemptive power of tears, and "tears are common among women." Unfortunately, the full redemptive power of women's prayer is blocked, because prayer is only heard when it is recited in synagogue,[28] and in these sinful generations, women do not attend synagogue for daily prayers. Leah makes it clear that in her view women should attend synagogue every day, morning and evening. But when they do come to synagogue, she notes, women often spend their time in idle chatter, comparing their clothes and jewelry, instead of praying with true devotion.[29]

Leah devotes considerable attention to her belief that proper prayer is for the sake of the Shekhinah (Divine Presence), the tenth *sefirah* or emanation of the Godhead, who mediates between the human and divine worlds. According to Jewish mystical teaching, the Shekhinah, like Israel, is in exile; and it is the goal of all true prayer and religious performance to end this exile and reunite her with her divine consort, Tiferet, the sixth *sefirah*.[30] The full and final reunification will only come in the era of messianic redemption; indeed, the redemption *is* the cosmic reunification. This is the redemption that women can bring about through their devoted and tearful prayer in synagogue.[31]

In a kabbalistic exegesis of Isaiah 1:12, Leah contrasts the devotion that the Shekhinah requires from the worshipers with the "trampling of the courts" that occurs when they instead engage in idle chatter in the synagogue. By further textual interpretation, Leah seeks to show that the problem with women's prayer is that women pray for their own material benefit, instead of for the sake of the exiled Shekhinah. With this argument, Leah polemicizes *against* the "simple" understanding of prayer as asking God for help and also against the recital of many popular *tkhines* whose purpose was to beg God for sustenance and livelihood.

Leah also takes up the question of women's obedience to their husbands, and, together with this, the famous Talmudic passage, "By what means do women acquire merit? By sending their sons to learn in the synagogue and their husbands to study in the schools of the rabbis, and waiting patiently for them to return home."[32] She is astonished that these vicarious acts could be the only means of women's acquiring merit, since all of the negative and most of the positive commandments that apply to men also apply to women. This cannot be what the Talmud meant. Rather, she argues, relying on a linguistic argument, the Talmud is actually asking, "Under what circumstances should women prevail over their husbands?" Under ordinary circumstances, women should obey their husbands. As Leah puts it, "In all the matters of this world [in which] it is fitting for him to be a man, let him be a man: 'Even a weaver is in charge in his own house!'"[33] But regarding "matters of the world to come," such as Torah study, the Talmud specifies that in this area women should prevail over their husbands and prevent them from neglecting Torah study or from causing such neglect on the part of their children.

In sum, Leah's introduction to the *Tkhine imohes* gives a mixed picture of women and their religious role. Her underlying assumption is that women *should* be present in the public domain of the synagogue (of course, in the women's section) and *can* and *should* engage in mystical, redemptive "prayer for the sake of heaven." Further, she argues that key religious texts about women have been misunderstood, to the detriment of women. Nonetheless, Leah states clearly that "a worthy woman does the will of her husband"; women's subordination to men is, under most circumstances, a fact of life.

While Leah Horowitz is easily documentable as a historical personage, this is not the case for Sarah, daughter of Mordecai (or Jacob) of Satanow, known as Sarah bas Tovim,[34] to whom the *Tkhine Shloyshe*

*she'orim* was attributed.[35] Sarah is a far more mysterious figure. All of the information we have about her comes from her own pen. No external documents have surfaced so far to corroborate Sarah's existence. In her *tkhines* she indicates that she was rich in her youth and became poor and was forced to become a wanderer. Some statements may indicate that she considered her writing of the *tkhine* to be a memorial for her after death because she had no children. Most unusually, no husband is mentioned; perhaps Sarah was unmarried. From the text, it is clear that Sarah knew a certain amount of Hebrew and was familiar with a number of Yiddish paraphrases and adaptations of classical Jewish sources. She was less learned than Leah and more rooted in the world of folk religious practice. An entire section of the *Shloyshe she-'orim* is a liturgy for the custom women had of making memorial candles from wicks that had been used to measure graves in the cemetery.[36]

Because of the great literary power and consequent popularity of the *Shloyshe she'orim*, impoverished male writers, composing *tkhines* as potboilers in the second half of the nineteenth century, made frequent pseudonymous use of Sarah's name, casting doubt on her actual existence.[37] In the course of time, Sarah bas Tovim became a figure of legendary proportions. A short story by the nineteenth-century writer, I. L. Peretz, probably drawing on material in oral tradition, depicts her as a sort of fairy godmother who appears magically to help pious women and girls who faithfully recite her *tkhines*.[38]

Thus, it is unclear whether there was a woman called Sarah bas Tovim who wrote all or most of the *Shloyshe she'orim*; and it is also unclear what the exact text of the work should be.[39] On balance, it seems likely that the author of much of this text was a woman, to whom I shall refer, for convenience, as Sarah bas Tovim. Whoever its author was, the text contains a distinctive and powerful literary voice, one that interweaves autobiography, homely and "womanly" concerns, and eschatological themes into one shining fabric:

> I, Sarah bas Tovim, I do this for the sake of the dear God, blessed be he and blessed be his name, and arrange, this second time, yet another beautiful new *tkhine* concerning three gates. The first gate is founded upon the three commandments which we women were commanded: [The acronym] *Hanna"h* is their name . . . that is to say, separating dough for *hallah*, observing menstrual avoidances [*niddah*], and kindling Sabbath lights [*hadlaqat ha-nerot*]. The second gate is a *tkhine* to

pray when one blesses the New Moon. The third gate concerns the Days of Awe.

I take for my help the living God, blessed be he, who lives forever and to eternity, and I set out this second beautiful new *tkhine* in Yiddish with great love, with great awe, with trembling and terror. . . . May God have mercy upon me and upon all Israel. May I not long be forced to be a wanderer, by the merit of our Mothers, Sarah, Rebecca, Rachel, and Leah. And my own dear mother Leah pray to God, blessed be he, for me, that my being a wanderer may be an atonement for me for my sins.

While parts of the *Shloyshe she'orim* are concerned with the holiness inherent in women's domestic and familial roles, the portion I wish to consider here, a description of the "women's Paradise," portrays women less traditionally, as powerful religious personalities and students of Torah. This description is part of the "gate" for the New Moon.[40] This "gate" draws heavily on external sources, works of Jewish mysticism adapted into Yiddish. It shows how women could use the materials made available to them by men, who were the popularizers and translators of kabbalistic texts. Sarah describes the women's paradise as follows:

There are also there in Paradise six chambers in which there are several thousand righteous women who have never suffered the pains of Hell. Bithia the Queen, daughter of Pharaoh,[41] is there. There is a place in Paradise where a curtain is prepared to be opened, which allows her to see the image of Moses our Teacher. Then she bows and says, How worthy is my strength and how knowing is my power! I drew such a light out of the water, I brought up this dear light! This happens three times a day.

In the next chamber, there are also thousands upon thousands upon myriads of women, and Serah daughter of Asher[42] is a queen. And every day it is announced three times, Here comes the image of Joseph the Righteous! Then she bows to him and says, Praised is my strength, and how worthy is my power, that I was privileged to tell my lord Jacob that my uncle was alive. And in the upper chamber, he studies Torah, and in the other chamber, they sing hymns and praises, and study Torah.

After describing the next two chambers, which are presided over by Jocheved (the mother of Moses) and Deborah, the passage concludes: "And the chambers of the matriarchs cannot be described; no one can come into their chambers. Now, dear women, when the souls are to-gether in paradise, how much joy there is! Therefore, I pray you to praise God with great devotion, and to say your prayers, that you may be worthy to be there with our Mothers." As I have shown else-where,[43] this remarkable passage derives from the *Zohar*, the great classic of medieval Jewish mysticism, via an intermediate source in Yiddish, the *Sefer Maʿasei Adonai*,[44] which contains translations and paraphrases of material from a variety of mystical works. Both Yiddish versions of this motif—that found in the *tkhine* and that found in the *Sefer Maʿasei Adonai*—differ from the original in ways that expand somewhat the spiritual aspirations deemed appropriate for women. It is important to note two significant features of this passage. First, it depicts women as *lernen toyre*. This phrase denotes "studying Torah," that is, the primary religious duty of Jewish men, from which women were excused or excluded. But in Paradise, at least according to the *Shloyshe sheʿorim*, women engage in this most holy of activities. The assertion that women could study Torah, even if only in Paradise, must have seemed quite revolutionary; it was expunged from some later editions of the text, which simply say that Joseph studied Torah in an upper chamber while the women sang God's praises below. (In-deed, the entire description of the women's Paradise is lacking in some late-nineteenth-century editions of this *tkhine*.) Second, and perhaps most striking is that Bithia and Seraḥ boldly proclaim their strength and their spiritual power. By depicting biblical women and the women in Paradise in this way, the text allowed the reciter of this *tkhine* to imagine herself in a radically different situation from that in which she lived. As she read this text, the woman could picture herself sur-rounded by myriads of righteous women, all devoting themselves to studying Torah and praising God.

## CONCLUSION

Sarah's vision would have been Paradise indeed for Reyna Basya, daughter of Isaac ben Hayyim Volozhiner, and wife of Naphtali Zevi Judah Berlin, both eminent leaders of the nineteenth-century Lithu-anian Jewish community. As her nephew records in his memoirs, she was driven to a state of distraction by "the disgrace of women, and the denigration of their value, in that they were forbidden to study Torah."[45] Living a century later than Leah Horowitz, Reyna Basya may represent the culmination of a trend in the religious history of Eastern European Jewish women. While still living a fully traditional Jewish life, Reyna Basya articulates, much more clearly than Leah, her pain at her exclusion from the religious world of Jewish men. It is not yet clear what caused the shift suggested by the evolution of the *tkhine* literature from a focus on a separate domain belonging to women as the heart of their religious lives to an effort, on the part of some learned women, to define a role for women in the male arenas of the synagogue and the house of study. Possible factors include the influence of hasidism, the rise of the *musar* yeshivot, and concern with the role of women in European society in general.

Be that as it may, this exploration of the *tkhine* literature has given us some important insights. *Tkhines* articulate both the sanctification of women's traditional roles and a critique of them. A woman content with a religious life focused on the home and family and a peripheral relationship to the men's world of prayer and study could use *tkhines* to render that life holy. Even the mundane domestic chore of baking bread could be understood as a sacred act shared with the ancient matriarchs and guarded by angels. And *tkhines* provided a range of views on the religious meaning of such bodily processes as menstruation and childbirth.

Nonetheless, there is a tension in the *tkhine* literature between the centering of women's religious life in the domestic domain and the aspirations to move beyond it found in some of the Eastern European authors. These women make use of rabbinic and mystical texts to shape a new vision of women's religious lives in which women's prayer was as significant as men's and where some women under some circumstances could study Torah. Whether the *tkhine* literature can be said to constitute a full-fledged religious language for women, however, is a question that must remain for future research.

## NOTES

An earlier version of this essay entitled "Traditional Yiddish Literature: A Source for the Study of Women's Religious Lives," was delivered as the Jacob Pat Memorial Lecture, Harvard University Library, 26 February 1987, and was published in pamphlet form by Harvard University Library in 1988. It is published here, in revised form, with the permission of the president and fellows of Harvard College. I also wish to express my gratitude to the National Endowment for the Humanities (NEH) and to Harvard Divinity School (HDS). An NEH fellowship for independent study and research in 1985, and a research associateship at HDS in 1986–87, gave me access to library resources and the necessary free time to pursue the questions I explore in this chapter.

1. *Berkhes* is the Western Yiddish word for the braided Sabbath bread, called *hallah* by some Eastern European Jews. The text is found in *Tkhines* (Amsterdam, 1648), col. [5c], and many later editions of the same collection, usually entitled *Seder Tkhines*. Titles of books whose text is entirely or primarily in Yiddish will be romanized according to their Yiddish pronunciation, even if all the words in the title are also in Hebrew. The Yiddish word *tkhine* (pl. *tkhines*) derives from the Hebrew *tehinnah* (pl. *tehinnot*), meaning "supplication." For a more detailed discussion of the *tkhine* literature, see my "Traditional Piety of Ashkenazic Women," in *Jewish Spirituality*, ed. Arthur Green, (New York, 1987), 2:245–75. I have used some language from that chapter in the present essay, especially in the discussion of the domains and occasions of women's religious lives.

2. For a more detailed discussion of the methodological issues involved in using popular Yiddish religious literature for the study of women's religious lives, see my "The Religion of Traditional Ashkenazic Women: Some Methodological Issues," *Association for Jewish Studies Review* 12 (1987): 73–94.

3. A late sixteenth-century book of *tkhines*, entitled *Ayn gor sheyne tkhine*, published in Prague or Cracow, has recently been acquired by the Jewish National and University Library, Jerusalem. This book was published at the initiative of women and may have been the first collection of *tkhines* specifically intended for female readers. I have not yet had a chance to examine this work, so I am not certain how it fits into the history of the genre.

4. As I have discussed elsewhere ("Traditional Piety," 249–52), the Hebrew models for *tkhines* were found in the new kabbalistic devotional literature for men created under the influence of the Lurianic revival. This raises important questions of the meaning of mysticism for women and nonlearned men. I treat the relationship of the *tkhines* to their Hebrew models (and related questions) at greater length in my forthcoming book, *Voices of the Matriarchs* (Boston, 1991).

5. I will refer to the Fürth edition of 1762 owned by the library of the Jewish Theological Seminary. It is unpaginated, but the individual *tkhines* are numbered.

6. The Mishnah (Shabbat 2:6) is the first source to specify that these religious acts are the particular duty of women. It phrases this in rather negative form: "For three transgressions women die in childbirth: for heedlessness in the laws of the menstruating woman [*niddah*], of the separation of a portion of the dough [in memory of the priestly tithe] [*hallah*], and the kindling of the [Sabbath] light [*hadlaqat ha-ner*]."

7. According to the rabbis (Pirqei R. Eliezer, chap. 45, *tosafot* to b. Rosh Hashanah 23a, s.v. *mi-shum*), this was a reward because women did not participate in the sin of the golden calf.

8. Women sometimes recited cemetery prayers in groups. In addition, a woman might engage another, more expert woman, to recite graveside prayers for her in her presence. See Gisela Suliteanu, "The traditional system of melopeic prose of the funeral songs recited by the Jewish women of the Socialist Republic of Rumania," in *Folklore Reseach Center Studies*, ed. Issachar Ben-Ami (Jerusalem, 1972), 3:291–349.

9. Interestingly, precisely these prayers are omitted from some later Eastern European editions of this collection, for example, Vilna, 1863. Perhaps in the nineteenth century people became more prudish about such topics; or else (as I suggest below) the focus of women's religious life shifts somewhat from the domestic to the communal domain.

10. B. Erubin 100b; Tanḥuma, beginning of Noah.

11. Thus the earliest editions. Some later editions say "with great joy."

12. Yom-Tov Levinsky, "Pitmat etrog ve-ʿorlat tinoq," *Yedaʿ ʿam* 1, nos. 5–6 (1949): 2–3; idem, "ha-Etrog ba-havai ha-yehudi," in *Sefer ha-moʿadim*, vol. 4, *Sukkot*, 2d. ed., ed. Yom-Tov Levinsky (Tel Aviv, 1951–52), 92–96, esp. 95–96.

13. Cf. also Herman Pollack, *Jewish Folkways in Germanic Lands (1648–1806)* (Cambridge, MA, 1971), 17.

14. Dov Noy, personal communication.

15. On the *Tsenerene* see Zinberg, A *History of Jewish Literature*, vol. 7, *Old Yiddish Literature from its Origins to the Haskalah Period* (Cincinnati, 1975) 129–39; Chone Shmeruk, "Di mizrekh-eyropeishe nuskhoes fun der Tsenerene (1786–1850)," in *For Max Weinreich on His Seventieth Birthday* (The Hague, 1964), 320–36 (later published in Hebrew translation, "ha-Nushaʾot ha-mizrah eyropeyot shel ha-ʾtseʾenah u-reʾenah'," in *Sifrut yidish be-polin*, ed. C. Shmeruk (Jerusalem, 1981), 147–64. For a (non-scholarly) English translation of this work, see *Tzʾenah urʾenah*, trans. by Miriam Stark Zakon, 3 vols. (Brooklyn, 1983–84).

16. See, e.g., Genesis Rabbah 15:8.

17. The text of the prayer that follows is the same as that found in *Seder tkhines u-vakoshes*.

18. *Tsenerene* (Amsterdam, 1702/1703), 4b.

19. For other, later references to this custom and prayer, see the articles by Levinsky cited in n. 12.

20. See Shmeruk, *Sifrut yidish be-polin*, 65. Isolated *tkhine* texts found within other works have been preserved from the sixteenth century. Short collections of *tkhines* were also published in Prague in the seventeenth century, but Prague stands in between Eastern and Western Europe.

21. On this question, see Niger, "Di yidishe literatur," 82–85, 88–94; Zinberg, *Old Yiddish Literature*, 251. Cynthia Ozick ("Notes toward Finding the Right Question," in *On Being a Jewish Feminist*, ed. Susannah Heschel [New York, 1983], 132–33) creates the erroneous impression that virtually all *tkhines* were forged by indigent male yeshiva students. Ozick relies for this information on an outdated article in the *Jewish Encyclopedia* 4:551 (New York, 1904).

22. Ber, of Bolechow, *Zikhronot R. Dov mi-Bolihov* (Berlin, 1922), 44. See also S. *Otsar siḥot ḥakhamim* (1913–14; rep. Benei-Beraq,1983–84), 42–43; and Haim Liberman, *Ohel Raḥel* (New York, 1979–80), 432–54. Liberman cites several sources referring to Leah.

23. *Encyclopaedia Judaica* (Jerusalem, 1972), s.v. "Horowitz, Jacob Jokel"; and Abraham Joshua Heschel, *The Circle of the Baal Shem Tov*, ed. Samuel H. Dresner (Chicago, 1985), 51, 55. For a recent study of women in Hasidism, see Ada Rapoport-Albert, "On Women in Hasidism, S. A. Horodecky and the Maid of Ludmir Tradition," in *Jewish History. Essays in Honour of Chimen Abramsky*, ed. Ada Rapoport-Albert and Steven J. Zipperstein (London, 1988), 495–525.

24. Many editions of a work entitled *Tkhine modeh ani* give Leah as the author. However, this work differs radically from *Tkhine imahot* in both substance and style; specifically, it contains a stereotypically "humble" view of women—much at odds

with Leah's own—and contains the prayers for sustenance and livelihood that were such anathema to Leah.

25. Very few extant editions contain the full, trilingual text. Of the two such editions known to me, neither mentions a date or place of publication. The first edition is probably the one found in the collection of the Jewish National and University Library (JNUL), Jerusalem, shelf mark R41 A460, vol. 6, no. 1. Liberman hypothesizes that it was published in Lvov at the press of Judith Rosanes (fl. 1788–1805). Another complete edition is found in the uncatalogued *tkhine* pamphlet collection of the Jewish Theological Seminary Library, New York. A third early edition, which contains all three sections of the *tkhine*, but paraphrases the introduction in Yiddish rather than retaining the original Hebrew, was published in Grodno in 1795–96. It is also in the collection of the JNUL, shelf mark R75 A284.

26. For a translation of the portion of the Yiddish text of the *Tkhine imohes* concerning the matriarchs, see my "Images of the Matriarchs in Yiddish Supplicatory Prayers," *Bulletin of the Center for the Study of World Religions* (Harvard University) 14 (1988): 44–51.

27. Jacob ben Asher's commentary to Exodus 38:8.

28. B. Berakhot 6a.

29. This particular criticism of women's behavior in synagogue is so widespread as to constitute a stereotype. Sarah bas Tovim makes the same criticism in the *Shloyshe She'orim*, although she describes frivolous behavior in synagogue as her own youthful sin. Thus, it is hard to know in this instance whether Leah's strictures against women's behavior in synagogue derive from her own observations or represent her acceptance of the stereotype.

30. The standard introduction to the history of Kabbalah is Gershom Scholem, *Major Trends in Jewish Mysticism* (New York, 1954). A recent major revision of Scholem's views can be found in Moshe Idel, *Kabbalah: New Perspectives* (New Haven, 1988). For an accessible entrée into the classic work of Jewish mysticism, see *Zohar, the Book of Enlightenment*, trans. Daniel Matt (New York, 1983); the introduction to this work contains an outline of the *sefirot*. The texts included in *Safed Spirituality*, trans. Lawrence Fine (Mahwah, NJ, 1984) give a sense of the mystical piety of the Lurianic revival, which seems to have influenced the authors of *tkhines*.

31. Leah is not alone in this concern. *Ayn sheyne naye tkhine oyf roshkhoydesh elul*, attributed to Hayyah bas Aryeh Leib, talks about how the Shekhinah weeps over the exile of Israel, and follows this by the statement that "proper prayer [is] when we weep and eagerly beg that we may be redeemed from exile." This text also contains the same critique (with the same prooftext from *Tiqqunei ha-Zohar* 22a) of prayer for material sustenance; but it is not as vociferous in its denunciation nor as explicitly kabbalistic. *Tkhine Imrei Shifre*, attributed to Shifrah bas Joseph (c. 1770) contains a kabbalistic interpretation of women's lighting of Sabbath candles, in which this act is in honor of the Shekhinah, and possesses redemptive and theurgic power. See my "Woman As High Priest: A Kabbalistic Prayer in Yiddish for Lighting Sabbath Candles," *Jewish History* 5 (1991).

32. B. Berakhot 17a.

33. A paraphrase of B. Megillah 12b. This proverbial expression means, approximately, that a man is king of his own castle.

34. Sarah's epithet means "daughter of good" or "notable people"; the *tovim* were a type of Jewish communal official. Tuwim is known as a surname among twentieth-century Polish Jews; some say that the poet Julian Tuwim (1894–1953) was a descendent of Sarah (Dov Noy, personal communication).

35. Another *tkhine*, entitled either *Sha ʿar ha-yiḥud ʿal ha-ʿolamot* or *Sheqer ha-heyn*, was also attributed to Sarah. This text is so rare that I have been unable to locate a copy. However, the portion of it quoted by Zinberg (*History*, 7:254–55) and shown by Liberman in facsimile (*Ohel Raḥel*, 453) convince me that the attribution is genuine; that is, the style is so similar that it is extremely likely that both of the *tkhines* attributed to Sarah are indeed written by the same author.

36. I discuss this portion of the text in my "Traditional Piety," 262–67.

37. On this controversy, see Zinberg, *History*, 7:252–54. Zinberg asserts that Sarah bas Tovim was indeed a historical figure. Using statements in her *tkhines* that give the names and places of residence of some of her male ancestors, he hypothesizes that she was probably the great-granddaughter of either Mordecai Zusskind (d. 1684) or Mordecai Gunzberg (d. 1688), both rabbis in Brisk (Brest-Litovsk). He may be right; but different editions of her works give somewhat different genealogies.

38. "Der Ziveg; oder, Sore bas Tovim," in I. L. Peretz, *Ale verk*, vol. 5, *Folkstimlekhe geshikhtn* (New York, 1947), 372–79.

39. While there are hundreds of editions of the *Shloyshe sheʿorim*, none of the early ones make any reference to date or place of publication. The earliest dated edition I have seen was published in Vilna, by Romm, in 1938, but I am convinced, on the basis of typography, that earlier editions were published in the eighteenth century. An additional problem is that the publishers of *tkhines*, including the *Shloyshe sheʿorim*, took great liberties with their texts. When no edition can be given clear priority, it is very difficult to establish the correct text.

40. I deal with the other "gates" in my "Traditional Piety."

41. Although a Bithia, daughter of Pharaoh, is mentioned in 2 Chronicles 4:18, it is not clear that she is the same person as the daughter of Pharaoh who rescued Moses (Exodus 2:5–10). The rabbis, however, made this identification and explained her name as meaning "daughter of God" (Leviticus Rabbah 1:3).

42. Serah, daughter of Asher, is mentioned in the Bible only in genealogical lists (Genesis 46:17, Numbers 26:46, 1 Chronicles 7:3). However, the Midrash portrays her as gently breaking the news that Joseph was alive by playing the harp and singing about it so that Jacob could hear (*Sefer ha-yashar*, Va-yiggash). For a fuller discussion of the rabbinic legends about Serah, see Joseph Heinemann, *Aggadot ve-toledoteihen* (Jerusalem, 1974) 56–63.

43. See my "Women in Paradise," *Tikkun: A Bi-monthly Jewish Critique of Politics, Culture and Society*, 2, no. 2 (April-May 1987): 43–46, 117–20.

44. The author of the *tkhine* used the Amsterdam edition of 1708 or an edition descended from it.

45. Baruch ha-Levi Epstein, *Sefer meqor barukh* (New York, 1954), pt. 4, chap. 46. Reyna Basya's anguished struggles to prove that it was permissible for women to study Torah (which obsessed her continually) and her nephew's pained but conscientious refutations of her arguments, culminating in her admission of defeat, make blood-curdling reading. Reyna Basya married Naphtali Ẓevi Judah Berlin (known as ha-Neẓiv) in 1831 (*Encyclopaedia Judaica* [Jerusalem, 1972] s.v. "Berlin, Naphtali Ẓevi Judah," col. 661). On the Jewish learned elite of Lithuania in this era see Immanuel Etkes, "Marriage and Torah Study Among the *Lomdim* in Lithuania in the Nineteenth Century," in *The Jewish Family: Metaphor and Memory*, ed. David Kraemer (New York, 1989), 153–78.

CHAPTER  **DEBORAH HERTZ**

*Emancipation through Intermarriage in Old Berlin*

Wealthy Jewish families in Berlin fought bitterly about the conversions and intermarriages of their daughters in the decades after Moses Mendelssohn died in 1786. In this essay I reconstruct the dramatic lives of twenty of these daughters. Many of these women began with arranged marriages to Jewish men, but their first marriages often ended in divorce. Conversion to Christianity often followed, and the next step was often a second marriage to a prominent gentile man. The question I ponder here is why it was the daughters and not the sons who departed kin and faith for a new life in the wider world.

The best way to begin to answer this question is to look at the extraordinary wealth of the Berlin Jewish elite. It was this wealth—and the culture adorning it—that made possible the daughters' adventures. The maxim of the eighteenth-century Prussian kings was to obtain the maximum economic benefit from the smallest number of actual Jews. Their success was reflected by the fact that somewhere between two-fifths and two-thirds of the adult men in the community were either "fabulously wealthy" or "wealthy," a distribution of affluence quite atypical for a European Jewish community.[1] The wealthy Jews in Berlin had earned their money in typical "court-Jewish" functions. They bought and sold metals and precious stones and served as the private bankers for the crown and for spendthrift nobles. By the last decades of the century some new functions were added to these old ones, as Jewish financiers became entrepreneurs. Sometimes willingly, sometimes coerced by the crown, Jews leased or owned workshops producing coins, wool, linen, silk, and ribbons.

To be sure, much of the wealth created by the Jewish elite was funneled into state coffers by means of the extensive taxes the community was forced to pay. Only infrequently did great wealth provide a release from humiliating regulations; even rich Jews were forced to pay the "animal" tax at the city gates. Yet the loyal financial services performed by so many of the community's leading members were eventually modestly rewarded by King Frederick the Great and his two eighteenth-century successors. Berlin's Jewish community had never been forced to live in a ghetto, and in the 1760s the richest families were given permission to build elaborate palaces in the center of town.[2]

As we shall see, the salon women's intermarriages came to pass partly because many Jews had the excess capital that many Prussian aristocrats lacked. High fertility rates and excessive subdivisions of landed estates meant that more and more Prussian noble families sent sons to Berlin to make their way. There they attended university to prepare for careers in the bureaucracy. Once in the urban setting, they often embarked on a life of luxury and even licentiousness, which was quite new in the Prussian context and often quite beyond their means.[3] Yet the banking system in Prussia was still primitive, and to obtain personal loans one had to rely on private family bankers. Here is where the Jewish merchants came into the picture. Discreet private loans to those who could afford the high interest rates was one way that the Jewish bankers increased their wealth even further. The coincidence of noble poverty, Jewish wealth, and the absence of a public banking system by which money could be loaned anonymously help to explain the larger context of the Jewish-noble intermarriages. Still, even when there may have been an economic motive, these marriages remain difficult to explain. For nobles to move beyond borrowing from Jewish fathers to marrying their converted daughters was a large and historic step into uncharted social territory. To understand why the Jewish women were ready to take this step, we must move beyond

Jewish wealth and explore the Jewish mastery of high culture that this wealth made possible.

Civic equality was not required for learning the skills of secular culture. Many decades before the 1812 Edict of Emancipation granted Prussian Jewry limited civic equality, Jews in Berlin were mastering the languages, scholarship, and daily life habits of the dominant culture. Even before Moses Mendelssohn became famous for his crusade to refashion Judaism according to rational and deistic principles, small circles of Jewish scholars in Berlin were learning philosophy, mathematics, and medicine. Later, inspired by Mendelssohn's example, Jewish men who came into adulthood in Berlin in the second half of the eighteenth century went further, publishing books and articles on secular themes. Newly rich Jews in Berlin, who had made their fortunes in the Seven Years' War, changed their lives in less intellectual ways. Their daughters' names came to sound less Jewish, as Malka called herself Amalie, Brendel called herself Dorothea, and Pessel called herself Philippine. The richest families built theaters in their homes, and their children pleaded with the community elders to be allowed to perform secular plays. Young men shaved their beards and donned powdered wigs, and their wives promenaded in the Thiergarten Park in parasols and silk dresses.

What was most distinctive about Berlin Jewry's assimilation in these years was that this wealth and this mastery of the dominant culture were crowned with a prize that could neither be purchased nor learned. That prize was social integration with the cream of the gentile society. This achievement was certainly without precedent in Berlin and was not accomplished to the same degree anywhere else in Europe at the time. What was especially distinctive was that this novel social integration was engineered by Jewish women, not Jewish men. Henriette Herz, Rahel Varnhagen, Dorothea Schlegel, Sarah Levy, Amalie Beer, and a host of more obscure women were celebrated for their social skills, conversational brilliance, and sometimes physical beauty as well. During the quarter century between 1780 and 1806, there were nine Jewish *salonières* who hosted some kind of social circle in Berlin, ranging from famous, regular, crowded gatherings to more irregular, modest entertaining. (There were also five salons led by gentile women.) An additional eleven Jewish women either attended one of the nine Jewish salons or were a sister or friend to one of the *salonières*. Born between 1761 and 1787, these women came into adulthood in the years when salons flourished in Berlin. By definition, they were a tiny sector of the Jewish world and, by the degree of their affluence, an unrepresentative sector. These women's salons introduced a light-hearted French style into the rather more somber Prussian intellectual world. At the same time, their salons constituted a miniature social utopia where noble and commoner, Jew and gentile seemed to leave their ascribed status outside the door. Precisely because the structures that made salons possible were changing so quickly, the salons were a fragile institution that only survived for a quarter century. As Rahel Varnhagen was later to remember, her salon circle dispersed abruptly after French troops occupied Berlin in 1806; the Jewish salons survived only as long as there was peace and prosperity in Berlin, wealthy Jews and Prussian nobles had mutually complementary economic needs, intellectual life was still informal, and the local intelligentsia was enthusiastic about French culture.[4]

The social glory achieved by the eighteenth-century Jewish *salonières* was never realized with such panache again either in Berlin or elsewhere in Germany. In later decades more poor Jews migrated into the city; and, at the same time, a stronger, more cohesive nobility increased the profits they received from their agricultural estates. The size of the intelligentsia grew, and intellectual institutions became more formal. In reaction to the Napoleonic occupation of 1806, the whole notion of salon culture came into question as French culture, Jews, and women became less exotically attractive for Prussian intellectuals. As salons gradually disappeared from the Berlin scene, so too a stage for wealthy, cultivated Jewish women vanished. But even though their special institution disappeared long before they were ready to "retire" as salon hosts, the salon women's lives had been permanently transformed. For the new social universe of salons and the new husbands they met there had seduced them to abandon the narrow world of traditional Judaism.

For some historians the Jewish salon women's readiness to leave Judaism was caused by the education they did or did not receive. According to this interpretation, Berlin Jewish women received too little traditional Jewish learning and too much decorative secular education.[5] There is some justice to this view. For several centuries before the salon era, it is undoubtably true that Jewish girls in Germany were denied the same education as their brothers. Jewish girls were not regularly trained in Hebrew or in Talmud, nor did Jewish law require their regular attendance at the synagogue. Indeed, a mid-eighteenth-century source records that girls were not even allowed to be in a house where tutors were training the community's boys in these subjects.[6] Girls and women in this era picked up bits and pieces of traditional learning mainly through study of the *Tsenerene*, a simplified Yiddish Bible composed of moral exhortations and parables.[7] The argument is that the salon women might not have become alienated from Judaism had they received a more rigorous Jewish education, which would have bonded them to their religious tradition.

According to this view, the community's failure to give these girls a solid religious training was only exacerbated by their exposure to a new world of secular novels, poetry, and plays. Tutors were hired to teach them proper German, French, and even English. They learned the harpsichord and were allowed to subscribe to lending libraries that circulated popular novels. Their brothers and husbands had fewer social incentives to improve their German or learn French, since their occupational choices were restricted narrowly to commerce and finance, where they worked mainly with other Jewish men and thus spoke Yiddish. Because their parents did not take their daughters' intellectual aspirations seriously, fathers allowed daughters to follow their own desires. There were practical matters that played a role too. Unlike most Jewish families in both Western and Eastern Europe at the time, the extraordinary wealth of the Berlin women's families meant that their labor was not needed in the home, the shop, or the family's commercial endeavors. Thus, the variety of practical skills a woman like Glückel of Hameln mastered a century earlier were no longer economically necessary to support the household.[8]

But a closer look at this explanation for the Jewish women's alienation from Judaism raises questions about whether education in the primary and adolescent years was the central arena where the decisive break with faith and family was forged. Was the girls' dilemma so unique? Few boys in Berlin received a rigorous Jewish education either. One problem with the boys' religious training was that their teachers were frequently young tutors from Poland who provided a rote, traditional pedagogy. Indeed, the inadequacies of contemporary religious education stimulated some wealthy young men to turn to secular studies, just as the women did.[9] Moreover, as support grew in the community for Moses Mendlessohn's credo that opening Jewish minds to secular intellectual skills could only aid in reforming Judaism, the opportunities to acquire worldly learning—once open only for sons of the wealthy—became more widely available. The Jewish Free School, directed by David Friedländer, offered a religious and a secular education to the city's younger and poorer boys.[10]

And what about the girls' secular instruction? Was it really merely decorative and frivolous? On the contrary, both Henriette Herz and Dorothea Schlegel received rigorous secular training from their fathers. Herz, for example, mastered French, English, Latin, and Hebrew while still at home and learned six more languages once her husband, Dr. Markus Herz, took over the mentor role in her life. Mendelssohn's oldest daughter, Dorothea, was also taught carefully by her father.[11] There is reason to doubt that early education was the decisive cause of the later differences in the men's and women's lives.

The weakness of the standard interpretation is underscored by looking at Jewish women's experiences in cities outside of Berlin. Their lives suggest that although some mastery of secular culture was useful in making glamorous gentile friends, accomplishing the first by no means guaranteed the second. Wealthy young Jewish women in Hamburg, Vienna, and Frankfurt had an early education similar to that of the Berlin women, but these women rarely enjoyed the social acceptance experienced by the salon women.[12]

If the kind of education the Berlin women received as adolescents was not central to their eventual departure from their faith, a closer inspection suggests that the women's social opportunities in their early twenties provided them with motives and chances to gain more secular intellectual skills on their own. For it was when they were already young adults that the sharp contrast in the male and female experience finally surfaced. The women made their entrée into gentile high society by participating in Berlin's many clubs, discussion societies, and, of course, salons. The Jewish men had great difficulties joining the city's prestigious intellectual clubs; eventually, they had to settle for forming their own alternative, parallel associations. This exclusion made it difficult for Jewish men to develop close friendships with their gentile counterparts.[13]

The Jewish women, on the other hand, enjoyed a startling success in salon society, and this experience made their intermarriages possible. To begin with, salon friends and salon performances stimulated the women to increased mastery of secular skills. More concretely, in salons they could meet glamorous potential marriage partners. That so many of these potential partners should have actually married the Jewish women they met in salons was shocking to their contemporaries. Few events would change the Jewish women's lives more dramatically than this, for marriage was the central social act for a woman in the eighteenth century. Whether she married at all, whom she married, and when she married affected a woman's standard of living, her social status, and her very ability to host a salon. To be sure, in the eighteenth century marriage also shaped men's lives in a decisive way. But for men marriage was only one of several institutions affecting their eventual social position.

It followed from the stupendous wealth of most of the salon women's fathers and the castelike character of the Jewish plutocracy that marriage was a central event in preserving and extending familial wealth and power. Moreover, arranged and early marriages were crucial if the alliance was to be made with precisely the right family. If the daughter was young, her virtue was sure to be intact. The peculiar way in which affluence and legal insecurity were combined in the conditions of life for the Jewish elite in Berlin made carefully chosen marriages particularly crucial. Rich Jewish fathers were eager to add well-connected and wealthy sons- and daughters-in-law to the family because both sets of parents usually belonged to a small, closed group of merchants in a monopolistic economic system. But since permission to live legally in the city (summarized in a *Schutzbrief,* or "letter of protection") was itself a crucial prize, money and connections were not the only relevant considerations in choosing a mate for one's child. Daughters could only inherit their father's *Schutzbrief* under special conditions. Since even the more privileged families could only pass their *Schutzbrief* on to their oldest son, younger sons were often married to women from outside the city. In order to maintain a minimum of intergenerational residential cohesion, all efforts were made to keep the daughters in Berlin by marrying them off to a firstborn local man who had inherited his father's *Schutzbrief.* There were, therefore, many reasons for parents in these circles to force an arranged marriage on an unwilling daughter.

There was little about the early years of most of the salon women's first marriages to indicate the marital breakdowns to come. All but two of the women married. The majority (fifteen of the twenty) married Jewish men. Only for the most famous brides is the process of the choice of groom known. Henriette was twelve when her father, director of the Jewish Hospital in Berlin, announced that he had chosen two men who were appropriate to become her husband. She had only to choose whether she preferred a rabbi or a physician. Having selected the latter, she promptly found herself engaged to Dr. Markus Herz, although she had only met him once. By the tender age of fifteen she was married to this genial but ugly man who was over twice her age. Nor did Moses Mendelssohn's daughter Dorothea have any choice in her marriage at nineteen to Simon Veit, a kindly businessman chosen by her father and altogether lacking in his bride's or her father's intellectual passions.

Even without more individual stories illustrating how marriages were arranged, there is other evidence suggesting that arranged marriage was indeed the rule among Berlin's Jewish elite. It cannot have been sheer chance that both bride and groom often came from the premier families in Berlin or elsewhere. Pessel Zulz, for instance, whose father owned a large silk manufactory, was married to Ephraim Cohen. The groom hailed from Holland; once in Berlin, he opened an enormous wool manufactory in the center of town employing hundreds of workers. Rebecca Itzig, one of the ten daughters born to Daniel and Miriam Itzig, married David Ephraim. Ephraim was the son of Veitel Heine Ephraim, one of the partners in a prosperous coin-minting operation during the Seven Years' War. The young couple's "poetry album," signed by visitors to their home between 1784 and 1796, shows a tight network of intimate siblings and other relatives.[14] The small number of eligible families from which appropriate spouses might be chosen was thus yet another constraint on marriage choice. The result was that the city's Jewish elite was extremely inbred.

The same combination of circumstances that resulted in arranged matches also resulted in an early age of marriage for the brides. It was best to ensure the proper alliance as soon as possible, even if that made for a rather long engagement. The age at which Jewish women married in different times and places has varied enormously, depending on the economic and legal constraints on mate choice. The average age of first marriage for the salon women was eighteen, several years younger than the age at which poorer Jewish women in Berlin married. A reconstruction of brides' ages of marriage from the complete list of 170 weddings involving two Jewish mates between 1780 and 1790 shows that the average Jewish woman in Berlin married at twenty-four, six years later than the average salon bride.[15] If the salon brides at eigh-

teen were young in contrast to other Jewish women who married in
Berlin in that period, they still married later in comparison to contemporary Jewish brides in Eastern Europe. In the eighteenth century, and
well into the nineteenth century, brides as young as thirteen were
reportedly a frequent occurrence.[16]

Some critics have blamed arranged marriages for driving young
women away from the faith, with negative consequences beyond the
era for the eventual fate of Judaism in modern Germany.[17] Yet at least
at the outset of their marital careers, it is by no means clear that all
the young brides were opposed to arranged and early marriages. Henriette Herz attributed her own enthusiasm for marrying young to the
privations of being a dependent daughter, as compared to the privileges of being a wife. She later remembered that she was content to
marry an older, unknown man if it meant being able to buy new bon-
nets and have her own hairdresser.[18] There was a general view that
married women led freer lives than single women did. With their husband's social and financial backing, they were surely freer to entertain
in style, as well as to expand their intellectual circles. All the successful *salonières*, with the exception of Rahel Varnhagen, were married
to wealthy Jewish men in the years when they hosted their salons.

One large problem in using past lives to evaluate the quality of a
marriage is the difficulty of finding adequate primary evidence to determine the experiental quality of particular relationships.

How "modern" were the first marriages of the salon women? Were
the partners "loving companions" even though the matches had usually been arranged by their parents? It is hard to answer this important
question. Overall, the answer is *no*; partners in arranged marriages do
not seem to have been very well matched. To be sure, evidence to
decide this issue is hard to come by. Even the actors' own testimony
in memoirs and letters requires delicate interpretation, insofar as such
statements may have reflected contemporary expectations and ideals
rather than their real feelings. One oblique, but nevertheless useful,
bit of evidence is the comparative ages of the brides and grooms. Even
if the spouses had little or no choice in the match and even if the
bride was still in her teens, surely the chances that the couple would
be "companions" would be enhanced if the two were closer rather
than further apart in age. We know the ages of six of the grooms who
married the eight Jewish salon women whose age of marriage is
known. The seventeen years between Henriette and Markus Herz was

decidedly unusual for this tiny group. In most of the other cases the age difference was no more than a year or two.

As for the feelings the spouses had toward each other, we are on even shakier ground in trying to determine how companionate the first Jewish marriages were. In only a few cases is anything recorded, either by or about one of the mates. Again, Henriette Herz's life is rare in its documentation. One chronicler of the Herzes' lives portrayed a rather distant relationship. According to this report Markus called Henriette "das Kind" (the child), and their bond was less that of a "happy marriage" than a "happy relationship." In this view, the absence of passion, as well as her childlessness, caused Henriette to look to "friends, literature and art" for her happiness. She also found companionship in her friendships, especially those with Dorothea Schlegel and Friedrich Schleiermacher.[19]

Dorothea's lack of delight in her first husband, Simon Veit, is also well documented. It is not clear how much of the problem lay in his physical appearance; he was described as "plain" and "not good looking." From their wedding day forward, Dorothea became "taciturn" and withdrawn. Friends noted that the two had little in common in their preferred languages and intellectual interests. He spoke mainly Yiddish and was involved in his business affairs, while she spoke French and German and kept up with the latest literary developments. Her famous father, Moses Mendelssohn, who came to worry about his children's fates in his last years, actually thought that his daughter Dorothea was happily married. Indeed, she badly wanted him to think this, so much so that she refused to give in to her friend Henriette Herz's pleas that she separate from Simon until her father died in 1786. But their eleven years together cannot have been without some contentment. Otherwise, it is difficult to explain Simon Veit's many kindnesses to Dorothea after their separation. His loyalty is a testimony to the survival of some strong bond between the two, even if it was not passion.[20]

Sometimes the kind of life-style great wealth allowed made the question of companionship or its lack less pressing. Karl August Varnhagen's description of the Cohen household, where he tutored the children, suggests that the fantastic wealth of some of the salon womens' husbands supported a way of life where companionship was not required for family harmony. The practice of husbands and wives living in different residences had long been typical of urban noble couples, especially in France but also to a lesser degree in Prussia. The Cohen household was a large and varied one, which included the numerous workers in Herr Cohen's adjoining wool factory, a clerk, and a tutor. Frequent visitors included Frau Cohen's mother and married sisters and a collection of local musical and literary personalities. At one point during Varnhagen's employment in the household, Herr Cohen was devoting his attentions to one Mademoiselle Seiler, a singer, and Varnhagen himself was carrying on a flirtation with Frau Cohen.[21] The apparent absence of a deep companionship between the Herzes, the Veits, and the Cohens seems to have been one result of arranged matches uniting mates of different ages and different degrees of involvement in secular culture. But as even these three cases show, a misguided arranged match did not necessarily result in a divorce. Henriette Herz stayed with Markus until his death in 1803; Philippine Cohen seems to have remained with her husband even after he fled Berlin because of bankruptcy in 1804; the Veits stayed together for eleven years before Dorothea departed for a new life with Friedrich Schlegel. For the other twelve of the salon women who married Jewish men, we are completely uninformed about the quality of their emotional lives. Yet five of the other twelve marriages endured until one of the spouses died.

The lives of the salon women who either chose or were forced to live without husbands vividly illustrate the hardships that the comfortably married probably sought to avoid. One classic case was Rahel Varnhagen. She did not marry until she was forty-one. She survived two failed engagements to Christian noblemen, and the Napoleonic Wars reduced her income drastically and introduced her to privations she had never before endured. It is not clear why she never married a Jewish man at the age her friends Herz and Veit did. Some have attributed her failure to marry a Jew to her family's decision not to provide her with a dowry of sufficient size. Yet Rahel Varnhagen's failure to marry traditionally was also caused by her own rebellion against Judaism and her attractiveness to prominent gentile suitors.[22]

In spite of all of the social and economic advantages a lasting marriage provided, nine (almost half) of the twenty salon women eventually divorced their Jewish husbands. It is rarely possible to be exact about the detailed causes of divorce on the interpersonal level. Of the nine divorcées, we know for certain that seven eventually remarried. One of those who did not was Rebecca Friedländer, who divorced

Moses Friedländer when she was twenty-three, then converted and changed her name to Regina Frohberg. But none of her gentile suitors, mostly noble military officials interested in literature, were actually willing to marry her. Her salon friends who also divorced their Jewish husbands—usually also when still in their twenties—had better luck than Friedländer in transforming noble suitors into husbands.[23] Indeed, five of the seven who remarried ended up with a noble husband; and the second husband of a sixth, Dorothea's Friedrich Schlegel, was ennobled after their marriage. Gentile husbands were found not only by those entering a second marriage. Three of the salon women's first marriages, including that of Rahel Varnhagen, were to gentile men.[24]

The salons played a key role in making some of the intermarriages possible, since the new partners literally met at these gatherings. Dorothea Veit met Friedrich Schlegel at Henriette and Markus Herz's salon, and Rahel first met Karl August Varnhagen at Philippine Cohen's, when he was employed there as a tutor.

Once having fallen in love with a gentile man she had met at a salon, a Jewish woman planning intermarriage would face less opposition from respectable Jews in these years than she would have in an earlier period. An older generation of acculturated Jews had done what they could to nip potential intermarriages in the bud. For instance, when the young Jewish woman Adele Ephraim was being courted by Franz von Leuchsenring, an intellectual of noble family, his friend Moses Mendelssohn threatened to cut off relations if he did not abandon his association with her.[25] In contrast, the salon women's contemporaries, Jewish and gentile alike, often actually encouraged intimacies between women and men born into different social realms. Not only did Henriette Herz suggest to Dorothea that she leave Simon Veit at the very outset of their marriage, but after Dorothea left her family, Herz continued to visit her in defiance of her own husband's wishes.[26]

But regardless of where the Jewish women met their gentile suitors, if they wished to marry them, they had to convert to Christianity. There was no civil marriage in Prussia until 1874; to marry a Christian one had to become a Christian. (Because both partners were Christians by the time they married, these marriages were technically not intermarriages; since a converted Jew remained a Jew in the eyes of most contemporaries, however, the term remains apt.) From what can be reconstructed, deciding to convert was a painful step for many of the salon women. Just as some of their gentile friends tried to supervise their marital choices, so, too, gentile salon friends sought to guide the women's religious choices. Friedrich Schleiermacher, for instance, long worked to convince both Henriette Herz and Rahel Varnhagen of the truths of Christianity. But rationalist exhortation by friends was by no means their only stimulus to conversion. Some have argued that the Jewish salon women's enthusiasm for the romantic views just then being formulated by the younger salon men led them to be particularly open to the mystical, pantheistic versions of Protestantism espoused by their friends. This, too, was a radical change in the climate of opinion. The deistic intellectuals of the previous generation, in contrast, had argued that since Judaism and Christianity shared a core of universal truths, enlightened Jews should strive to reform Judaism rather than to become Christians.[27]

We have seen thus far that the deficiencies of the Jewish women's educations and the deistic attitude of their friends both played a role in the decision many of the women made to change their faith. But obviously, the willingness of prestigious suitors to become husbands provided an incentive of a more immediate, more personal kind. Almost all of the women's conversions were connected with marriages to gentiles. The seven divorced salon women who remarried all converted, and the three women whose first marriages were intermarriages also converted. An additional six women converted but never intermarried, either because suitors declined to become husbands or because Jewish husbands converted alongside their wives. In one single instance, that of Henriette Herz, conversion seems to have been chosen out of authentic conviction, with no would-be gentile husband waiting in the wings. This leaves, at most, three of the twenty salon women who died in the religion into which they had been born.[28]

The strong association between conversion and intermarriage, especially intermarriage to noblemen, suggests that one reason the women changed religions was social opportunism and craving for the higher positions possessed by Christians in a radically unequal society. Indeed, for many intermarriages there is evidence of this motive. Yet whatever desires for status propelled them into a new, Christian world, many of the women retained strong ties to friends and relatives who remained Jewish. Although the salon women had access to a glamorous social world that was for the most part closed to their parents, brothers, and husbands, many also showed a loyalty to their still-

Jewish families (especially to their mothers, if not to their first Jewish husbands). Often this loyalty resulted in poverty and loneliness at a vulnerable time. Not all was immediately abandoned for social advancement. Herz lost governess positions because she would not convert while her mother was alive; Dorothea Schlegel would also not convert and marry Friedrich until after her mother's death. Nor was it simply the pull of family ties that bound a minority of the salon women to their faith. Sara Levy, Amalie Beer, and Fanny von Arnstein (Levy's *salonière* sister who lived in Vienna) all had a principled position against conversion and argued against it to friends and relatives considering such a step.[29] All three, it should be noted, had lasting marriages to Jewish men.

But it would be wrong to discount social ambition as a motive. However wealthy members of the Jewish elite were, the Jewish community was far below most commoners and all nobles in terms of civic rights and privileges. And in the Prussian context, before the modest changes of the reforms of 1807–14, there was little hope that the nobility's privileges and prestige would be curtailed. Becoming a noble was a very heady opportunity in this setting, which is why this tiny cluster of six Jewish-noble and four Jewish-commoner marriages was significant in the context of Jewish life in Germany. That not merely gentile but noble gentile families would accept Jewish women as daughters- and sisters-in-law was quite a new and serious turn of events in Jewish-German history. Not that there had been no Jewish-gentile contact or no conversion in Berlin earlier in the century. But such social contacts had been mainly between men, with the limited purpose of either scholarly or commercial exchange. Nor had the wives and daughters of Berlin's court-Jewish families then had much informal, purely social contact with the families of the princes whom their husbands and fathers served financially. An analysis of Berlin conversion records collected by Nazi genealogists during the Third Reich provides statistical evidence of a distinct shift in the gender and the class of the converts in the salon years. At the same time that the salon women began to marry their prominent suitors, the Berlin conversion statistics show that the rate of adult female conversion began to overtake the rate of male conversions.[30] There was also a change in the class of the converts: in the pre-1770 years, the (mainly male) converts tended to be poor; but in the salon years, the (mainly female) converts were more often wealthy, compared to the previous era.

These changes suggest that the salon women's experiences were part of a wider pattern among Berlin Jews.

Once they had converted, the divorcées could marry the gentile suitors they had met in salons. What were these second marriages like? Were they more companionate than the women's first marriages? One reason to think that the intermarried spouses might have been "loving partners" is that several of the gentile grooms were writers affiliated with the early romantic literary movement. A strong critique of ar-ranged marriages, for their effect both on individuals and on the wider society, was a major theme in romanticism. Certainly, several of the more famous intermarriages do seem to have been companionate matches. Dorothea and Friedrich Schlegel, Rahel and Karl August Varnhagen von Ense, and Julie (Saaling) and Karl Heyse were clearly friends as well as spouses. Other couples, such as Marianne Meyer and Prince von Reuss, were definitely not companions, maintaining sepa-rate residences and mixing in quite different social circles. Unfortu-nately, information is far too sparse on the remaining intermarried couples to determine which trend was the rule.

But even if companionate relationships were the dominant trend, it would be wrong to conclude that mates would have chosen each other only because of their mutual emotional resonance, that looks, status, and wealth played no role at all. Even though the very exis-tence of these intermarriages shows that the choice of mates was now formally very much freer than ever before, the direction the women moved when they chose their own mates does not seem to have been a random one. For when we examine the personal and material quali-ties of the intermarried spouses, the total sum of many partners' "ledg-ers" of status, wealth, looks, and intellectual skills seems to have been roughly equal, although not at all similar in their parts. The noble husbands were rich in status but often poor in property or personal qualities. The converted brides tended to be rich in money, and many were also rich in beauty and cultivation. Yet their Jewish origin was still a very large drawback indeed; for the fact of the matter was that neither the noble nor the commoner gentile grooms who married the salon brides tended to be the pick of the crop. Rahel Varnhagen, Marianne Meyer, and Sara Meyer all married gentile men with one objective "defect" or other. The men were too old or too young, titled but poor, or brilliant but unemployed. Yet regardless of how poor or unattractive a noble groom might have been, his title was of overriding value to a would-be Jewish bride. For her Jewish origins, even if formally covered over with a new religion, would undoubtedly be a source of embarrassment to the groom. In an era when the status of a new in-law would typically affect the parents and siblings of both mates, taking on a once-Jewish relative was a major decision not just for individuals but for entire families. It would certainly ease the pain if she had compensatory qualities, money being only the most obvious.[31] To be sure, the financial assistance that gentile grooms might expect to gain from a once-Jewish bride was not always large or even a sure thing. In cases of strong parental objections, a public legal battle might be required for a converted Jewish woman to receive her inheritance. But even if the family money was by no means always ready to hand, marriage to a woman from these circles might at least provide access to the Jewish financial elite. As crucial as money was, it would be a serious mistake to think that it was the only counterbalancing possession that the status-poor salon brides offered their status-rich gentile grooms. The Jewish brides were often attractive and articulate. Their dark good looks matched the romantic ideology of many of the salon men, just as their cultivation and conversational skills fit them for the romantic ideal of woman as inspirational Muse.

This very external analysis suggests that many of the couples did indeed possess complementary qualities. Good looks, sophistication, and money could be traded for a noble name. Still, it does not follow that emotional motives were lacking. To ignore the women's emotional reasons for choosing a particular mate would be especially inappropriate since these husbands were freely chosen: the historic novelty of these marriages rests precisely on the fact that they were *not* arranged. The mutually attractive exchange of the man's status for the woman's wealth is not the whole story, for the institutional setting of the salon legitimized the Jewish women as brides for noble men. The salon had once been an exclusively noble institution, and leading salons was an activity that "dusted" Jewish women with a noble aura.[32]

Ten intermarriages do not constitute a pattern. Still, these intermarriages are noteworthy because they were the culmination of the considerable social success rich Jewish women in Berlin enjoyed in those years. Their successes were unusual at the time, and they are also anomalous in comparison to the experiences of Jewish women in nineteenth-century Germany.[33] Thus, interpreting the meaning of the intermarriages is as important as assessing their causes. Prussia has long been viewed as a land where upward mobility was blocked by a rigid social structure, a social structure that also retarded the lively contact among social classses so useful elsewhere in the development of political democracy.[34] Historians may have overlooked the Berlin Jewish women's swift social integration because it was experienced by women rather than by men. Marriage was one of the few ways for families to exchange status for wealth without challenging the closed male occupational hierarchy. Therefore, women sometimes had more opportunities for upward mobility than men did. For when status was exchanged for wealth, the woman usually brought the wealth, the man the status.

Yet the opportunity to change one's social position so radically must have made life emotionally confusing for the women involved. Seen from a long distance, their behavior has been judged as the socially opportunistic betrayal of their religion and their people. Yet much other evidence suggests that this was not how the women saw their own acts. Rather, they seem to have viewed their salon circles, conversions, and intermarriages as victories in an often-painful fight for personal freedom. In the eighteenth-century setting this fight for emancipation could not, by definition, be a fight to free oneself from the constraints of established society or a fight for the legitimation of one's religious or gender group. Emancipation for the Jewish salon women meant integration into the dominant upper-class culture and society, the model of civilized humanity.[35] In this way the salon women experienced at an early date and in a gender-specific way the basic conflict between group loyalty and individual emancipation that would torment so many European Jews in the two centuries to follow.

## NOTES

Some of the women discussed in this essay had several last names in the course of their lives. Here, their married names are used, unless they are known by their birth names.

1. Hannah Arendt (*The Origins of Totalitarianism* [Cleveland, 1958], 16, n. 6) has claimed that "two-thirds of the 600 families in Berlin in this era were rich." Raphael Mahler (*A History of Modern Jewry 1780–1815* [London, 1971], 127) esti-

mated that 45 percent of 450 Jewish families in Berlin in this era were either "fabulously wealthy" or "wealthy."

2. Many existing regulations were not being observed by the last decades of the eighteenth century. See "The Struggle for the Emancipation of the Jews in Prussia," an appendix to Henri Brunschwig's *Romanticism and Enlightenment in Eighteenth-Century Prussia* (Chicago, 1974).

3. On the crisis of the Prussian nobility in this era, see the chapter on Prussia in A. Goodwin, *The European Nobility in the Eighteenth Century* (London, 1953) or Fritz Stern, "Prussia," in *European Landed Elites in the Nineteenth Century*, ed. David Spring (Baltimore, 1977).

4. I look at three dimensions of socializing to decide which social events should be called salons: regular meetings but without invitations; discussion about intellectual matters; and guests belonging to different social classes. Not all of Berlin's fourteen salons met all three criteria; they are used as an "ideal type," not a strict definition. Varnhagen's nostalgic quote is cited in Hannah Arendt, *Rahel Varnhagen: The Life of a Jewess* (London, 1957), 99.

5. A good example of this view can be found in Max Brod, *Heinrich Heine* (Berlin, 1935), 70; see also Solomon Liptzin, *Germany's Stepchildren* (New York, 1944), 26, for a most condemnatory analysis of what the salon women did with their secular education.

6. See J. Eschelbacher, "Die Anfänge allgemeiner Bildung unter den deutschen Juden vor Mendelssohn," in *Beiträge zur Geschichte der deutschen Juden* (Frankfurt a. Main, 1916), 168–77; and M. Güdemann, *Geschichte des Erziehungswesens und der Kultur der Abendländischen Juden* (Vienna, 1884), vol. 1.

7. See Robert S. Rosen, Introduction, to *The Memoirs of Glückel of Hameln*, trans. Marvin Lowenthal (New York, 1977), xiv; and chapter 7 above.

8. See *The Memoirs of Glückel of Hameln*, for an example of the important role wives could play in the family's commercial enterprises at the beginning of the eighteenth century.

9. See Moritz Stern, *Beiträge zur Geschichte der jüdischen Gemeinde zu Berlin* (Berlin, 1926).

10. Michael Meyer, *The Origins of the Modern Jew: Jewish Identity and European Culture in Germany, 1749–1824* (Detroit, 1967), 58.

11. On Herz's education, see Julius Furst, ed., *Henriette Herz: Ihr Leben und ihre Erinnerungen* (Berlin, 1858), 19; on Dorothea Mendelssohn Schlegel's training, see Margareta Hiemenz, *Dorothea v. Schlegel* (Freiburg i. Breisgau, 1911), 6 and M. Kayserling, *Die jüdischen Frauen in der Geschichte, Literatur, und Kunst* (Leipzig, 1879), 183. For Rahel Varnhagen, see the most detailed biography of her, Otto Berdrow, *Rahel Varnhagen: Ein Lebens- und Zeitbild* (Stuttgart, 1902).

12. Rich, comparative information on the Jewish women in these other cities can be found in M. Kayserling, *Die jüdischen Frauen;* on the overall situation of the Jewish communities in these cities in this period, see Helga Krohn, *Die Juden in Hamburg 1800–1850* (Hamburg, 1967); I. Kracauer, *Geschichte der Juden in Frankfurt a. Main 1150–1824* (Frankfurt a. Main, 1927); Hans Tietze, *Die Juden Wiens* (Leipzig, 1933); Hans Jager-Sunstenau, "Die geadelten Judenfamilien im vormärzlichen Wien," (Ph.D. diss., Vienna, 1950).

13. See my *Jewish High Society in Old Regime Berlin* (New Haven, 1988), 86–95. On the major all-Jewish clubs, see Ludwig Lesser, *Chronik der Gesellschaft der Freunde in Berlin* (Berlin, 1842); on Jews' attempts to join the Freemasons, see Jacob Katz, *Jews and Freemasons in Europe 1723–1939* (Cambridge, 1970), chap. 3. My analysis

here is based on a collective biography compiled from biographies, memoirs, and letters, including one hundred persons who attended at least one of the fourteen salons that met in Berlin between 1780 and 1806. See my "Intermarriage in the Berlin Salons," *Central European History* 16 (1983): 314, for tables analyzing the social, religious, and gender composition of these one hundred salon participants.

14. See my "Intermarriage," 316–17, n. 25–27, for information on these family networks.

15. These data have been compiled from the complete roster of Jewish marriages published by Jacob Jacobson, *Jüdische Trauungen in Berlin 1773–1859* (Berlin, 1968). For background in customs of Jewish marriages in Germany in this era, see Herman Pollack, *Jewish Folkways in Germanic Lands (1648–1806): Studies in Aspects of Daily Life* (Cambridge, UK, 1971), 29–39.

16. See David Biale, "Love, Marriage, and the Modernization of the Jews," in *Approaches to Modern Judaism*, ed. Marc Lee Raphael (Chico, California, 1983), 7.

17. Harry Abt, "Dorothea Schlegel bis zu ihrer Vereinigung mit der Romantik" (Ph.D. diss., Frankfurt a. Main, 1925).

18. See Furst, *Henriette Herz*, 11. On arranged marriages among German Jewry in general, see Biale, "Love, Marriage"; and for the nineteenth century, Marion Kaplan, "For Love or Money: The Marriage Strategies of Jews in Imperial Germany," *Leo Baeck Institute Year Book* 28 (1983): 263–300.

19. See Kayserling, *Die jüdischen Frauen*, 199.

20. Ibid., 183.

21. Karl August Varnhagen von Ense, *Denkwürdigkeiten des eigenen Lebens*, ed. Karl Leutner (East Berlin, 1954), 81.

22. See Arendt, *Rahel Varnhagen*, 3. For a fuller account of her financial situation, see Berdrow, *Rahel Varnhagen*, 144–45. One scholar who claimed that Levin was "poor" is Kay Goodman, in her stimulating "Poesis and Praxis in Rahel Varnhagen's Letters," *New German Critique* 27 (1982): 123–40.

23. On Friedländer, see Paul Heyse, *Jugenderinnerungen und Bekenntnisse* (Berlin, 1901), 6; Jacobson, *Jüdische Trauungen*, 440; Hannah Arendt, *Rahel Varnhagen*, 107; Ludwig Geiger, "Marie oder die Folgen des ersten Fehltritts, ein unbekannter Roman," *Zeitschrift fur Bücherfreunde*, n.s. 9, no. 1 (1917): 58–62.

24. See my "Intermarriage," 326, n. 47, for details and documentation.

25. See Karl August Varnhagen von Ense, *Denkwürdigkeiten und vermischte Schriften*, vol. 4 (Leipzig, 1843), 494.

26. See Furst, *Henriette Herz*, 11.

27. A useful way to understand the contrast between the enlightened, deistic approach to conversion and the romantics' views is through study of David Friedländer's 1799 proposal that Berlin Jews should voluntarily undergo "dry" baptism to become "rationalist" Christians. The best summaries in English of the debate about dry baptism can be found in Alfred D. Low, *Jews in the Eyes of the Germans* (Philadelphia, 1979), 176–80 and H. D. Schmidt, "The Terms of Emancipation 1781–1812," *Leo Baeck Institute Year Book* 1 (1955): 28–51.

28. One of the three who probably converted was Jette Stieglitz, whose father (Benjamin Ephraim) and husband (Dr. Israel Stieglitz) both converted. See Jacobson, *Trauungen*, 349. Two of the Jewish salon women we know did not convert were Sara Levy and Amalie Beer. On Henriette Mendelssohn and her unhappy life, see Hertz, "Intermarriage," 324, n. 45.

29. On Sara Levy's position on conversion, see Nahida Ruth Lazarus, *Das jüdisches Weib* (Berlin, 1922), 153; on Fanny von Arnstein's position, see Hilde Spiel, *Fanny*

*von Arnstein, oder, Die Emanzipation* (Frankfurt a. Main, 1962), 83. Very little has been published about Beer; see Jacobson, *Jüdische Trauungen*, 317; the Beer-Meyerbeer papers (files 1, 6); the Rabbi Leopold Stein papers; and the Baer Family papers—all at the archives of the Leo Baeck Institute in New York City.

30. The discussion of conversion trends in eighteenth-century Germany is based on my reconstruction of a set of conversion records called the *Judenkartei* compiled by Nazi genealogists and now in the Evangelisches Zentralarchiv in West Berlin. See my "Seductive Conversion in Berlin, 1770–1809," in *Jewish Apostasy in the Modern World*, ed. Todd Endelman (New York, 1987). Useful data on conversions throughout Germany in this era can be found in Jacob Katz, *Out of the Ghetto: The Social Background of Jewish Emancipation, 1770–1870* (New York, 1978), chap. 3.

31. It has been difficult to find out the financial details of Jewish-Jewish, as well as of converted-Christian, marriages. The few marriage contracts from eighteenth-century Jewish marriages in Germany found in the archives of the Leo Baeck Institute do not contain specific financial details; and contracts from Christian marriages (which might have involved a converted partner) are difficult to find because notarial records have not been systematically preserved in Germany. On Veit's inheritance, see Margaretha Hiemenz, *Dorothea Schlegel*, 18.

32. This analysis derives from the splendid work of Carolyn Lougee, *Le paradis des femmes: Women, Salons, and Social Stratification in Seventeenth Century France* (Princeton, 1976).

33. See Marion Kaplan, *The Jewish Feminist Movement in Germany* (Greenwood, CT, 1979), chap. 2; and chapter 9 below.

34. See Ralf Dahrendorf, *Society and Democracy in Germany* (Garden City, 1967).

35. Phyllis Mack of Rutgers University stressed this point in her comment on an earlier version of this essay presented at the Columbia University Seminar on Women and Society.

This essay contains in abridged and somewhat altered form material which appeared in chapters 6 and 7 of the author's *Jewish High Society in Old Regime Berlin* (New Haven, 1988). We thank Yale University Press for permission to reprint this material here.

**9** **MARION A. KAPLAN**

*Tradition and Transition: Jewish Women in Imperial Germany*

---

With few exceptions the written history of the Jews is the history of Jewish men. Yet the lives of Jewish women often differed profoundly from those of their fathers, husbands, and sons. This is certainly the case with imperial Germany.[1] This essay, surveying 1870–1918, the period between the founding of Germany and the end of World War I, examines the extent to which conditions specific to women (such as their primary role in the home and family and exclusion from politics, most forms of public employment, and higher education) influenced their behavior and attitudes; it suggests, as well, that Jewish women, for reasons that were often beyond their control, remained the guardians of tradition in a period in which German Jews were undergoing a variety of processes of adaptation to German society.

Many Jews in nineteenth-century Germany tried to overcome anti-Jewish sentiment by modernizing their religion and themselves. Some even dropped religious practice altogether. They flaunted their Germanness as they privatized their Jewishness. But most were unwilling or unable[2] to surrender their identity as Jews entirely. A collective consciousness and self-consciousness prevented them from blending altogether into the dominant society. Rather than rejecting their Jewish identities entirely through assimilation, therefore, the larger number of German Jews "acculturated" by accepting the external, objective behavior and standards of the dominant culture. They adapted to styles of dress and manners of speech,[3] moved out of predominantly Jewish neighborhoods into newer ones (often forming new "ghettos"), accommodated to contemporary middle-class attitudes toward work and achievement, and evinced a deep loyalty to the fatherland. They saw no contradiction between their Germanness and their Jewishness. Yet their sentiments[4] and their perceptions often separated them from the rest of the population. They were also distinguished by their career patterns, celebration of Jewish holidays and life-cycle events, and attitudes toward conversion and intermarriage. Their social contacts, too, often isolated them from other Germans,[5] since they "had an emotional affinity with each other, which drew them together and tended to exclude Gentiles."[6] The culture of the Jewish minority mixed an ancient heritage and contemporary German bourgeois practice but was identical to neither.[7]

The extent of Jewish integration into the German occupational and social structure was determined both by the limits of the majority's acceptance of Jews and by the willingness and ability of Jews to make use of the possibilities offered them. Jewish women, however, at least before the 1890s, were segregated from the mainstream far more severely as women than as Jews. I shall present an overview of the role of women in the home and the religious-ethnic community—the two areas of women's predominant activity. I shall also examine changes in Jewish women's educational and employment activities as indications of their integration into German society.

In order to find women within their social context, a variety of sources have been utilized. Jewish newspapers and organizational bulletins and records provide useful information. Statistical sources for women, at least on a national level (as well as for some provinces, including Prussia) are also available. Memoirs, although mainly limited to middle-class women, come closest to presenting women as whole persons engaged in the private and public spheres. Other sources include letters by and to women; diaries by women and men; prescriptive essays; rabbinical essays, conference speeches, and resolutions; oral history; and assorted archival collections at the Leo Baeck Institute in New York.

Women were not aware of the importance of their lives, thus they left few or no records. They seem to have written few memoirs; and those they wrote most often describe the lives of their fathers or husbands.[8] Women's associations, as well, left far fewer records than equally or less important men's organizations. This was due, in part, to the lack of funds; the smaller office staffs; and the voluntary, sporadic assistance women's groups had at their disposal compared to the wealthier and professionally run male groups. But again, it was also due to the women's lack of appreciation of their own work and historical worth.

If there is one valid generalization that can be made about Jewish women in this period, it is that the overwhelming majority were housewives. Single, married, or widowed, paid or unpaid workers, they performed the tasks associated with running a home. Even if they hired other women to do the more menial chores, the responsibility of the home was theirs. In Imperial Germany, rapid industrialization, falling fertility rates, and the middle-class status of a majority of German Jews affected the role of the housewife;[9] also, as the number of children per family declined,[10] the functions of bourgeois women were redefined. Women's work became more administrative and cultural and less physical. In Germany, which experienced a rapid and compressed period of industrialization, commercial and economic pressures on men were intense. Housewives were expected to provide islands of serenity in a madly industrializing world,[11] and Jewish women, in addition, were to maintain Judaism in the face of rapid secularization.

The nineteenth century witnessed the disengagement of society from religion, the "downgrading of religion to a denominational category and concomitantly the end of the primacy of Judaism and Jewishness as an all-embracing influence dominating both social life and the conduct of the individual."[12] Jews experienced the uneven process of secularization along with other Germans. The great majority of Jewish women in Imperial Germany, like most of the female population, experienced these changes from their primary position in the home where they were protected from the front lines of change and were expected to cushion the family from its shock waves. Ironically, they were often blamed for the contradictions and dislocations of modernity, even as their responsibilities in the home and to the family interfered with their exposure to the modernizing influences to which their husbands were subjected. Thus, Jewish women did not always experience economic mobility and urbanization in the same way as Jewish men: there was often a time lag resulting from the gender limitations imposed upon them.

Within the political boundaries of Imperial Germany, the important dates for women also differed from men's. The year 1900, when the new German Civil Code (of 1895) was put into effect, raising the status of women above that of minors, was an important date for the lives of women. Also 1908, the year of vast educational reforms and the abolition of the *Vereinsgesetz* (which had banned women's participation in political organizations) had gender-specific implications.[13] Furthermore, while improved infant health (beginning around 1900) and the precipitous decline in Jewish fertility (particularly in the 1880s) may have influenced the quality of both male and female lives, they markedly reduced women's physical burdens and affected their lives more immediately.[14]

## JEWISH WOMEN IN THE HOME AND FAMILY: THE TENACITY AND DECLINE OF JEWISH CUSTOMS

Much of Jewish ritual observance takes place in the home, in a familial setting. While traditional Judaism relegated women to a peripheral role in the synagogue, it placed them on a pedestal in the home; family life and the religious observance of the Sabbath, holidays, and dietary laws were most clearly women's domain. Women's relationship to their religion, then, is best measured by the extent of their maintenance of "Jewishness" in the home, both in specific practices and in sentimental attachments, rather than by synagogue attendance or by other public behavior.

Women shaped the milieu in which traditional sentiments were reinforced. As mothers and grandmothers, they impressed their offspring as much with their feelings about their religion as with their attachment to religious practices. Looking back over a lifetime, memoir writers seemed more affected by their mothers' attitudes to their religion as it was revealed in the home (whether positive or negative) than by their fathers' attendance at synagogues or their own religious instruction or synagogue participation.[15]

This informal transmission of religious feelings and identification through observance in the home was women's domain. Rural Jews throughout the entire Imperial era waxed almost elegiac when they described the importance of the mother's (and often grandmother's) preparation of the Sabbath.[16] The distinctive Sabbath atmosphere, traditional foods, white tablecloth and finer tableware, candles, special clothing, and family gathering, mentioned over and over again in memoirs, was attributed to the mother's efforts.[17] Women also took special care in the preparations for the major holidays.[18] The most strenuous of these, described with a sense of exhaustion, was Passover.[19] House cleaning often began in January, climaxing in March or April with an all-night exchange of kitchenware and a carefully executed replacement of the year-round dishes with the Passover ones. While both parents participated in the final ritual, the symbolic search for *chometz* (leaven), it was the women who had actually prepared the family for the holiday.

These were not simply rural phenomena. In the cities, too, memoirs overwhelmingly indicate that Jews (and particularly women) were conscious of the Jewish calendar and the tradition of particular rituals and foods on holidays. Urban Jews often reduced the number of holidays they celebrated and minimized the religious content, especially second-generation citydwellers. Yet in all but a minority of families they were aware of, and attempted to commemorate, the major holidays, if only by a family reunion and a traditional meal.

While it is impossible to determine whether Jews observed such rituals as a result of real spirituality or simply family traditions, communal custom, or a "semi-conscious feeling of solidarity with the rest of Jewry,"[20] there is no doubt that Orthodox religious observance declined in the period under study. (Only fifteen percent of German Jews could still be classified as Orthodox at the turn of the century.)[21] However, there is no evidence to indicate that people felt less "Jewish" simply because they practiced an abbreviated and modernized form of their religion. Their participation in updated versions of their parents' rituals indicated an acknowledgement of their Jewish group identity. While they and their religion acculturated, they did not assimilate.

Furthermore, it was in some ways easier for women to consider themselves religious than it was for men. Women experienced less dissonance between religious practice and their daily routine. Whereas men faced obstacles to the performance of their religious duties resulting from their business obligations and travels, women remained in their home environment, over which they could exert some control. Since women were excluded from many rituals to begin with, their actions had less relationship to religious sentiment than those of men. For example, the daughter of the Orthodox leader Esriel Hildesheimer wrote that whereas the men and boys prayed at sunset, the women and girls read short stories and fairy tales to each other while finishing their mending.[22] When men began to neglect their observances, it may have indicated some degree of waning religiosity. Women, however, could continue their forms of religious participation without any break in their previous patterns or feelings.

Even among more secular, urban, bourgeois Jews, who no longer observed dietary rules or the Sabbath and whose religious behavior was often a conglomerate of Christian and Jewish forms (Christmas trees and bar mitzvah were not uncommon), it was frequently the women in the family who were the last bastions regarding the enforcement of dietary laws and other traditions.[23] They were also the ones who left memories of Judaism with their children.[24] Recollections of a grandmother's religiosity were shared by Sigmund Freud's son: "On Saturdays we used to hear her singing Jewish prayers in a small but firm and melodious voice. All of this, strangely enough in a Jewish family, seemed alien to us children who had been brought up without any instruction in Jewish ritual."[25] These examples suggest that women may have resisted the complete abandonment of their religious heritage in the only acceptable manner of female opposition: quietly, within the shelter of the home.

Even when women abandoned certain rituals, there was probably a time lag between husbands and wives. Anna Kronthal (b. 1862, in Poznan) noted that her mother fasted all day on Yom Kippur, which she spent in the synagogue. Her father, on the other hand, had an easier time of it: "After a hearty breakfast it is easier to fast."[26] During their engagement Freud promised his very religious fiancée that something of the "essence" of Judaism would "not be absent" from their home, although after their marriage he persuaded her to drop all religious practice. She did this, but at the end of Freud's life husband and wife were still bickering because Martha wished to light candles on the Sabbath.[27]

Obviously, there were women who gradually dropped the observance of most rituals, particularly second-generation urbanites. Some preferred a more secular approach, others a more convenient one: one woman convinced her husband that it was foolish to forgo lunch on Yom Kippur.[28] And there were women who for social reasons assumed that a denial of their Jewish identity, religious and otherwise, would improve their position in gentile society. Yet these were the minority.

Conversion and intermarriage statistics for the Imperial era, for example, show Jewish men to have been the group consistently more prone to cut their ties with Judaism and Jewish society.[29] When women intermarried, economic necessity and lack of available Jewish partners were primary causes. The wealthy Jewish woman who married the penniless Prussian aristocrat or officer was a well known, but not particularly representative, type, and her heyday probably came earlier.[30] One finds that more Jewish males in mixed marriages had middle-class incomes than Jewish females. In marriages between non-Jewish men and Jewish women, commentators remarked that the latter most often came from the lower classes.[31] These women bore more children and experienced more stillbirths than non-Jewish women married to Jewish men, leading one demographer to conclude that Jewish women married to gentile men lived at a "significantly lower standard of living" than those with a Jewish husband.[32] Further, intermarried Jewish women were more likely than Jewish men to assimilate entirely (perhaps another reason for their greater hesitancy to involve themselves in such a union). In general, the children of mixed marriages did not grow up as Jews, but the offspring of Jewish fathers were more likely to be brought up within the Jewish faith than those of Jewish mothers.[33] The extent to which these women did assimilate suggests that class status influenced women's allegiance to their religion and community. Without middle-class means it may have become increasingly more difficult to maintain traditional loyalties.

As in the case of intermarriage, female conversion, too, was more often necessitated by serious economic need than male conversion. The latter was frequently a means toward achieving promotion and social acceptance rather than assuring one's basic sustenance. Tax records of Berlin converts in the years 1873–1906, indicate that 84 percent of female converts (as compared to 44 percent of male converts) fell in the lowest income categories.[34] Until 1880, comparatively few women converted. Between 1873 and 1906 women were one-fourth of all converts. By 1908 their share had increased to 37 percent and by 1912 to 40 percent of all conversions.[35] The entrance of women into paid employment and the growth of anti-Semitism contributed to this sudden increase.[36] The Jewish press gave evidence to support this theory. One could read of the Jewish teacher who sought employment in vain until she converted or the Jewish domestic who also converted in order to find employment.[37]

Despite increasing rates of conversions and intermarriage, most Jewish women kept to a small group of Jewish friends and were enclosed in a family circle. Women's relegation to this private sphere discouraged them, more than men, from assimilatory behavior. Even Jewish feminists, who would seek the emancipation of the individual from traditional sociocultural constraints, clung to the notion of the family as the cornerstone of Judaism.[38]

Women found communality and sociability within the family. They were responsible for kinship networks and for the care of grandparents and orphans—in short, for the moral and material support, the continuity and organization, of an often geographically dispersed family system. Frequently this was left to the oldest woman in the family. When her grandmother died, Eva Ehrenberg (b. 1891, in Frankfurt a. Main) recalled her mother's assuming responsibility for the family network: "so that the connections would be maintained."[39] The aged were seen as family responsibilities and assets. Grandparents often lived within walking distance of their grandchildren in towns and big cities alike. They frequently moved in with their children when they became widowed. A single woman would also live with an aging mother or father, often giving up her own ambitions to care for her parent.[40]

Jewish women participated in cousin clubs, initiated vacations with other family members, and planned regular family gatherings. Frequently, such meetings led to discussions of possible marriage partners, with women considering the likelihood of two personalities meshing and men talking over the financial prerequisites.[41] Naturally, it was easier to maintain intimate family connections in the towns. Yet even when heightened mobility threatened to tear these ties apart, women, in particular, traveled to visit relatives. Whereas boys left home for an apprenticeship or the university, girls left home in order to maintain family connections.

## WOMEN IN THE RELIGIOUS COMMUNITY

Traditional Jewish religious practice (which, as Jewish feminist leader between 1904 and 1938 Bertha Pappenheim charged,[42] viewed women basically in biological terms, as sexual beings) does not require female participation in most synagogue rituals. When women did attend services, they sat segregated in a gallery or rear area apart from the men. At mid-nineteenth century, their religious education consisted of a mixture of morals, religion, and reading and writing (German and Judaeo-German).[43] Their education was minimal; one woman (b. 1844) recalled that when she borrowed a prayer book in the women's gallery, she found notations in the margins suggesting the appropriate emotion or reaction, such as "One cries at this point." She commented, "The majority of women recited the prayers without understanding anything."[44] This generalization was no longer true during the Imperial era, when Hebrew was taught to some women. Still, women read the *tkhines* (a devotional book, written in Judaeo-German) or German prayers while Hebrew services went on below them and often took the opportunity to chat with other women. Witnesses and participants decried the lack of decorum in the galleries where the "second-class citizens of God" sat.[45]

During the nineteenth century, a few attempts were made to rectify this situation. Some leaders of Reform (Liberal) Judaism were sensitive to the roles of women in the organized religion. In part, they sought to maintain women's allegiance, but mostly they were embarrassed lest gentile society should observe the Oriental customs evident in the relegation of Jewish women to second-class status.

The leaders of Reform placed the status of women on the agenda of their synod at Breslau in 1846. They proclaimed as atavistic and "an insult to the free personality of woman" the segregation of women, the absence of confirmation, the male blessing thanking God for not having been born a woman, the ban on women in choirs, and the law of *halitzah* (which demands a brother-in-law's permission for the remarriage of a childless widow).[46] Yet this conference made few practical improvements in women's status in the synagogue except in the tiny Reform congregation of Berlin. Still, the religion and its adherents did acculturate to some of the traditions of the majority. Confirmation and the double-ring wedding ceremony caught on in Reform congregations. Reform Rabbis argued that boys and girls should be confirmed, although they denied that confirmation meant the same thing as in Christianity. In Judaism there was no definite age at which girls began their obligation to obey the laws; thus, "once again, the female sex [was] here treated as less capable, as in Oriental custom."[47] Rabbinic and lay leaders suggested that the education of both boys and girls "should climax with a solemn act in a sacred place."[48] This custom gained wider acceptance during the last decades of the Imperial era and was supported by Jewish feminists, who insisted that girls should receive equal religious preparation.[49]

Women, themselves, were sometimes involved in modifying religious practice: female pressure, for example, led to the introduction of double-ring ceremonies in Reform congregations.[50] This may have been particularly true outside the institutional setting of the synagogue. For example, in rural regions, many Jewish home rituals, like the preparations for birth and childbed and baby-naming ceremonies (*Holekrash*), were led by women and informed by local custom or superstition.[51]

Despite some changes, however, Jewish law and Jewish tradition, reinforced by the sexism of German society, remained remarkably resistant to female intrusion. Thus, the good intentions of reformers and some superficial modifications did not alter a woman's role in the synagogue. She still sat in a women's section, read a women's Bible, and, more often than not, did not even attend but prayed at home. In 1908 a Reform organization, the Vereinigung für das liberale Judentum in Deutschland, formulated a platform noting that special emphasis was to be placed on the greater participation of women in organized religion and the community.[52] Its guidelines added that the participation of women was indispensable and that they should receive an equal share of religious duties, as well as rights. Yet theory did not quickly translate into action. In the years before the World War there was no agitation for religious equality from any quarter, and even demands for women's votes in community concerns were opposed or ignored. In sum, Jewish women's exclusion from participation in the synagogue pointed to the centrality of the home in their personal connection to Judaism. Such gender-specific observance was probably perceived as less important by both women and men. The latter had greater respect for public observance, to the point that their memoirs typically skirt over their mothers' private observances. Women, too, accepted the hegemonic values placing greater importance on the public sphere. Still, many continued to perform rituals and evince religious sentiment, however belittled or overlooked, in the private sphere. Thus, historians know far more about the perceived inferiority of women's rituals than about women's actual neglect of religion.

Women's exclusion from the synagogue did not extend to Jewish communal activities: this is where women found work, demonstrated competence, and built self-esteem in the public sphere. Religious tradition as well as practical necessity encouraged the continuation of the charitable activities that had originated in the medieval ghetto. Even as the milieu of the ghetto disappeared and Jews no longer operated in an exclusively Jewish framework, Jewish women continued traditional charitable societies. Men rigidly excluded them from the management of communal affairs but allowed them to extend their practical housekeeping to the community at large. Thus, women found an outlet for their organizing talents and charitable propensities in voluntary associations. They donated their spare time to benevolent societies, including those that engaged in poor relief, aid to sick and pregnant women, and the preparation of female corpses for burial (*chevra kadisha*). During the nineteenth century, growing numbers of Jewish women's groups, paralleling the growth of German women's associations, began to broaden their welfare activities. Their ministrations were well-meaning and basic, and there was personal contact between donors and recipients. Women's societies continued to grow and modernize in the late nineteenth century, expanding their interests (particularly in the area of girls' education and child welfare) and creating impressive social and economic enterprises.

Distinctive among these groups was the Jüdischer Frauenbund (League of Jewish Women), founded in 1904 by Bertha Pappenheim. Combining feminist goals with a strong sense of Jewish identity, the Jüdischer Frauenbund came to enroll about 20 percent of all Jewish women in Germany and played a vital role within the Jewish community. Among its concerns were equal participation of women with men in the Jewish community, providing career training for Jewish women, and combatting all forms of immorality, especially white slavery (prostitution).[53]

In 1908, with the abolition of the *Vereinsgesetz* (banning women's involvement in political organizations), many formerly all male Jewish organizations, such as the Centralverein, suddenly became aware of a pool of potential new members and began sponsoring women's meetings. Despite a few token spokeswomen (Henriette May, Ernestine Eschelbacher, and Henriette Fürth), however, the Centralverein, and similar groups, sought the membership, rather than the leadership, of women.[54]

Although attention has been called to the German-Jewish women who participated in the work of the nonsectarian German Women's movement and in the advancement of social work, the majority of organized Jewish women remained within Jewish local or national organizations. Even among the Jewish women most active in broader social welfare or feminist activities, many donated their efforts to specifically Jewish endeavors as well.[55] Jewishness—the modernized practice of their religion—as well as a strong sense of solidarity with other Jews, defined their identity more than has been recognized by historians and more than they themselves may have realized. As time went on (particularly after the World War), the organized Jewish community and Jewish friendship networks and charity and cultural associations, rather than the strict observance of traditional Jewish customs, provided the vehicle for Jewish identity.

## INTEGRATION INTO MAINSTREAM EDUCATION AND EMPLOYMENT

Both Jewish and German patriarchal traditions impeded women's pursuit of education. Too much education was "unfeminine": a woman would not perform her other duties and would neglect her family if she became too learned. Similarly, too much reading of any sort was considered not only distracting, but positively dangerous to women's health. Thus, most girls' schools, particularly at the primary level (*Volksschule*) gave their pupils an education that concentrated on reading, writing, arithmetic, and "feminine" subjects such as art, music, and literature. At the middle level (*Mittelschule*), girls might attend a nine-year course (*höhere Töchterschule* or *höhere Mädchenschule*;

it offered ten years after reforms in 1901 and 1908), which they completed by fifteen or sixteen years of age. Thereafter, the upper-middle-
class girl might receive some music, literature, and language instruction at home from a private tutor.

In 1908 a major reorganization of the Prussian school system introduced subjects necessary to university entrance into girls' curricula.
Even then, girls' education concentrated on domestic science, elementary education, and child care, with some religious instruction,
languages, and literature appended. Only in the first decade of the
twentieth century did German universities admit women, years behind other Western industrial nations.

Whereas Jewish men were well integrated (and overrepresented
with regard to their percentage of the general population) in the German higher-education system, particularly in the *Gymnasium* (college
preparatory high school) and university, Jewish women, by virtue of
gender rather than religious or ethnic affiliation, were excluded from
both. Until the 1890s the only education open to them, the *Volks-
schule* or the *höhere Töchterschule*, shaped their understanding of German history and culture and their experience with non-Jewish peers.
Most Jewish girls in this period attended private or public *Volksschule*;
and an increasingly and disproportionately high percentage (approximately 42 percent of Jewish girls in Prussia in 1901 compared to 3.7
percent of gentile girls) went to the *höhere Töchterschule*.[56] In cities,
where such schools were located, these percentages were sharply
higher.[57] The decision to send one's daughter for extra schooling was
likely influenced by the urban, middle-class status of German Jews and
their aspirations for the social regard that attended those who excelled
in German education, as well as by the traditional Jewish veneration
for learning. Moreover, *höhere Töchterschule* implied a certain class
status or upward mobility. Not only did it consist of a formal curriculum, but girls who attended it also received extracurricular enrichment paid for by their parents. This included dancing lessons and
balls, as well as music, drawing, and singing lessons. The after-school
programs of German-Jewish girls were exact replicas of the German
middle-class prescription for elevated womanhood.

No matter whether they received minimal training or the more
elaborate accoutrements of a "class-appropriate" education, the majority of Jewish girls were integrated into German classrooms; there
they had their first sustained (and frequently harsh) experience with

the non-Jewish world.[58] Discrimination against them could start as early as kindergarten and continue through the uppermost school years.

This period of life often left strong memories, and it is not unusual to find memoirs in which the authors insist that they did not come into contact with anti-Semitism. Nevertheless, they invariably do recall at least one such occurrence and describe it in a way that shows it left an indelible impression. Toni Ehrlich (b. 1880, in Breslau), the only Jew in a class of twenty, remembered an incident in which a pupil, asked to dictate a grammatical sentence, responded, "The Jews crucified our Savior."[59] When she invited a classmate to her home she was turned down, because the girl's parents would not let their daughter visit a Jew. Encounters with anti-Semitism were often fleeting moments in the classroom or sewing circle, sometimes barely perceptible, most often quickly repressed or excused as atypical. Yet the effects of rejection left Jews with a peculiar sensitivity to their status as outsiders. They cut so deeply as to be remembered and often denied a lifetime later.

In the lower and middle schools, Jewish girls, much like their gentile counterparts, also experienced the consequences of gender discrimination. These effects were less obvious to them, because their socialization and role indoctrination prevented all but a few from demanding much more. They shared the culturally determined expectations and psychologically internalized marginality that set them apart from boys. Therefore, of the two, sexism and anti-Semitism, girls were more aware of the latter (even as they sometimes repressed it) as part of the legacy of childhood experiences.

In contrast, Jewish women who sought a higher education were keenly conscious that sexism, rather than anti-Semitism, was the predominant obstacle in their paths. Anti-Semitism was certainly not absent, particularly since the entrance of women into these male sanctuaries coincided with the growth of racial anti-Semitism in Germany. Authors of memoirs often allude to the double burden of being a woman and a Jew, but the antifemale biases of their professors, their parents, and their Jewish male counterparts had the most stinging effect.

The doors of higher education finally opened to women in 1908. Thereafter, Jewish women were highly represented; although their actual numbers were small.[60] By 1911 German-Jewish women made up

11 percent of all women students at Prussian universities (189 women).[61] Social acceptance was another thing. As women and as Jews, they were outsiders. It was clear to them that their teachers, professors, and, frequently, parents approved neither their educational, nor their career, aspirations.[62]

The commercial success of German Jewry in the late nineteenth century had relegated most women to an entirely domestic role. Much like their gentile counterparts, Jewish men, whether they were wealthy or still aspiring to bourgeois respectability, considered it beneath their dignity and a sign of financial failure if their wives or daughters were employed. Thus, only a minority of native-born German-Jewish women were integrated into the work force. Those who worked outside the home were affected by sexism and by anti-Semitism. Women who demanded careers (and there were always some who did) precipitated family crises. Middle-class parents considered public employment unladylike and improper for their daughters. When the daughters (born in the 1870s) of a wealthy banker in Mainz insisted on helping out in his bank, their father reluctantly agreed. But they had to hide in a back office, "because it would have hurt the firm's reputation [for them] to be seen there."[63] Thus, gender discrimination (as well as class pretensions) made it unlikely that most Jewish women would avail themselves of the public world of work as a path toward integration.

By 1882, when the first comprehensive employment statistics were published, 11 percent of all Jewish women in Prussia (compared to 21 percent of gentile women) were employed. By 1895 a German census indicated that 39,427 Jewish women were employed. Twelve years later these figures showed a 36 percent increase to 53,747, or 18 percent of Jewish women.[64]

Those women who ventured out either despite their affluence and cultural conditioning or because of economic need confronted anti-Semitism. Whereas growing numbers of middle-class women entered the world of work in the late nineteenth century, anti-Semitism closed the doors of many of the new "women's careers" (teaching, nursing, post and telegraph operation) to Jews.[65] The few who did struggle through the hostile university often found their opportunities severely limited by a mixture of anti-Semitism and misogyny. As late as 1919, Jewish newspapers warned women of pronounced anti-Semitism in teaching,[66] while anti-female attitudes and restrictions prevailed in most professions.

Even when anti-Semitism was not a direct obstacle to integration, Jewish women did not adapt to a "German" job distribution. While their occupational profile more nearly approximated that of the general German population than did the profile of Jewish men, Jewish women, like Jewish men, were found most often in commercial sectors and were thereby segregated by occupation.[67] Thus, Jewish women found themselves in traditionally "Jewish" job categories, which were attacked by anti-Semites as parasitic, and criticized by Jewish leaders as indicative of an "unhealthy job distribution." This predominance of women in commerce was due to several factors. Sixty-four percent of Jewish working males (for reasons having to do with historical discrimination against Jews and the resulting formation of certain skills and predilections) were engaged in commerce; and family businesses provided jobs for female relatives. Fully 30 percent of Jewish women in commercial enterprises were "family assistants."[68] Also, the majority of Jews lived in cities, where trade or office jobs in industry offered young women opportunities for employment. Therefore, women's choice of occupation was closely related to the position of Jews in Germany. Job status, on the other hand, was gender-related. Jewish women were found in positions inferior to men and held the vast majority of the least remunerative and least respected jobs.

In the first decades of the twentieth century, Jewish women increasingly appeared in the public spheres of higher education and work. But the double burden of being women and Jews plagued them. Discrimination against them as Jews continued to influence their choice of jobs and careers, while rigid sex role stereotypes continued to affect their job status within the Jewish community.

## CONCLUSION

Jewish women's experiences and perceptions in accomodating to the majority culture in Imperial Germany were different from men's due to their socialization, their primary loyalties to home and family, and the sexism of both Jewish tradition and the general society. Women appear to have clung longer than men to both the religious and social ties of the Jewish community, and they were integrated into the realms of education, employment, and politics later. Although Jewish women acculturated, looking, dressing, and speaking like their neighbors, their intense involvements with their families and with the Jewish community in concert with endemic anti-Semitism inhibited their total assimilation. They maintained their Jewishness even as they accomodated to the majority.

## NOTES

This essay is an abridged and somewhat altered version of the author's "Tradition and Transition: The Acculturation, Assimilation, and Integration of Jews in Imperial Germany: A Gender Analysis," *Leo Baeck Institute Year Book* [hereafter *LBI Year Book*] 27 (1982): 3–35. Readers should consult the original essay for theoretical analyses and for more detailed documentation that the present format allows. We thank the *Leo Baeck Institute Year Book* for permission to reprint this new version of the essay here.

1. Among historians of this period who do offer glimpses of women's lives are Jacob Toury, *Soziale und politische Geschichte der Juden in Deutschland, 1847–1871* (Düsseldorf, 1977); Monika Richarz, ed. *Jüdisches Leben in Deutschland: Selbstzeugnisse zur Sozialgeschichte im Kaiserreich* (Stuttgart, 1979); Jacob Katz, *Out of the Ghetto* (Cambridge, MA, 1973).

2. See Ismar Schorsch, *Jewish Reactions to German Anti-Semitism, 1870–1914* (New York, 1972); Peter Pulzer, "Why Was There a Jewish Question in Imperial Germany?" *LBI Year Book* 25 (1980): 142.

3. Jews were careful to speak proper German, but many maintained a language loyalty to Judeo-German as well. On Jewish uses of their own distinct language, see my "Gender Analysis," 6.

4. Gershom Scholem, "On the Social Psychology of the Jews in Germany, 1900–1933," in *Jews and Germans from 1860 to 1933: The Problematic Symbiosis*, ed. David Bronsen (Heidelberg, 1979), 17.

5. This extended to Austrian Jews as well: "In one way we all remained Jewish," wrote Freud's son. "We moved in Jewish circles, our friends were Jews, our doctor, our lawyer were Jews" (quoted in Egon Schwartz, "Melting Pot or Witches' Cauldron? Jews and Anti-Semites in Vienna at the Turn of the Century," in *Jews and Germans*, ed. Bronsen, 276–77.

6. Charlotte Wolff, *Hindsight: An Autobiography* (London, 1980), 6.

7. Marion Berghahn (*German Jews in England, 1933–1980: Assimilation, Integrity, and Ethnicity* [London, 1982]) makes this point and argues that ethnic culture is not a way station en route to homogenization but a form of social life.

8. See, e.g., Toni Cassirer, "Aus meinem Leben mit Ernst Cassirer," Memoir Collection, Leo Baeck Institute, New York [hereafter LBI], p. iii. Even if women

wrote as many memoirs as men, they or their relatives did not find it as important to publish or bequeath them.

9. Jacob Toury (*Soziale und politische Geschichte*, 114) estimated that in 1871–1874 about 60 percent of German Jews were part of an upper and middle tax bracket; between 15 percent and 35 percent were either petty bourgeois or fell into the lowest tax bracket; and between 5 percent and 25 percent could be termed marginal or poor.

10. According to John Knodel (*The Decline of Fertility in Germany, 1871–1939* [Princeton, 1974], 136–47, 246–63), Jews probably started to reduce their family size several decades prior to German unification. Throughout the Imperial era they were well ahead of the rest of the non-Jewish population in family planning, although the latter, too, reduced its family size. Also see Steven Lowenstein, "The Pace of Modernisation of German Jewry in the Nineteenth Century," *LBI Year Book* 21 (1976): 56.

11. Gerda Lerner, *The Majority Finds Its Past. Placing Women in History* (New York, 1979), 132; L. von Stein (1886) in Jürgen Zinnecker, *Sozialgeschichte der Mädchenbildung* (Weinheim, 1973), 116, 118.

12. Hermann Greive, "Zionism and Jewish Orthodoxy," *LBI Year Book* 25 (1980): 188.

13. The civil code raised women's status by dropping the husband's guardianship and disciplinary rights over his wife. It gave her rights to her own earnings, but husbands were awarded final authority over the wealth or property she brought into the marriage. The *Vereinsgesetze* were laws of association instituted by Prussia and many other states in the mid-nineteenth century. They banned women (and minors) from participation in political organizations, interpreting "political" broadly.

14. Infant mortality figures improved very little before 1900 in Germany, England, or France. Jews generally had better rates than the surrounding German population. See Knodel, *Decline of Fertility*, 155–74 and my "Gender Analysis," 11, n. 31 for documentation on infant mortality, as well as declining Jewish fertility rates.

15. For one example, see Richarz, *Jüdisches Leben*, 298–99.

16. See, e.g., Richarz, *Jüdisches Leben*, 158–59.

17. Bruno Stern, *Meine Jugenderinnerungen an eine Kleinstadt und ihre jüdische Gemeinde* (Stuttgart, 1968), 93.

18. Esther Calvary, Memoir Collection, LBI, 11; Clara Geismar, Memoir Collection, LBI, 20–23, 42–44.

19. Henriette Hirsch, Memoir Collection, LBI, 9.

20. Scholem, "Social Psychology," 18.

21. Schorsch, "Jewish Reactions," 19.

22. Calvary, Memoir Collection, LBI, 19.

23. Adele Rosenzweig (b. 1867 at Ahlen, moved to Kassel in 1872) recalled that her family kept a kosher kitchen until her mother died. At that point her grandmother refused to visit their home because it was no longer kosher. Rivka Horwitz, ed. "Jugenderinnerungen," *Bulletin des Leo Baeck Instituts* 16–17, nos. 53–54 (1977–78): 144.

24. For examples, see Richarz, *Jüdisches Leben*, 298–99.

25. Quoted by David Aberbach, "Freud's Jewish Problem," *Commentary*, June 1980, 37.

26. Anna Kronthal, *Posner Mürbekuchen, Jugend-Erinnerungen einer Posnerin* (Munich, 1932), 27.

27. Quoted by David Aberbach, "Freud's Jewish Problem," 37.

28. Richarz, *Jüdisches Leben*, 346.

29. See my "Gender Analysis," 16–17, for statistical breakdowns on inter-marriage.

30. Arthur Ruppin, *Die Juden der Gegenwart* (Berlin, 1918), 162; and chapter 8 above.

31. Max Marcuse, *Über die Fruchtbarkeit der Christlich-jüdischen Mischehe* (Bonn, 1920), 16.

32. Ibid., 12.

33. *Israelitisches Gemeindeblatt* (Cologne), 8 May 1908, p. 186; *Zeitschrift für Demographie und Statistik der Juden* (Berlin) [hereafter ZDSJ], July 1906, pp. 107–8. This is despite the halachic ruling in which the mother determines the Jewishness of her child.

34. ZDSJ, January 1908, 13.

35. Toury (*Soziale und politische Geschichte*, 60) suggests that in all of Germany approximately 11,000 Jews converted between 1800 and 1870. Thereafter, between 1870 and 1900, 11,500 conversions took place. See also *Im deutschen Reich*, August 1913, pp. 339, 342.

36. *Im deutschen Reich*, August 1913, p. 342; see also my "Gender Analysis," 18.

37. *Im deutschen Reich*, October 1896, p. 505; *Israelitisches Gemeindeblatt* (Cologne), 3 November, 1905, pp. 439–40.

38. Rahel Strauss, "Ehe und Muttterschaft," in *Vom jüdischen Geiste: Ein Aufsatzreihe*, ed. Der Jüdische Frauenbund (Berlin, 1934), 21. On German Jewish women's feminist activities, see my *The Jewish Feminist Movement in Germany: The Campaigns of the Jüdischer Frauenbund, 1904–1938* (Westport, CT, 1979) and "German-Jewish Feminism in the Twentieth Century," *Jewish Social Studies* 38 (1976): 39–53.

39. Eva Ehrenberg, *Sehnsucht-mein geliebtes Kind* (Frankfurt a. Main, 1963), 24. This theme runs through most women's memoirs.

40. For an example, see Hirsch, Memoir Collection, LBI, 65. Sophie Diamant (b. 1879, in Mainz) lived with her aging mother long after her five brothers and sisters left home. At thirty-one she married, and her mother moved into her home shortly thereafter ("Familiengeschichte Schlesinger," Memoir Collection, LBI).

41. Philippine Landau, *Kindheitserinnerungen: Bilder aus einer rheinischen Kleinstadt des vorigen Jahrhunderts* (Dietenheim, 1956), 30. Introductions by relatives could mean introductions to relatives. Marriages between two relatives occurred more often among Jews than people of other religions. See my "For Love or Money: Jewish Marriage Strategies in Imperial Germany," in *The Marriage Bargain: Women and Dowries in European History*, ed. Marion A. Kaplan (New York, 1985), 152–53.

42. Johanna Meyer Collection, no. 877 (XI, 2), LBI. On the remarkable career of Bertha Pappenheim (1859–1936), activist, author, and founder of the feminist *Jüdischer Frauenbund*, see my "Bertha Pappenheim: Founder of German-Jewish Feminism," in *The Jewish Woman: New Perspectives*, ed. Elisabeth Koltun (New York, 1976), 149–63.

43. Mordechai Eliav, *Jewish Education in Germany in the Period of Enlightenment and Emancipation* [Hebrew] (Jerusalem, 1960), chap. 11 and pp. 271–79.

44. Geismar, Memoir Collection, LBI. 73.

45. Wolff, *Hindsight*, 47. For information on the *tkhines*, see Chava Weissler, "The Religion of Traditional Ashkenazic Women: Some Methodological Issues," *Association for Jewish Studies Review* 12 (1987): 73–94; and chapter 7 above.

46. David Philipson, *The Reform Movement in Judaism* (New York, 1967), 218.

47. Isaac Asher Francolm, "Simplicity Not Pomp," in *Das Rationale Judentum*

(1840), excerpted by W. Gunther Plaut, ed. and trans. *The Rise of Reform Judaism. A Sourcebook of Its European Origins* (New York, 1963), 174.

48. Ibid.

49. *Allgemeine Zeitung des Judentums*, 30 January 1914, p. 4.

50. Joseph Aub, "One or Two Wedding Rings?" in *Rise of Reform*, ed. Plaut, 218.

51. For descriptions of the ceremonies surrounding childbirth, see Jacob Picard, "Childhood in the Village," in *LBI Year Book* 4 (1959): 280; Edmond Uhry, Memoir Collection, LBI, 111; Stern, *Meine Jugenderinnerungen*, 116.

52. Gunther Plaut, *The Growth of Reform Judaism: American and European Sources until 1948* (New York, 1965), 68.

53. See my "German-Jewish Feminism," 39–40 and *Jewish Feminist Movement.*

54. See my "Gender Analysis," 24.

55. Ibid., 26.

56. ZDSJ, September 1909, p. 141.

57. In 1897 in Berlin, 60.17 percent of Jewish girls went to such schools compared to 9.6 percent of gentile girls (*ZDSJ*, August 1909, p. 120).

58. Only a slight majority of Jewish children attended Volksschule at all, and of this number a minority attended a Jewish Volksschule. See my "Gender Analysis," 27 for statistical breakdowns.

59. Ehrlich, Memoir Collection, LBI, 21.

60. Baden allowed women to matriculate in 1901 (Universities of Heidelberg and Freiburg). Prussia was the last to allow women to matriculate, in 1908. In 1905 there were eighty full-time women students in Germany; in 1910 there were 1,867; and in 1914 there were 4,126.

61. ZDSJ, April 1913, p. 61; February 1914, p. 31; June 1914, pp. 86–87. In 1911 Jewish students made up 8 percent of the male population at the universities in Prussia.

62. See my "Gender Analysis," 30 for a variety of contemporary responses.

63. Diamant, "Familiengeschichte Schlesinger," Memoir Collection, LBI, 8.

64. ZDSJ, May 1911, pp. 79–80; and see my "Gender Analysis," 32.

65. Jewish women wished to become teachers despite the well-known difficulties they would face. In 1911, in fact, the majority of Prussian-Jewish female students took subjects leading to teaching careers. But in the prewar era many graduates were forced to content themselves with jobs as librarians, substitute teachers, or private tutors or teachers.

66. See, e.g., ZDSJ, January-March 1919, p. 4.

67. See my "Gender Analysis," 33 for statistical breakdowns.

68. ZDSJ, April 1905.

## Gender and the Immigrant Jewish Experience in the United States

When East European Jews migrated to the United States in the late nineteenth and early twentieth centuries as part of that vast wave labeled the New Immigration, women were an important component of the newcomers. In fact, because this was a family migration, women constituted a greater proportion of Jewish immigrants than of any other immigrant population of the time.[1] Yet in much of U.S. Jewish historiography women make scarcely more than a cameo appearance. Those who achieved fame or fortune in the public arena, such as Jennie Grossinger or Emma Goldman (to cite two very disparate figures), are duly noted. However, the historical experience of ordinary women is subsumed in that of the Jewish community as a whole; and the history of the Jewish community as a whole, like all history, has been retold from the vantage point of Jewish men. The perceptions, achievements, and institutions of men define the historical record of U.S. Jewry.

The development of the field of women's history, however, has alerted us to the distinctive nature of women's historical experience not only within the family but also at work and in the community.

Gender has taken its place, alongside class and ethnicity, as an essential category of historical analysis. Defined as "the socially and culturally constructed aspects of the division of the sexes,"[2] as an analytic category *gender* enables us to reexamine and refine assumptions about historical development that are derived from the experience of one-half of the population alone. It also prods us to take note of hierarchies within culture and society. In the words of Joan Wallach Scott, in an important recent theoretical essay, "Gender is a constitutive element of social relationships based on perceived differences between the sexes, and gender is a primary way of signifying relationships of power."[3]

The complex interplay of gender, social class, and religio-ethnic culture shaped the ways in which Jewish women participated in the economic, cultural, religious, and political life of the immigrant Jewish community and U.S. society. Even as Jewish women shared a common heritage, living space, and some institutions, values, and aspirations with their husbands and brothers, they also created a female culture and constructed a community different from the organized community of Jewish men. Within the Jewish community women found their situation defined and limited primarily by their gender and class, while in the society at large they confronted the additional disability conferred by their ethnicity. The incorporation of the experience of women into the saga of East European Jews in the United States stimulates a rethinking of such familiar issues as social mobility, the processes of acculturation and integration, and the definition of community and politics. Similarly, sensitivity to the different forms of discourse about gender and to the concomitant differences in social behavior among ethnic groups is necessary to prevent the homogenization of experience that is all too common in the history of immigrant women in the United States.[4] Immigrant Jewish women shared many of the characteristics of other early-twentieth-century U.S. immigrant women, but their experience was influenced by their Jewishness as well as their gender (itself constructed by a Jewish culture in transition and by the particular historical situation of Jews in Eastern Europe).

Immigrant Jewish women had their roots in an East European Jewish culture in which the roles of men and women were clearly differentiated, particularly in the religious realm. Positions of status within the public sacred sphere as well as seats of power within the commu-

nity as a whole were reserved for men, as was access to the study of
Jewish texts. Boys were raised to master those texts, to assume their
rightful place within the synagogue and community, and to serve as
the heads of their family. Girls, on the other hand, were given little
or no formal education but learned at their mother's skirts the skills
that were essential for maintaining a kosher home and sustaining a
family.

East European Jewish culture offered women contradictory messages. Although their status was clearly inferior to men's, within the
secular sphere women were given a great deal of autonomy in order to
support their families and to provide social welfare through their own
charitable associations. Because the full-time scholar was the masculine cultural ideal (though a reality for only an infinitesimally small
elite) and because of dire economic conditions, economic activity was
recognized as appropriate and normal for women. Thus, in addition to
performing their household tasks, women also participated in what we
would call the public sphere of marketplace life and, to a lesser extent,
communal life.[5]

By the end of the last century, the impact of urbanization and of
such ideologies as Haskalah (Enlightenment) and socialism had enhanced the status of Jewish women. Both Haskalah and socialism
attacked the disabilities that women suffered under Jewish law and
proclaimed a theoretical commitment to female equality, thereby reinforcing the assertiveness and sense of competence that traditional
Jewish culture had tolerated among women in the world of practical
affairs.[6] Since evidence indicates that the Jews who migrated from
Eastern Europe were recruited overwhelmingly from areas that had
suffered the most disruption of the traditional Jewish economy and
culture, secular ideologies wielded considerable influence within the
immigrant Jewish community. Although, as we shall see, immigrant
Jewish women retained distinctly different roles from immigrant men,
they were often granted more autonomy in matters of work and leisure
than was the case for women in some other ethnic communities.

This was so despite the fact that within the family circle girls,
especially the eldest, were expected to assume more responsibility
than were boys. They were assigned traditional female tasks of household chores and child care for younger siblings, in addition to paid
labor. One immigrant woman remarked, "I always used to help my
mother. . . . I never let her wash a floor." Another described how her

parents depended on her as an adolescent to accompany them and translate for them in their contacts with English-speaking personnel. "Oh yes, they depended on me," she concluded. "My brother really enjoyed his life—I had the responsibilities."[7] A three-generation comparative study of Jewish, Italian, and Slavic women confirms her remark. It discovered that of the three ethnic groups, Jewish women of the first generation were overwhelmingly the most likely to perceive sex distinctions in their parents' treatment of them and their brothers (not that they were necessarily discriminated against more: it's possible they were more sensitive to differential treatment). More than 95 percent of them complained that their brothers had been favored by their parents.[8]

If boys and girls were the recipients of different parental expectations of behavior at home, they also approached the major aspect of life outside the home—wage labor—with perspectives shaped by their gender. The place, type, and significance of work differed substantially for women and for men in the immigrant Jewish community. While full-time, lifelong and highly paid employment replaced the mastery of Jewish texts as the gender ideal for Jewish men in the United States, Jewish women, like their sisters in other ethnic groups, saw work outside the home as a temporary phenomenon, limited to the hopefully brief period between the completion of their education and their marrying. For women work was a function of their place in the life cycle. Because immigrant Jewish men were highly skilled and well endowed with entrepreneurial talent relative to other immigrants, married Jewish women worked outside the home in much smaller numbers than did other immigrant women. For example, a U.S. Senate report on immigrant work patterns revealed that in 1911 1 percent of immigrant Jewish wives in New York City were officially employed as compared with 36 percent of their female Italian neighbors. (East European Jewish and Italian immigrants are often compared because of the coincidence of their mass migration to the United States and the proximity of their settlement, though in different urban immigrant neighborhoods, in several cities.) While there was considerable local variation and the New York City disparity is the most extreme, the pattern generally holds true.[9] These ethnic differentials increased with the passage of time as the majority of Jewish men experienced relatively rapid upward social mobility. The ability of many immigrant Jewish men to provide for their families without the employment of their wives (but often with the wages of their children) led to a decline between 1910 and 1925 in the percentage of employed Jewish women while the percentage increased among other ethnic groups.[10]

The full-time housewife thus appeared sooner in immigrant and second-generation Jewish communities than among other immigrant groups. Jewish women experienced more rapid mobility than other immigrant women, but their experience of mobility was vicarious and left them dependent on their husbands for their status. The decision to work outside the home was not left to women themselves. Indeed, immigrant Jewish men—and undoubtedly many women as well—shared the cultural norms prevalent among both European immigrants and the middle-class U.S. public that declared that wives working outside the home reflected the failure of their husbands to fulfill their responsibilities. Except when prolonged unemployment or illness dictated otherwise, Jewish men insisted that their wives abandon outside employment. Some immigrant Jewish women, interviewed in the mid-1970s when they were between seventy and ninety years old, expressed their regret at the absence of choice and pointed to the negative consequences of their early retirement. As one commented, "If a wife worked, the husband couldn't dominate as much as he could with a girl who depended on him for all the income. When men came home from work . . . they were kings in the house."[11] Housewives worked, too, but their work was not generally reflected in official statistics and perhaps was not even considered as real work by the women themselves. They helped their husbands in mom-and-pop stores, did piecework at home, or took in boarders to supplement the family's income. Sydney Stahl Weinberg's oral history project on elderly immigrant Jewish women in New York has found that while all forty-six women in the study had worked outside the home at some point in their married lives, most initially denied that they had worked after marriage and volunteered the information that they had entered the labor force during the Depression or after their children were grown only late in the interview.[12] When immigrant Jewish women entered the labor force in their youth, they found their job placement affected by their gender. Like their brothers, they generally secured employment through family contacts. Not surprisingly, they concentrated in the typical Jewish trades, particularly in the garment industry. Because of their work experience in Eastern Europe, their literacy, and the Jewish devaluation of unskilled manual labor, they tended to be more highly skilled than other employed immigrant women. However, they were less likely than their brothers to hold white collar jobs. Thus, in New York City in 1905 when more than 45 percent of immigrant Jewish men were employed in white-collar positions, only 27 percent of their sisters were so employed.[13] Within broad categories of jobs, as well, there were important gender distinctions. In the garment shops the most highly paid positions were regularly assigned to men, the less remunerative jobs to women. Women working full-time in the clothing trades scarcely earned 60 percent of their brothers' wages.[14] The sons and daughters of immigrants were also segregated by gender in the labor market. Jewish immigrants prepared their sons for careers as business entrepreneurs and later as professionals; their daughters were trained to become clerical workers, department store saleswomen, and schoolteachers. In the settlement houses, clubs and classes were segregated by gender. Following the prevailing pattern for women, the Baroness de Hirsch Training School for girls in New York, to cite one example, offered courses in millinery, cooking, washing machine operating, hand sewing, and dressmaking.[15] The aspirations that young women developed were therefore limited by prevailing cultural values of appropriate gender behavior. Second-generation Jewish women eagerly accepted the U.S. female dream of clerical work and teaching. By 1914 some observers commented, inaccurately, that Jewish women had already replaced U.S.-born and Irish women as the single largest element among New York City schoolteachers.[16] Because of the cultural disparagement of employment for married women, internalized values, and actual discrimination, the work worlds of women and men were distinct.

Although paid employment occupied relatively little of an adult woman's life, the significance attached to the work experience by the woman herself and by the community as a whole appears to have had a strong impact on immigrant Jewish women. One study by Virginia Yans-McLaughlin found that Jewish women employed in garment factories, in contrast to their Italian fellow workers, saw themselves as autonomous beings in control of their own lives.[17] Sydney Stahl Weinberg's interviews also revealed that immigrant Jewish women felt that work conferred freedom. Their parents respected that freedom; while they expected their daughters to contribute to the family's income, many allowed them to decide for themselves how much of their earnings they would hand over. In most Italian families, on the other hand, employed daughters were expected to give their parents their entire pay and received a modest allowance in return. Thus, work conveyed the status of autonomous adult to young Jewish women though it did not necessarily do so to the daughters of other ethnic groups.[18] As one immigrant Jewish woman (from Pittsburgh) recounted, "The best part was when I got a job for myself and was able to stand on my own feet."[19] The sense of competence and independence experienced in the workplace in their youth appears to have remained with immigrant and second-generation Jewish women even after their retirement into the home.

Jewish women displayed their sense of autonomy in a number of ways. The norms of their community permitted them considerable freedom in choosing their work and their leisure activities. For example, it was considered socially acceptable for them to attend public lectures and meetings at night unchaperoned, and they did so. After marriage, Jewish women expressed their desire for enhanced control over their own lives by seeking birth control information and becoming efficient users of contraception. Jewish women flocked to hear birth control lectures in Yiddish given by such prominent radicals as Emma Goldman and Rose Pastor Stokes and then wrote them letters asking for further information. When Margaret Sanger opened one of her early birth control clinics in the Jewish neighborhood of Brownsville in Brooklyn in 1916, women lined up outside on opening day even though the dispensing of birth control information was then illegal.[20] The rapid decline in Jewish fertility within one generation provides statistical evidence of the impact of increased female autonomy on the family lives of the entire Jewish community and is a central aspect of the historical experience of Jewish women in the last century.

Their early work experience often introduced Jewish women to another arena in which to exercise their autonomy, politics. Like their brothers, Jewish women proved to be fervent union activists. Gentile observers often commented on the high level of union participation and social consciousness displayed by Jewish working women. As the Women's Trades Union League, an association of middle-class female reformers and working-class women dedicated to improving working conditions for women, reported in 1909, "The Jewish women are quick to organize, and the League has found in several trades that the membership of the union was wholly Jewish, while the other nationalities working in the same trade were non-union."[21] A contemporary investigator from the Russell Sage Foundation also commended the "public spiritedness" of the Jewish girl and her "sense of relationship to a community larger than the family or the personal group of which she happens to be a member."[22] The labor historian Alice Kessler-Harris found that Jewish women were "responsible for at least one quarter of the increased number of unionized women (in America) in the second decade of the twentieth century."[23] In New York City before World War I, female Jewish garment workers constituted the majority of unionized women workers and the majority of the membership of the Women's Trade Union League. Indeed, Jewish women emerged as union leaders and displayed their steadfastness to the union cause during protracted and bitter strikes in the garment industry. The female shirtwaistmakers strike of 1909, in which Jewish women predominated, for example, was the largest strike by women until that time in the United States. The historian of the International Ladies Garment Workers' Union (ILGWU) commented of that strike that "though the principal union officials were men and the direction of the strike was in the hands of men, the women played a preponderant part in carrying it through. It was mainly women who did the picketing, who were arrested and fined, who ran the risk of assault, who suffered ill-treatment from the police and the court."[24] The success of the strike demonstrated that women could be counted on on the picket line and in the shops.

Despite their dedication to the union cause, Jewish women labor leaders found themselves discriminated against by the male union leadership, which was ambivalent at best about women working outside the home. When Pauline Newman, for example, organized a group of Philadelphia candymakers in 1910 and sought a charter for them from the International Bakery and Confectionary Workers' Union, the parent union delayed so long in issuing the charter that the local group fell apart.[25] Because women were considered merely temporary members of the work force, pushing down wages, even progressive unions like the ILGWU were reluctant to invest substantial efforts and resources in their unionization. Moreover, despite their theoretical commitment to the equality of women and men, male union leaders seem to have had difficulty in accepting women like Pauline Newman, Fannia Cohn, Rose Pesotta, and Rose Schneiderman in positions of authority. Within the union leadership ranks these women often felt isolated.[26] The garment unions also colluded in the sexual division of labor in the industry, with the higher-paid jobs reserved exclusively for males; the Protocols of the Dress and Waist Trade of 1913, accepted by union and management alike, established a wage scale in which the lowest salary for male jobs exceeded the highest pay for female jobs. Finally, male union leaders did not see the sexual harassment of women workers as an issue worthy of their attention.[27] Thus, gender considerations limited the effectiveness of trade unions in dealing with specific needs of women workers.

Gender also affected women's economic fortunes. In spite of their relative autonomy within the family and in their social life, the immigrant Jewish women who could not count on a husband's wages suffered from the limited job opportunities available to women, as well as their lack of experience. As in many societies, they and their children were the primary victims of poverty. The absence, disability, or death of the male breadwinner threw working-class families into disarray. Widows and their children accounted for the largest budget item in cash relief funds disbursed by the United Hebrew Charities in New York City before World War I. Moreover, economic circumstances, easy geographic mobility, and separation incurred in the migration process led thousands of Jewish men to desert their wives and children. Abandoned women and their families constituted the second largest item on the United Hebrew Charities cash relief budget, receiving 14.6 percent of the relief disbursed in 1905.[28] So seriously did the Jewish community treat this social problem that it established a National Desertion Bureau in 1911 to locate missing Jewish husbands.[29] The statistics are likely to understate the scope of the problem, for many deserted wives sought assistance from public charity with great reluctance, some only years after their husbands left them.[30] The establishment of Jewish orphan asylums in this period also offers poignant testimony to the difficulties experienced by women in supporting their children in the absence of their husbands, for many children placed in orphanages had one surviving parent. Some Jewish women, faced with the harsh working conditions and the brutally low wages available to them in factories and with families offering little emotional support, chose (or were lured into) prostitution as the alternative. A 1910 study of 647 prostitutes released from the Bedford Kills Reformatory found that Jewish women constituted 19 percent of the group, about equal to their proportion of New York City's population.

By 1924 the percentage of Jewish women among those arrested for prostitution in New York had fallen to 11 percent, although the Jewish population had increased.[31] Yet it is important to recognize in prostitution a gender-specific, as well as a class-specific, response to poverty and limited options.

Just as women were largely segregated in job categories and experienced work and poverty differently from men, so, too, their experiences with education were linked to their gender. Like Jewish men, Jewish women internalized the value of education, which was so prominent a part of East European Jewish culture. Their opportunities to express their passion for education, however, were far more restricted than were their brothers'. To put it another way, they shared the ethnic cultural and class factors that led to a higher percentage of immigrant and second-generation Jews in high school and college than other immigrant groups, but their gender prevented them from achieving parity with their brothers.

Although older children of both sexes, whose financial contribution was usually necessary for the survival of the family in its early years in the United States, were likely to begin work in garment shops in early adolescence while their younger, sometimes U.S.-born, siblings were able to prolong their education, girls' aspirations for education were deemed less worthy of consideration than boys'.[32] Immigrant families with limited resources to invest in education chose the strategy of expending them on their sons, on whom the responsibility of supporting a family would fall. It is not surprising, then, that a 1950 New York census survey indicated that among foreign-born Jews aged twenty-five to forty-four, the mean number of years of education for men was 10.9, while for women it was 9.7. And these figures represented a narrowing of the discrepancy that had existed in earlier years.[33] It was not uncommon to remove a daughter from school and send her to work in order to maintain a son in high school or college. One such story, that of Bessie, a department store girl with a brother in the College of the City of New York, was retold in the pages of *McClure's Magazine* in 1903.[34] Another immigrant Jewish woman, Ella Wolff, described how her father removed her from school over the opposition of the school principal, who had even threatened to have him imprisoned.[35] Yet a third woman, who became a worker in a garment shop at the age of thirteen in the early years of this century remarked in an interview, "I accepted my responsibility to help support my family even though this meant I wouldn't go to high school. I wanted to go to school but I knew this was not possible."[36] As the daughter of an immigrant family living in Pittsburgh commented, with some exaggeration, of the milieu in which she grew up, "The boys all went to college, but the girls worked to help the boys through."[37]

Even when young women were allowed to graduate from high school and attend college, in New York City they found the doors of their brothers' preferred public college closed to them. In fact, women were not admitted to the famed College of Arts and Sciences, the main undergraduate school of the City College of New York, until 1950. Instead, they would attend the Normal College (later called Hunter College), where they could prepare for the preeminent female profession of teaching. By 1916, young Jewish women of East European origin accounted for fully one-quarter of the graduates of Hunter College.[38] According to a study by Leonard Dinnerstein, in the 1920s Jewish girls were more likely to attend high school and college than the daughters of other ethnic groups; and by 1934 more than 50 percent of female college students in New York were Jewish.[39] As immigrant and second-generation families prospered, the gender difference in education narrowed substantially. By 1950, for example, native-born Jewish women between the ages of twenty-five and forty-four averaged 12.4 years of schooling, while their brothers' mean was 12.7 years.[40]

Most immigrant and second-generation Jewish women could not afford the luxury of college, though. To acquire the education they sought, they turned to adult education courses which were offered free of charge in the evenings to working women. In two separate studies, one conducted on the eve of World War I in New York City and the other in the mid-1920s in Philadelphia, gentile observers commented on the disproportionate representation of Jewish women in the evening classes. In Philadelphia in 1925, for example, 70 percent of the night school students were Jewish women.[41]

If Jewish women enjoyed more limited opportunities to acquire advanced secular education than their brothers, they were even more restricted in their access to a religious education. In immigrant neighborhoods only a relatively small percentage of Jewish children were given a formal Jewish education. Several surveys conducted in the first three decades of this century discovered that just twenty-five percent of school-age children were studying in a cheder, or afternoon Hebrew school.[42] Of those, the vast majority were boys; for a formal religious education was deemed at best unnecessary, and at worst inappropriate, for girls. One immigrant woman testified to the norms of her community with her remark, "I was the only girl attending Hebrew school."[43] Most girls acquired their Jewish knowledge in a less formal manner. As one woman who grew up in Pittsburgh commented, "I had received a strong sense of Jewish commitment from my childhood experiences in a very Jewish home, but my sister and I did not receive a religious education—my brother did."[44] Just as the Jewish socialization of boys and girls had differed in the East European shtetl and city, so it continued to differ in the immigrant ghetto and second-generation neighborhood. While immigrant Jewish boys received less Jewish education than had been the case in the shtetl, the communal ideal still prescribed for them the study of at least the rudiments of a literate Jewish culture. For the majority of those who failed to do so, the break with the East European experience was a radical one. Jewish girls, on the other hand, had always derived their Jewish knowledge and identity from observation and celebration within the home. They continued to do so in the immigrant period, acquiring what anthropologist Barbara Myerhoff, in her study of elderly immigrant Jews living in Venice, California, called "domestic Judaism." As one of her female informants put it, "You know Judaism is really what happens in the family, and this makes it something a woman knows best."[45]

The Jewish identity of Jewish women, then, was integrally connected with home and family life rather than with institutions and seems to have been characterized by continuity (at a low level of formal instruction) rather than disruption. In the absence of contact with Jewish educational institutions it may have been sustained longer than was the case with Jewish men, whose traditional role was played out in synagogue and house of study. It would be of interest to discover whether this domestic foundation of Jewish identity enabled some working- and middle-class twentieth-century U.S. Jewish women to display the patterns of behavior that Marion Kaplan found among German Jewish women at the end of the nineteenth century, such as a greater degree of ritual observance than among their husbands and a tendency to serve as the transmitters of Jewish identity within the family circle.[46]

Because immigrant Jewish women had fewer institutional affiliations than men, the community they defined for themselves was less dependent on formal institutions than was the Jewish community that emerges in our classic history texts. Perhaps the most important gender-linked form of community was the urban neighborhood. While men, women, and children shared the stoops and sidewalks of immigrant and second-generation Jewish neighborhoods, at least during the daytime the neighborhood was the special turf of women. Women often looked to their neighbors as their particular community. Moreover, they used the neighborhood as the locus of their political activity. Historians have often asserted that Jewish housewives, particularly in immigrant settlements, were apolitical. Had they looked to the neighborhood rather than to the unions or to formal meetings under the auspices of political parties, they would have found evidence of a high degree of female political activity. The social consciousness that so many observers noted among Jewish working women did not disappear after marriage; it simply changed its place and mode of operation.

Jewish women used the neighborhood for grassroots political organizing, both sporadic and sustained. At least three major gender-linked issues engaged their attention in the first two decades of this century: food prices, rising rents, and women's suffrage. The earliest and most dramatic incident of women's neighborhood-based political activity occurred in New York City in 1902, when the price of kosher meat soared from twelve cents to eighteen cents a pound. Concerned that they would not be able to stretch their husbands' wages to provide meat for their families, middle-aged housewives (their average age was thirty-nine) organized a boycott of kosher butcher shops, which spread from the Lower East Side to Williamsburg and Harlem and attracted the attention of all the New York City newspapers because the women milled in the street, broke into butcher shops, and flung meat onto the sidewalks. The leaders of this movement used their presence in the neighborhood to good advantage. They utilized a house-to-house canvas to provide information to their constituency and to collect bail funds for women who had been arrested. Further, they were on hand to enforce the boycott, through a combination of moral and physical suasion. Thus, they went so far as to inspect the *cholent* (Sabbath stew) pots of women en route to the bakery on Friday afternoon in order to ensure that the Sabbath meal would be a meatless one. Relying on their recognition as respected figures in the neighborhood, they also interrupted synagogue services on the Sabbath in order to gain the support of male worshipers for their cause and to secure rabbinic endorsements. Within the neighborhood the leaders also organized large protest meetings to spur on their troops and provided political leaflets to maintain the momentum of their movement. Thus, with the neighborhood as their base, they combined the most current political concept of the mass strike and boycott with such traditional Jewish concerns as *kashrut* (observance of the Jewish dietary laws) and the resort to the synagogue as an institution concerned with communal justice.[47] Through the neighborhood they seem to have transcended the divisions, religious and secular, radical and liberal, that divided the organized immigrant Jewish community.

Similar tactics appeared in subsequent food riots and boycotts (e.g., New York City, 1917),[48] as well as in rent strikes and suffrage campaigns. Thus, hailing the meat boycott as their model, Jewish housewives played an active role in Lower East Side rent strikes in 1904 and 1907–8. Beginning with a house-to-house canvas, women strike leaders promoted neighborhood solidarity by collecting written pledges of refusals to pay rent.[49]

The suffrage campaigns on the Lower East Side, where support for female suffrage was higher than in any other immigrant neighborhood in New York City in the state elections of 1915 and 1917, also took extensive advantage of the neighborhood network of women. While most historians have focused on large, often citywide, rallies and on the pronouncements of the leadership of the suffrage movement (which was reluctant to acknowledge Jewish support), Elinor Lerner's pioneering study of the suffrage vote in individual election districts has revealed that immigrant Jewish women did painstaking community organizing on the issue for years and were instrumental in getting out the vote.[50] Young working-class women in the garment unions provided the initiative for undertaking intensive public activity on the Lower East Side beginning in 1907, as well as much of the membership for the Wage Earners' League of the Woman Suffrage party. In the Woman Suffrage party itself Jewish women constituted 17 percent of the founding members and 64 percent of the members in the most highly Jewish assembly districts. In four of those districts Jewish women served as chairpersons and coordinated the propaganda campaign. Incidentally, those four districts had the highest prosuffrage vote in all of Manhattan in 1915. Married women, too, like their working sisters, played a role in organizing the suffrage campaign both on the Lower East Side and in more affluent Harlem. Mary Beard, historian and suffragist, happily noted that "[the] army of tenement mothers and working women [who marched in the last suffrage parade] ought to stir the sluggish to action."[51] Yiddish leaflets addressed tenement mothers directly, appealing to their desire to solve their housing and food problems by touting the power of the ballot box.

Most importantly, Jewish women applied the techniques they had developed in the meat boycott and rent strikes to the suffrage campaign. In 1911 Lavinia Dock, South Manhattan organizer for the Woman Suffrage party, commended "the splendid captains and workers [who] were making woman suffrage known in shops and homes and even in the political life of the district." These activities, she noted, "represented the most sincere kind of propaganda work, personal interviews, street meetings and earnest argumentation."[52] On the Lower East Side, Jewish women were particularly assiduous in carrying out a neighborhood canvass. Trudging up tenement stairs, they went from flat to flat to speak about women's suffrage. For each visit they recorded in a card file the attitude of each voter toward the issue and the type of literature distributed to the household.[53]

Even women who were not actively involved in the campaign were aware of, and interested in, the issue. In her reports on the neighborhood, Lavinia Dock, who worked on the staff of the Henry Street Settlement, pointed out in 1911 that women and children she met in the settlement knew many details of the victory of suffrage in Washington State and that Jewish women, on their own initiative, consulted with her on the issues of suffrage and becoming citizens. In 1915 she was able to report that the neighborhood canvass yielded a 75-percent approval rate for women's suffrage among Jews on the Lower East Side, a figure suggesting that Jewish culture now affirmed the acceptability of a secular public role for women.[54] Not surprisingly, after the suffrage amendment was ratified, Jewish women registered to vote in large numbers.

While much of our information is from New York City, scattered evidence from other communities suggests that women performed similar communal-political tasks elsewhere as well. For example, the first mass suffrage meeting in Philadelphia was organized and attended for the most part by Jews.[55] One Pittsburgh woman reminisced, "I was one of the girls who marched for women's suffrage. I was not a speaker.

I was one of those we called 'Jimmy Higgins' in the Socialist Party—who sells literature, gives out literature, carries the platform."[56]

It was in their neighborhoods, then, that immigrant women, primarily of the working class, constructed a female community. Through the neighborhood network they provided advice and emotional support for each other as well as acting on issues of broad social consequence.

When immigrant women and their second-generation daughters did affiliate with formal communal institutions, they did so in institutions that were by and large segregated by gender. *Landsmanshaft* societies, which provided social services and companionship for immigrants hailing from the same town, generally boasted a "ladies auxiliary" through which women participated in the affairs of the society. Upwardly mobile immigrant women adapted to the norms of U.S. Jewish life by joining the synagogue sisterhoods that had emerged at the end of the nineteenth century and had become nationally organized in the second decade of the twentieth. Sisterhoods were seen as the most acceptable mode for middle-class Jewish women to express their religious commitments, for in the United States the public expression of piety was increasingly linked with the female gender. The synagogue sisterhood offered a venue for Jewish women to apply their domestic skills, such as food preparation and decoration of the sanctuary, to the formerly masculine domain of the synagogue without disrupting the hierarchy of status within the congregation itself.[57] It was "Americanization," then, that provided a new public religious focus for women's Jewish identity.

With upward mobility and the increasing leisure time it provided, immigrant women and their daughters also joined such Jewish women's organizations as Hadassah and the National Council of Jewish Women, which built on a triple legacy: traditional Jewish philanthropy, the nineteenth-century Ladies Aid Society, and the U.S. Women's Club movement. These Jewish women's organizations enabled women to take their talents and energy outside their own households in a socially approved manner; in a Jewish version of what has been called "domestic feminism," civic concern became an expression of domestic responsibility writ large. Some historians have pointed out that Jewish women's social welfare associations were often more involved in the general civic affairs of their region than were parallel local men's organizations. Because of their concern with such "women's issues" as family stability, health, and child care, they may have retained an interest in causes associated with the Progressive movement longer than did male-dominated Jewish communal institutions.[58] Although these women's organizations never openly challenged the primacy of the home and domestic responsibilities as the proper central focus of women's lives, they reconfigured the boundaries between the domestic and public spheres. In teaching administrative skills and conferring public positions of authority and responsibility upon their members, they also expanded the range of appropriate female behavior. The impact of these organizations on the self-definition of their activists deserves further attention.[59]

Since immigrant Jewish women experienced work, domestic responsibility, and community differently from their male peers, it would be worthwhile to explore what values they contributed to Jewish associations such as *Landsmanshaftn* and synagogues or secular organizations. At least one labor historian has suggested, for example, that female organizers were the initiators of the advanced educational, cultural, and recreational programs that ultimately became the pride of the Jewish garment unions.[60] For them, the realization of the ideals of the Labor movement could not be limited to higher wages or improved working conditions alone but included the creation of a community offering workers the potential for self-improvement and for life-enriching leisure. Were there other female visions of community expressed implicitly in the educational, cultural, social, and philanthropic activities of the major Jewish women's organizations?

The largely domestic religious experience of immigrant Jewish women and how they transmitted their concepts of Judaism and Jewishness to their children in an era of little formal Jewish education could perhaps be explored through memoirs, diaries, and literature to gain a fresh perspective on the adaptation of Judaism in the United States.[61] While the "feminization" of nineteenth- and twentieth-century U.S. Christianity has been the object of study, a parallel trend in U.S. Jewish life has yet to be fully investigated. The religious functions of women's philanthropic societies and sisterhoods also deserve sustained attention. The relatively high level of gender segregation in traditional Judaism and even in modernized forms of Judaism necessitates the explicit study of the religious, as well as the social, experience of Jewish women.[62]

The historical experience of immigrant Jewish women embraced work and family, politics and social welfare, friendship groups and neighborhood. We can understand their experience and its significance only if we expand our definition of the historical arena, ask questions that do not presume male experience as the norm, and look for new sources of information. As we have seen, oral history, when combined with more traditional documentation, has much to offer in facilitating the integration in historical narrative of the private and public dimensions of women's lives and of human experience in general. By including gender as one of their tools of analysis, historians of U.S. Jewry will produce a more complex and nuanced account of the transformation of the Jewish community and its culture on U.S. soil.

## NOTES

1. Simon Kuznets, "Immigration of Russian Jews to the U.S.: Background and Structure," *Perspectives in American History* 9 (1975): 94–95. In 1880, on the eve of the mass immigration of East European Jews to the United States, there was a U.S. Jewish community of 250 thousand, mostly made up of well-acculturated and middle-class Jews of German origin and liberal Jewish practice. The entry, between 1881 and 1914, of almost two million Jews from Eastern Europe to the United States profoundly altered the U.S. Jewish community. For a documentary study of U.S. Jewish women prior to the mass arrival of immigrants from Eastern Europe, see Ann Braude, "The Jewish Woman's Encounter with American Culture," in *Women and Religion in America*, vol. 1, *The Nineteenth Century: A Documentary History*, ed. Rosemary Radford Ruether and Rosemary Skinner Kelly (San Francisco, 1981), 150–92.

2. For a theoretical discussion of gender, see Gayle Rubin, "The Traffic in Women: Notes on the 'Political Economy' of Sex," in *Toward an Anthropology of Women*, ed. Rayna R. Reiter (New York, 1975), 157–210.

3. Joan Wallach Scott, *Gender and the Politics of History* (New York, 1988), 42; see also Gerda Lerner, *The Majority Finds Its Past* (New York, 1979), 161–64.

4. This has been the case particularly with two recent comparative studies of Jews and Italians: Judith E. Smith, *Family Connections: A History of Italian and Jewish Immigrant Lives in Providence, Rhode Island 1900–1940* (Albany, NY, 1985) and Elizabeth Ewen, *Immigrant Women in the Land of Dollars* (New York, 1985). Both of them focus on class and gender similarities to the virtual exclusion of religioethnic specificities. In part, this blurring of ethnic difference is due to their ignorance of the languages spoken by the immigrants (Smith of Yiddish, Ewen of both Yiddish and Italian).

5. Bernard Farber, Charles Mindel, and Bernard Lazerwitz, "The Jewish American Family," in *Ethnic Families in America*, ed. Charles Mindel and Robert Habenstein (New York, 1976), 354.

6. Charlotte Baum, Paula Hyman, and Sonya Michel, *The Jewish Woman in America* (New York, 1976), 71–89.

7. Sydney Stahl Weinberg, *The World of Our Mothers: The Lives of Jewish Immigrant Women* (Chapel Hill, 1988), 153; idem, "The World of Our Mothers: Family, Work, and Education in the Lives of Jewish Immigrant Women," *Frontiers* 7 (1983): 73. A shorter version of the latter quote appears in idem, *World*, 160; on the responsibilities of daughters in general, see pp. 151–60 and also Smith, *Family Connections*, 114–16, 118.

8. Corinne Azen Krause, *Grandmothers, Mothers, and Daughters: An Oral History Study of Ethnicity, Mental Health, and Continuity of Three Generations of Jewish, Italian, and Slavic-American Women* (n.p., n.d.) 48–53.

9. Elizabeth Pleck, "A Mother's Wages," in *A Heritage of Her Own*, ed. Nancy F. Cott and Elizabeth H. Pleck (New York, 1979), 372. In other cities the disparity was smaller. See also Smith, *Family Connections*, 47–48. Smith finds a reduced differential between Italian and Jewish wives because she includes unofficial work, such as caring for boarders and helping out in shopkeeping, in her calculations.

10. Barbara Klaczynska, "Why Women Work: A Comparison of Various Groups, Philadelphia 1910–1930," *Labor History* 17 (1976): 83–86; Caroline Manning, *The Immigrant Woman and Her Job* (Washington, 1930), 23–24.

11. Ewen, *Immigrant Women*, 231. Ewen cites taped interviews (on file in the Tamiment Library of New York University) with four immigrant Jewish women on this subject: the citation is from one pseudonymously referred to as "Judith Weissman."

12. Weinberg, "World," 77; idem, *World*, 262.

13. Thomas Kessner and Betty Caroli, "New Immigrant Women at Work: Italians and Jews in New York City 1880–1905," *Journal of Ethnic Studies* 5, no. 4 (1978): 21, 25. See also Smith, *Family Connections*, 68, 70.

14. Lloyd Gartner, "East European Immigrant Jews on the Lower East Side, 1890–1893," *American Jewish Historical Quarterly* 53, no. 3 (1964): 271.

15. Sherry Gorelick, *City College and the Jewish Poor* (New Brunswick, NJ, 1981), 214–15.

16. *McClure's Magazine* cited in Rudolph Glanz, *The Jewish Woman in America* (New York, 1976), 1:66–67; Weinberg, *World*, 196.

17. Virginia Yans, cited in Weinberg, "World," 74, 78; Weinberg, *World*, 190.

18. Weinberg, *World*, 187–92.

19. Cited in Corinne Azen Krause, "Urbanization without Breakdown: Italian, Jewish, and Slavic Immigrant Women in Pittsburgh," *Journal of Urban History* 4, no. 3 (1978): 296.

20. Elinor Lerner, "American Feminism and the Jewish Question," in *Anti-Semitism in American History*, ed. David Gerber (Urbana, 1986), 308 and this article's earlier draft which has more detail on this subject (p. 11) than the published version. I would like to thank Elinor Lerner for sharing this manuscript with me.

21. Women's Trade Union League [WTUL], *Annual Report* (1908–9), 7. On the involvement of the WTUL with working-class immigrant women, see Nancy Schrom Dye, "Creating a Feminist Alliance: Sisterhood and Class Conflict in the New York Women's Trade Union League, 1903–1914," in *Class, Sex, and the Woman Worker*, ed. Milton Cantor and Bruce Laurie (Westport, CT, 1977), 225–45.

22. Mary Van Kleeck, *Artificial Flower Makers* (New York, 1913), 34–35.

23. Alice Kessler-Harris, "Where Are the Organized Women Workers?" *Feminist Studies* 3 (1975): 102.

24. Louis Levine, *The Women's Garment Workers: A History of the International Ladies' Garment Workers' Union* (New York, 1924), as cited in Baum, Hyman, and Michel, *Jewish Woman*, 143.

25. Alice Kessler-Harris, *Out to Work* (New York, 1982), 157.

26. Idem, "Organizing the Unorganizable: Three Jewish Women and Their Union," in Cantor and Laurie, *Class, Sex*, 152–58.

27. Baum, Hyman, and Michel, *Jewish Woman*, 135–36; Ewen, *Immigrant Women*, 260.

28. Reena Sigman Friedman, "'Send Me My Husband Who Is in New York City': Husband Desertion in the American Jewish Immigrant Community, 1900–1926," *Jewish Social Studies* 44, no. 1 (1982): 1.

29. Ibid.

30. Ibid., 14.

31. Edward J. Bristow, *Prostitution and Prejudice: The Jewish Fight against White Slavery 1870–1939* (New York, 1982), 162, 283–84.

32. Weinberg, *World*, 151–52, 173–77.

33. Ibid., 290.

34. Cited in Glanz, *Jewish Woman*, 1:66–67.

35. Kessler-Harris, *Out to Work*, 126–27.

36. Cited in Ewen, *Immigrant Women*, 100.

37. Ida Cohen Selavan, *My Voice Was Heard* (New York, 1981), 93.

38. Gorelick, *City College*, 123.

39. Leonard Dinnerstein, "Education and the Advancement of American Jews," in *American Education and the European Immigrant*, ed. Bernard Weiss (Urbana, 1982), 47; Jacob Rader Marcus, *The American Jewish Woman, 1654–1980* (New York, 1981), 132.

40. For the decline in gender differentials in education within the third generation of U.S. Jews, see Chaim Waxman, *America's Jews in Transition* (Philadelphia, 1983), 145. For the 1950 figures, see Weinberg, *World*, 290.

41. Mary Van Kleek, *Working Girls in Evening Schools* (New York, 1914) and Manning, *Immigrant Woman*, 27.

42. Judah Pilch, ed., *A History of Jewish Education in the U.S.* (New York, 1969), 67–68, 82–83.

43. Selavan, *My Voice*, 43.

44. Ibid., 61.

45. Barbara Myerhoff, *Number Our Days* (New York, 1978), 234.

46. Marion Kaplan, "Priestess and Hausfrau: German Jewish Women in the Family," in *The Jewish Family: Myths and Reality*, ed. Steven M. Cohen and myself (New York, 1986), 62–81; and see chapter 9 above.

47. For a detailed analysis of this incident, see my "Immigrant Women and Consumer Protest: The New York City Kosher Meat Boycott of 1902," *American Jewish History*, 70, no. 1 (1980): 91–105.

48. On the food riots and boycotts that erupted in February and March 1917, see Ewen, *Immigrant Women*, 176–82.

49. Daphne Kis, "The Political Role of Women in Community: New York's Lower East Side, 1900–1910," (Hampshire College, 1976, typescript), 58–80; Ewen, *Immigrant Women*, 126–27.

50. Elinor Lerner, "Jewish Involvement in the New York City Women Suffrage Movement," *American Jewish History*, 70, no. 4 (1981): 444–53.

51. Ibid., 447.

52. Ibid., 449–50.

53. Ibid., 451–52.

54. Ibid., 456.

55. Elinor Lerner, "American Feminism," (ms.), 9.

56. Selevan, *My Voice*, 203.

57. Jenna Weissman Joselit, "The Special Sphere of the Middle-Class American Jewish Woman: The Synagogue Sisterhood, 1890–1940," in *The American Synagogue: A Sanctuary Transformed*, ed. Jack Wertheimer (New York, 1987), 206–30; and chapter 12 below. On the growing feminization of the Reform synagogue, see Faith Rogow, "Gone to Another Meeting: A History of the National Council of Jewish Women" (Ph.D. diss., State University of New York, Binghamton, 1988), 59–121.

58. William Toll, *The Making of an Ethnic Middle Class: Portland Jewry over Four Generations* (Albany, NY, 1982), 331. See also Evelyn Bodek, "'Making Do': Jewish Women and Philanthropy," in *Jewish Life in Philadelphia, 1830–1940*, ed. Murray Friedman (Philadelphia, 1983), 161.

59. On the construction of new boundaries between public and private, see Beth Wenger, "Jewish Women and Voluntarism: Beyond the Myth of Enablers," *American Jewish History* 79, no. 1 (1989): 16–36. On the impact of the National Council of Jewish Women, see Rogow, "Gone to Another Meeting"; and Sue Levi Elwell, "The Founding and Early Programs of the National Council of Jewish Women: Study and Practice of Jewish Women's Religious Expression" (Ph.D. diss., Indiana University, 1982); and chapter 12 below. A history of Hadassah focusing on its impact on its members is a major desideratum.

60. Kessler-Harris, "Organizing the Unorganizable," 155.

61. See, in particular, Ann Douglas, *The Feminization of American Culture* (New York, 1978).

62. See chapter 12 on aspects of U.S. Jewish women's spiritual lives.

CHAPTER **11** **JOAN RINGELHEIM**

*Women and the Holocaust: A Reconsideration of Research*

---

> Thinking is like the veil of Penelope: it undoes every morning what it had finished the night before.
>
> Hannah Arendt,
> "Thinking and Moral Considerations"

Even a cursory look at studies about the Holocaust would indicate that the experiences and perceptions of Jewish women have been obscured or absorbed into descriptions of men's lives. The similarity among Jewish victims of the Nazi policy of destruction has been considered more important than any differentiation, including (or especially) that of gender. It is not surprising, then, that until quite recently there has been no feminist perspective in Holocaust scholarship.[1]

Although the research on women and the Holocaust is only just beginning, it already has taken a problematic and troubling direction. Since my own work has been instrumental in setting this course, I am going to make it my case study for analysis and criticism. Using fragments of stories Jewish women survivors have told me in interviews, I will recapitulate the asssumptions, hypotheses, and categories I have used in my interpretation and explore what is problematic in this approach. I want to look particularly at the influence of *cultural feminism* on my own work and pose some new questions for myself and others.

## INTERVIEW DATA

When I began research, I assumed that gender must have counted for something and that focusing on women's experience would yield new questions and new data: If you were Jewish, in what ways did it matter whether you were a man or a woman? Did gender cause any difference in policies, actions, or reactions of either the Nazis or those opposed to them? In what ways did sexism function in the racist ideology against Jews and other so-called non-Aryans? Is there, for instance, anything to be seen in statistics about the number of men killed as compared to women, differences among those selected to die, or distinctions in types of work assigned? Did the Nazis prolong and intensify an already-existing sexism against Jewish women as they prolonged, intensified, and even elaborated anti-Semitism against the Jews as a whole?[2] In what ways was sexism maintained and intensified under Nazism by the Jews themselves?

Were women's experiences during the Holocaust different from men's in some respects? Were there differences in work, relationships, roles, and maintenance possibilities or capabilities ( i.e., what a person did or tried to do simply to keep going, to make it from day to day)?[3] Do women and men possess different maintenance skills? Because of traditional gender roles, are women better able to bear conditions of deprivation?

At the initial stages of research, I suggested that traditional attitudes and responses towards women, as well as gender-defined conditions, made women especially vulnerable to abuse of their sexuality and their maternal responsibility—vulnerable to rape and other forms of sexual exploitation, murder of themselves and their children, the necessity of killing their own or other women's babies, and forced abortion—whether in the ghettos, in resistance groups, in hiding, passing as a gentile, or in the camps. I believed it important, moreover, to explore the claim of some survivors and scholars that women's capacities for enduring the trauma of dislocation, starvation, loss of traditional support structures, and physical and mental abuse were different from, and sometimes greater than, men's.[4]

These assumptions and ideas shaped the form of an interview schedule with a twofold aim: (1) to recapture the Holocaust experience as a whole and (2) to establish women's sense of their particular experience within it: what was done to them (their *vulnerabilities*), and what they did (their *resources*). I began each of the twenty interviews I conducted with some general questions about life prior to the Holocaust: family background, relationships, education, class, and so on. I wanted the women to start their stories in a way that seemed comfortable, even familiar. I expected to be able to hear their understanding of themselves both as Jews and as women from the narrative structures they devised. I asked further questions as needed to clarify or expand an idea or to raise a topic not yet mentioned. In particular, I asked about the things that seemed related to their lives as women: sexuality, sexual abuse, family, children, relationships, food, resistance, and passivity. I asked questions about choices, decisions, and problems. What did they tell me?[5]

In their descriptions of the tragedy of Jews during the Holocaust, the women interviewed discussed women's particular victimization. They spoke of their sexual vulnerability, concerns that men either described in different ways or, more often, did not describe at all.[6] Almost every woman referred to the humiliating feelings and experiences surrounding her entrance to the camp (for my interviewees this was Auschwitz): being nude; being shaved all over (for some, being shaved in a sexual stance, straddling two stools); and being observed by men, both fellow prisoners and SS guards. Their stories demonstrate shared fears about, and experiences of, sexual vulnerability as women, not only about mortal danger as Jews.

Some women remember the ways in which sex was used as a commodity in the ghettos; sexual exchanges for food or other goods involved Jewish men at least as often as—perhaps more often than—they did Nazi authorities. S. spoke of her experiences in Theresienstadt, the so-called model ghetto in Czechoslovakia. She was about twenty:

> Women survived partly by brains. I worked in the office, in supply, in the education office. I wasn't doing badly. . . . To . . . [a certain] point you were autonomous . . . you could lead your own life . . . people could get married. You also survived by your male connections. It was the males who had the main offices, who ran the kitchens. . . . [The] *Judenrat* [Jewish governing council] [was] running [the ghetto and the Jewish men] *used* it. And did they *use* it. *Did* they use it. That was how

you survived as a woman, through the male. I was done in by one. I suppose I didn't sleep high enough, to put it bluntly. Because in that society, that was the only way you could survive.

Her experiences with sexual abuse did not end when she was sent to Auschwitz. Once when she was working in *Kanada* an SS officer approached her as she began to take a nap.[7] He tried to wake her by kicking the bunk on which she was resting. She knew what he wanted (she had noticed him staring at her) and feigned sleep, pushing him away or moaning as if he were part of a dream. S. claimed that he would not have forced her to have sex; he would only have had relations if she agreed because a prisoner could report the SS. In such cases the prisoner had some "power," she said, because it was a crime for an SS to have sexual relations with Jews. This SS man went away. Another time S. was not so lucky: she was raped by a prisoner.

At the time of the Warsaw Ghetto, G. was about fifteen years old. She remembered seeing a young SS officer spot beautiful Jewish women, go to their houses, and rape them. Afterwards, he would shoot them. He always came prepared with a horse-drawn hearse. Since G. was quite pretty, her mother and cousin made paste from flour and water and put it on her face with the hope that she would be less vulnerable if less attractive. She was afraid but never really "knew if it was better to look prettier or terrible."

About three years later G. was in a camp near Lublin and Maidanek, and the commandant decided to open up the gates between the men's and women's camps. "The men came. I was pretty young then. Strangest thing—so many of these men tried right away to screw . . . [they were] like a horde of animals . . . I had the vision for a long, long time—this horde of sick men jumping." She was only watching, and this is all she remembers. It was one of her worst memories from the Holocaust.

Although there are many stories about sexual abuse, they are not easy to come by. Some think it inappropriate to talk about these matters; discussions about sexuality desecrate the memories of the dead or the living or the Holocaust itself. For others, it is simply too difficult and painful. Still others think it may be a trivial issue. One survivor told me that she had been sexually abused by a number of gentile men while she was in hiding when she was about eleven years old. Her comment about this was that it "was not important . . . except to me." She meant that it had no significance within the larger picture of the Holocaust. But why should ideas about the Holocaust as a whole exclude these women's experiences—exclude what is important to women and thus make the judgment that women's experiences as women are trivial? These aspects of women's daily lives—vulnerability to rape, humiliation, and sexual exchange, not to speak of pregnancy, abortion, and fear for one's children—cannot simply be universalized as true for all survivors.

It would be wrong to suggest that abuse characterized the whole of women's sexual experiences during the Holocaust. Some women speak about heterosexual love relationships, great passions, or small romances in the ghettos, the resistance groups, and even in the camps. They also speak of liaisons created out of loneliness, friendship, the need for help, or even the desire to experience sex before death.

In camps that were sex-segregated as most were, deep friendships occurred among the women that sometimes developed into sexual relationships. Thus far, no woman has talked to me about such experiences as her own. S. did say that she knew of lesbian relationships and that "it wasn't an issue; wherever you could get warmth, care, and affection, that was good. That was all that mattered."[8] Her view is not the common one that I have encountered. More often, those interviewed showed hostility about the issue; attitudes toward lesbian relationships in the camps seem at best ambivalent and require careful study.

Coping with pregnancy, childbirth, and infant care made Jewish women particularly vulnerable in other ways to physical abuse and mental anguish, whether through abortion by choice, forced abortion, bearing a child, being killed with a child as its actual or supposed mother, bearing a child and not being able to feed it, or killing a baby because its cries jeopardized other people or because if the baby were found (at least in Auschwitz) both Jewish mother and baby would be killed.[9] I heard one child survivor say that all adults were enemies to children,[10] but women with children may have been more vulnerable than anyone except children by themselves.

What I am trying to make graphic is the complexity of these Jewish women's lives because of the connections between biology and sexism. There are particular vulnerabilities, such as pregnancy and abortion, resulting from women's biology; others, created by sexism, perpetuate violence against women in the form of humiliation, molestation, rape, and sexual exchange. These vulnerabilities, as well as the sheer terror, degradation, and genocide perpetrated by the Nazis against the Jews, existed for Jewish women in the Holocaust.

Besides their special vulnerability, the other topic I discussed with the women I interviewed was their special resources. Survivors testify to gender difference in this regard. A number of observers had the impression that women survived better than men, that women "tended to outlive" men, at least in comparable situations.[11] Such perceptions need to be examined.

Study of the Holocaust requires more specific research on the comparative survival rates of women and men than is represented in the sporadic opinions and unrepresentative surveys now available.[12] Without such statistics we have only impressions and speculations, a series of questions rather than answers. Were more women killed than men? What was the relation between work and survival? If some sorts of work could save lives, did women and men have similar chances to do it? What was the pattern of food distribution between women and men, among women, and among men; were women eating the same amount as men or sharing their portions more than men did? Are there biological differences to account for the dissimilarities mentioned by survivors and scholars about the effects of starvation?

Some of the differences perceived do appear to be related to gender: women transformed starving into communal sharing of recipe stories; they exchanged sex for food, rather than the reverse; they altered rags into clothes; and mutual isolation into relationships or surrogate "families." Women were able to transform their habits of raising children or their experience of nurturing into the care of nonbiological family. Men, when they lost their role in the protection of their own families, seemed less able to transform this habit into the protection of others. Men did not remain or become fathers as readily as women became mothers or nurturers. Do women apply and modify previous gender roles more easily than men?[13]

The so-called trivial, everyday activities of which the women speak constitute the necessary but not sufficient conditions for their survival. "Women's work"—activities centering around food, children, clothing, shelter, social relations, warmth, and cleanliness—may be regarded as the only meaningful labor in time of such dire necessity. It is only with such trivial—and often trivialized—concerns that life among the oppressed becomes possible. And it is important to look at what this means both to women and to men, whose relationships to necessity have traditionally been quite different in both European and other cultures.

Because of the material conditions and social relations that characterize their lives, women are able to create or recreate "families" and so provide networks for maintenance that may be related to survival rates. Awareness of such responses (and of such variables as class, age, and nationality) is crucial to understanding the lives of the women I spoke to.[14] Excerpts from the following three interviews give some preliminary sense of how a few women have spoken about the importance of relationships to their survival.[15]

## Rose

Rose, from a poor family, was born in Hungary in 1919. She was trained as a hairdresser and was deported to Auschwitz in March of 1942. After a year on an outside demolition crew she began work in the sauna, cutting the hair of the incoming prisoners.

> There were mountains of dead bodies outside of the barracks which were picked up by trucks every morning. If you had to go to the bathroom [diarrhea was rampant and getting to the latrine difficult], then you went to the bathroom on top of them. Didn't think twice about it. You had no feelings. [Yet] I knew a young girl from Holland, Eva, who was brought to Block 25 [a kind of holding pen for women going to be gassed]. Eva was fifteen or sixteen, and got diarrhea which was enough for them to take you away. Took her to Block 25 and I knew where she was going to go. . . . I sneaked there and took her something to eat. . . . My heart was aching for her. You know, here I was walking over dead bodies and it didn't bother me, but it bothered me to see a young girl like this go and nothing I could do for her. There was still feelings . . . I couldn't cry too much . . . I felt so bad for her and when you got close to these barracks in Block 25, you can't imagine what you saw in there. Just can't imagine—half-crazy, laid on top of one another, lost their minds . . . horrible."

At about the time Rose got her job in the sauna (1943), Rollie came to Auschwitz from Greece with two sisters. The youngest, Teresa (Rollie's favorite), got sick and died. Rollie was beside herself and wanted to commit suicide. Rose met her.

If it wasn't for me, she wouldn't be alive. We helped each other. We had to cling . . . you had to have somebody. We helped each other. She considers me her best friend, her mother, her father, everything . . . I considered her as my daughter [Rose was then twenty-four; Rollie was eighteen]. This I felt for her. I was sheltering her. . . . When I had typhus, all I wanted was an apple. Who can get an apple there? [Rollie] sold her bread to exchange for an apple that I should get it.

A small incident. In the chronicle of concentration camp horrors it may even appear to be minuscule. For Rose, it is small only because it takes a short time to tell. It is an emblem of life for her.

That time you don't think what kind of relation; you just think, I got somebody here I can talk to, somebody close by. That's all what you think about . . . I fought going off my mind. I thought of taking my life [on the electrified wires that surrounded the camp and forgetting] the whole thing. But . . . I gotta live. This woman told me, I'm gonna be free, I'm gonna go to America to see my father. [That] gave me alot. . . . Got Rollie here and she's still a baby—this was how I was thinking about her. Can't do that [commit suicide or lose her mind]. You know, there was always something that was stopping me. Now here was little Eva, she goes in Block 25 and I just want to see her once more—was always something that I say "No, I am not gonna do that." Didn't let myself go.

Rose gave her own reasons for the ways in which women kept themselves and others going and explained what it meant that they did so: Women were

picking each other like monkeys [for lice]. Never remember seeing the men do it. The minute they had lice they just left it alone; the women have a different instinct. Housewives. We want to clean. . . . Somehow the men, . . . the [lice] ate them alive. . . . [During roll call] the women holding each other and keeping each other warm. . . . Someone puts their arm around you and you remember. . . . Can you imagine how much it meant to us over there! Men were crouching into themselves—maybe five feet apart [Rose demonstrated how the men she saw put their arms around their own bodies, rather than around the next person for warmth]. . . . I think more women survived. . . . As much as I saw in Auschwitz, the men were falling like flies. The woman was somehow stronger. . . . Woman friendship is different than man friendship you see. . . . We have these motherly instincts, friend instincts more. If two or three women are friends they can be closer than two or three men. [Men] can be nice to each other, talk to each other, have a beer with each other. But that's as far as it goes, you know? But that's what was holding the woman together because everybody had to have somebody to lean on, to depend on. The men, no . . . the men didn't do that. Men were friends there too. They talked to each other but they didn't, wouldn't, sell their bread for an apple for the other guy. They wouldn't sacrifice nothing. See, that was the difference.


## Susan

Susan was born in Vienna in 1922 and moved to Czechoslovakia in 1938 with her mother and father. She was deported to Theresienstadt in 1942 and to Auschwitz in January 1943. In the first month there she worked as a typist in the political department. She was sent back to the regular prison population because one of the women in her group was caught passing food and the entire group was punished for it. Susan got typhus soon after returning to the regular camp population.

She had become part of a group of Jewish women from Berlin, and

> without them, I wouldn't have gotten through this illness. They helped me through a good eight days of 103- to 104-degree temperature. . . . I remember like today, every morning standing in roll call, standing close, braced—walked out with their arms under me. These women supported me physically . . . emotionally and spiritually. I was supposed to go to the hospital block [this usually meant death] and my *blockalteste* [blockleader] Ilka, with whom I had established a relationship let me stay in the barracks for a day while she covered for me. This was my day of crisis. Without this protection, I would have died. . . . Always part of some group of women for whom you went through fire. . . . Maybe it was egotistical. You knew your group cared for you. . . . It was the reciprocity that kept you alive and going."

I asked if one needed affection:

> Oh yes. Yes, you did, oh yes, you did. Women amongst each other . . . for warmth, for feeling of someone caring. That you needed. Most basic point, it kept you warm if you were cuddled. Yes, we were affectionate. Even later in *Kanada* when we were quite comfortable . . . you slept four in a bunk next to each other; sure you cuddle up every so of-

ten—that was quite natural. That was not out of the ordinary. When people let themselves go, they also lost touch with other people.

Groups were formed in *Kanada*: "It was a different sort of friendship than in outside *kommandos*. There, it was a matter of survival. Don't know what men did. From what I read, it was not [the same]. The only way you had it with men [was] if they were commmunists or part of religious groups. . . . There was less of a need for support in *Kanada* because we could get necessities."

So in *Kanada*, the women formed different groups made up of people sharing the same interests or people who thought alike. In Susan's opinion, these friendships among like-minded people—instead of groups united for maintenance—were possible because death was not imminent in this situation. Friendships here seemed more relaxed and were formed not out of sheer necessity but instead out of mutual sympathy for each other.

### Judy

Judy is the youngest of these women. Born in 1929 in Hungary, she came to Auschwitz when she was fifteen in May 1944. Unlike Rose and Susan, she arrived with her family. They were separated on arrival. Judy was the only one who survived.

She was in Auschwitz for about nine months. She did speak of friendships with the girls in her bunks; she was in a barrack with about one thousand fifteen-year-old girls. She "mothered" those in her bunk whose education and experience were different from hers. She told them stories from such books as *Gone with the Wind* and *My Son, My Son* and from Deanna Durbin and Shirley Temple movies. In November she was sent on a transport to a labor camp, Guben, near Berlin. She was "brought to work in a factory soldering electrical equipment. The conditions were better here. Only fifty people to a room. Each bunk had two or three people. Each person received a blanket. They slept on a wooden board, with no mattress or pillow."

That first evening she had just fallen asleep, when someone came into the room and turned on the lights: "'Is there anyone here from Uzhorod [her hometown]?' It was Emu, the sister of a childhood friend [who was looking for her sister]. Even though I was not her sister, there was excitement and from that moment I had somebody and that meant everything to me . . . meant life to me."

Emu was there with her sister-in-law, Rosie. They were between ten and twelve years older than Judy. Emu worked in the kitchen and Rosie in the clothing warehouse.

> I became attached to both of them. . . . I got a coat right away from Rosie. . . . [Emu] always had an extra potato or two for me. She would see to it that I got the thicker part of the soup, not the liquid. Every so often, she would have an extra piece of bread which I joyously took back to my room and then shared with the few who were around me who didn't have that fortune as I did. I felt extremely lucky because of the friendship of these two women. They were very devoted, very caring, very kind and . . . good to me.

Her hope and strength were building. She thought the war would be over soon. However, they were evacuated to Bergen Belsen on a death march. It was cold and snowing; they had no water or food. Judy wanted them to leave her: "I was weak and my feet were blistered and bleeding. But they wouldn't let me go, they dragged me when I couldn't walk, and stood close by when the guards were near so they wouldn't see me." Somehow they managed. "I ate snow off of the person's shoulder in front of me or pulled frozen roots from the ground."

Judy was simply taken into the lives of Emu and Rosie; there were no discussions, no negotiations. They seemed to trust each other in what they did with and for each other. Is it partly because they were not total strangers? They do not *ask* Judy to go on; they simply don't let her fall. The acts push and sustain. It isn't the will to live that gets Judy through; it is a practice, a set of behaviors between one and the others.

They finally arrived at Bergen Belsen. Rosie had taken some jewelry with her from Guben for possible bartering. They stuffed the pieces in their mouths as they went through the showers. Judy said that conditions were awful. They slept on the floor. They hardly had any food and "no sanitation . . . people dying by the minute. We were given one meal a day. Often there was no bread. Eventually [there were] lice everywhere. [We were] continually and totally infested by lice [that] carried the typhus germ."

They each got typhus. Rosie was first.

We would drag her to where we could manage to get a little water . . . keep her supported between us, walking, so she's not lying down all the time. Tried to wash her face and slap her face gently. [Tried] to breathe life into her. Somehow these two ladies found a source . . . [and traded] their jewelry for aspirin, some food, sugar cubes, extra pieces of bread. Every time they acquired an extra bite of food they would share it with me as if I was a one-third partner. That was the most amazing thing. I just couldn't believe that. . . . It wasn't mine at all. [Yet] they never even considered not sharing.

After Rosie got better, Emu got very sick. . . . She developed huge welts—spotted typhus. She was very bosomy and had welts underneath her bosom that were festering. . . . I remember Rosie lifting her breast and me blowing on it to air it, to try to help this . . . to just lift it away from the wound so that the wound would reach some air . . . We would force feed her and she would say, "I can't swallow it. Let me die. I can't live anymore. I can't get up." "No! You can. You've come this long, and you're not going to go now. You can and you have to and you will." Just the way they did on the death march for me. We were encouraging this way in Bergen-Belsen.


Judy also got sick. Emu and Rosie did what they could to keep her alive. They still had a piece of jewelry. "They traded it for some cheese and bread. [We] shared it in honor of my sixteenth birthday. It was some sixteenth birthday under those kinds of conditions." Judy was sick for a few days: "I was shivering and my teeth were shaking. I was sure I was not going to live. Someone burst into the room and said, 'All our guards are gone. English soldiers are all over the place.' . . . I couldn't walk. My friends dragged me outside into a sunny, spring day. Liberation, April 15, 1945, about 1:00 p.m. I took this day as my new birthday."

Obviously Rose, Susan, and Judy survived because the Nazis did not kill them; and they were liberated. Ultimately, survival was luck. But that tells us very little if we want to find out about their maintenance strategies and how these strategies relate to their survival. "Luck" does not tell us how they committed to life in a world meant for death. In other words, they survived because the Nazis did not kill them; but they lived (trying to be human) because of what they did. Surviving is different from living.[16]

While other things may have been needed in order to keep going, such as inside work, extra food, cleanliness, willingness to risk, and physical and psychological strength, friendships and relationships are central to the stories of Judy, Susan, and Rose.[17] An important clue to these women's understanding of how they carried on, such acts of friendship also suggest questions that need to be asked of others about their experiences. These women recognized that isolation and separation were created by the Nazi system in the camps. They also knew that if strength mattered—if it was even possible—it could only exist with others. In their "families" they created the possibilities for material and psychological strength. Their relationships—their conversations, singing, story telling, recipe sharing, praying, joke telling, gossiping—helped them to transform a world of death and inhumanity into one more act of human life.

## ANALYSIS AND CRITICISM

> "What I propose . . . is very simple: it is nothing more than to think what we are doing."
> Hannah Arendt, *The Human Condition*

The language and perspective above recapitulate some of the research I had completed before May 1984, when I came to see serious problems in my work arising at least in part from my unconscious use of cultural feminism as a frame through which to view Jewish women survivors.[18] Cultural feminism informed the assumptions posited, hypotheses created, and the conclusions reached. Since cultural feminism has also been reflected in the work of many involved in women's studies and feminist theory, I have come to believe that the perspective it offers must be changed.

Cultural feminism was a reaction against at least two views: (1) radical feminism's position that women are an oppressed class and (2) the position of both New Left politics and radical feminism that personal liberation is impossible without widespread social change. This reaction shifted the territory of liberation from an insistence on the need for changing material conditions to a belief in changing the inner life, consciousness, culture and so on. Brooke, an early 1970s feminist critic of cultural feminism, called it "the belief that women will be freed via an alternate women's culture."[19]

While those who originally espoused cultural feminism may have thought, and even intended, that women would rise up and revolt once their consciousness was changed, the result was something else again. The putative politics of revolution turned into a politics of accomodation for individual and personal solutions. Cultural feminism developed not simply as a tactic for battling the antiwoman line in a sexist world but as a detour around it without violent revolution; without confronting the state, family, marriage, or organized religion, and without eliminating institutions intent upon keeping women in their place. This detour became a new strategy and ideology.

The "liberation" that cultural feminism invokes is from women's past. From that re-collection comes the discovery or development of a separate women's culture and community based upon the belief that women and men are in some sense radically different. Such re-collection, cultural feminists would argue, can create (and this is true) a positive class consciousness as well as (and this is questionable) a genuinely different society. Proponents of cultural feminism offer cultural and/or biological explanations for gender differences, but embedded in both is the judgment that the feminine or the female is superior to the masculine or the male. Thus, cultural feminism overthrows a theory of masculine superiority for its opposite rather than standing such an idea on its head or throwing it out the window.

On these terms, cultural feminism celebrates woman—her values and the art, music, sexuality, mothering, and so on that spring from them. In her article "Female Nationalism," Ti-Grace Atkinson succinctly characterizes cultural feminism as "the search for a *mythical history*, the *cult of femaleness*, the *glorification of motherhood*, *naturalism*, and *separatism*, [making] "female consciousness the source and arbiter of world reality."[20]

Thus, cultural feminism entrenches us in a reactionary politics of personal or life-style change, in liberation of the self, and is not truly concerned with bringing about fundamental changes in the ordering of human society or even solidarity with other women. While cultural feminists speak about a kind of universal woman, in fact they privilege some women over others. Cultural feminists *say* they consider all women, but *refer* only to lesbians, mothers, straight women, white women, middle-class women, women against pornography, or any number of others. Ann Oakley is right when she says that while not all solidarity with women demonstrates feminist consciousness, "there can be no feminist consciousness without female solidarity."[21] And if female solidarity is to have political import, there must be an active, progressive movement.

Cultural feminism, in glorifying the female past, unintentionally accepts oppression. The very "femininity" that seemed oppressive earlier in the Women's movement has now been made sacred. Can we so blithely reclaim and make right what has caused so much oppression without some careful scrutiny of our motives and politics? Without such a critical examination we damage not only our politics but also our research. We so much want to justify or support our positive reinterpretations of women's values, beliefs, and practices that our critical faculties become quiescent when we discuss these issues. The claim of female superiority is not at issue so much as the nature of gender differences and the kind of woman who best exemplifies them.

What does all of this mean for our research strategies? We must resolve not to use research either to valorize oppression, or to blunt or negate its effects. To excavate women's past, to begin to know and understand what has been "hidden from history," does not mean that we use that "herstory" as a model for women's liberation. Our task must be to contribute to a strategy for changing, not simply reinterpreting and obfuscating, women's lives.

The archaeological perspective that we have had on women's culture must be reexamined. Why do we take this point of view? How do we want to use it? Against what are we fighting? What new world are we making? Does our work sustain or even reinforce oppression? Are we articulating ways to understand and combat oppression? How does our work further the liberation of women? And if it does not, in what sense is it feminist?

Political and philosophical or conceptual errors are not far apart from each other. Analysis of my own work on women and the Holocaust has to turn on a critique of both my political and my philosophical perspective on the material and on the world. My use of cultural feminism as a frame (albeit unconsciously), changed respect for the stories of the Jewish women into some sort of glorification and led to my conclusion that these women transformed "a world of death and inhumanity into one more act of human life." It was important, perhaps even crucial for me to see choices, power, agency, and strength in womens's friendships, bonding, sharing, storytelling, and conversations in the camps and ghettos, in hiding, and passing as a gentile. And indeed, there are inspiring stories and people, moving tales of help, devotion, and love. However, they describe incidents and are not at the center of the Holocaust. They need to be put into perspective.

The Holocaust is a story of loss, not gain. After all, most Jews in Europe were killed. In addition, one fourth to one half of the Sinti and Roma population was killed. Perhaps ten to fifteen thousand homosexul men were killed. The list goes on. Even if we can find differences—even if women did maintain themselves better than men—how is this a real gain? We need to look critically, moreover, at the many ways in which women maintained themselves; their strategies were not always positive, and so a most difficult question has to be asked: "What have the victims wrought?"[22]

It is interesting to look at differences between women and men. It is even interesting to see, if we can, whether women maintained themselves either better than or (perhaps more accurately) differently from men. However, the discovery of difference is often pernicious because it helps us to forget the oppression that is the context of these supposed strengths, and to ignore the possibility that they may be only apparent. To suggest that among the Jews who lived through the Holocaust, women rather than men survived better is to move toward acceptance or valorization of oppression even if one uses a cultural, not a biological, argument. Oppression does not make people better; oppression makes people oppressed. There is no sense in fighting or even trying to understanding oppresssion as long as we maintain that the values and practices of the oppressed are not only better than those of the oppressor but in some objective sense "a model [for] humanity and the new society."[23] This is not to say that there are no differences between men and women in the ways that they relate to institutions or in their values. It is to question our interpretations of the conceptual and political import of such differences.

My attempt, then, to emphasize friendships among women in the camps gives a false or misleading impression that oppression is only external and not internal as well. Why the silence about the internalized oppression of the Jewish women survivors? To avoid another dimension of the horror of the Holocaust or of oppression in general? In the work represented above, I seemed to be saying that in spite of rape, abuse, the murder of babies; in spite of starvation, separations, losses, terror, violence, in spite of everything ugly and disgusting, women bonded, loved each other. Rose said, "That's what was holding the woman together." Must we not ask, How many women? At what cost? For how long? Under what conditions?

"Can you imagine what it meant," Rose said to me, "to have affection in spite of the dirt, disease, stench?" I don't doubt that it meant a great deal. It isn't that the statement is necessarily false but that the focus on friendship, affection, and so on distorted our understanding of a larger situation in which that experience may have played only a small role. The bonding was limited and exclusive. It wasn't a bonding against the enemy in solidarity with women. Did the terror of isolation and death *not* affect the women because they bonded? Perhaps these friendship stories cover a deeper and more troubled story of intrigue, bitterness, hurt, pain, and brutality. What else happened in the groups? Between the groups? The talk about friendship allowed those of us who heard the stories to admire these women, even to receive some peace and comfort. It helped to lessen the terrible surrounding sounds of the Holocaust. This "woman-centered" perspective was misguided.

Perhaps it was the only way I could have begun. Perhaps this emphasis on something like achievements was a necessary stage. On the other hand, perhaps it was too frightening to look at women and the Holocaust without having a way out. It is only human, even for a feminist, to look for something that will make the horror less horrible or even negligible. We have a need for the appearance of order as well as for real order; and when that need arises from a desire for solace or peace in a disturbed world (or from the belief that structural change in society is either impossible or too risky), we can be misled.

Yet if the perspective and questions were wrong, the work is not useless. Rather it requires a different political and philosophical context. Different questions must be asked of the survivors, and different interpretations made of their replies. To reconstruct the research on women and the Holocaust, we must begin with new questions:

1. What does oppression do to us? What is its process and effect? What is the price of survival? Of oppression? Can anything good come out of oppression?

2. Is women's culture liberating? How can it be if it was nourished in oppression? Can we ever forget the price we pay as oppressed

women? Should we? How does a belief that we can *survive* oppression affect our determination to *fight* oppression? If we glorify "the feminine" from a presumably feminist perspective, how do we avoid valorizing oppression in order to criticize and organize against it? Are we unwilling to confront the damage of oppression and how it has killed us? How we kill each other? If sexism makes women better able to survive, why get rid of it? Does suffering make us better people? If these questions make sense, are there real dangers in the work of Mary Daly, Carol Gilligan, Nancy Chodorow, Adrienne Rich, Dorothy Dinnerstein, and others who begin from a position of difference and end with the judgment (or at least do not deny the judgment) that women, in values, skills, and (some suggest) even biological makeup, are superior to men? In sum, does cultural feminism in spite of itself, glorify the oppression of women? To what extent does cultural feminism, with its emphasis on women's values, skills, and so on, contribute to this kind of perspective and itself become part of the problem we have to solve as feminists? How break this dangerous alliance between trying to understand oppression and needing to mythologize our strengths in or in spite of oppression? How envision a liberated future without an appeal to an oppressive past?

3. Do we lie in order to survive, no matter what the level of oppression?[24] Do the women survivors of the Holocaust lie? Engage in self-deception? Bad faith? Just not tell the truth? Mythologize in order to keep surviving? Does the women's understanding of themselves during the Holocaust differ from what happened? Is the only possibility for survival of any kind the creation of some "cover story" for an individual or a people? How often do survivors say things because they have a sense of obligation to their group, as women or as Jews? Are there patterns to these transformations? Do we have the right as researchers to uncover this story? An obligation? How do we as researchers transform the stories we hear? How should we?

4. Is it a methodological and theoretical mistake to look at women and the Holocaust from the vantage point of their difference from men rather than from that of oppression? Why do many women survivors believe women survived better than men? Does it have to do with the reality of the Holocaust or with women's return to traditional roles and expectations afterward? Is it the only thing to hold onto in a world that pays so little attention to them either as women or as survivors? Why do men believe that women survived better?

5. Were women's friendships in the camps really as crucial, in a positive sense, as those interviewed say? Is there more to the story than the women are likely to report no matter what questions are posed? Are these groups more like a form of tribalism than a form of friendship? What does it mean that the women use the term *family* to describe their groups? If biological family loyalties were often a hindrance to the survival of individuals during the Holocaust outside the camps, to what extent did families, surrogate or biological, hamper women in the camps? Why is it important for us to believe that these friendships were so central to their stories? What is at stake?

6. What is resistance? Is anything an oppressed woman does an act of resistance? Is survival resistance? What if a woman kills herself? Does suicide then become resistance? If suicide is sometimes an act of resistance, is it always so? Is dying resistance? Is courage resistance? Is singing on the way to the gas chamber resistance? Is maintaining the Jewish religion resistance? Is stealing resistance? Is hiding resistance? Escape? Is helping resistance? Is sabotage? Is killing the enemy resistance? See how the term becomes neutralized and, worse, destroyed! Such slippage in language suggests that all Jews became heroes or martyrs and all women heroines. Can that possibly make sense of what happened? Do descriptions of the lack of active or armed resistance against the enemy (either by the Jews or women or others) have to lead us not only to defend what they did but also to glorify it, to make of it what it was not? And so we reach what has become a common feminist position: survival is resistance. Certain values, described as feminine virtues, may get some women through but do not seem to offer most women the resources for fighting the enemy, for genuine resistance. They do not, that is, push one to "cripple or damage" or stop the enemy or even to try.[25] Manipulation of the system is not resistance even though it can mean survival. Do women know more about the manipulation of systems than about resistance to systems? What is the relationship between manipulation and survival? If we believe that survival is resistance, we may end up with the notion that armed or active resistance is not a priority or that it stands on equal footing with living through the Holocaust in any way possible.[26] Is survival a good no matter what the cost? What do we say about cooperation or even collaboration for survival? What about sexual exchanges for food or protection? Is the term *resistance* supposed to describe a kind of heroism about almost anything and anybody?

The phrase "resistance is survival" is a mystification in response to which at least one final question can be posed: What do we say about the dead?

7. What does transformation of female gender roles really mean in the face of the oppression and genocidal murder perpetrated during the Holocaust? Is our ability to transform ourselves a liability, or are only certain kinds of transformations liabilities? Did any genuine transformations actually take place? Do women become "liberated" in the process of these transformations in sex-segregated circumstances? Or merely more deeply embedded in these roles? How did these transformations affect their lives after the Holocaust?

8. Did anyone really survive the Holocaust?

9. How can I be true to the material given me by those I have interviewed? How be true to the women? What does that mean? What are my obligations as a woman? As a Jew? As an historian? As a philosopher? As a feminist?

10. What are the political effects or consequences of studying women and the Holocaust? What is the philosophical yield?

These questions and the critique out of which they come not only have enabled me to see where I have been, but also show me in what direction I need to move.[27]

---

> Comprehension, . . . means the unpremeditated, attentive
> facing up to, and resisting of reality—whatever it may be.
> Hannah Arendt, *The Origins of Totalitarianism*

## NOTES

---

This essay is an abridged and revised version of my "Women and the Holocaust: A Reconsideration of Research," *Signs: Journal of Women in Culture and Society* 10, no. 4 (1985): 741–61. Copyright 1985 by Joan Ringelheim, reprinted with my permission. Readers should consult the original essay for more detailed documentation than the present format allows.

1. See *Proceedings of the Conference, Women Surviving: The Holocaust*, ed. Esther Katz and myself (New York, 1983); and my three papers, "The Unethical and the Unspeakable: Women and the Holocaust," *Simon Wiesenthal Annual* 1 (1984): 69–87; "Communities in Distress: Women and the Holocaust" (Institute for Research in His-

tory, 1982, typescript); and "Resources and Vulnerabilities" (Institute for Research in History, 1983, typescript). See also Sybil Milton, "Women and the Holocaust: The Case of German and German-Jewish Women," in *When Biology Became Destiny: Women in Weimer and Nazi Germany*, ed. Renate Bridenthal, Attina Grossman, and Marion Kaplan (New York, 1984), 297–333; idem, "Issues and Resources," in *Proceedings of the Conference*, ed. Katz and myself, 10–21; Vera Laska, ed., *Women in the Resistance and in the Holocaust* (Westport, CT,1983); Marlene Heinemann, *Gender and Destiny: Women Writers and the Holocaust* (Westport, CT, 1986).

2. See Gisela Bock, "Racism and Sexism in Nazi Germany: Motherhood, Compulsory Sterilization, and the State," *Signs: Journal of Women in Culture and Society* 8, no. 3 (1983): 400–421.

3. I decided to use the term *maintenance* rather than the more customary *survival* because whether one survived or was murdered was determined by the Nazis or by one's "fate" (i.e., luck); whereas *maintenance* was determined by the victims, to some degree.

4. See my "The Unethical and the Unspeakable," 84.

5. Unless otherwise indicated, the subsequent quotes are from my interviews with Jewish women survivors. I have done twenty-eight interviews with twenty women. Most of the interviews were three hours long; a few lasted between six and ten hours. They were all in English. For the purposes of this paper I have culled some fragments to illuminate issues and concerns. For clarity, I have sometimes added words or explanations in brackets.

6. Twelve out of twenty of the survivors interviewed mentioned fear of rape, feelings of sexual humiliation, or instances of sexual exchange. Two of the twenty said they were raped. Another said she was almost raped.

7. *Kanada* was a section of the *Effektenkammer*, storehouse for the valuables— clothes, jewelry, and so on—of the prisoners who entered Auschwitz. Those who worked there were considered an elite *kommando* (work crew).

8. See also *Proceedings of the Conference*, ed. Katz and myself, 73–74 and 141–42; and Sybil Milton, "Women and the Holocaust," 315–16.

9. See my "The Unethical and the Unspeakable," 74–75, 78 and "Resources and Vulnerabilities," 20; and *Proceedings of the Conference*, ed. Katz and myself, 40–41.

10. Yaffa Eliach, "The Holocaust and the Family" (paper presented at Lehigh University, 1984).

11. Elmer Luchterhand, "Social Behavior of Concentration Camp Prisoners: Continuities and Discontinuities with Pre- and Postcamp Life," in *Survivors, Victims, and Perpetrators*, ed. Joel Dimsdale (New York, 1980), 273.

12. See Alexander Donat, "Jewish Resistance, in *Out of the Worldwind*, ed. Albert H. Friedlander (New York, 1968), 62; Leonard Tushnet, *The Uses of Adversity: Studies of Starvation in the Warsaw Ghetto* (New York, 1966), 27; Sybil Milton, "Women and the Holocaust," 307–8; idem, "Issues and Resources," 15–19; Raul Hilberg, ed., *Documents of Destruction* (Chicago, 1971), 40–41; Germaine Tillion, *Ravensbruck* (New York, 1975), 39, 230; Lucjan Dobroszycki, ed., *The Chronicle of the Lodz Ghetto* (New Haven, CT, 1984), esp. lvii; see also n. 27 below.

13. See my "Communities in Distress," 35 and 43, n. 27 and *Proceedings of the Conference*, ed. Katz and myself, 176.

14. See my "The Unethical and the Unspeakable," 80.

15. The interviews with Rose and Judy took place in May 1982. Susan was interviewed in August 1979. I have had subsequent conversations with Judy and Susan.

Again, the quotations are from these interviews unless otherwise stated. Ten among the seventeen other women survivors interviewed (1981–84) also spoke of relationships with other women as being significant.

16. See my "Communities in Distress," 33–34.

17. These categories were worked out in a converation with Susan Cernyak-Spatz and Pamela Armstrong in August 1982. See also Milton, "Issues and Resources," 17–19; idem, "Women and the Holocaust," 311–15.

18. I was first made aware of these problems when I read Ti-Grace Atkinson, "Female Nationalism"—published in French as "Le Nationalisme Feminin," in *Nouvelles questions féministes* 6–7 (Spring, 1984): 35–54—in an unpublished English version. Subsequent discussions with Atkinson—about cultural feminism, feminist theory and politics, philosophy, and women and the Holocaust—demonstrated that the impasse I had reached had much to do with my unknowing adherence to cultural feminism.

19. Brooke, "Retreat to Cultural Feminism," in *Feminist Revolution: Redstockings of the Women's Liberation Movement* (New York, 1975), 79, 83.

20. Atkinson, "Female Nationalism," 35, 53.

21. Ann Oakley, *Subject Women* (New York, 1981), 278.

22. Hope Weissman to the author, June 1984.

23. See Barbara Burris, "The Fourth World Manifesto," in *Radical Feminism*, ed. Anne Koedt, Ellen Levine, and Anita Rapone (New York, 1973), 356.

24. See Adrienne Rich, *On Lies, Secrets, and Silence: Selected Prose, 1966–1978* (New York, 1979), 189: "In the struggle for survival we tell lies."

25. Suggested by Raul Hilberg in "Bibliography and the Holocaust" (paper presented at the Scholar's Conference, New York City, 1981).

26. Compare my "The Unethical and the Unspeakable," 75–81.

27. POSTSCRIPT (New York City, July, 1989): When this paper was finished I turned my attention to the issue of women's survival. I focused on one of the most prominent questions from my previous work: Did women survive better than men? In order to answer the question factually rather than anecdotally, I analyzed various documents from the *Einsatzgruppen* operations; the Lodz, Warsaw and Theresienstadt ghettos; the labor camps; and the displaced persons camps. They suggest that more Jewish women than men were killed in the extermination process by 12–14 percent. This information formed the framework for my research following the publication of the original version of this essay in *Signs*. I am now in the process of completing a book on women and the Holocaust that discusses what these figures mean through consideration of such issues as resistance, survival, anti-Semitism and sexism, and genocide and sexism.

**12** **ELLEN M. UMANSKY**

*Spiritual Expressions: Jewish Women's Religious Lives in the Twentieth-Century United States*

With few exceptions,[1] previous studies of Jewish spirituality have assumed, either explicitly or implicitly, that the study of Jewish texts and regular participation in public worship have always been the central elements of traditional Jewish life. Indeed, if one examines Judaism through the lens of male experience, as most of these studies have done,[2] study and prayer *have been* central features of the lives of (male) traditional Jews. Early feminist studies of the religious lives of Jewish women, including those by Paula Hyman and Rachel Adler, shared the assumption that the study of religious texts and participation in public worship constituted what Hyman labeled the "heart and soul of traditional Judaism."[3] Women's exclusion from these areas made them little more than "peripheral" Jews (i.e., radically different from men, who do not take into account "the objective reality of women's lives, self-concept and education").[4]

Without denying these conclusions, more recent feminist studies have recognized that to view study and communal worship as the heart and soul of traditional Judaism and then to focus on how women were excluded from (or sought to gain acceptance in) these areas is to accept an essentially androcentric vision of Judaism. This vision, focusing on the activities of men, universalizes their experiences and assigns them primary importance and at the same time minimizes or ignores the reality of women's religious lives.

Recognizing the importance of gender in the shaping of Jewish identities, past and present, I shall reconstruct, primarily through the writings of women, how twentieth-century U.S. Jewish women have understood and lived Judaism. Jewish spirituality is not necessarily equated with the study of religious texts or participation in communal worship. Nor is it assumed that women's traditional exclusion from these aspects of religious life has made them feel peripheral. Rather, the questions I ask are, What has been the nature of Jewish women's religious lives in the United States? How has gender helped shape these experiences? How have Jewish women defined spirituality in general and Jewish spirituality in particular? How have women's experiences of Judaism broadened our understanding of what the heart and soul of Judaism really is?

## WOMEN AS SPIRITUAL BEINGS

At the beginning of the twentieth century, most native-born U. S. Jewish women (generally of German-Jewish origin and Reform in orientation) accepted the commonly held U.S. assumption that women were religious by nature. As early as the 1830s, religion was seen to be a special concern of women, with their homes functioning as havens from an increasingly corrupt secular world. By the end of the century, U.S. middle class ladies were expected to be spiritual exemplars. It was they who were to impart spiritual values to their children and husbands, creating a religious, moral atmosphere within the home. As religion became associated with what Ann Douglas has labeled "feminine influence,"[5] women's activities, both in and outside of the home, began to reflect women's growing conviction that it was up to them to share their own understanding of true religion with others. Literary women began to write religious novels and spiritual autobiographies; wealthy, philanthropic women formed social, educational, and charitable organizations; and some audacious women, seeking to impart their religious capacities directly, sought admission to religious seminaries and, with or without the benefit of ordination, began to preach publicly.

An increasing number of women all over the country began to form study groups for their own religious edification. Meeting at one another's homes, they would study the Bible or some other religious text. Christian Science, for example, which arose in the 1880s and achieved its greatest growth during the first three decades of the twentieth century, often took root in local communities through study groups organized and led by women that met on a regular basis to read and study Mary Baker Eddy's *Science and Health with Key to the Scriptures.* After several years, many of these groups established themselves as Christian Science churches, erecting their own places of worship and establishing formal ties with the mother church in Boston.

Some native-born Jewish women eagerly participated in non-sectarian charitable, educational, and philanthropic organizations. Notable among such women was Maud Nathan (1862–1946), a wealthy Jew of Sephardic descent who was active in the New York Exchange for Women's Work and the Women's Auxiliary of the Civil Service Reform Association. She helped found, and later served as president of, the Consumers' League of New York, an organization intended to ameliorate, through consumer pressure, the working conditions for women and children in New York City department stores.

Other elite Jewish women began to create women's organizations specifically for Jews. By the turn of the century, for example, few Jewish communities in the United States lacked a "ladies' aid society." Attempting to extend their help beyond the Jewish community, members engaged in such activities as visiting hospitals, establishing loan funds for the poor, and offering cultural events to which all women were invited. In Chicago, for instance, the Chicago Women's Aid, an association founded in 1862 as the Chicago Young Ladies' Aid, helped to introduce penny lunches in schools, hired a dietician, and provided the Associated Jewish Charities with a visiting nurse. It also took an active interest in, and provided financial support for, the Sheltering Home and Crèche for Poor Jewish Children. Chicago also had two ladies' sewing societies. These societies hired poor women to sew clothing, which would then be distributed to the needy.[6] For their members, these Jewish societies functioned as both social and spiritual outlets. They not only afforded Jewish women the opportunity to meet other women of similar backgrounds and socioeconomic class but also enabled them to bring their "feminine influence" into the larger community, providing other, less fortunate women with adequate clothing, food, and shelter so that they, too, might transform their homes into pious havens.

Similar motivations compelled the women, both Jewish and non-Jewish, who worked to establish and run settlement houses. Lillian Wald (1867–1940), perhaps U.S. Jewry's best-known female social worker, championed such causes as child welfare, public health nursing, vocational guidance, and the establishment of scholarships for talented children. Born in Cincinnati into a prosperous middle-class family, the well-educated Wald turned to social service, especially nursing, as a means of helping others. Though she felt more comfortable at meetings held by the humanistic Ethical Culture Society than she did at synagogue services, Wald continued to identify herself as a Jew, at least culturally.[7] Certainly her efforts to help others were conditioned to a great extent by her own upbringing, specifically, what she had been taught to regard as women's sensitive and moral nature.

Like Goldie Stone, an acculturated Lithuanian immigrant who worked with members of the native-born female Jewish elite in Chicago to create social and philanthropic opportunities for impoverished East European Jewish immigrants, Lillian Wald might simply have summed up her faith in the phrase, "Be kind."[8] Yet many of the Jewish women who engaged in social reform explicitly described their activities as an outgrowth of women's particular religious mission.

Julia Richman (1855–1912), for example, a leading Jewish educator who assisted Jewish immigrants through her work with the Educational Alliance in New York and who, in 1903, became the first Jew to serve as district superintendent in the New York City school system, spoke of the obligation of Jewish women to minister to the moral and physical needs of less fortunate Jews. Though it is important, she asserted, for all men and women to assist us in our religious mission, it is up to women, particularly those who are mothers, to ensure that future generations of Jews are acquainted with Jewish history and literature by imparting religious values to their children and by actively supporting religious school education. "Only with the aid of our Rabbis," she maintained, "can the women hope to improve our schools; only with the aid of our women can the Rabbis hope to gain real influence over their flock." The key to the "permanence of all true, earnest, spiritual American Judaism," she insisted, rests with women, for it is our responsibility to ensure that the highest spiritual aims permeate not only the classroom but also the home.

It is every mother's obligation, she said, to teach her children, while they are still young, *true Judaism*, that is, the acknowledgment and sensing of God's daily presence. "Take your children to the Religious School at a very early age," she advised.

> Select for them a teacher who loves little ones and who loves God. What do these babies care about Adam and Eve, or the order of creation? Introduce them to the wonders of plant and animal life. *Show them God* in the bursting seed, in the budding flower, in the bird-producing egg, in the glorious sunshine. Let them see God and learn to love Him for His blessings which they share. Let them be made to feel that God means protection, that to Him they owe love and respect and gratitude and loyalty. Make God the starting point and the goal. Love of God, confidence in God, fear, not of God, but of His disapproval, these are the steps by which to develop the feeling of moral obligation, first to the world, then to Judaism.[9]

Equating both spirituality in general and Jewish spirituality in particular with inner piety and moral obligation, Richman believed that women's religious nature gave them a special responsibility to help tap the spiritual potential of others.

One finds similar sentiments expressed in speeches and essays written by Minnie Louis (1841–1922), an educator and social reformer who worked with Julia Richman in New York. In a paper entitled "The Influence of Women in Bringing Religious Conviction to Bear upon Daily Life," read at the Triennial Congress of the National Council of Women in 1895 and subsequently published in the *American Hebrew*, Louis defined *religion* as the "cognition of something beyond, above us, yet ever with us, leading us into a realm of thought that broadens and brightens and nourishes as we advance in it. . . . It is an intuition, a primary truth." Describing woman as "the ozone of the metaphysical atmosphere," she maintained that women's altruistic nature, especially prevalent in mothers, made them instinctively seek the religious as an area of life in which they might exert their greatest influence and activity. Addressing herself to all women, she insisted,

It is we with our "sanative conscience" that must turn in the full, strong
light, and make chancel, aisle and transept, lectern and pew, glow in
the sunbeams of a new spirituality. Let us turn all into lecture halls,
study halls and libraries for young and old, for men and women, for
aristocrat and plebian, for employer and employee; turn them into hospitals for the sick, into homes for the homeless and helpless, and have
our priests guard *them* until the complete education has come to all,
and built in *each* heart a Temple for God, made *every* home a Temple
for him, and *every* voice to sing with one accord—"The Fatherhood of
God, the Brotherhood of Man!" . . . Then, oh women!, we will not
glory in our influence, but with humble heart will say, "Blessed art
thou, O Lord, who hast made us as we are."[10]

In other works, written at the turn of the century, Minnie Louis
focused on Jewish spirituality more explicitly. "Judaism," she
maintained,

is to me, *per se*, religion; the amalgamation of every virtue, the be-all
and end-all of every possible aspiration. . . . It is the spirit of Divinity
reaching down into every soul to help it climb up to its supernal height;
it is the strong yet tender power that lifts the soul to that spirit and
bears it aloft on pinions of love and mercy above the irritations of
human weakness. It is condensed in those talismanic words, "do justice, love mercy, and walk humbly with thy God."[11]

Extolling the virtues of Sunday school education, Louis made a particular appeal to Jewish women to help cultivate the "pure spiritual
character" of their children and, acknowledging their own paucity of
knowledge, to convey to their offspring the importance of learning
about both Judaism's history and its religious spirit.

By the beginning of the twentieth century, Jewish women's organizations proliferated among the native-born elite on both a local and
national level, again with the aim of spreading their members' "feminine influence" throughout the U.S. Jewish community. Most notable
were the local sisterhoods—established as social, educational, and
philanthropic organizations—that by the second decade of the century were in existence in almost every Reform temple in the country.
By 1913, these groups were coordinated on a national level as the
National Federation of Temple Sisterhoods.[12] The National Women's
League of the United Synagogue of America, founded in 1918 and

renamed the Women's League for Conservative Judaism in 1972, engaged in similar activities.[13]

The National Council of Jewish Women, which was founded in 1893 following the first Congress of Jewish Women, organized by Hannah Greenbaum Solomon (1858–1942) as part of the Parliament of Religions held at the Chicago World's Fair, was unusual in its independence from any male-dominated religious movement. The leadership of the National Council coordinated the educational, religious, and philanthropic work of local chapters (helping to guide this work through the creation of a national platform) and sought to unite Jewish women of different social and religious backgrounds. The Council succeeded to some extent in this endeavor, although the overwhelming majority of its early members were of German origin and were religiously identified as Reform. Seeking to tap the spiritual potential of their members and subsequently, through specific philanthropic and educational efforts, to help them exert a moral influence over the U.S. Jewish community as a whole, early leaders of Council, like Rebekah Kohut (1864–1951), president of the New York section, firmly believed that on every Jewish woman "is laid the duty of being God's missionary in the fullest sense of the word. We are not necessarily to win souls by an aggressive propaganda," she maintained, "which too often repels rather than attracts, but simply by the quiet force of a beautiful example. Every true Jewess is a priestess, and by the very strength of her unobtrusive belief is a witness for religion; and when faith in God is the source of her virtues, truth and integrity, gentleness and purity the foundation stones of her life, then truly she is a priestess in Israel."[14]

While the particular religious style that Julia Richman, Minnie Louis, and Rebekah Kohut used, invoking the fatherhood of God and the brotherhood of man, quoting the prophets, serving as witness to God, and engaging in a particular religious mission, reflected their own attachment to the teachings of Reform Judaism, their belief in the innate spirituality of women (i.e., in women's intuitive awareness of God's presence) and their ability to exert a religious influence over others was shared by other Jewish women, both immigrants and native-born, who did not affiliate or identify with Reform. Cultural Jews, like Lillian Wald, undoubtedly came to this belief through prevalent late-nineteenth-century U.S. notions of true womanhood and true religion. More traditional Jewish women, especially those who immigrated to the United States from Eastern Europe, may have come to believe in women's innate religiosity directly or indirectly from the writings of Samson Raphael Hirsch, the nineteenth-century founder of modern Orthodoxy, and his successors. These writers justified traditional Judaism's exclusion of women from positive, time-bound commandments on the grounds that women, because they were innately spiritual, did not need external, time-bound reminders of how one could serve God. It is as likely, however, that such women were influenced both by traditional Judaism's encouragement of women's private devotions and by the books of devotional prayers written specifically for Jewish women during the late nineteenth and early twentieth centuries.

During the medieval and early modern period, loose translations of the prayer book into the vernacular were written for, and made available to, East European Jewish women. Also available were *tkhines*, petitionary prayers written in Yiddish for—and sometimes by—women.[15] In the United States, by the middle of the nineteenth century, prayer translations for women began to appear in English as well. For the most part, these translated texts were not read in the synagogue but in the home. By the early twentieth century, books of devotional prayers written by traditional rabbis specifically for women were also published in the United States. These books, like Rabbi Abraham Hirschowitz's *Religious Duties of the Daughters of Israel*, published in English in 1902, contained prayers and private meditations focusing on women's own home-centered activities rather than on the communal experiences of the Jewish people.

Hirshowitz's book, for example, offered elaborate explanations for women's three special mitzvot (commandments concerning preparing the Sabbath loaves, kindling Sabbath lights, and observation of family purity regulations); discussed laws concerning *kashrut*, the dietary rules for which women assumed greatest responsibility; and contained prayers to be recited on such occasions as one's wedding day, the birth of a child, and recovery from illness. Also included were morning and evening prayers for mothers to teach to their children.[16] This book, and others like it, helped foster a sense of religiosity that was personal rather than communal, rooted primarily in private devotions that reflected the reality of traditional women's daily lives.

As Sydney Stahl Weinberg has noted, many East European immigrant women refused to abandon Orthodoxy, even if that refusal made the process of acculturation to the United States both difficult and painful. Yet many of these women discovered that their preservation of traditional Judaism within the home held a significance in the United States that it lacked in Europe, where the synagogue had been viewed as the central institution of Jewish religious life. In the United States, "where economic pressures made religious learning apparently irrelevant to daily life, women's domestic practices became major rather than peripheral components in transmitting a sense of Jewish identification to children."[17] Women communicated this sense of Jewish identity by conveying the importance of Jewish ethnicity (an aspect of Jewish life primarily transmitted through the preparation of certain foods), Jewish peoplehood (through the celebration of the Sabbath and festivals and often through the taking in of fellow Jewish immigrants as boarders), and Jewish spirituality as both moral obligation and inner piety.

As immigrant women became acculturated, they increasingly joined women's organizations founded by native-born Jews. By the 1920s and 1930s, for example, thousands had become members of the National Council of Jewish Women and Hadassah, the enormously successful women's Zionist organization co-founded and led by Henrietta Szold (1860–1945) in 1912. Not all of these women, of course, were Orthodox or even religious. Yet even those who identified themselves simply as cultural Jews shared with Szold the belief that the perpetuation of both Jews and Judaism depended on Jewish repatriation to Palestine. In numerous speeches Szold appealed to Jewish women—as those capable of exerting the greatest influence on the young—to convince their families and their communities that Jewish survival depended on Zionist efforts. While Hadassah's goals were not explicitly spiritual, Hadassah provided hundreds of thousands of Jewish women with the opportunity to engage in important Jewish philanthropic, educational, cultural, and even political activities. Indeed, if one understands Jewish spirituality as extending beyond study and prayer, then raising money to send a contigent of nurses to Palestine, helping the poor, working for Jewish-Arab rapprochement—in short, working for practical change—can be a reflection, as they were for Szold, of religious and moral convictions. Thus, one can view participation even in seemingly nonreligious organizations like Hadassah as ways in which many Jewish women throughout the twentieth century have sought to give their own understanding of Jewish self-identity greater public expression.

## LITERARY WOMEN

Throughout the late nineteenth and early twentieth centuries, some women attempted to articulate their own feelings about Jewish self-identity, including their understanding of spirituality in general and Jewish spirituality in particular, through short stories, semiautobiographical novels, magazine articles, and, occasionally, explicitly theological works. Josephine Lazarus' *Spirit of Judaism*, for example, published in 1896, called for the creation of a new, universal religion through which liberal Judaism and liberal Christianity might be united. Her work sparked continuing theological discussions and debates among liberal Jews during the early years of the twentieth century. On a more popular level the works of such immigrant writers as Mary Antin (1881–1949) and Anzia Yezierska (1885–1970) consciously reflected on what the immigrant experience meant to them as Jews and as women.

Yezierska, in particular, in six short story collections and novels published between 1920 and 1932, angrily denounced what she perceived as the subordinate, if not inferior, role of women within traditional Jewish life. Throughout her writings, her alienation and sense of exclusion from a traditional Judaism that she believed held few if any spiritual possibilities for women is palpable. Judaism, she maintained, was a religion created by and for men. As Sara Smolinsky, the heroine of her most popular novel, *Bread Givers*, laments, women's prayers don't count (i.e., women are excluded from being counted in the traditional prayer quorum) because the traditional Jewish view is that God simply doesn't listen to women. Her father, she recalls, had taught her that "women had no brains for the study of God's Torah"; yet "they could be the servants of men who studied the Torah. Only if they cooked for the men, and washed for the men and didn't nag or curse the men out of their homes; only if they let the men study Torah in peace, then, maybe, they could push themselves into Heaven with the men, to wait on them there."[18] Rejecting her father's faith, Sara, like Yezierska herself, comes to view spirituality as an awareness of one's own potential followed by the resolve to "become a person," that is, to tap into inner resources that make self-growth and self-fulfillment possible despite external obstacles that might be in the way.

One finds similar sentiments expressed in the short stories and novels of Elizabeth Stern (1890–1954), who immigrated to the United States with her parents at the age of three. While her works are tinged with less bitterness and anger than those of Yezierska, they, too, describe traditional Judaism as an outdated male creation that fails to take the spiritual aspirations of modern women seriously (although, in her view, it also fails, for different reasons, to take the spiritual aspirations of modern men seriously). In her semiautobiographical novel, *I Am a Woman—and a Jew*, published in 1925, she also rejects Reform Judaism, concluding that for most of its adherents it offers little more than Jewish social unity.

One finds in Stern's writings, far more than in those of Yezierska, a sense of religious struggle. Unlike Yezierska's Sara Smolinsky, for example, who leaves her father's home and the spiritual inheritance that was to be her possession, Stern's Leah Morton (the pseudonym under which she published her autobiographical novel) continues to struggle, unwilling to leave her father's world completely. While her initial rejection of Judaism begins long before she leaves home, she attempts to discover, even after her departure, a religious way to again identify herself as Jewish.

It is unclear how many of the particulars of Leah Morton's spiritual search were in fact autobiographical. Yet we do know that despite Elizabeth Stern's struggle to identify religiously as a Jew in order to find personal meaning and to create a link between her world and that of her parents, by 1928 she had come to the conclusion that true faith was neither Jewish nor non-Jewish but universal. Acknowledging that her religious break with Judaism was final, she subsequently joined the Philadelphia Ethical Society, a branch of the Ethical Culture Society, where she found a faith that "came from the truth of intellectual processes."[19] At first her religious break from Judaism did not signal a disavowal of Jewish ethnicity; for, as she concludes at the end of her novel, "I am [a Jew] before everything. Perhaps not in my work or in my daily life. But in that inner self that cannot change, I belong to my people."[20] By the end of her life, however, it seems that even her ethnic ties had been broken. Becoming a member of the Religious

Society of Friends around 1941, an attraction that undoubtedly grew out of her lifelong commitment to pacifism, she devoted much time and energy to various Quaker organizations. When she died in 1954, she was buried as a Quaker.

Not all early-twentieth-century Jewish literary women, of course, turned their backs on Judaism. Mary Antin, for example, while rejecting Judaism as a religious faith, never completely abandoned either religious observance or explicitly Jewish causes. Undoubtedly, others continued to find meaning in Judaism as a religious heritage. Indeed, numerous social reformers like Maud Nathan and organization women like Hannah Greenbaum Solomon and Rebekah Kohut published memoirs describing their continuing allegiance to the Jewish community and to the Jewish religious values that had been instilled in them. Studies of early-twentieth-century U.S. Jewish women writers who detailed their feelings about Judaism as a personal religious faith still need to be undertaken.

More recently, short stories and memoirs by women looking back at Jewish religious life in the early twentieth century have further expanded our understanding of Judaism through the lens of women's experiences. Kate Simon's *Bronx Primitive* (1982), a poignant memoir of growing up in an immigrant neighborhood in the 1920s, details her recollections of her family's early life in the United States. Describing her parents' adaptation to their new environment, and their falling off in religious observance, Simon remembers the moment when her mother announced she would no longer light Sabbath candles:

> My mother had put two candlesticks on the big round dining table, lit them, and placed a white cloth on her head. She began to talk to them in the same singsong that Uncle David murmured when he bound his arm with black leather strips and swayed back and forth. It was talking to God, we had been told, and women did it only on Friday night, the only time God had for women. In the middle of a phrase my mother took off her headcloth, blew out the candles, and, turning to my astonished father, said—in Polish, which we still spoke sometimes—"No more. I never believed it, I don't now. And I don't have to do it to please my mother, or anyone, here."[21]

In contrast, other contemporary writers, often drawing on the experiences of their own mothers and grandmothers, have described the significance many immigrant women continued to attach to religious observance. Harriet Rosenstein, writing in 1974, recalls spending time with her grandmother, helping her transfer "her gold-brown *challahs* from the oven to a long mahogany sideboard in the dining room," letting them cool "on the special sabbath cloth she had herself embroidered."[22] She describes her grandmother's devoutness: her kissing her fingers and pressing them to the mezuzah attached to the doorpost every time she entered her bedroom, praying in Hebrew "like a woman possessed" as she got undressed each evening.

Other recent fiction has focused on the spiritual lives of contemporary Jewish women. In such works as Esther Broner's *Weave of Women* (1978) and Nessa Rapoport's story "The Woman Who Lost Her Names" (1980) we find reflections, not only on the traditional exclusion of women from much of Judaism's public religious life but also on how women today can reclaim the power of naming, deciding for themselves what is religiously significant and learning to tap their own spiritual potential. Thus, the community of women described in Broner's novel work to create new rituals that reflect the reality of women's lives, while Rapoport's heroine demands the right to create a new name for her daughter.

In her 1981 novel, *Preparing for Sabbath*, Rapoport describes spirituality as trying "to serve God and devote [her] life to Him." Yet unlike so many women writers of the late nineteenth and early twentieth century, she refuses to believe that men and women possess different spiritual natures. "I'm sick of hearing," her heroine, Judith Rafael, asserts,

> about how women have a different spirituality. I'm sick of being taught how important it is [for men] to put on a *tallis* [prayer shawl] and *tefillin* every morning and then to be told that women don't need concrete symbols because they have some magical female ability to sanctify themselves. You don't expect women to bring *Shabbes* [Sabbath] in just by thinking about it. You expect them to light candles. Why should it change for other prayers? Sure a woman can *daven* [pray] every morning if she choses. But the physical act of wrapping yourself in a *tallis*, of reciting the blessing for *tefillin*, knowing that for centuries Jews have expressed their bond with God in just this way—there is no substitute. A man who *davens* every day with *tefillin* knows his prayer is incomplete without it, but a woman's prayer has nothing physical, actual, to say: I am here.[23]

Further, without denying the importance of cultivating a sense of inner piety, Rapoport's heroine recognizes that *Jewish* spirituality cannot be discovered without studying religious texts. "Judaism," she insists, "is a religion that loves knowledge, and women who are untrained have nothing."[24] Here, even more than in "The Woman Who Lost Her Names," Rapoport's heroine refuses to accept passively the religious role that her forefathers have carved out for her. She demands the right not only to articulate her own understanding of Jewish spirituality but also to claim access for women to the spiritual paths that Judaism has denied them.

## WOMEN AS RELIGIOUS LEADERS

Early in the twentieth century, when women like Maud Nathan and Hannah Solomon received invitations to preach from Reform pulpits, they assumed—as did their audience—that these invitations were recognitions of their public prominence and effective public speaking. None of these women aspired to become religious leaders, nor were they viewed as such by their contemporaries. During the 1890s, however, there was such a female religious leader. Ray Frank (1865–1945?), a journalist from Oakland, California, apparently became a popular Jewish preacher, traveling up and down the Pacific coast, addressing Jewish audiences and helping to establish Jewish congregations. Her activities as a religious leader were short-lived, though, ending in 1898 with her marriage to Simon Litman and her subsequent decision to devote herself to her husband and home.

It wasn't until the early 1920s that U.S. Jewish women, (although even then only a handful) began to seriously consider becoming religious leaders.[25] At Hebrew Union College (HUC), the rabbinical seminary of the Reform movement, Martha Neumark (b. 1900?), daughter of a faculty member, took courses in the college's rabbinical program, hoping to receive ordination. In 1921 she petitioned the faculty to be assigned to lead High Holy Day services in the fall should a pulpit be available. When the faculty vote on the matter ended in a tie, it was left to Kaufman Kohler, president of the college, to reach a decision. Kohler approved Neumark's petition, subject to subsequent approval by the congregation in question. He then suggested to the board of governors that a joint faculty-board committee be formed to consider the larger issue that Neumark's petition had indirectly raised, that of women's rabbinic ordination.

Although the final report adopted by the committee maintained that given Reform Judaism's commitment to women's equality there was no logical reason why women should not be entitled to receive a rabbinical degree, it went on to assert that for practical reasons women's admission to Hebrew Union College's rabbinical program should be discouraged. The matter was then referred to the HUC faculty (who concluded that "in view of the fact that Reform Judaism has in many other instances departed from traditional practice, it cannot logically and consistently refuse the ordination of women"), the Central Conference of American Rabbis (CCAR—this Reform rabbinical group similarly affirmed that women could not "justly be denied the privilege of ordination"), and finally, in 1923, to the board of governors as a whole, who effectively vetoed the HUC faculty and CCAR recommendations by voting that "no change should be made in the present practice of limiting to males the right to matriculate for the purpose of entering the rabbinate."[26]

In 1925, in an article published in the *Jewish Tribune*, Martha Neumark reflected on her desire to become the first woman rabbi in the United States and on the few experiences she had had as a religious leader. Describing the first time she led a synagogue service (during the summer of 1920), she wrote:

> I shall never forget the occasion. The curious, yet sympathetic interest of the congregation (the women relished the idea more than the men did), the unique quality of the event, the generous approval of my father. . . . It was as I incanted the Hebrew that the witchery and charm of the service surged through me. I began to feel the value of ritual in a religious service . . . [and since then] have come to believe that ritual and ceremony are invaluable adjuncts to a religious communion.[27]

Defining *spirituality* as an awareness of God's presence and the desire to commune with him, Neumark suggested that perhaps women were even better suited for the Reform rabbinate than men, since most of the congregants who attended services were women, who could better identify with a woman rabbi's "spiritual struggles." Maintaining that an effective rabbi should not only be learned but also a sympathetic listener willing to share her or his struggles with members of the congregation, Neumark concluded that even if the religious concerns of women rabbis and their female congregants were not identical, at least "their paths of spiritual storm" would better coincide.

In the years prior to World War II, two other women unsuccessfully sought to become U.S. Reform rabbis, Irma Levy Lindheim (1886–1978), a Zionist who entered Hebrew Union College in 1922 during the height of the Martha Neumark controversy, and Helen Hadassah Levinthal, who in 1939 completed the rabbinic program at Rabbi Stephen Wise's progressive New York seminary, the Jewish Institute of Religion (JIR—which subsequently merged with HUC) but was refused ordination.[28] By the 1950s, however, the Reform movement once again formally addressed the issue of women's becoming rabbis. In part, at least, this issue was raised in response to the activities of Paula Ackerman (1893–1989), the widow of William Ackerman, rabbi of (Reform) Temple Beth Israel in Meridian, Mississippi.

Following her husband's death in November 1950, Paula Ackerman was asked by the congregation to become their spiritual leader. Although she had received no rabbinical training, she could read Hebrew, had previously conducted religious services at the temple when circumstances forced her husband to be absent, and had long served as a religious school teacher, both in Meridian and in her hometown of Pensacola, Florida. After several weeks of hesitation she accepted the congregation's offer and from January 1951 until September 1953, led services, preached sermons, and performed marriages, funerals, and conversions. In so doing, she became the first woman to serve as a spiritual leader of a mainstream U.S. Jewish congregation.

When Paula Ackerman was asked to become the religious leader of Temple Beth Israel, she had neither the formal training nor the personal inclination to do so. Yet, as she told me in one of many conversations I had with her, during the month that the congregation had given her to reach a decision, she prayed to God to guide her. Spontaneously opening her heart to God, looking to him for an answer, she came to believe that God was calling her to become a religious leader. This conviction was strengthened by what she took to be a number of religious signs, one of which stood out particularly clearly:

> At the time the congregation came to me, I was scheduled to have a hysterectomy. I was 57 years old and still menstruating. I didn't want

to have the operation. What's more, I didn't think I should read from the Torah if I were menstruating. Well, I prayed to the Lord for guidance and from the moment I thought I would say yes to the congregation, my periods stopped completely. I went to my gynecologist and told her about it. She said, "Don't feel that it's gone. Often, a shock like you've had with your husband's death and the congregation wanting you to carry on could make it stop. It could come back after several years." Well, I have never seen it. And I never needed to have the hysterectomy. Wouldn't you think the Lord was telling me something?[29]

After assuming her congregational duties, Ackerman continued to pray for guidance. Each morning before going to her office, she would enter the temple sanctuary, prostrate herself before the ark (containing the Torah scrolls), and silently ask God for continued strength and wisdom. On the pulpit and later on the lecture circuit Ackerman was apparently a powerful speaker. She never wrote out her sermons or lectures; instead, she spoke from notes that helped remind her of the religious themes she wanted to convey. Equating both spirituality in general and Jewish spirituality in particular with inner piety and an awareness of God's daily presence, Paula Ackerman actively sought to cultivate her religious nature and to share her faith with others.

During her tenure as "lay rabbi" of Temple Beth Israel, Ackerman was accorded a good deal of respect, by both local clergy (Jewish and non-Jewish) and Reform rabbis throughout the country (a few of whom co-officiated at weddings with her); but it wasn't until 1956 that Nelson Glueck, then president of Hebrew Union College, formally supported the recommendation of a CCAR committee advocating women's ordination as rabbis and their admittance into the CCAR after completing the HUC-JIR rabbinical program. Over ten years later, as the burgeoning feminist movement began to create new expectations among women themselves, women began to apply, and were accepted for admission, to the college. Since 1972 and the ordination of Sally Priesand as the movement's first U.S. Reform rabbi,[30] well over a hundred women have been ordained. Women are also ordained in the smaller, Reconstructionist movement (and have been admitted into the rabbinical program since the movement's rabbinic college first opened in 1968). The Conservative movement, following a protracted and sometimes bitter struggle, voted in 1983 to allow the ordination of women.

Yet over fifty years ago, long before women's ordination as rabbis (or investiture as cantors, another development that has occurred in the Reform and Conservative movements in recent years), one Jewish woman successfully assumed leadership of a small, Jewish religious movement in New York City. Her name was Tehilla Lichtenstein (1893–1973), and the movement she led was called (and is still called) the Society of Jewish Science.[31]

The movement's origins go back to the first three decades of the twentieth century when as many as forty thousand U.S. Jews, two-thirds of whom were women, became involved with the teachings of Christian Science. Primarily appealing to an urban Jewish middle class, including both native-born Jews and acculturated immigrants, Christian Science held out the promise of relief from physical suffering as well as what seemed to many an intense religious faith and a satisfying concept of God. In response to this defection of so many Jews, three Reform rabbis—Alfred Geiger Moses, Morris Lichtenstein and Clifton Harby Levy—began to espouse a concept of Jewish spirituality they identified as Jewish Science. Seen as a Jewish alternative to Christian Science, Jewish Science offered a vision of health and happiness set within a context that was explicitly Jewish. Of the three founders, only Lichtenstein formed a group that is still in existence today, a group that was led for the thirty-five years following his death by his widow, Tehilla.[32]

Although she saw herself as Morris Lichtenstein's disciple, the spiritual visions that Tehilla Lichtenstein came to express in hundreds of sermons delivered between 1939 and her death in 1973 differed from those of her husband. To a large extent, they were shaped by gender. Morris Lichtenstein, an ordained rabbi, emphasized the fundamental principles of Judaism. Tehilla, who had received a limited Jewish education and had spent the eighteen years of her married life primarily as a wife and mother, emphasized the daily experiences through which these fundamentals might be revealed.

Drawing upon both her experiences and her imagination, Tehilla Lichtenstein most frequently used personal examples related to motherhood, marriage, and the home. Thus, she described human progress as going forward "like vacuum machines, picking up the bad with the good." In giving advice "about ruling others and yielding to others," she reminded her congregants that just as "there is not much joy in . . . anxious and intense motherhood," so it was important to know when to leave one's friends alone. In describing God's love for humanity, she often compared running to God with running to one's mother, for from both, she maintained, we look for strength, knowing that both will be there. "Mother's love," she wrote, "is on this earth, the nearest thing, the closest thing, to the love that God bears for mankind. Mother's love is of the same substance, it is of the same divine fabric, and expresses itself in the same boundless way."[33]

Believing in God as both personal (i.e., concerned with individual fears and aspirations) and universal (Creator of the world and all within it), Tehilla Lichtenstein spoke of the importance of a God concept that could both satisfy the mind and fill the heart. Such a concept, she held, could be found within Judaism along with a belief in the possibility of achieving a relationship with the divine. To find God, she insisted, we have only to open ourselves to God's reality, recognizing that God is a force and a power, a presence for happiness, achievement, healing, and indeed "anything that will enhance and enrich and ennoble our individual lives." She was convinced that Jewish Science could offer its adherents a means of achieving this communion, by contending and proving that "God is good, that God expresses Himself in love, and that God answers prayer."[34]

## CONTEMPORARY EXPRESSIONS

In the last twenty years, as the second wave of feminism has influenced thousands of U.S. Jewish women, encouraging them both to explore their own understanding of spirituality and to articulate and share their religious visions, we have gained greater access to the nature and content of Jewish women's religious lives. What is more, as many contemporary Jewish women have achieved a greater knowledge of the Hebrew language and of Jewish texts, their religious lives have come to differ radically from the lives of previous generations.

One still finds in the writings of many Jewish women the identification of spirituality with inner piety and Jewish spirituality with communion with God and obeying God's teachings (including those that focus on ethics and morality). Yet this understanding of spirituality, primarily found among women who either identify themselves as Reform Jews or grew up in the Reform movement, may have less to do with gender than with the teachings of Reform Judaism itself. As first articulated in nineteenth-century Germany, Reform Judaism viewed ethical monotheism, that is, belief in One God and observance of God's moral teachings, to be the "essence" of Judaism. While in the last one hundred years, particularly in the United States, Reform has gained a greater appreciation for traditional ceremonies and observances, it still views moral behavior (seen in light of God's covenant with Israel) as central. Indeed, for many, if not most Reform Jews, the ethical realm is more central than study and public prayer. As Reform rabbi Laura Geller noted in an address to members of the Central Conference of American Rabbis in 1987:

> Raised in the Reform Judaism of the 1950's and early '60s, I learned that being Jewish meant being concerned with *Tikkun Olam* [repairing the world, making it whole], although I didn't learn the Hebrew expression until much later. My earliest Jewish memory is not of candle lighting or *kiddush*, or even the Four Questions [asked by the youngest child present at the Passover seder]. It is, rather, a memory of sneaking down to the living room after I had been put to bed and overhearing my mother and father discuss with members of our Temple's Social Action Committee the propriety of buying a house as a "straw" . . . [that is,] buying a house in a segregated neighborhood in order to sell it to a black family. We should do this, they explained, because we are Jewish. Being Jewish meant being involved with *Tikkun Olam*.[35]

While a focus on "Jewish values" more than on "Jewish skills" may be particularly characteristic of Reform Judaism, what does seem to be a common thread running through the spiritual visions of many contemporary U.S. Jewish women is a willingness to share their own experiences, what Geller calls the "Torah of our lives as well as the Torah that was written down." From deeply personal sermons written by Reform, Reconstructionist, and Conservative women rabbis,[36] to poems such as Merle Feld's "Meditation on Menstruation," "Healing after a Miscarriage," and "Birthing Blessings,"[37] Savina J.Teubal's "Simchat Hochmah" (literally, the celebration of acquiring wisdom), a ritual written for the celebration of her sixtieth birthday, and Penina Adelman's fertility ritual for the biblical Hannah (written, at least in part, as an expression of her "frustration, despair and uncertainty" as to whether or not she herself could bear a child)[38] these varied spiritual expressions reveal a sense of spirituality that is to a great extent gender based.

The desire to forge a link between individual experience and Jewish teachings as a way to find personal meaning in Jewish rituals, observances, and texts may simply reflect the historical reality that the male framers of Jewish liturgy and law were not particularly concerned with women's spirituality. Thus, women have been forced to create new rituals, stories, and blessings that forge a connection between religious faith and the realities of their everyday lives. Or, as the work of the psychologist Carol Gilligan has suggested in another context, it may indeed echo a "different voice," rooted in women's own inner natures. In either case, however, these newer, spiritual expressions, like those articulated by previous generations of women, have been shaped by such cultural and social factors as current beliefs about women's nature, access to Jewish learning, and, specifically, the study of Jewish texts. The increasing feminist awareness, within U.S. society in general and the U.S. Jewish community in particular has also created an atmosphere among both traditional and liberal Jews that has encouraged women to find their own voices and to articulate their own spiritual visions.

## CONCLUSION

A study of Jewish women's religious lives in the United States in the twentieth century calls into question the centrality of study of religious texts and participation in public worship to the religious experience of all Jews. Certainly, such activities have not been central to Jewish women's religious lives, yet it is also true that study and worship have not been central features of Jewish self-identity for most twentieth century U.S. Jewish men. My point is that while the relationship of most male Jews in the United States to Judaism is discontinuous with the relationship of most of their forefathers, the relationship of most of their female counterparts to Judaism has shared a great deal with the Jewish involvement of previous generations of women. Largely ignorant of Hebrew and of Jewish texts, they have been barred (in more traditional synagogues) from full participation in public worship and, until recently, from serving as religious leaders. Rabbinic social policy and Jewish women themselves have seen their special responsibility as the inculcation of religious values in their children, the transmission of moral values to the larger community, and the creation of a Jewish atmosphere within the home. Still, some twenti-eth-century U.S. Jewish women, acting in a context of rapid social change, have through their organizational involvement and religious leadership and through the oral and written expression of their spiri-tual awakening and growth helped to transform the shape and content of Jewish women's religious lives and options. In so doing they have reminded us that Jewish women and men have always pursued a vari-ety of spiritual paths.

## NOTES

1. See, e.g., Chava Weissler's "Women in Paradise," *Tikkun* 2, no. 2 (1988): 43–46; idem, "Traditional Piety of Ashkenazic Women," in *Jewish Spirituality*, 2 vols., ed. Arthur Green (New York, 1987), 2:245–75; and chapter 7 above.

2. Notable recent examples include Barry W. Holtz, ed., *Back to the Sources: Reading the Classic Jewish Texts* (New York, 1984), especially Holtz's introduction; Green, *Jewish Spirituality*, which, with the exception of Weissler's chapter in the sec-ond volume, implicitly equates Jewish spirituality with male spirituality; and most of the articles on Judaism and Jewish religious life in Mircea Eliade, ed., *The Encyclopedia of Religion*, 16 vols. (New York, 1986).

3. Paula Hyman, "The Other Half: Women in the Jewish Tradition," in *The Jewish Woman*, ed. Elizabeth Koltun (New York, 1976), 105–13. Rachel Adler, "The Jew Who Wasn't There: *Halacha* and the Jewish Woman," in *On Being a Jewish Femi-nist*, ed. Susannah Heschel (New York, 1983), 12–18.

4. "Peripheral Jews" from Adler, "Jew Who Wasn't There," 13–14; "objective reality . . . " from Hyman, "The Other Half," 112.

5. Ann Douglas, *The Feminization of American Culture* (New York, 1977), 79ff.

6. Jacob Rader Marcus, ed., *The American Jewish Woman: A Documentary History* (New York, 1981), 465–67.

7. June Sochen, *Consecrate Every Day: The Public Lives of Jewish American Women 1880–1908* (Albany, NY, 1981), 129.

8. Marcus, *American Jewish Woman*, 604.

9. Julia Richman, "Report of National Committee on Religious School Work," in *Piety, Persuasion, and Friendship: A Sourcebook of Modern Jewish Women's Spirituality*, ed. myself and Dianne Ashton (Boston, forthcoming)—originally presented at the annual meeting of the National Council of Jewish Women, 1896. *Piety, Persuasion, and Friendship* includes other writings of Richman as well.

10. Minnie D. Louis, "The Influence of Women in Bringing Religious Conviction to Bear upon Daily Life," in *Piety, Persuasion and Friendship*, ed. myself and Ashton.

11. Minnie D. Louis, "Religious Schools," in *Piety, Persuasion and Friendship*, ed. myself and Ashton.

12. June Sochen (*Consecrate Every Day*, 68) notes that by 1928 over three hun-

dred temples were represented and membership had grown to 55 thousand; see chapter 10 above.

13. According to Pamela Nadell (*Conservative Judaism in America: A Biographical Dictionary and Sourcebook* [Westport, CT, 1988], 330–31), 26 local sisterhoods affiliated with the league upon its founding in 1918. By 1925, 230 sisterhoods had joined, totalling twenty thousand members. The smaller number of members in the Women's League (in comparison to the Reform movement's National Federation of Temple Sisterhoods) probably reflects the smaller size of the Conservative movement at that time.

14. Rebekah Kohut, "Address at First Annual Convention of the National Council of Jewish Women [1896]," in *Piety, Persuasion, and Friendship*, ed. myself and Ashton.

15. On the *tkhines* literature, see Weissler, "Traditional Piety," and chapter 7 above.

16. Abraham Hirschowitz, ed., *Religious Duties of the Daughters of Israel* (New York, 1902).

17. Sydney Stahl Weinberg, *The World of our Mothers* (Chapel Hill, 1988), 140; and chapters 9–10 above.

18. Anzia Yezierska, *Bread Givers* (1925; rep. New York, 1975), 9–10.

19. See my introduction to *I Am a Woman—And a Jew* by Leah Morton (1926; rep. New York, 1986), xv.

20. Morton, *I Am a Woman*, 362.

21. Kate Simon, *Bronx Primitive: Portraits in a Childhood* (New York, 1982), 90.

22. Harriet Rosenstein, "The Fraychie Story," in *The Woman Who Lost Her Names: Selected Writings by American Jewish Women*, ed. Julia Wolf Mazow (New York, 1980), 41.

23. Nessa Rapoport, *Preparing for Sabbath* (New York, 1981), 147–48.

24. Ibid., 148.

25. As early as 1903, however, Henrietta Szold began attending classes at the Conservative movement's Jewish Theological Seminary in New York City, the only woman allowed to do so at that time. Had the Conservative movement considered ordaining her, perhaps Szold might have become a rabbi rather than going on to express her spiritual gifts in the founding of Hadassah.

26. For a fuller discussion, see my "Women in Judaism: From the Reform Movement to Contemporary Jewish Religious Feminism," in *Women of Spirit: Female Leadership in the Jewish and Christian Traditions*, ed. Rosemary Ruether and Eleanor McLaughlin (New York, 1977), 339ff.

27. Martha Neumark's "The Woman Rabbi," featured in Ann D. Braude, "Jewish Women in the Twentieth Century: Documents," in *Women and Religion in America*, vol. 3, ed. Rosemary Radford Ruether and Rosemary Skinner Keller (New York, 1986), 162.

28. On Lindheim and Levinthal, see Linda Gordon Kuzmack, *The Emergence of the Jewish Women's Movement in England and the United States, 1881–1933* (Columbus, OH, 1990), chap. 7.

29. See my "Paula Ackerman: Reform's Lost Woman Rabbi," *Genesis 2*, no. 17 (June-July, 1986): 18–20.

30. Though Priesand was the first woman to be ordained by a Reform rabbinical seminary, she was not the first woman to be ordained a Reform rabbi. In the late 1930s, Regina Jonas completed rabbinic studies at the Berlin Academy for the Science of Judaism. When ordination was denied because of her sex, R. Max Dienemann of

Offenbach took the unusual step of privately granting her a Hebrew rabbinical diploma. She functioned briefly as a rabbi, but was imprisoned at the Theresienstadt concentration camp in 1940 and died soon after.

31. In all probability, membership never exceeded five hundred, although thousands of Jews learned of the teachings of Jewish Science through books, lectures, radio broadcasts, and subscriptions to the *Jewish Science Interpreter*, the society's monthly publication.

32. For a fuller account of the Jewish attraction to Christian Science, and the development of Jewish Science as a separate movement, see my *From Christian Science to Jewish Science: Spiritual Healing and American Jews* (forthcoming).

33. These examples and others like them are explored more fully in my "Piety, Persuasion, and Friendship: Female Jewish Leadership in Modern Times," in *Embodied Love: Sensuality and Relationship As Feminist Values*, ed. Paula M. Cooey et al. (San Francisco, 1987), 198ff.

34. Tehilla Lichtenstein, "Do We Believe in a Personal God?" (sermon), n.d., Mss. CO1 no. 22, box no. 2, American Jewish Archives, Cincinnati.

35. Published in the *Central Conference of American Rabbis Yearbook* (1987), this paper, entitled "Encountering the Divine Presence," is included in *Piety, Persuasion and Friendship*, ed. myself and Ashton.

36. See, e.g., sermons by Reform rabbis Laura Geller and Shira Milgrom, Conservative rabbi Amy Eilberg, and Reconstructionist rabbi Sheila Weinberg in *Piety, Persuasion and Friendship*, ed. myself and Ashton.

37. Ibid.

38. Adelman's ritual can be found in Penina V. Adelman, *Miriam's Well* (Fresh Meadows, NY, 1986), 84ff. For her reflection on the ritual's creation, see Penina V. Adelman, "The Womb and the Word: A Fertility Ritual for Hannah," in *Piety, Persuasion and Friendship*, ed. myself and Ashton, which also contains Teubal's ritual with personal reflections on its creation.

# INDEX